AMERICA
IN QUOTATIONS

D1523503

AMERICA
IN QUOTATIONS

Edited by
Bahman Dehgan

McFarland & Company, Inc., Publishers
Jefferson, North Carolina, and London

LIBRARY OF CONGRESS CATALOGUING-IN-PUBLICATION DATA

America in quotations / edited by Bahman Dehgan.
p.   cm.
Includes indexes.

ISBN 0-7864-1586-X (softcover : 50# alkaline paper) ∞

1. United States—Quotations, maxims, etc.   I. Dehgan, Bahman.
PN6084.U53A44   2003
973—dc21   2003007617

British Library cataloguing data are available

Manufactured in the United States of America

Cover photograph: ©2002 PhotoSpin

*McFarland & Company, Inc., Publishers
Box 611, Jefferson, North Carolina 28640
www.mcfarlandpub.com*

CONTENTS

Contents

Contents

PREFACE

America in Quotations is a collection of quotes—serious and humorous—about America and Americans: national characters, life, history, geography, military affairs, politics, society, art, literature, culture, and so on. Although American and non–American contributors have an equal share, the most important criterion has been the quality of every quotation. For this reason unfamiliar selections and unknown writers have a significant place in the work. It has 19 main topics and every main topic is divided into subtopics, which are listed alphabetically. For example:

The Nation: America, Patriotism, etc.
The American People: Americans, Blacks, Indians, etc.
Places: Boston, California, Chicago, Cities, Los Angeles, New York, Niagara Falls, Travel, etc.
The Individual: Aging, Heroes, House and Home, Life, Men, Success, Women, Youth, etc.
Human Relations: Conversation, Family, Love, Marriage, Parents, Sex, etc.
Social Life: Cars, Education, Health Care, Sport, Leisure, Society, Thanksgiving, Work, etc.
Culture and Media: Art, Culture, Hollywood, Journalism, Movies, Music, Theater, Television, etc.

Politics and Government: Congress, Democracy, Democrats, First Lady, Kennedy, Politics, Presidency, Nixon, etc.
War and the Military: American Revolution, The Military, NATO, Vietnam War, World War II, etc.
International Relations: Canada, Cuba, England, Europe, World, etc.

Quotes within subtopics are listed in chronological order, and I have tried to find exact dates of the quotations (composition and/or publication). If there is any obscurity I have omitted the date and substituted birth and death dates of the author. When it is absolutely necessary—for a better understanding of some quotes—a very short biographical notice has been given. The time span of the remarks is from the 17th century to the present, and everywhere, America(n) means (of) U.S.A.

This collection can be used as a reference work or just as interesting reading or browsing. Cross-references and the indexes at the end facilitate searching. Comprehensiveness of topics, objectivity and "informative insight" of the sayings are the main features for the compilation. Therefore, I have tried to avoid "general" and "propagandistic" (for or against) sentences. Besides the Internet, which has been a great help, I have used many sources, first- and second-hand, American and non–American.

Although *America in Quotations* is about "American affairs," I, as a Persian, have had a special interest in compiling it. My grandfather published some editorials in his newspaper *Haqiqat* (in Tehran) on Persian-American relationships in the 1920s, and my father wrote many articles in Persian about important American events during the 1950–70 period. I myself followed United States–Iran relations during the Iranian Revolution in 1978–79 and afterwards with great enthusiasm. So this work is the result and continuation of this interest.

I would like to thank James Walch for his useful suggestions, and my wife Minoo for her understanding and support. I hope that you find this book useful and informative, and I welcome any comments from the readers.

Bahman Dehgan

THE NATION

America

1. Young man, there is America—which at this day serves for little more than to amuse you with stories of savage men and uncouth manners; yet shall, before you taste of death, show itself equal to the whole that commerce which now attracts the envy of the world.—**Edmund Burke:** Second Speech on Conciliation with America; 22 March 1775; *Works* vol. 2

2. I look upon North America as the only great nursery of freemen left on the face of the earth.—**Jonathan Shipley,** English clergyman: 1774; *Dictionary of National Biography*

3. America is a model of force and freedom & moderation—with all the coarseness and rudeness of its people.—**Lord Byron:** letter, 12 October 1821

4. America is a land of wonders, in which everything is in constant motion and every change seems an improvement.... No natural boundary seems to be set to the efforts of man; and in his eyes, what is not yet done is only what he has not yet attempted to do.—**Alexis de Tocqueville:** *Democracy in America* (1835)

5. America is great because America is *good.* If America ever ceases to be good it will cease to be great.—**Alexis de Tocqueville,** 1805–59: attrib.

6. America, thou half-brother of the world; With something good and bad of every land. —**Philip James Bailey:** *Festus* (1839)

7. My toast would be, may our country always be successful, but whether successful or otherwise, always right.—**John Quincy Adams,** 1767–1848

8. O America because you build for mankind I build for you.—**Walt Whitman:** *By Blue Ontario's Shore* (1856)

9. Asylum of the oppressed of every nation.—**Anonymous:** phrase used in the Democratic platform of 1856

10. America is the only place where man is full grown!—**Oliver Wendell Holmes, Sr.:** *The Professor at the Breakfast-Table* (1860)

11. America means opportunity, freedom, power.—**Ralph Waldo Emerson,** 1803–82: *Uncollected Lectures* (1932)

12. The office of America is to liberate, to abolish kingcraft, priestcraft, caste, monopoly, to pull down the gallows, to burn up the bloody statutebook, to take in the immigrant, to open the doors of the sea and the fields of the earth.—**Ralph Waldo Emerson:** 1867; *Journals* (1909–14)

13. A country of young men.—**Ralph Waldo Emerson:** *Society and Solitude* (1870)

14. America is an adorable woman chewing tobacco.—**Auguste Bartholdi,** French sculptor of Statue of Liberty: comment made during fund-raising trip for Statue in 1871; *New York Times*, 3 May 1986

15. Talleyrand once said to the first Napoleon that the United States is a giant without bones.

Since that time our gristle has been rapidly hardening.—**James A. Garfield**, 1831–81

16. I am lost in wonder and amazement. It is not a country, but a world. The West I liked best. The people are stronger, fresher, saner than the rest. They are ready to be taught. The surroundings of nature have instilled in them a love of the beautiful, which but needs development and direction. The East I found a feeble reflex of Europe; in fact, I may say that 1 was in America for a month before I saw an American.—**Oscar Wilde:** *St Louis Daily Democrat*, 26 February 1882

17. America is one long expectoration.—**Oscar Wilde:** newspaper interview, 1882

18. A wholesale, and not a retail country.—**G. A. Sala:** *America Revisited* (1882)

19. Though I have kind invitations enough to visit America, I could not, even for a couple of months, live in a country so miserable as to possess no castles.—**John Ruskin:** *Praeterita* (1885–89)

20. America excites an admiration which must be felt on the spot to be understood.—**James Bryce:** *The American Commonwealth* (1888)

21. The United States—bounded on the north by the Aurora Borealis, on the south by the precession of the equinoxes, on the east by the primeval chaos, and on the west by the Day of Judgement.—**John Fiske**, 1842–1901: *Bounding the United States*

22. It is by the goodness of God that in our country we have those three unspeakably precious things: freedom of speech, freedom of conscience, and the prudence never to practice either of them.—**Mark Twain:** *Following the Equator* (1897)

23. One loves America above all things, for her youth, her greenness, her plasticity, innocence, good intentions, friends, everything.—**William James:** letter to Mrs. Henry Whitman, 1899

24. Little of beauty has America given the world save the rude grandeur God himself stamped on her bosom; the human spirit in this new world has expressed itself in vigor and ingenuity rather than in beauty.—**W. E. B. Du Bois:** *The Souls of Black Folk* (1903)

25. The land of unlimited possibilities.—**Ludwig Max Goldberger:** *Land of Unlimited Possibilities* (1903)

26. Our country is too big for union, too sordid for patriotism, too democratic for liberty. —**Fisher Ames:** letter to Thomas Dwight, 26 October 1903

27. America has a new delicacy, a coarse, rank refinement.—**G. K. Chesterton:** *Charles Dickens* (1906)

28. As for America, it is the ideal fruit of all your youthful hopes and reforms. Everybody is fairly decent, respectable, domestic, bourgeois, middle-class, and tiresome. There is absolutely nothing to revue except that it's a bore.—**Henry Brooks Adams:** letter, 17 December 1908

29. American society is a sort of flat, freshwater pond which absorbs silently, without reaction, anything which is thrown into it. —**Henry Brooks Adams:** letter, 20 September 1911

30. America lives in the heart of every man everywhere who wishes to find a region where he will be free to work out his destiny as he chooses.—**Woodrow Wilson:** speech, Chicago, 6 April 1912

31. America, my country, is almost a continent and hardly yet a nation.—**Ezra Pound:** 1912; *Patria Mia* (1950)

32. America is a young country with an old mentality.—**George Santayana:** *Winds of Doctrine* (1913)

33. America is a tune. It must be sung together.—**Gerald Stanley Lee:** *Crowds* (1913)

34. "A country without conversation," said a philosopher. "The big land has a big heart," wrote a kindly scholar; and by the same post from another critic, "that land of crushing hospitality!" "It's hell, but it's fine," an artist told me. "El Cuspidorado," remarked an Oxford man brilliantly. But one wiser than all the rest wrote, "Think gently of the Americans. They are so very young; and so very anxious to appear grown up; and so very lovable."—**Rupert Brooke:** *Letters from America* (1916)

35. The things that will destroy America are prosperity-at-any-price, peace-at-any-price, safety-first instead of duty-first, the love of soft living, and the get-rich-quick theory of life. —**Theodore Roosevelt:** letter, 10 January 1917

36. We go forth all to seek America. And in the seeking we create her. In the quality of our search shall be the nature of the America that we created.—**Waldo Frank:** *Our America* (1919)

37. God's own country.—**Anonymous:** 1921

38. Oh, America, the sun sets in you.
Are you the grave of our day?
—**D. H. Lawrence:** *Birds Beast, and Flowers* (1923)

39. America is still a government of the naïve, by the naïve, and for the naïve.—**Christopher Morley:** *Inward Ho!* (1923)

40. America makes prodigious mistakes, America has colossal faults, but one thing cannot be denied: America is always on the move. She may be going to Hell, of course, but at least she isn't standing still.—**E. E. Cummings:** May 1927; George J. Firmage (ed.) *A Miscellany* (1958)

41. It is veneer, rouge, aestheticism, art museums, new theaters, etc. that make America impotent. The good things are football, kindness, and jazz bands.—**George Santayana:** letter to Van Wyck Brooks, 22 May 1927

42. You are as various as your land.—**Stephen Vincent Benét:** *John Brown's Body* (1928)

43. The United States is just now the oldest country in the world, there always is an oldest country and she is it, it is she who is the mother of the twentieth century civilization. She began to feel herself as it just after the Civil War. And so it is a country the right age to have been born in and the wrong age to live in.—**Gertrude Stein:** *Transition*, Fall 1928

44. America is fundamentally the land of the overrated child.—**Hermann A. Keyserling:** *America Set Free* (1929)

45. France was a land, England was a people, but America, having about it still that quality of the idea, was harder to utter—it was the graves at Shiloh and the tired, drawn, nervous faces of its great men, and the country boys dying in the Argonne for a phrase that was empty before their bodies withered. It was a

willingness of the heart.—**F. Scott Fitzgerald:** *Saturday Evening Post* (New York), 19 October 1929

46. America is the last abode of romance and other medieval phenomena.—**Eric Linklater:** *Juan in America* (1931)

47. The only things that the United States has given to the world are skyscrapers, jazz, and cocktails. That is all. And in Cuba, in our America, they make much better cocktails. —**Federico García Lorca,** Spanish poet and dramatist: interview 1933; *Obras Completas* vol. 3 (1986)

48. It's a great country, but you can't live in it for nothing.—**Will Rogers,** 1879–1935

49. America is the greatest of opportunities and the worst of influences.—**George Santayana:** *The Last Puritan* (1935)

50. America.... It is a fabulous country, the only fabulous country; it is the only place where miracles not only happen, but where they happen all the time.—**Thomas Wolfe:** *Of Time and the River* (1935)

51. America is the most grandiose experiment the world has seen, but, I am afraid, it is not going to be a success.—**Sigmund Freud,** 1856–1939: Ronald W. Clark *Freud: The Man and His Cause* (1980)

52. Yes, America is gigantic, but a gigantic mistake.—**Sigmund Freud:** Ernest Jones *Memories of a Psychoanalyst* (1959)

53. In the United States there is more space where nobody is than where anybody is. That is what makes America what it is.—**Gertrude Stein:** *The Geographical History of America* (1936)

54. "I'm glad I'm American," she said. "Here in Italy I feel that everybody's dead. Carthaginians and old Romans and Moorish pirates and medieval princes with poisoned rings." —**F. Scott Fitzgerald,** 1896–1940: *The Crack-Up* (1945)

55. America is the country where you buy a lifetime supply of aspirin for one dollar, and use it up in two weeks.—**John Barrymore,** 1882–1942: Evan Esar (ed.) *The Dictionary of Humorous Quotation* (1949)

56. America—rather, the United States—seems to me to be the Jew among the nations. It is resourceful, adaptable, maligned, envied, feared, imposed upon. It is warm-hearted, overfriendly; quick-witted, lavish, colorful; given to extravagant speech and gestures; its people are travelers and wanderers by nature, moving, shifting, restless; swarming in Fords, in ocean liners; craving entertainment; volatile. The _schnuckle_ among the nations of the world. —**Edna Ferber:** _A Peculiar Treasure_ (1939)

57. I like it here, just because it is the Great Void where you have to balance without handholds.—**W. H. Auden:** letter to Naomi Mitchison, 1942

58. A country whose national motto has been "root, hog, or die."—**Denis William Brogan:** _The American Character_ (1944)

59. I have never been able to look upon America as young and vital but rather as prematurely old, as a fruit which rotted before it had it chance to ripen.—**Henry Miller:** _The Air-Conditioned Nightmare_ (1945)

60. I take SPACE to be the central fact to man born in America. I spell it large because it comes large here. Large and without mercy. —**Charles Olson:** _Call Me Ishmael_ (1947)

61. America is rather like life. You can usually find it in what you look for. It will probably be interesting, and it is sure to be large.—**E. M. Forster:** _Listener_ (London), 4 September 1947

62. God bless the U.S.A., so large,
So friendly, and so rich.
—**W. H. Auden,** 1907–73: "On the Circuit"

63. I don't see America as a mainland, but as a sea, a big ocean. Sometimes a storm arises, a formidable current develops, and it seems it will engulf everything. Wait a moment, another current will appear and bring the first one to naught.—**Jacques Maritain,** French philosopher: _Reflections on America_ (1948)

64. I feel most at home in the United States, not because it is intrinsically a more interesting country, but because no one really belongs there any more than I do. We are all there together in its wholly excellent vacuum.—**Wyndham Lewis,** British author: _America and Cosmic Man_ (1948)

65. America is a passionate idea or it is nothing. America is a human brotherhood or it is a chaos.—**Max Lerner:** _Actions and Passions_ (1949)

66. America is not only big and rich, it is mysterious; and its capacity for the humorous or ironical concealment of its interests matches that of the legendary inscrutable Chinese. —**David Riesman:** _The Lonely Crowd_ (1950)

67. America is a large, friendly dog in a very small room. Every time it wags its tail, it knocks over a chair.—**Arnold Toynbee:** BBC _News Summaries,_ 14 July 1954

68. America, which has the most glorious present still existing in the world today, hardly stops to enjoy it, in her insatiable appetite for the future.—**Anne Morrow Lindbergh:** _Gift from the Sea_ (1955)

69. America has meant to the world a land in which the common man who means well and is willing to do his part has access to all the necessary means of a good life.—**Alvin Saunders Johnson**

70. America is so vast that almost everything said about it is likely to be true, and the opposite is probably equally true.—**James T. Farrell:** Introduction to H. L. Mencken _Prejudices: A Selection_ (1958)

71. All America is an insane asylum.—**Ezra Pound:** c. 1958; Penelope Niven _Carl Sandburg_ (1991)

72. America is so big, and everyone is working, making, digging, bulldozing, trucking, loading, and so on, and I guess the sufferers suffer at the same rate.—**Saul Bellow:** _Henderson the Rain King_ (1959)

73. When I first arrived in the States a shrewd American said to me: "A European coming to America for the first time, should skip New York and fly directly to Kansas. Start from the Middle. The East will only mislead you."—**Lord Kinross:** _The Innocents at Home_ (1959)

74. America is a hurricane, and the only people who do not hear the sound are those fortunate if incredibly stupid and smug White Protestants who live in the center, in the serene eye of the big wind.—**Norman Mailer:** _Advertisements for Myself_ (1959)

75. America is a nation created by all the hopeful wanderers of Europe, not out of geography and genetics, but out of purpose.—**Theodore H. White:** *Making of the President* (1960)

76. The American experience stirred mankind from discovery to exploration, from the cautious quest for what they knew (or what they thought they knew) was out there, to an enthusiastic reaching to the unknown.—**Daniel J. Boorstin,** 1914–

77. A country which one should never go to for the first time.—**Jawaharlal Nehru,** 1889–1964: *Sunday Times,* 27 January 1980

78. For this is what America is all about. It is the uncrossed desert and the unclimbed ridge. It is the star that is not reached and the harvest that is sleeping in the unplowed ground.—**Lyndon B. Johnson:** inaugural presidential address, 20 January 1965

79. It's like Britain, only with buttons.—**Ringo Starr:** interview BBC-TV, 1965

80. America is somewhat like Palestine before Christ appeared—a country full of minor prophets.—**Peter Ustinov:** *Illustrated London News,* 1968

81. The land of the dull and the home of the literal.—**Gore Vidal:** *Reflections upon a Sinking Ship* (1969)

82. I don't measure America by its achievement, but by its potential.—**Shirley Chisholm:** *Unbought and Unbossed* (1970)

83. A land of boys who refuse to grow up.—**Salvador de Madariaga,** 1886–1978: Sagittarius and D. George: *The Perpetual Pessimist*

84. From the beginning America was a place to be discovered.—**Peter Schrag:** *The Vanishing American* (1972)

85. One comes to the United States—always, no matter how often—to see the future. It's what life in one's own country will be like, five, ten, twenty years from now.—**Ehud Yonay:** *New York Times,* 26 November 1972

86. America may be violent, greedy and colonialist but my God, it's interesting.—**Paul Newman:** *Today,* 6 January 1973

87. History had created something new in the USA, namely crookedness with self-respect or duplicity with honor.—**Saul Bellow:** *Humboldt's Gift* (1975)

88. The most important American addition to the World Experience was the simple surprising fact of America. We have helped prepare mankind for all its later surprises.—**Daniel J. Boorstin:** Reith Lecturer, October 1975; *The Exploring Spirit: America and the World Experience* (1976)

89. A great old-movie museum.—**Anthony Burgess:** "David Susskind Show," 4 January 1976

90. That's the old American way—if you get a good thing, then overdo it.—**Phil Walden:** *Rolling Stone,* 1 July 1976

91. We become not a melting pot but a beautiful mosaic. Different people, different beliefs, different yearnings, different hopes, different dreams.—**Jimmy Carter:** speech at Pittsburgh, Pennsylvania, 27 October 1976

92. America is a country that doesn't know where it is going but is determined to set a speed record getting there.—**Laurence J. Peter:** *Peter's Quotations* (1977)

93. You come to the United States not knowing what to expect. Then all your worst prejudices are confirmed.—**John Fowles:** *Daniel Martin* (1977)

94. What the people want is very simple. They want an America as good as its promise.—**Barbara Jordan:** speech, 1977

95. America is not a melting pot. It is a sizzling cauldron.—**Barbara Mikulski:** *Chicago Tribune,* 8 January 1978

96. I begin to think that America *is* an entertainment industry.—**Russell Davies:** *Observer Review,* 5 March 1978

97. Two problems of our country—energy and malaise.—**Jimmy Carter:** at town meeting in Bardstown, Kentucky, 31 July 1979

98. I was given a bed in which four people could have slept without ever being introduced. Everything in America is on wide screen.—**Quentin Crisp:** *How to Become a Virgin* (1981)

99. The biggest difference between ancient Rome and the USA is that in Rome the common man was treated like a dog. In America he sets the tone. This is the first country where the common man could stand erect.—**I. F. Stone**, 1907–89: Clive James *Flying Visit* (1984)

100. Our flag is red, white and blue, but our nation is a rainbow—red, yellow, brown, black and white—and we're all precious in God's sight. America is not like a blanket—one piece of unbroken cloth, the same color, the same texture, the same size. America is more like a quilt—many patches, many pieces, many colors, many sizes, all woven and held together by a common thread.—**Jesse Jackson**: speech before the Democratic National Convention, 16 July 1984

101. America is like an unfaithful lover who promised us more than we got.—**Charlotte Bunch**: *Passionate Politics* (1987)

102. The spirit is at home, if not entirely satisfied, in America.—**Allan Bloom**: *The Closing of the American Mind* (1987)

103. The genius of America is that out of the many, we become one.—**Jesse Jackson**: Democratic National Convention, Atlanta, Georgia, 20 July 1988

104. A rigid America is also weak and vulnerable, because it sacrifices its unique strength: the energy of people who think they can always make something new of their lives.—**James Fallows**: *More Like Us* (1989)

105. Let's not be too tough on our own ignorance. It's the thing that makes America great. If America weren't incomparably ignorant, how could we have tolerated the last eight years?—**Frank Zappa**: 1989

106. Making duplicate copies and computer printouts of things no one wanted even one of in the first place is giving America a new sense of purpose.—**Andy Rooney**, 1920– : Robert Byrne *The Fourth 637 Best Things Anybody Ever Said* (1990)

107. America is still mostly xenophobic and racist. That's the nature of America.—**Jerry Garcia**: *Rolling Stone*, 30 November 1989

108. America is like one of those old-fashioned six-cylinder truck engines that can be missing two sparkplugs and have a broken flywheel and have a crankshaft that's 5000 millimeters off fitting properly, and two bad ball-bearings, and still runs. We're in that kind of situation. We can have substantial parts of the population committing suicide, and still run and look fairly good.—**Thomas McGuane**: *Sunday Correspondent*, 1 April 1990

109. America is a country that seems forever to be toddler or teenager, at those two stages of human development characterized by conflict between autonomy and security.—**Anna Quindlen**: 29 July 1990; *Thinking Out Loud* (1993)

110. Disneyland is a white pioneer's idea of what America is. Wacky American animals. American conviviality, zappy, zany, congenial and nice, like a parade of demented, bright Shriners.—**Jonathan Miller**, 1934– : Jon Winokur (ed.) *The Portable Curmudgeon Redux* (1992)

111. The real America that Whitman proclaimed and Thoreau decoded.—**Allen Ginsberg**, 1926– : Robert I. Fitzhenry (ed.) *The Harper Book of Quotations* (1993)

112. Perhaps this is our strange and haunting paradox here in America—that we are fixed and certain only when we are in movement. —**Tom Wolfe**, 1931–

113. The metaphor of the melting pot is unfortunate and misleading. A more accurate analogy would be a salad bowl, for, though the salad is an entity, the lettuce can still be distinguished from the chicory, the tomatoes from the cabbage.—**Carl N. Degler**

114. The United States is like the guy at the party who gives cocaine to everybody and still nobody likes him.—**Jim Samuels**

115. America's greatest strength, and its greatest weakness, is our belief in second chances, our belief that we can always start over, that things can be made better.—**Anthony Walton**

116. America once had the clarity of a pioneer axe.—**Robert Osborn**: Connie Robertson (ed.) *The Wordsworth Dictionary of Quotations* (1996)

117. America is like a bar-room drunk. One minute it brags about its money and muscle, and then for the next hour it bleats into its beer about failure and hopelessness.—**Henry Southworth Allen:** *Going Too Far Enough* (1994)

118. America today is capable of terrific intolerance about smoking, or toxic waste that threatens trout. But only a deeply confused society is more concerned about protecting lungs than minds, trout than black women.—**Garry Wills:** *New York Daily News*, 21 November 1994

119. America must be described in romantic terms…. America is a romance in which we all partake.—**Newt Gingrich:** *To Renew America* (1995)

120. The US is without doubt the greatest show on the road. Brutal, indifferent, scornful and ruthless it may be, but it's also very smart. As a salesman it's out on its own. And its most saleable commodity is self-love. The US has actually educated itself to be in love with itself.—**Harold Pinter:** *Guardian*, 4 December 1996

The Dream and the Ideal

See also PAST AND FUTURE: Future; SOCIAL LIFE: Progress

121. Americans are not a perfect people, but we are called to a perfect mission.—**Andrew Jackson,** 1767–1845, 7th president

122. It would be well, there can be no doubt, for the American people as a whole, if they loved the Real less, and the Ideal somewhat more.—**Charles Dickens:** *American Notes* (1842)

123. The mission of the United States is one of benevolent assimilation.—**William McKinley,** 1843–1901: Laurence J. Peter *Peter's Quotations* (1977)

124. America was established not to create wealth but to realize a vision, to realize an ideal—to discover and maintain liberty among men.—**Woodrow Wilson:** address, Chicago, 12 February 1912

125. Sometimes people call me an idealist. Well, that is the way I know I am an American. America is the only idealistic nation in the world.—**Woodrow Wilson:** speech at Sioux Falls, South Dakota, 8 September 1919

126. There is nothing the matter with Americans except their ideals. The real American is all right; it is the ideal American who is all wrong.—**G. K. Chesterton:** *New York Times*, 1 February 1931

127. The American dream was that within this system every man could become an owner. It has been said that every soldier of Napoleon carried in his knapsack a marshal's baton, and in the early days of this century it seems to have been thought that every young American carried in his lunch box a roll of ticker tape.—**Dean Acheson:** address, Law Club of Chicago, 22 January 1937

128. I believe in America because we have great dreams—and because we have the opportunity to make those dreams come true.—**Wendell L. Wilkie,** 1892–1944: Robert Andrews *The Concise Columbia Dictionary of Quotations* (1987)

129. The American ideal, after all, is that everyone should be as much alike as possible. —**James Baldwin:** *Commentary* (New York), February 1948

130. It is said that Americans are businessmen. This is not so. They are idealist, with a slightly naïve realism.—**Edouard Herriot:** 1952; Colin Bingham (ed.) *Wit and Wisdom* (1982)

131. They proclaimed to all the world the revolutionary doctrine of the divine rights of the common man. That doctrine has ever since been the heart of the American faith.—**Dwight D. Eisenhower:** referring to the founding fathers; speech at the Columbia University Bicentennial dinner, 30 May 1954

132. Give the American people a good cause, and there's nothing they can't lick.—**John Wayne,** 1907–79

133. Of all the nations in the world, the United States was built in nobody's image. It was the land of the unexpected, of unbounded hope, of ideals, of quest for an unknown perfection. It is all the more unfitting that we should offer ourselves in images. And all the more fitting that the images which we make wittingly or unwittingly to sell America to the world should come back to haunt and curse us.—**Daniel J. Boorstin:** *The Image* (1962)

134. If the American dream is for Americans only, it will remain our dream and never be our destiny.—**René de Visme Williamson**

135. Each [American] would shape his image [of the ideal American] a little differently, but the main ingredients would include a bit of Thomas Jefferson, Alexander the Great, the Statue of Liberty, Henry Ford and the Ford Foundation.—**Dean Acheson,** 1893–1971: Colin Bingham (ed.) *Wit and Wisdom* (1982)

136. America is not just a power: it is a promise. It is not enough for our Country to be extraordinary in might; it must be exemplary in meaning.—**Nelson A. Rockefeller:** *Unity, Freedom and Peace: A Blueprint for Tomorrow* (1968)

137. America is not so much a nightmare as a non-dream. The American non-dream is precisely a move to wipe the dream out of existence. The dream is a spontaneous happening and therefore dangerous to a control system set up by the non-dreamers.—**William S. Burroughs:** *The Job: Interviews with Daniel Odier* (1969)

138. We suffer primarily not from our vices or our weaknesses, but from our illusions.—**Daniel J. Boorstin:** *Time*, 12 November 1979

139. The American Dream has run out of gas. The car has stopped. It no longer supplies the world with its images, its dreams, its fantasies. No more. It's over. It supplies the world with its nightmares now: the Kennedy assassination, Watergate, Vietnam....—**J. G. Ballard:** *Métaphors*, No. 7, 1983

140. America is too great for small dreams.—**Ronald Reagan:** speech to Congress, 1 January 1984

141. For decades nobody has asked America, What do we care about? What do we stand for? What are our priorities?—**Steve Jobs:** *Marknads tendenser* (Stockholm), March 1992

142. For other nations, Utopia is a blessed past never to be recovered; for Americans it is just beyond the horizon.—**Henry Kissinger,** 1923–: attrib.; Antony Jay *The Oxford Dictionary of Political Quotations* (1997)

143. I am the living attestation of the American dream. I am the extolment of this great nation.—**Don King,** American boxing promoter: *Independent on Sunday*, 10 March 1996

Founding

See also LAW AND ORDER: Constitution

144. The historic glory of America lies in the fact that it is the one nation that was founded like a church. That is, it was founded on a faith that was not merely summed up after it had existed; it was defined before it existed.—**G. K. Chesterton,** 1874–1936: Ted Goodman (ed.) *The Forbes Book of Business Quotations* (1997)

145. Ours is the only country deliberately founded on a good idea.—**John Gunther:** *Inside U.S.A.* (1947)

146. America is the only country ever founded on the printed word.—**Marshall McLuhan,** 1911–80

147. The only country in the world actually founded on liberty—the only one. People went to America to be free.—**Margaret Thatcher,** 1925–

148. America wasn't founded so that we could all be better. America was founded so we could all be anything we damn well pleased.—**P. J. O'Rourke,** 1947– : *Rolling Stone*

Patriotism

See also NATION: Minorities

149. Americans rightly think their patriotism is a sort of religion strengthened by practical service.—**Alexis de Tocqueville:** *Democracy in America* vol. 1 (1835)

150. I was born an American; I will live an American; I shall die an American.—**Daniel Webster:** speech in the Senate, 17 July 1850

151. My country, right or wrong; if right, to be kept right; and if wrong, to be set right!—**Carl Schurz:** speech in the Senate, 29 February 1872

152. We pause to ... recall what our country has done for each of us and to ask ourselves what we can do for our country in return.—**Oliver Wendell Holmes, Sr.:** speech at Keene, New Hampshire, 30 May 1884

153. What this country needs is a good hard bloody war to revive the vice of patriotism on which its existence as a nation depends.—**Ambrose Bierce:** letter, 15 February 1911

154. Our whole duty, for the present, at any rate, is summed up in the motto America first.—**Woodrow Wilson:** speech, New York, 20 April 1915

155. In the great fulfillment we must have a citizenship less concerned about what the government can do for it and more anxious about what it can do for the nation.—**Warren G. Harding:** speech at the Republican National Convention, 7 June 1916

156. There can be no fifty-fifty Americanism in this country. There is room here for only hundred per cent Americanism.—**Theodore Roosevelt:** speech, Saratoga, New York, 19 July 1918

157. Patriotism is easy to understand in America; it means looking out for yourself by looking out for your country.—**Calvin Coolidge:** speech, Northampton, Massachusetts, 30 May 1923

158. Intellectually I know that America is no better than any other country; emotionally I know she is better than every other country.—**Sinclair Lewis:** interview in Berlin, 29 December 1930

159. When an American says that he loves his country, he means that he loves an inner air, an inner light in which freedom lives and in which a man can draw the breath of self-respect.—**Adlai Stevenson:** speech at New York City, 27 August 1952

160. What do we mean by patriotism in the context of our times? I venture to suggest that what we mean is a sense of national responsibility ... a patriotism which is not short, frenzied outbursts of emotion, but the tranquil and steady dedication of a lifetime.—**Adlai Stevenson:** speech at New York City, 27 August 1952

161. I love America more than any other country in this world, and, exactly for this reason, I insist on the right to criticize her perpetually. —**James Baldwin:** *Notes of a Native Son* (1955)

162. The love of Americans for their country is not an indulgent, it is an exacting and chastising love; they cannot tolerate its defects. —**Jacques Maritain:** *Reflections on America* (1958)

163. Ask not what your country can do for you—ask what you can do for your country. —**John F. Kennedy:** inaugural address as president, 20 January 1961

164. American patriotism is generally something that amuses Europeans, I suppose because children look idiotic saluting the flag and because the consitution contains so many cracks through which the lawyers may creep.—**Katharine Whitehorn:** *Roundabout* (1962)

165. The patriots are those who love America enough to see her as a model to mankind. —**Adlai Stevenson:** *Harper's Magazine*, July 1963

166. What we need are critical lovers of America—patriots who express their faith in their country by working to *improve* it.—**Hubert H. Humphrey:** *Beyond Civil Rights* (1968)

167. I'm very critical of the U.S., but get me outside the country and all of a sudden I can't bring myself to say one nasty thing about the U.S.—**Saul Alinsky,** 1909–72

168. Patriotism, to be truly American, begins with the human allegiance.—**Norman Cousins,** 1915–90: Laurence J. Peter *Peter's Quotations* (1977)

169. As you begin your tour of the United States, you may as well know that one American national trait which irritates many Americans and must be convenient for our critics is that we relentlessly advertise our imperfections.—**Henry Cabot Lodge,** 1902–85

170. A loyal American is one who gets mad when an alien cusses the institutions he cusses. —*Huntington Herald*

171. I like America, just as everybody else does. I love America, I gotta say that. But America will be judged. —**Bob Dylan:** 26 November 1979, Tempe, Arizona; John Bauldie (ed.) *Wanted Man* (1990)

172. You can't prove you're an American by waving Old Glory. —**Helen Gahagan Douglas:** *A Full Life* (1982)

173. At its truest, American patriotism has a sort of abstraction about it that makes it uniquely difficult and valuable: it is a devotion not to a specific physical place, gene pool, cuisine, or cultural tradition, but to a political and social vision, a promise and the idea of freedom—an idea not much honored elsewhere in the world or in history. At its worst, American patriotism degenerates into a coarse form of national self-congratulation. —**Lance Morrow:** *Fishing in the Tiber* (1988)

174. It seems that American patriotism measures itself against an outcast group. The right Americans are the right Americans because they're not like the wrong Americans, who are not really Americans. —**Eric Hobsbawm:** *Marxism Today* (London), January 1988

175. I am loving before I am patriotic, I am human before I am American. —**A. F. Shaw**

THE AMERICAN PEOPLE

Americans

176. A people who are still, as it were, but in the gristle, and not yet hardened into the bone of manhood. —**Edmund Burke:** Speech on Conciliation with America, 1774-5; *Works* vol. 2

177. It is part of the American character to consider nothing as desperate, to surmount every difficulty by resolution and contrivance. —**Thomas Jefferson:** letter to Martha Jefferson, 28 March 1787

178. They have in the course of twenty years acquired a distinct national character for low, lying knavery. —**Robert Southey:** letter to Walter Savage Landor, 1812

179. I would rather ... have a nod from an American, than a snuff-box from an Emperor. —**Lord Byron:** letter, 8 June 1822

180. The Americans are excessively pleased with any kind of favourable expressions, and never forgive or forget any slight or abuse. It would be better for them if they were a trifle thicker-skinned. —**Samuel Taylor Coleridge:** *Table Talk* (1830)

181. Other nations have been called thin-skinned, but the citizens of the Union have, apparently, no skins at all; they wince if a breeze blows over them, unless it be tempered with adulation.—**Frances Trollope:** *Domestic Manners of the Americans* (1832)

182. If an American were condemned to confine his activity to his own affairs, he would he robbed of one half of his existence.—**Alexis de Tocqueville:** *Democracy in America* vol. 1 (1835)

183. The Americans, in their intercourse with strangers, appear impatient of the smallest censure and insatiable of praise.—**Alexis de Tocqueville:** *Democracy in America* (1835–40)

184. Their demeanour is invariably morose, sullen, clownish and repulsive. I should think there is not, on the face of the earth, a people so entirely destitute of humour, vivacity, or the capacity for enjoyment.—**Charles Dickens:** *Martin Chuzzlewitt* (1843–4)

185. We are a puny and fickle folk. Avarice, hesitation, and following are our diseases. —**Ralph Waldo Emerson:** *Nature, Addresses and Lectures* (1849)

186. We Americans are the peculiar, chosen people—the Israel of our time; we bear the ark of the liberties of the world.—**Herman Melville:** *White Jacket* (1850)

187. The American is nomadic in religion, in ideas, in morals.—**James Russell Lowell:** *Fireside Travels* (1864)

188. I hate this shallow Americanism which hopes to get rich by credit, to get knowledge by raps on midnight tables, to learn the economy of the mind by phrenology, or skill without study, or mastery without apprenticeship. —**Ralph Waldo Emerson:** *Society and Solitude* (1870)

189. It appears the Americans have taken umbrage. The deuce they have! Whereabouts is that?—*Punch*, British humorous periodical: 1872

190. What though people had plenty to eat and clothes to wear, if they put their feet upon the tables and did not reverence their betters? The Americans were to her rough, uncouth, and vulgar—and she told them so.—**Anthony Trollope:** on Frances Trollope's *Domestic Manners of the Americans*; *Autobiography* (1883)

191. When an American says, "Come and see me," he *means* it.—**Wilkie Collins,** 1824–89:

Catherine Peters *The King of Inventors: A Life of Wilkie Collins* (1993)

192. The American imagination is peculiarly sensitive to the impression of great size. "A big thing" is their habitual phrase of admiration. —**James Bryce:** *The American Commonwealth* (1888)

193. I am not *an* American. I am *the* American.—**Frank Fuller** 1827–1915: Mark Twain, personal notebook, 1897

194. We are the lavishest and showiest and most luxury-loving people on the earth; and at our masthead we fly one true and honest symbol, the gaudiest flag the world has ever seen. —**Mark Twain:** *Diplomatic Pay and Clothes* (1899)

195. We have to be despised by somebody whom we regard as above us, or we are not happy; we have to have somebody to worship and envy, or we cannot be content. In America we manifest this in all the ancient and customary ways. In public we scoff at titles and hereditary privilege, but privately we hanker after them, and when we get a chance we buy them for cash and a daughter.—**Mark Twain:** *My Autobiography*

196. What a horror it is for a whole nation to be developing without the sense of beauty, and eating bananas for breakfast.—**Edith Wharton:** letter to Sara Norton, 19 August 1904

197. The American people abhor a vacuum. —**Theodore Roosevelt:** speech in Cairo, Illinois, 3 October 1907

198. As for America, it is the ideal fruit of all your youthful hopes and reforms. Everybody is fairly decent, respectable, domestic, bourgeois, middle-class, and tiresome. There is absolutely nothing to revile except that it's a bore.—**Henry Brooks Adams:** letter to Charles Milnes Gaskell, 17 December 1908

199. It's a complex fate, being an American. —**Henry James,** 1843–1916: *New York Times Book Review,* 24 July 1977

200. We are an uprooted people, newly arrived, and *nouveau riche.* As a nation we have all the vulgarity that goes with that, all the scattering of soul.—**Walter Lippmann:** *Drift and Mastery* (1914)

201. Americans are eminently prophets; they apply morals to public affairs; they are impatient and enthusiastic. Their judgments have highly speculative implications, which they often make explicit; they are men with principles, and fond of stating them. Moreover, they have an intense self-reliance; to exercise private judgment is not only a habit with them but a conscious duty.—**George Santayana:** *Character and Opinion in the United States* (1920)

202. All his life he [American] jumps into a train after it has started and jumps out before it has stopped; and never once gets left behind, or breaks a leg.—**George Santayana:** *Character and Opinion in the United States* (1920)

203. The curse of me & my nation is that we always think things can be bettered by immediate action of some sort, *any* sort rather than no sort.—**Ezra Pound,** American poet: letter to James Joyce, 7–8 June 1920

204. A tough but nervous, tenacious but restless race; materially ambitious, yet prone to introspection, and subject to waves of religious emotion. A race whose typical member is eternally torn between a passion for righteousness and a desire to get on in the world.—**Samuel Eliot Morison:** *Maritime History of Massachusetts* (1921)

205. The American people, taking one with another, constitute the most timorous, sniveling, poltroonish, ignominious mob of serfs and goose-steppers ever gathered under one flag in Christendom since the end of the Middle Ages. —**H. L. Mencken:** *Prejudices* Third Series (1922)

206. The essential American soul is hard, isolate, stoic, a killer.—**D. H. Lawrence:** *Studies in Classic American Literature* (1922)

207. America is neither free nor brave, but a land of tight, iron-clanking little wills, everybody trying to pot it over everybody else, and a land of men absolutely devoid of the real courage of trust, trust in life's sacred spontaneity. They can't *trust*, life until they can *control* it.—**D. H. Lawrence:** letter, 27 September 1922

208. In every American there is an air of incorrigible innocence, which seems to conceal a diabolical cunning.—**A. E. Housman,** 1859–1936, British poet: Frederic Prokosch *Voices: A Memoir* (1983)

209. Above all, we know that although Americans can be led to make great sacrifices, they do not like to be driven.—**Herbert Hoover,** 1874–1964

210. Americans are getting like a Ford car—they all have the same parts, the same upholstering and make exactly the same noises.—**Will Rogers:** 1928; *Autobiography of Will Rogers* (1949)

211. We don't know what we want, but we are ready to bite somebody to get it.—**Will Rogers:** 1928; *Autobiography of Will Rogers* (1949)

212. Every true American likes to think in terms of thousands and millions. The word "million" is probably the most pleasure-giving vocable in the language.—**Agnes Repplier:** *Times and Tendencies* (1931)

213. The American people never carry an umbrella. They prepare to walk in eternal sunshine.—**Alfred E. Smith:** speech, 1931

214. The Americans are a queer people; they can't rest.—**Stephen Leacock,** 1869–1944: Fred J. Ringel *America as Others See It* (1932)

215. The three great American vices seem to be efficiency, punctuality and the desire for achievement and success. They are the things that make the Americans so unhappy and so nervous.—**Lin Yutang:** *The Importance of Living* (1937)

216. In America, everybody is, but some are more than others.—**Gertrude Stein:** *Everybody's Autobiography* (1938)

217. Perhaps this is our strange and haunting paradox here in America, that we are fixed and certain only when we are in movement. —**Thomas Wolfe,** 1900–38: *You Can't Go Home Again* (1940)

218. Nothing so challenges the American spirit as tackling the biggest job on earth. Americans are stimulated by the big job—the Panama Canal, Boulder Dam, Grand Coulee, Lower Colorado River developments, the tallest building in the world, the mightiest battleship.—**Lyndon B. Johnson:** speech to Congress, 30 April 1941

219. No man has a right in America to treat any other man tolerantly, for tolerance is the assumption of superiority.—**Wendell Lewis Willkie,** 1892–1944

220. The shell is America's most active contribution to the formation of character. A tough hide. Grow it early.—**Anaïs Nin:** *The Diary of Anaïs Nin* vol. 4 (1944–47)

221. There is no crime in the cynical American calendar more humiliating than to be a sucker.—**Max Lerner:** *Actions and Passions* (1949)

222. We are a people with a faith in each other, and when we lose that faith we are weak, however heavily armed. We are a people with a faith in reason, and the unending pursuit of new knowledge; and when we lose that faith we are insecure, though we be ever so heavily armed. We are a people with a faith in God, and a deep sense of stewardship to our Creator, the Father of us all; and when that is no longer Strong within us, we are weak and we are lost, however heavily armed with weapons—with atomic weapons—we may be.—**David E. Lilienthal:** *This I Do Believe* (1949)

223. Americans are willing to go to enormous trouble and expense defending their principles with arms, very little trouble and expense advocating them with words. Temperamentally we are ready to die for certain principles (or, in the case of overripe adults, send youngsters to die), but we show little inclination to advertise the reasons for dying.—**E. B. White:** *New Yorker,* 23 September 1950

224. Americans cheerfully assume that in some mystic way love conquers all, that good outweighs evil in the just balance of the universe and at the eleventh hour something gloriously triumphant will prevent the worst before it happens.—**Brooks Atkinson:** *Once Around the Sun* (1951)

225. [His] mentality was one that bad been remarked upon as being peculiarly American since the nation had been born—the restless, erratic insight and imagination of a gadgeteer. —**Kurt Vonnegut:** *Player Piano* (1952)

226. We cling to a bourgeois mediocrity which would make it appear we are all Americans, made in the image and likeness of George Washington, all of a pattern, all prospering if we are good, and going down in the world if we are bad.—**Dorothy Day:** *The Long Loneliness* (1952)

227. The standardized American is largely a myth created not least by Americans themselves.—**Irwin Edman,** 1896–1954: *The Uses of Philosophy* (1955)

228. Perhaps I am still very much of an American. That is to say, naïve, optimistic, gullible. In the eyes of a European, what am I but an American to the core, an American who exposes his Americanism like a sore. Like it or not, I am a product of this land of plenty, a believer in superabundance, a believer in miracies.—**Henry Miller:** *A Devil in Paradise* (1956)

229. The Yankee is one who, if he once gets his teeth set on a thing, all creation can't make him let go.—**James T. Farrell:** Introduction to H. L. Mencken *Prejudices: A Selection* (1958)

230. Americans are suckers for good news. —**Adlai Stevenson:** speech, 8 June 1958; *New York Times,* 9 June 1958

231. The growing American characteristically defends himself against anxiety by learning not to become too involved.—**Edgar Z. Friedenberg:** *The Vanishing Adolescent* (1959)

232. Always the path of American destiny has been into the unknown. Always there arose enough of reserves of strength, balances of sanity, portions of wisdom to carry the nation through to a fresh start with ever-renewing vitality.—**Carl Sandburg:** on 96th anniversary of Lincoln's Gettysburg address, *New York Times,* 20 November 1959

233. Being American is not a matter of birth. We must practice it every day, lest we become something else.—**Malcolm Wallop,** 1929–68: *Imprimis*

234. I don't think they're brash, that's a stereotype from the past, the Americans these days are cool and shut off, they've got glass or ice between them and the rest of the world.—**Doris Lessing:** *Golden Notebook* (1962)

235. Never have people been more the masters of their environment. Yet never has a people felt more deceived and disappointed. For never has a people expected so much more than the world could offer.—**Daniel J. Boorstin:** *The Image* (1962)

236. [Americans] expect to eat and stay thin, to be constantly on the move and ever more neighborly... to revere God and be God.—**Daniel J. Boorstin:** *Newsweek*, 26 February 1962

237. Americans ... are not only hospitable in emergency but radiant. The most lavishly helpful people in the world, accepting the burden of nuisances as if they were bunches of hothouse flowers, all the more delightful because unexpected.—**Pamela Hansford Johnson:** *Night and Silence* (1963)

238. In America few people will trust you unless you are irreverent.—**Norman Mailer:** *The Presidential Papers* (1963)

239. Frustrate a Frenchman, he will drink himself to death; an Irishman, he will die of angry hypertension; a Dane, he will shoot himself; an American, he will get drunk, shoot you, then establish a million-dollar aid program for your relatives. Then he will die of an ulcer.—**Stanley Rudin:** *New York Times*, 22 August 1963

240. The Americans have always been food, sex, and spirit revivalists.—**Edward Dahlberg:** *Alms for Oblivion* (1964)

241. No people require maxims so much as the American. The reason is obvious: the country is so vast, the people always going somewhere, from Oregon apple valley to boreal New England, that we do not know whether to be temperate orchards or sterile climate.—**Edward Dahlberg:** *Alms for Oblivion* (1964)

242. Bond smoked like Peter Lorre, drank like Humphrey Bogart, ate like Sydney Greenstreet, used up girls like Errol Flynn ... then went to a steam bath and came out looking like Clark Gable.—**Harry Reasoner:** on Ian Fleming's character James Bond in numerous films; *Journal-American* (New York), 13 August 1964

243. For every five well-adjusted and smoothly functioning Americans, there are two who never had the chance to discover themselves. It may well be because they have never been alone with themselves.—**Marya Mannes:** *Vogue*, 1 October 1964

244. The Americans will always do the right thing... after they've exhausted all the alternatives.—**Winston Churchill,** 1874–1965

245. Americans are big boys. You can talk them into almost anything. [Just] sit with them for half an hour over a bottle of whiskey and be a nice guy.—**Nguyen Cao Ky:** 1965; Robert C. Mason *Chicken-hawk* (1983)

246. The Americans are a funny lot; they drink whiskey to keep them warm; then they put some ice in it to make it cool; they put some sugar in it to make it sweet, and then they put a slice of lemon in it to make it sour. Then they say "here's to you" and drink it themselves.—**B. N. Chakravarty:** *India Speaks to America* (1966)

247. Americans—like omelettes:
there is no such thing
as a pretty good one.
—**W. H. Auden:** *Marginalia* (1965–68)

248. In a land in which the tough guy is admired, politeness is widely considered to be effeminate.—**Ashley Montagu:** *The American Way of Life* (1967)

249. America knew what it would be. For more than three centuries, the word "American" designated a man who was defined not by what he had done, but by what he would do.—**Octavio Paz:** *Tri Quarterly* (1968)

250. One trouble with Americans is that we're fixers rather than preventers.—**James Doolittle:** *Guideposts*, 1969

251. Scratch an American and you get a Seventh Day Adventist every time.—**Lord Hailsham:** *Observer*, 1 June 1969

252. The compulsion to do good is an innate American trait. Only North Americans seem to believe that they always should, may, and actually can choose somebody with whom to share their blessings. Ultimately this attitude leads to bombing people into the acceptance of gifts.—**Ivan Illich:** *Celebration of Awareness* (1969)

253. The average American is for the underdog, but only on the condition that he has a chance to win.—**Bill Vaughan:** *The Kansas City Star*, 1970

254. Americans do at the end of the day what they don't like to do at noon.—**Dean Acheson,** 1893–1971: *Time*, 30 June 1980

255. The ideal American type is perfectly expressed by the Protestant, individualist, anticonformist, and this is the type that is in the process of disappearing. In reality there are few left.—**Orson Welles,** 1915–85: Andrew Sarris (ed.) *Hollywood Voices* (1971)

256. Among the things Americans invented or improved is the poker game, financial shenanigans, the art of stock exchange speculation, the rackets, and ingenious petty swindles. —**Luigi Barzini:** *Reflections 1972* (1972)

257. Americans see history as a straight line and themselves standing at the cutting edge of it as representatives for all mankind. They believe in the future as if it were a religion; they believe that there is nothing they cannot accomplish, that solutions wait somewhere for all problems, like brides.—**Frances Fitzgerald:** *Fire in the Lake* (1972)

258. America … just a nation of two hundred million used car salesmen with all the money we need to buy guns and no qualms about killing anybody else in the world who tries to make us uncomfortable.—**Hunter S. Thompson:** 1972; Robert Andrews *The Concise Columbia Dictionary of Quotations* (1987)

259. The four cornerstones of character on which the structure of this nation was built are: Initiative, Imagination, Individuality and Independence.—**Edward V. Rickenbacker,** 1890–1973: Ted Goodman (ed.) *The Forbes Book of Business Quotations* (1997)

260. The average American suffers from two delusions, one that God is dead and the other that there is a difference between brands of cigarettes.—**Philip K. Dick,** 1928–82

261. You will find the Americans much like the Greeks found the Romans: great, big, vulgar, bustling people more vigorous than we are and also more idle, with more unspoiled virtues but also more corrupt.—**Harold Macmillan,** 1894–1986

262. It may be that the most interesting American struggle is the struggle to set oneself free from the limits one is born to, and then to learn something of the value of those limits.—**Greil Marcus:** *Mystery Train* (1975)

263. Americans have been conditioned to respect newness, whatever it costs them.—**John Updike:** *A Month of Sundays* (1975)

264. We Americans are a peculiar people. We are for the underdog no matter how much of a dog he is.—**A. B. Chandler:** *Reader's Digest*, November 1975

265. America is still the best hope. But the Americans themselves will have to be the best hope too.—**Jorge Luis Borges:** *Time*, 5 July 1976

266. We are of course a nation of differences. Those differences don't make us weak. They're the source of our strength. The question is not when we came here but why our families came here. And what we did after we arrived.—**Jimmy Carter:** speech at Al Smith Dinner, New York City, 21 October 1976

267. Hunter Thompson's disease, … an incurable, fatal malady suffered by those who feel that Americans can be as easily led to beauty as to ugliness, to truth as to public relations, to joy as to bitterness.—**Kurt Vonnegut:** *New Times*, 10 December 1976

268. Americans (as seen from a distance) were known to get things done, ruthlessly, meticulously, quickly, against all obstacles.—**Luigi Barzini:** *O America* (1977)

269. All I would ask of Americans is that you go on being yourselves—valiant without being fanatical, individualistic without being foolhardy, skeptical without being cynical, open-minded without being indecisive, generous without being naive, patriotic without being nationalistic, and good without being perfect.—**Peter Jay:** *New York Times*, 13 October 1977

270. The duty of our generation of Americans is to renew our nation's faith—not focused just against foreign threats, but against the threat of selfishness, cynicism and apathy.—**Jimmy Carter:** *Time*, 5 February 1979

271. The American conviction that one should not kick a man when he is up.—**Henry Fairlie:** *Spectator*, 24 May 1980

272. In England you have to know people very intimately indeed before they tell you about the rust in their Volvo. It has never surprised me that there are fifty million Roman Catholics in America, and nearly as many psychiatrists: bean-spilling is the national mania. —**Alan Coren:** *Sunday Times*, 21 June 1981

273. It is an American characteristic not to stop running even after you have arrived. —**Clive James:** *Observer*, 1981

274. [College students] think that they, by being Americans, and well-to-do, bring privilege to what they touch. This vanity is becoming an empty caste arrogance. Ignorant people in preppy clothes are more dangerous to America than oil embargoes. —**V. S. Naipaul:** *New York Times*, 21 December 1981

275. Americans are overreaching; overreaching is the most admirable and most American of the many American excesses. —**George F. Will:** *Statecraft as Soulcraft* (1984)

276. Americans usually believe that nothing is impossible. —**Lawrence S. Eagleburger,** 1930–   : Henry O. Dormann *The Speaker's Book of Quotations* (1987)

277. Americans may have no identity, but they do have wonderful teeth. —**Jean Baudrillard:** *America* (1986)

278. They're the experts where personality is concerned, the Americans; they've got it down to a fine art. —**Alan Bennett:** *Talking Heads* (1988)

279. It has always been cited as an irrepressible symptom of America's vitality that her people, in fair times and foul, believe in themselves and their institutions. —**Alistair Cooke:** *America Observed* (1988)

280. Americans have begun to understand that trouble does not start somewhere on the other side of town. It seems to originate inside the absolute middle of the homemade cherry pie. —**June Jordan:** *Moving Towards Home: Political Essays* (1989)

281. He knew them. Americans. They killed each other over dinner, shot one another for sport, mugged old ladies in the street. Help like that he didn't need. —**T. Coraghessan Boyle:** *East Is East* (1990)

282. Free people have a serious problem with place, being in a place, using up a place, deciding which new place to rotate to. Americans ricochet around the United States like billiard balls. —**Walker Percy:** *Signposts in a Strange Land* (1991)

283. Anyone who believes that the competitive spirit in America is dead has never been in a supermarket when the cashier opens another checkout line. —**Ann Landers,** 1918–   : Louis E. Boone (ed.) *Quotable Business* (1992)

284. The self is now the sacred cow of American culture, self-esteem is sacrosanct. —**Robert Hughes:** *Culture of Conservatives* (1993)

285. Americans have a special horror of letting things happen their own way, without interference. They would like to jump down their stomachs, digest the food, and shovel the shit out. —**William S. Burroughs,** 1914–   : Connie Robertson (ed.) *The Wordsworth Dictionary of Quotations* (1996)

Americans Abroad

See also INTERNATIONAL RELATIONS: World

286. That strange blend of the commercial traveler, the missionary and the barbarian conqueror, which was the American abroad. —**Olaf Stapledon:** *Last and First Men* (1930)

287. There is no substitute for the riches gained on a lifetime basis by the young American who studies or works abroad. —**Letitia Baldridge:** *Of Diamonds and Diplomats* (1968)

288. America has a history of political isolation and economic self-sufficiency; its citizens have tended to regard the rest of the world as a disaster area from which lucky or pushy people emigrate to the Promised Land. Alternatively, they think of other nations as mere showplaces for picturesque scenery, odd flora and fauna and quaint artifacts. The American tourist abroad therefore wears clothes suitable for a trip to a disaster area, or for a visit to a museum or zoo: comfortable, casual, brightly colored, relatively cheap: not calculated to arouse envy or pick up dirt.—**Alison Lurie:** *The Language of Clothes* (1981)

289. Americans have always been eager for travel, that being how they got to the New World in the first place.—**Otto Friedrich:** *Time*, 22 April 1985

290. Americans go from one dreary Holiday Inn to another and are searching desperately for their sanitized lavatory seats and their iced Coca-Cola. Americans are rather like bad Bulgarian wine. They don't travel well.—**Bernard Falk:** BBC-TV, April 1986; *Travel Weekly*, 1 May 1986

291. If a foreign country doesn't look like a middle-class suburb of Dallas or Detroit, then obviously the natives must be dangerous as well as badly dressed.—**Lewis H. Lapham:** *Money and Class in America* (1988)

292. Tips for Americans traveling abroad:
—Carry the Koran;
—Paint a red dot on your forehead;
—Wear sandals;
—Never ask how the Mets are doing.
—**Mark Russell:** Robert Byrne *The Fourth 637 Best Things Anybody Ever Said* (1990)

293. You can always tell a Midwestern couple in Europe because they will be standing in the middle of a busy intersection looking at a windblown map and arguing over which way is west. European cities, with their wandering streets and undisciplined alleys, drive Midwesterners practically insane.—**Bill Bryson:** *The Lost Continent* (1989)

294. Americans get nervous abroad. As a result they tend either to travel in groups or bomb Libya.—**Miles Kington:** *Independent*, 29 March 1989

295. There are few certainties when you travel. One of them is that the moment you arrive in a foreign country, the American dollar will fall like a stone.—**Erma Bombeck:** *When You Look Like Your Passport, It's Time to Go Home* (1991)

Blacks

See also CULTURE AND MEDIA: Music

296. To be a poor man is hard, but to be a poor race in a land of dollars is the very bottom of hardships.—**W. E. B. Du Bois:** *The Souls of Black Folk* (1903)

297. An American, a Negro … two souls, two thoughts, two unreconciled strivings; two warring ideals in one dark body, whose dogged strength alone keeps it from being torn asunder.—**W. E. B. Du Bois:** *The Souls of Black Folk* (1903)

298. Exaggerated self-importance is deemed an individual fault, but a racial virtue.—**Kelly Miller:** *The American Negro* (1908)

299. The treatment of the Negro is America's greatest and most conspicuous scandal.—**Gunnar Myrdal:** *An American Dilemma* (1944)

300. The American Negro problem is a problem in the heart of the American. It is there that the interracial tension has its focus. It is there that the decisive struggle goes on.—**Gunnar Myrdal:** *An American Dilemma* (1944)

301. The Negro problem is a white man's problem.—**Franz Schoenberner:** *Confessions of a European Intellectual* (1946)

302. Please stop using the word "Negro." We are the only human beings in the world with fifty-seven variety of complexions who are classed together as a single racial unit. Therefore, we are really truly colored people, and that is the only name in the English language which accurately describes us.—**Mary Church Terrell:** letter to the editor; *Washington Post*, 14 May 1949

303. It is only in his music, which Americans are able to admire because a protective sentimentality limits their understanding of it, that the Negro in America has been able to tell his story.—**James Baldwin:** *Partisan Review*, November 1951

304. At the root of the American Negro problem is the necessity of the American white man to find a way of living with the Negro in order to be able to live with himself.—**James Baldwin:** *Harper's Magazine*, October 1953

305. The Negro is America's metaphor.—**Richard Wright,** 1908-60: *New York Times*, 5 October 1995

306. I'll tell you what's at the bottom of it. If you can convince the lowest white man that he's better than the best coloured man, he won't notice you're picking his pocket. Hell, give him someone to look down on and he'll empty his pockets for you.—**Lyndon B. Johnson:** to Bill Moyers during the 1960 presidential campaign; Robert Dallek *Lone Star Rising* (1991)

307. From adolescence to death there is something very personal about being a Negro in America.—**J. Saunders Redding,** 1906-88: Janet Cheatham Bell (ed.) *Famous Black Quotations* (1995)

308. A Negro woman has the same kind of problems as other women, but she can't take the same things for granted.—**Dorothy Height,** 1912- : Terri L. Jewell *The Black Woman's Gumbo Ya-Ya* (1993)

309. The Negro was invented in America. —**John Oliver Killens,** 1916- : Janet Cheatham Bell (ed.) *Famous Black Quotations* (1995)

310. I want to be the white man's brother, not his brother-in-law.—**Martin Luther King, Jr.:** *New York Journal-American*, 10 September 1962

311. The Negro's great stumbling block in his stride toward freedom is not the White Citizen's Councilor or the Ku Klux Klanner, but the white moderate is more devoted to order than to justice.—**Martin Luther King, Jr.:** letter from Birmingham Jail; *Why We Can't Wait* (1963)

312. Segregation now, segregation tomorrow and segregation forever!—**George Wallace:** inaugural address as Governor of Alabama, January 1963; *Birmingham World*, 19 January 1963

313. Just being a Negro doesn't qualify you to understand the race situation any more than being sick makes you an expert on medicine. —**Dick Gregory:** *Nigger* (1964)

314. Being a star made it possible for me to get insulted in places where the average Negro could never hope to go and get insulted.

—**Sammy Davis, Jr.,** American actor, singer, and dancer: *Yes I Can* (1965)

315. But suppose God is black? What if we go to Heaven and we, all our lives, have treated the Negro as an inferior, and God is there, and we look up and He is not white? What then is our response?—**Robert F. Kennedy,** 1925-68

316. The Negro needs the white man to free him from his fears. The white man needs the Negro to free him from his guilt.—**Martin Luther King, Jr.,** 1929-68: obituary, *New York Times*, 7 April 1968

317. To be a Negro in America is to hope against hope.—**Martin Luther King, Jr.:** *Chaos or Community* (1967)

318. If I do something good then I am an American, but if I do something bad then I am a Negro.—**Tommie Smith:** Christopher Brasher *Mexico 1968* (1968)

319. I suggested [in 1966] that we use the panther as our symbol and call our political vehicle the Black Panther Party. The panther is a fierce animal, but he will not attack until he is backed into a corner; then he will strike out.— **Huey Newton:** *Revolutionary Suicide* (1973)

320. The absence of [George] Wallace is not the presence of justice.—**Jesse Jackson:** *Time*, 17 May 1976

321. We too often condemn blacks who succeed and excel, calling them Uncle Toms.—**Jesse Jackson:** *Sepia*, September 1976

322. The vogue of the New Negro ... had all of the character of a public relations promotion. The Negro had to be "sold" to the public in terms they could understand.—**Nathan Huggins:** *Harlem Renaissance* (1977)

323. It is the black poet who bridges the gap in tradition, who modifies tradition when experience demands it, who translates experience into meaning and meaning into belief.—**Henry Louis Gates, Jr.:** Dester Fisher and Robert B. Stepto *Afro-American Literature* (1979)

324. For perhaps the last fifty years there has been a growing distrust, even hatred, between black men and black women. It has been nursed along not only by racism on the part of whites, but also by an almost deliberate ignorance on the part of blacks about the sexual politics of their experience in this country.—**Michele Wallace:** *Black Macho and the Myth of the Superwoman* (1978)

325. No other group in America has so had their identity socialized out of existence as have black women. When black people are talked about the focus tends to be on black *men*; and when women are talked about the focus tends to be on *white* women.—**Bell Hooks:** *Ain't I a Woman?* (1981)

326. America is deeply rooted in Negro culture: its colloquialisms, its humor, its music. —**Sonny Rollins:** *Freedom Suite* (1983)

327. As long as the colored man look to white folks to put the crown on what he say ... as long as he looks to white folks for approval ... then he ain't never gonna find out who he is and what he's about.—**August Wilson, Jr.:** *Ma Rainey's Black Bottom* (1984)

328. The white man discovered the Cross by way of the Bible, but the black man discovered the Bible by way of the Cross.—**James Baldwin:** *Evidence of Things Not Seen* (1985)

329. [Blacks] fought for the right to check into a hotel; today we are fighting to have enough money to check-out.—**Benjamin L. Hooks:** *USA Today*, 30 June 1986

330. It's hard being black. You ever been black? I was black once—when I was poor.—**Larry Holmes:** *Spectator*, 11 July 1987

331. Have you always been a Negro or are you just trying to be fashionable?—**Alvin Sargent:** *Julia* TV-series; Robert Byrne *The Fourth 637 Best Things Anybody Ever Said* (1990)

332. Black people are the only segment in American society that is defined by its weakest elements. Every other segment is defined by its highest achievement. We have to turn that around.—**Jewell Jackson McCabe:** Brian Lanker *I Dream a World* (1989)

333. As a matter of racial pride we want to be called blacks. Which has replaced the term Afro-Americans. Which replaced Negroes. Which replaced colored people. Which replaced darkies. Which replaced blacks.—**Jules Feiffer,** 1929- : William Safire *Language Maven Strikes Again* (1990)

334. This [racism] is something that white America is going to have to work out themselves. If they decide they want to stop it, curtail it, or to do the right thing then it will be done, but not until then.—**Spike Lee:** *Roger Ebert's Home Movie Companion* (1990)

335. To be black and an intellectual in America is to live in a box. On the box is a label, not of my own choosing.—**Stephen Carter:** *Reflections of an Affirmative Action Baby* (1992)

336. There are those who believe Black people possess the secret of joy and that it is this that will sustain them through any spiritual or moral or physical devastation.—**Alice Walker:** *Possessing the Secret of Joy* (1992)

337. In this country American means white. Everybody else has to hyphenate.—**Toni Morrison:** *Guardian*, 29 January 1992

338. Black people have always been America's wilderness in search of a promised land.—**Cornel West:** *Race Matters* (1993)

339. When Negroes are average, they fail, unless they are very, very lucky. Now, if you're average and white, honey, you can go far. Just look at Dan Quayle. If that boy was colored he'd be washing dishes somewhere.—**Annie Elizabeth Delany:** *Having Our Say: The Delany Sisters' First 100 Years* (1993)

340. Rule 1 is take what you can, give up what you must. Rule 2 is take it whenever, however, and from whomever. Rule 3 is, if you are not ready to abide by the first two rules, you are not qualified for a career in politics.—**William L. Clay:** advice to blacks in politics; *Just Permanent Interests* (1993)

341. When we're unemployed, we're called lazy; when the whites are unemployed it's called a depression.—**Jesse Jackson,** 1941-

Immigrants

See also THE NATION: Patriotism

342. Alien, *n*. An American sovereign in his probationary state.—**Ambrose Bierce:** *The Devil's Dictionary* (1906)

343. Every immigrant who comes here should be required within five years to learn English or leave the country.—**Theodore Roosevelt:** *Kansas City Star*, 27 April 1918

344. Without comprehension, the immigrant would forever remain shut out—a stranger in America. Until America can release the heart as well as train the hand of the immigrant, he would forever remain driven back upon himself, corroded by the very richness of the unused gifts within his soul.—**Anzia Yezierska:** *Hungry Hearts and Other Stories* (1920)

345. America our nation has been beaten by strangers who have bought the laws and fenced off the meadows and cut down the woods for pulp and turned our pleasant cities into slums and sweated the wealth out of our people and when they want to they hire the executioner to throw the switch.—**John Dos Passos:** *The Big Money* (1936)

346. The making of an American begins at that point where he himself rejects all other ties, any other history; and himself adopts the vesture of his adopted land.—**James Baldwin:** *Partisan Review*, Nov-Dec 1951

347. It almost seems that nobody can hate America as much as native Americans. America needs new immigrants to love and cherish it.—**Eric Hoffer:** *Reflections on the Human Condition* (1973)

348. My folks are immigrants and they fell under the spell of the American legend that the streets were paved with gold. When Papa got here he found out three things: (1) The streets were not paved with gold; (2) the streets were not paved at all; (3) he was supposed to do the paving.—**Sam Levenson,** 1911–80: Louis E. Boone (ed.) *Quotable Business* (1992)

349. Illegal aliens have always been a problem in the United States. Ask an Indian.—**Robert Orben,** 1927– , American editor and writer

350. My literary agenda begins by acknowledging that America has transformed *me*. It does not end until I show how I (and the hundreds of thousands like me) have transformed America.—**Bharati Mukherjee:** Janet Sternburg (ed.) *The Writer on Her Work* vol. 2 (1991)

Indians

See also HISTORY: Discovery

351. I went to America to convert the Indians; but oh, who shall convert me?—**John Wesley:** *Diary*, 24 January 1738

352. The only good Indian is a dead Indian.—**Philip H. Sheridan:** at Fort Cobb, January 1869, attrib.

353. We must act with vindictive earnestness against the Sioux, even to their extermination, men, women, and children. Nothing less will reach the root of the case.—**W. T. Sherman,** 1831–88: dispatch to president Grant; Robert Debs Heinl, Jr. *Dictionary of Military and Naval Quotations* (1966)

354. We took away their country and their means of support, broke up their mode of living, their habits of life, introduced disease and decay among them and it was for this and against this they made war. Could anyone expect less?—**Philip H. Sheridan:** 1878; Thomas C. Leonard *Above the Battle* (1978)

355. The pious ones of Plymouth, who, reaching the Rock, first fell upon their own knees and then upon the aborigines.—**William Maxwell Evarts,** 1818–83: attrib.; *Louisville Courier-Journal*, 4 July 1913

356. What law have I broken? Is it wrong for me to love my own? Is it wicked for me because my skin is red? Because I am Sioux; because I was born where my fathers lived; because I would die for my people and my country?—**Sitting Bull (Tatanka Iyotake):** to Major Brotherton, recorded July 1881; Gary C. Anderson *Sitting Bull* (1996)

357. When the white man came, we had the land and they had the Bibles. Now they have the land and we have the Bibles.—**Chief Dan George**

358. White America assumes, inevitably and frighteningly, the Red Indian nature—little by little.—**D. H. Lawrence:** letter to E. H. and Achsah Brewster, May 1921

359. Not that the Red Indian will ever possess the broad lands of America. At least I presume

not. But his ghost will.—**D. H. Lawrence:** *Studies in Classic American Literature* (1924)

360. This country was a lot better off when the Indians were running it.—**Vine Victor Deloria, Jr.:** *New York Times Magazine*, 3 March 1970

361. The Indian knows his village and feels for his village as no white man for his country, his town, or even for his own bit of land. His village is not the strip of land four miles long and three miles wide that is his as long as the sun rises and the moon sets. The myths are the village, and the winds and rains. The river is the village, and the talking bird, the owl, who calls the name of the man who is going to die.—**Margaret Craven:** *I Heard the Owl Call My Name* (1973)

362. Whoever the last true cowboy in America turns out to be, he's likely to be an Indian.—**William Trogdon:** *Blue Highways* (1983)

363. For the American Indian, the ability of all creatures to share in the process of ongoing creation makes all things sacred.—**Paula Gunn Allen,** American Indian poet and writer: *The Sacred Hoop* (1986)

364. We are the land. To the best of my understanding, that is the fundamental idea that permeates American Indian life.—**Paula Gunn Allen:** *The Sacred Hoop* (1986)

365. Indians think it is important to remember, while Americans believe it is important to forget.—**Paula Gunn Allen:** *The Sacred Hoop* (1986)

366. Our tribe unraveled like a coarse rope, frayed at either end as the old and new among us were taken.—**Louise Erdrich:** *Tracks* (1988)

367. It is impossible to come into contact with Native American spirituality and not be struck with the immensity of the gratitude expressed.—**Anne Wilson Schaef:** *Meditations for Women Who Do Too Much* (1990)

368. She realized that white people rarely concerned themselves with Indian matters, that Indians were the shadow people, living almost invisibly on the fringes around them, and that this shadowy world allowed for a strange kind of freedom.—**Linda Hogan:** *Mean Spirit* (1990)

369. In America, the Indian is relegated to the obligatory first chapter—the Once Great Nation chapter—after which the Indian is cleared away as easily as brush, using a very sharp rhetorical tool called an "alas."—**Richard Rodriguez:** *Harper's Magazine*, November 1991

370. Before you guys came along, we hunted and fished when we wanted to, the women did all the work, and we paid no taxes. And you thought you could improve on this system? Indians have to deal with four "B.C.":s: Before Christ, Before Columbus, Before Custer, and before Costner.—**Adam Fortunate Eagle,** Native American Artist: World Affairs Conference, University of Colorado, 1993

Minorities

See also THE NATION: Patriotism

371. Let us have done with British-Americans and Irish-Americans and German-Americans, and so on, and all be Americans…. If a man is going to be an American at all let him be so without any qualifying adjectives; and if he is going to be something else, let him drop the word American from his personal description.—**Henry Cabot Lodge:** address, 21 Dec 1888

372. An entirely new factor has appeared in the social development of the country, and this factor is the Irish-American, and his influence. To mature its powers, to concentrate its action, to learn the secret of its own strength and of England's weakness, the Celtic intellect has had to cross the Atlantic. At home it had but learned the pathetic weakness of nationality; in a strange land it realized what indomitable forces nationality possesses. What captivity was to the Jews, exile has been to the Irish: America and American influence have educated them.—**Oscar Wilde,** Anglo-Irish playwright and author: *Pall Mall Gazette* (London), 13 April 1889

373. You cannot become thorough Americans if you think of yourselves in groups. America does not consist of groups. A man who thinks of himself as belonging to a particular national group in America has not yet become an American.—**Woodrow Wilson:** address at Convention Hall, Philadelphia, Pennsylvania, 10 May 1915

374. There is no room in this country for hyphenated Americans. The one absolutely certain way of bringing this nation to ruin, of preventing all possibility of it continuing to be a nation at all, would be to permit it to become a tangle of squabbling nationalities.—**Theodore Roosevelt:** speech, New York City, 12 October 1915

375. I know that the White House was designed by [James] Hoban, a noted Irish-American architect, and I have no doubt that he believed by incorporating several features of the Dublin style he would make it more homelike for any president of Irish descent. It was a long wait, but I appreciate his efforts.—**John F. Kennedy:** on himself with Irish descent; address to the Irish Parliament in Dublin; *New York Times*, 28 June 1963

376. American Danish can be doughy, heavy, sticky, tasting of prunes and is usually wrapped in cellophane. Danish Danish is light, crisp, buttery and often tastes of marzipan or raisins; it is seldom wrapped in anything but loving care.—**R. W. Apple, Jr.:** *New York Times*, 22 November 1978

377. Irish Americans are about as Irish as black Americans are African.—**Bob Geldof,** Irish rock singer: *Observer*, 22 June 1986

The Public and Public Opinion

---

378. I believe there is no country, on the face of the earth, where there is less freedom of opinion on any subject in reference to which there is a broad difference of opinion, than in this.—**Charles Dickens:** letter to John Forster, 24 February 1842

379. No one ever went broke underestimating the taste of the American public.—**H. L. Mencken,** 1880–1956: Laurence J. Peter (ed.) *Peter's Quotations* (1977)

380. In America, public opinion is the leader. —**Frances Perkins:** *People at Work* (1934)

381. There exists in the world today a gigantic reservoir of good will toward us, the American people.—**Wendell Lewis Willkie:** *One World* (1943)

382. The trouble with the American public is that it thinks something is better than nothing.—**Alfred Stieglitz,** 1864–1946: Robert I. Fitzhenry *Barnes & Noble Book of Quotations* (1986)

383. The United States is a country where public opinion plays an important role. Nothing can be achieved or endure without it, and its veto is final. It is more spontaneous than anywhere else in the world and also more easily directed by efficient propaganda than in any other country.—**André Siegfried:** *America at Mid-Century* (1955)

384. American public opinion is like an ocean —it cannot be stirred by a teaspoon.—**Hubert H. Humphrey:** speech, 11 October 1966

385. It has always been an urgent necessity in America to filter the popular voice through political institutions, in place of the social habits which filter it, at an earlier stage, in Europe. —**Henry Fairlie:** *Spectator*, 29 March 1980

386. What the American public doesn't know, is exactly what makes them the American public.—**Dan Aykroyd:** *Tommy Boy* (film), 1995

PLACES

Alaska

387. Nature was the killer, like a living murderous enemy surrounding a stockade.—**Edna Ferber:** *Ice Palace* (1958)

388. You are no longer an Arctic frontier. You constitute a bridge to the continent of Asia and all its people.—**Dwight D. Eisenhower:** speech, 12 June 1960

389. A handful of people clinging to a subcontinent.—**John McPhee:** *Coming into the Country* (1977)

390. [Alaska is] not a state, it's an experience.—**John Denver:** *Chicago Tribune*, 16 August 1978

391. Our biggest, buggiest, boggiest state.—**Edward Abbey:** *A Voice Crying in the Wilderness* (1989)

392. I'd read somewhere that nine out of ten adults in Alaska had a drinking problem. I could believe it. Snow, ice, sleet, wind, the dark night of the soul: what else were you supposed to do?—**T. Coraghessan Boyle:** *If the River Was Whiskey* (1989)

Baltimore

393. A Baltimorean is not merely John Doe, an isolated individual of *Homo sapiens*, exactly like every other John Doe. He is John Doe of a certain place—of Baltimore, of a definite *house* in Baltimore.—**H. L. Mencken:** *Prejudices* Fifth Series (1926)

394. Baltimore is such a lousy town, Francis Scott Key went out in a boat to write *The Star Spangled Banner.*—**Billy Martin:** Colin Jarman *The Guinness Dictionary of Poisonous Quotes* (1991)

Boston

395. Their hotels are bad. Their pumpkin pies are delicious. Their poetry is not so good.—**Edgar Allan Poe:** *Broadway Journal* (1845)

396. Boston's a hole, the herring-pond is wide.—**Elizabeth Barrett Browning**, 1806–61: "Mr. Sludge"

397. A Boston man is the east wind made flesh.—**Thomas Gold Appleton**, 1812–84: attrib.

398. Boston runs to brains as well as to beans and brown bread. But she is cursed with an army of cranks whom nothing short of a straitjacket or a swamp-elm will ever control.—**William Cowper Brann**, 1855–98: *The Iconoclast* (1898–1903)

399. Tomorrow night I appear for the first time before a Boston Audience—4,000 critics.—**Mark Twain**, 1835–1910: Colin Jarman *The Guinness Dictionary of Poisonous Quotes* (1991)

400. I come from the city of Boston,
The home of the bean and the cod,
Where Cabots speak only to Lowells,
And Lowells speak only to God.
—**Samuel C. Bushnell:** "Boston" (1905)

401. The society of Boston was and is quite uncivilized but refined beyond the point of civilization.—**T. S. Eliot:** *Little Review* (1918)

402. It is not age which killed Boston, for no cities die of age; it is the youth of other cities.—**W. L. George:** *Hail Columbia!* (1921)

403. A Bostonian—an American, broadly speaking.—**George E. Woodberry,** 1855–1930: Robert I. Fitzhenry (ed.) *Barnes & Noble Book of Quotations* (1987)

404. When I go abroad I always sail from Boston because it is such a pleasant place to get away from.—**Oliver Herford,** 1863–1935: Jon Winokur (ed.) *The Portable Curmudgeon Redux* (1992)

405. Well-bred Bostonians today deprecate the dourness, grimness, and bigotry of their forefathers—but they are intensely proud of them.—**Dixon Wecter:** *The Saga of American Society* (1937)

406. Boston is a moral and intellectual nursery always busy applying first principles to trifles.—**George Santayana,** 1863–1952: Daniel Cory (ed.) *Santayana: The Later Years* (1963)

407. A steel engraving with no color at all. —**John P. Marquand:** *Point of No Return* (1949)

408. I guess God made Boston on a wet Sunday.—**Raymond Chandler:** letter to Bernice Baumgarten, 21 March 1949

409. If you hear an owl hoot: "To whom" instead of "To who" you can make up your mind he was born and educated in Boston.—**Anonymous:** *F.P.A.'s Book of Quotations* (1952)

410. I have just returned from Boston. It is the only thing to do if you find yourself up there. —**Fred Allen:** letter to Groucho Marx, 12 June 1953

411. In Boston the night comes down with an incredibly heavy, small-town finality. The cows come home; the chickens go to roost; the meadow is dark. Nearly every Bostonian is in his house or in someone else's house, dining at the home board, enjoying domestic and social privacy.—**Elizabeth Hardwick:** *Harper's Magazine*, December 1959

412. Clear out eight hundred thousand people and preserve it as a museum piece.—**Frank Lloyd Wright,** 1867–1959: Colin Jarman *The Guinness Dictionary of Poisonous Quotes* (1991)

413. In Boston serpents whistle at the cold. —**Robert Lowell,** 1917–77: "Where the Rainbow Ends"; Louis Untermeyer (ed.) *Modern American Poetry* 8th ed. (1962)

414. Boston is one of the few American cities that regrets the past ... Boston's like England. Up to its ears in yellowing photographs.—**Penelope Gilliatt:** *A State of Change* (1967)

415. Wendell Phillips. He was about the only Bostonian of his time who wore no middle name and he was therefore considered half naked.—**Frank Sullivan,** 1892–1976: *A Garland of Ibids*

416. The place where the tide goes out and never comes back.—**Anonymous:** Laurence J. Peter *Peter's Quotations* (1977)

417. A festering mud puddle.—**Ellis Arnall:** Laurence J. Peter *Peter's Quotations* (1977)

418. It is one of the three cities in the world where the girls wear the ugliest shoes.—**Frank Zappa:** *Boston,* December 1978

419. A city with champagne tastes and beer pocketbooks.—**Alan Friedberg:** *Time,* 16 July 1979

420. This is a town where there are three pastimes: politics, sports, and revenge.—**Lawrence C. Moulter:** *New York Times,* 17 February 1993

California

421. A queer place—in a way, it has turned its back on the world, and looks into the void Pacific. It is absolutely selfish, very empty, but not false, and at least, not full of false effort. —**D. H. Lawrence:** letter to J. M. Murphy, 24 September 1923

422. A state peculiarly addicted to swift enthusiasms. It is a seed-bed of all manner of cults and theories, taken up, and dropped, with equal speed.—**Charlotte Perkins Gilman,** 1860–1935: *The Living of Charlotte Perkins Gilman* (1935)

423. A fine place to live—if you happen to be an orange.—**Fred Allen:** *American Magazine,* December 1945

424. A tragic country—like Palestine, like every Promised Land.—**Christopher Isherwood:** *Horizon* (London), 1947

425. They are a very decent generous lot of people out here and *they don't expect you to listen....* It's the secret of social ease in this country. They talk entirely for their own pleasure. Nothing they say is designed to be heard. —**Evelyn Waugh:** *The Loved One* (1948)

426. The department-store state. The most of everything and the best of nothing.—**Raymond Chandler:** *The Little Sister* (1949)

427. Nothing wrong with southern California that a rise in the ocean wouldn't cure.—**Ross MacDonald:** *The Drowning Pool* (1950)

428. Nobody can tell about this California climate. One minit its hot and the next minit its cold, so a person never knows what to hock. —**Anita Loos:** *A Mouse Is Born* (1951)

429. The Screwy State.—**Robert Graves,** 1895–1985: Jon Winokur (ed.) *The Portable Curmudgeon* (1987)

430. That advance post of civilization, with its flavourless cosmopolitanism, its charlatan philosophers and religions, its lack of anything old and well-tried, rooted in tradition and character.—**J. B. Priestley:** *Thoughts in the Wilderness* (1957)

431. It's a scientific fact that if you stay in California you lose one point of your IQ every year.—**Truman Capote:** *Breakfast at Tiffany's* (1958)

432. In California everyone goes to a therapist, is a therapist, or is a therapist going to a therapist.—**Truman Capote,** 1924–84: Fred Metcalf *The Penguin Dictionary of Modern Humorous Quotations* (1986)

433. Where the twentieth-century is a burning and shining neon light, and where, anyway, cows are rarely seen out-of-doors nowadays. —**Malcolm Muggeridge:** *Observer*, 11 April 1965

434. A place in which a boom mentality and a sense of Chekhovian loss meet in uneasy suspension; in which the mind is troubled by some buried but ineradicable suspicion that things had better work here, because here, beneath that immense bleached sky, is where we run out of continent.—**Joan Didion:** 1965; *Slouching Towards Bethlehem* (1968)

435. A tragic country—like Palestine, like every Promised Land.—**Christopher Isherwood:** *Exhumations* (1966)

436. San Narciso lay near L.A. Like many named places in California it was less an identifiable city than a grouping of concepts—census tracts, special purpose bond-issue districts, shopping nuclei, all overlaid with access roads to its own freeway.—**Thomas Pynchon:** *The Crying of Lot 49* (1966)

437. Where you can't run any farther without getting wet.—**Neil Morgan:** *Saturday Review*, 23 September 1967

438. Southern California, a veritable paradise of statuspheres.—**Tom Wolfe:** *The Pump House Gang* (1968)

439. It used to be said that you had to know what was happening in America because it gave us a glimpse of our future. Today, the rest of America, and after that Europe, had better heed what happens in California, for it already reveals the type of civilisation that is in store for all of us.—**Alistair Cooke,** British broadcaster: *Talk About America* (1968)

440. Californians are the biggest collection of losers who ever met on one piece of real estate. —**David Karp:** *New York Times*, 1968

441. From time to time the continent shifts, and everything that isn't fastened down slides into Southern California.—**Frank Lloyd Wright:** 1867–1959

442. All creative people should be required to leave California for three months every year. —**Gloria Swanson,** 1897–1983: Abby Adams *An Uncommon Scold* (1989)

443. Switzerland and Burgundy and Yorkshire and Scotland and Spain.—**Alistair Cooke:** *America* (1973)

444. Whatever starts in California unfortunately has a tendency to spread.—**Jimmy Carter:** Robert Shogun *Promises to Keep* (1977)

445. The apparent ease of California life is an illusion, and those who believe the illusion will live here in only the most temporary way. —**Joan Didion:** *The White Album* (1977)

446. A place with lots of warm weather and lots of cold people.—**Vanessa Redgrave:** *US*, 28 June 1977

447. A wet dream in the mind of New York. —**Erica Jong:** *How to Save Your Own Life* (1978)

448. I have seen the future and it plays.—**John Morgan:** 1978

449. Too fruity and nutty by half.—**George Gale:** *Spectator*, 23 September 1978

450. A place in which a boom mentality and a sense of Chekhovian loss meet in uneasy suspension.—**Joan Didion:** *New York Times Magazine*, 17 June 1979

451. A society in which a sense of history is continually sacrificed to a dream of the future. —**A. Alvarez:** *Observer*, 21 October 1979

452. In California, marriage is a felony.—**Joanne Astral:** "Evening at the Improv," NBC-TV, 1982

453. The West coast of Iowa.—**Joan Didion,** 1934–

454. Californians invented the concept of lifestyle. This alone warrants their doom.—**Joan Didion**

455. Southern California, where the American Dream came too true.—**Lawrence Ferlinghetti,** 1919–

456. Living in California adds ten years to a man's life. And those extra ten years I'd like to spend in New York.—**Harry Ruby**

457. There's nothing wrong with Southern California that a rise in the ocean level wouldn't cure.—**Ross MacDonald**

458. Most people in California came from somewhere else. They moved to California so they could name their kids Rainbow or Mailbox, and purchase tubular Swedish furniture without getting laughed at. Your "lifestyle" (as they say) is your ethics. This means that in California you don't really have to do anything, except look healthy, think good thoughts and pat yourself on the back about what a good person you are.—**Ian Shoales:** Jon Winokur (ed.) *The Portable Curmudgeon* (1987)

459. I spent two miserable years in California. But it was Barbara Stanwyck who said: "The best place to be miserable is California."—**Andrei Konchalovsky,** Russian director: *Knave*, October 1986

460. Californians are good at planning for the earth-quake, while simultaneously denying it will happen.—**Sheila Ballantyne:** *Life on Earth* (1988)

461. As one went to Europe to see the living past, so one must visit Southern California to observe the future.—**Alison Lurie,** 1926– : Abby Adams *An Uncommon Scold* (1989)

462. I wouldn't live in California. All that sun makes you sterile.—**Alan Alda,** 1936– : Colin Jarman *The Guinness Dictionary of Poisonous Quotes* (1991)

463. California reminds me of the popular American Protestant concept of Heaven: there is always a reasonable flow of new arrivals; one meets many—not all—of one's friends; people spend a good deal of their time congratulating one another about the fact that they are there; discontent would be unthinkable; and the newcomer is slightly disconcerted to realize that now, the devil having been banished and virtue being triumphant, nothing terribly interesting can ever happen again.—**George F. Kennan,** 1904– : Jon Winokur (ed.) *The Portable Curmudgeon Redux* (1992)

464. If it's worth doing, California will do it to excess.—**Anonymous:** fall 1996

465. All things start in California and spread to New York, then to London, and then throughout Europe.—**Stelios Haji-Ioannou:** *Wall Street Journal*, 9 December 1996

Chicago

466. Chicago sounds rough to the maker of verse;
One comfort we have—Cincinnati sounds worse.
—**Oliver Wendell Holmes, Sr.:** "Welcome to the Chicago Commercial Club," 14 January 1880

467. Perhaps the most typically American place in America.—**James Bryce:** *The American Commonwealth* (1888)

468. I have struck a city—a real city—and they call it Chicago.... I urgently desire never to see it again. It is inhabited by savages.—**Rudyard Kipling:** *American Notes* (1891)

469. Satan (impatiently) to Newcomer: The trouble with you Chicago people is, that you think you are the best people down here; whereas you are merely the most numerous.—**Mark Twain:** *Following the Equator* (1897)

470. Gigantic, willful, young,
Chicago sitteth at the northwest gates.
—**William Vaughn Moody:** *An Ode in Time of Hesitation* (1901)

471. Could anything be more indicative of a slight but general insanity than the aspect of the crowd on the streets of Chicago?—**Charles Horton Cooley:** *Human Nature and the Social Order* (1902)

472. First in violence, deepest in dirt, lawless, unlovely, ill-smelling, irreverent, new; an overgrown gawk of a—village, the "tough" among cities, a spectacle for the nation.—**Lincoln Steffens:** *The Shame of the Cities* (1904)

473. In the twilight, it was a vision of power.
—**Upton Sinclair:** *The Jungle* (1906)

474. Chicago is a product of modern capitalism, and like other great commercial centers is unfit for human habitation.—**Eugene Debs:** 1908; Colin Jarman *The Guinness Dictionary of Poisonous Quotes* (1991)

475. Chicago is unique. It is the only completely corrupt city in America.—**Charles Merriam:** 1911

476. Hog Butcher for the World,
Tool Maker, Stacker of Wheat,
Player with Railroads and the Nation's Freight Handler;
Stormy, husky, brawling,
City of Big Shoulders.
—**Carl Sandburg:** *Chicago Poems* (1916)

477. A city of terror and light, untamed.—**W. L. George:** *Hail Columbia!* (1921)

478. I adore Chicago. It is the pulse of America.—**Sarah Bernhardt,** 1844–1923

479. I am going to St. Petersburg, Florida, tomorrow. Let the worthy citizens of Chicago get their liquor the best they can. I'm sick of the job—it's a thankless one and full of grief. I've been spending the best years of my life as a public benefactor.—**Al Capone:** 1927

480. There's only one thing for Chicago to do, and that's to move to a better neighborhood. —**Herman Fetzer:** c. 1930; Robert McLaughlin *The Heartland* (1967)

481. It's one of the most progressive cities in the world. Shooting is only a sideline.—**Will Rogers:** 22 June 1930

482. Chicago will give you a chance. The sporting spirit is the spirit of Chicago.—**Lincoln Steffens:** *The Autobiography of Lincoln Steffens* (1931)

483. Eventually, I think Chicago will be the most beautiful great city left in the world. —**Frank Lloyd Wright:** 1939

484. I've reported murders, scandals, marriages, premieres and national political conventions. I've been amused, intrigued, outraged, enthralled and exasperated by Chicago. And I've come to love this American giant, viewing it as the most misunderstood, most underrated city in the world. There is none other quite like my City of Big Shoulders.—**Irv Kupcinet:** "Kup's Column," 1941

485. Chicago's South side is like a vast, unorganized lunatic asylum. Nothing can flourish here but vice and disease.—**Henry Miller:** *The Air-Conditioned Nightmare* (1945)

486. The greatest and most typically American of all cities. New York is bigger and more spectacular and can outmatch it in other superlatives, but it is a "world" city, more European in some respects than American.—**John Gunther:** *Inside U.S.A.* (1947)

487. The last copy of the *Chicago Daily News* I picked up had three crime stories on its front page. But by comparison to the gaudy days, this is small-time stuff. Chicago is as full of crooks as a saw with teeth, but the era when they ruled the city is gone forever.—**John Gunther:** *Inside U.S.A.* (1947)

488. A façade of skyscrapers facing a lake, and behind the façade every type of dubiousness. —**E. M. Forster:** letter, 5 June 1947

489. Chicago seems a big city instead of merely a large place.—**A. J. Liebling:** first to designate Chicago "The Second City," 1949

490. Like loving a woman with a broken nose, you may well find lovelier lovelies. But never a lovely so real.—**Nelson Algren:** *Chicago: City on the Make* (1951)

491. It's a joint where the bulls and the foxes live well and the lambs wind up head-down from the hook.—**Nelson Algren:** *Chicago: City on the Make* (1951)

492. I give you Chicago. It is not London and Harvard. It is not Paris and buttermilk. It is American in every chitling and sparerib. It is alive from snout to tail.—**H. L. Mencken,** 1880–1956

493. There was no need to inform us of the protocol involved. We were from Chicago and knew all about cement.—**Groucho Marx,** 1895–1977

494. I'm a little hoarse tonight. I've been living in Chicago for the past two months, and you know how it is, yelling for help on the way home every night. Things are so tough in Chicago that at Easter time, for bunnies the little kids use porcupines.—**Fred Allen,** 1894–1956: *Much Ado About Me* (1956)

495. I like to go to Marshall Field's in Chicago just to see how many things there are in the world that I do not want.—**Mother Mary Madeleva:** *My First Seventy Years* (1959)

496. Here is the difference between Dante, Milton, and me. They wrote about hell and never saw the place. I wrote about Chicago after looking the town over for years and years.—**Carl Sandburg,** 1878–1967: Harry Golden *Carl Sandburg* (1961)

497. Hell has been described as a pocket edition of Chicago.—**Ashley Montagu:** *The American Way Of Life* (1967)

498. Chicago was a town where nobody could forget how the money was made. It was picked up from floors still slippery with blood.—**Norman Mailer:** *Miami and the Siege of Chicago* (1968)

499. In most places in the country, voting is looked upon as a right and a duty, but in Chi-cago it's a sport. In Chicago not only your vote counts, but all kinds of other votes—kids, dead folks, and so on.—**Dick Gregory:** *Dick Gregory's Political Primer* (1972)

500. That's great advertising when you can turn Chicago into a city you'd want to spend more than three hours in.—**Jerry Della Femina**

501. Chicago has a strange metaphysical elegance of death about it.—**Claes Oldenburg,** 1929–

502. A pompous Milwaukee.—**Leonard Louis Levinson,** 1905–74: Laurence J. Peter (ed.) *Peter's Quotations* (1977)

503. An October sort of city even in spring.—**Nelson Algren,** 1909–81: *Newsweek,* 13 August 1984

504. I don't have any great love for Chicago. What the hell, a childhood around Douglas Park isn't very memorable. I remember the street fights and how you were afraid to cross the bridge cause the Irish kid on the other side would beat your head in. I left Chicago a long time ago.—**Benny Goodman:** *King of Swing* (1976)

505. A town with a Queen Anne front and a Queen Mary back.—**Paul H. Doauglas:** *New York Times,* 1977

506. Chicago is not the most corrupt American city, it's the most theatrically corrupt.—**Studs Terkel:** "Dick Cavett Show," 9 June 1978

507. Merely a place to change trains.—**Gaetano Merola:** *New York Times,* 21 November 1978

508. I'm impressed with people from Chicago. Hollywood is hype, New York is talk, Chicago is work.—**Michael Douglas,** 1944– , American actor: Robert Byrne (ed.) *The 637 Best Things Anybody Ever Said* (1982)

509. There are almost no beautiful cities in America, though there are many beautiful parts of cities, and some sections that are glorious without being beautiful, like downtown Chicago. Cities are too big and too rich for beauty; they have outgrown themselves too many times.—**Noel Perrin:** *Third Person Rural* (1983)

510. A lot of real Chicago lives in the neighborhood taverns. It is the mixed German and Irish and Polish gift to the city, a bit of the old country grafted into a strong new plant in the new.—**Bill Granger:** 1983

511. A city of contradictions, of private visions haphazardly overlaid and linked together. If the city was unhappy with itself yesterday—and invariably it was—it will reinvent itself today.—**Pat Colander:** *New York Times*, 5 May 1985

512. This vicious, stinking zoo, this mean-grinning, mace-smelling boneyard of a city; an elegant rockpile of a monument to everything cruel and stupid and corrupt in the human spirit.—**Hunter S. Thompson,** 1939–   : Jon Winokur (ed.) *The Portable Curmudgeon* (1987)

513. The place where bulls and foxes dine very well, but lambs end up head down on the hook.—**Ward Just:** *Jack Gance* (1988)

514. My first day in Chicago, September 4, 1983. I set foot in this city, and just walking down the street, it was like roots, like the motherland. I knew I belonged here.—**Oprah Winfrey**

515. I think that's how Chicago got started. A bunch of people in New York said, "Gee, I'm enjoying the crime and the poverty, but it just isn't cold enough. Let's go west."—**Richard Jeni**

516. Anywhere in the world you hear a Chicago bluesman play, it's a Chicago sound born and bred.—**Ralph Metcalfe**

517. Sharks are as tough as those football fans who take their shirts off during games in Chicago in January, only more intelligent.—**Dave Barry:** *Sex and the Single Amoeba: What Every Teen Should Know*

518. Most cities have a smell of their own. Chicago smells like it's not sure.—**Alan King:** Colin Jarman *The Guinness Dictionary of Poisonous Quotes* (1991)

519. I miss everything about Chicago, except January and February.—**Gary Cole**

Cincinnati

520. When the end of the world comes, I want to be in Cincinnati because it's always twenty years behind the times.—**Mark Twain,** 1835–

1910: attrib.; *Chronicle of Higher Education*, 4 September 1991

521. A hundred years ago Cincinnati was often called *Porkopolis* because so many hogs were butchered and processed there.—**J. C. Furnas:** Laurence J. Peter *Peter's Quotations* (1977)

522. I wish I were on a Cincinnati street corner holding a clean dog.—**Anonymous**

Cities

See also CULTURE AND MEDIA: Architecture

523. The cities of America are inexpressibly tedious. The Bostonians take their learning too sadly: culture with them is an accomplishment rather than an atmosphere; their "Hub," as they call it, is the paradise of prigs. Chicago is a sort of monster-shop, full of bustle and bores. Political life at Washington is like political life in a suburban vestry. Baltimore is amusing for a week, but Philadelphia is dreadfully provincial; and though one can dine in New York, one could not dwell there.—**Oscar Wilde:** *Court and Society Review* (London), March 1887

524. The government of cities is the one conspicuous failure of the United States.—**James Bryce:** *The American Commonwealth* (1888)

525. There is no part of the world where nomenclature is so rich, poetical, humorous, and picturesque as the United States of America. All times, races, and languages have brought their contribution. Pekin is in the same State with Euclid, with Bellefontaine, and with Sandusky. Old, red Manhattan lies, like an Indian arrowhead under a steam factory, below Anglified New York. The names of the States and Territories themselves form a chorus of sweet and most romantic vocables: Delaware, Ohio, Indiana, Florida, Dakota, Iowa, Wyoming, Minnesota, and the Carolinas.—**Robert Louis Stevenson:** *Across the Plains* (1892)

526. In Boston they ask, "How much does he know?" In New York, "How much is he worth?" In Philadelphia, "Who were his parents?"—**Mark Twain:** *North American Review* (Iowa), January 1895

527. There are just three big cities in the United States that are *story cities*—New York, of course, New Orleans, and best of the lot, San Francisco.—**Frank Norris**, 1870–1902: Laurence J. Peter *Peter's Quotations* (1977)

528. American cities are being littered with a disorder of unsystematized foundations and picturesque [architectural] legacies, much as I find my nursery floor littered with abandoned toys and battles and buildings when the children are in bed after a long wet day.—**H. G. Wells:** "The Future in America" (1906)

529. I think of American cities as enormous agglomerations in whose inmost dark recesses innumerable elevators are constantly ascending and descending, like the angels of the ladder. —**Arnold Bennett:** *Those United States* (1912)

530. The European traveller in America is struck by two peculiarities: first, the extreme similarity of outlook in all parts of the U.S. (except the old South), and second the passionate desire of each locality to prove that it is peculiar and different from every other. The second of these is, of course, the cause of the first.—**Bertrand Russell:** 1930; *In Praise of Idleness and Other Essays* (1935)

531. America is a nation with no truly national city, no Paris, no Rome, no London, no city which is at once the social center, the political capital, and the financial hub.—**C. Wright Mills:** *The Power Elite* (1956)

532. American cities are like badger holes ringed with trash.—**John Steinbeck:** *Travels with Charley* (1962)

533. The very development of the American city has removed poverty from the living, emotional experience of millions upon millions of middle-class Americans.—**Michael Harrington:** *The Other America* (1963)

534. The real illness of the American city today, and especially of the deprived groups within it, is voicelessness.—**Harvey Cox:** *The Secular City* (1966)

535. The reason American cities are prosperous is that there is no place to sit down.—**Alfred J. Talley:** A. K. Adams (ed.) *Cassell's Book of Humorous Quotations* (1969)

536. New York is one of the capitals of the world and Los Angeles is a constellation of plastic, San Francisco is a lady, Boston has become Urban Renewal, Philadelphia and Baltimore and Washington wink like dull diamonds in the smog of Eastern Megalopolis, and New Orleans is unremarkable past the French Quarter. Detroit is a one-trade town, Pittsburgh has lost its golden triangle, St. Louis has become the golden arch of the corporation, and nights in Kansas City close early. The oil depletion allowance makes Houston and Dallas naught but checkerboards for this sort of game. But Chicago is a great American city. Perhaps it is the last of the great American cities.—**Norman Mailer:** *Miami and the Siege of Chicago* (1968)

537. I didn't say I wouldn't go into ghetto areas. I've been in many of them and to some extent I would say this: If you've seen one city slum you've seen them all.—**Spiro T. Agnew,** Republican vice-president: *Detroit Free Press,* 19 October 1968

538. The big cities of America are becoming Third World countries.—**Nora Ephron:** lecture, San Francisco, 4 November 1983

539. Being blunt with your feelings is very American. In this big country, I can be as brash as New York, as hedonistic as Los Angeles, as sensuous as San Francisco, as brainy as Boston, as proper as Philadelphia, as brawny as Chicago, as warm as Palm Springs, as friendly as my adopted home town of Dallas, Fort Worth, and as peaceful as the inland waterway that rubs up against my former home in Virginia Beach.—**Martina Navratilova,** Czech-born American tennis player: *Martina Navratilova—Being Myself* (1985)

540. In some parts of the world, people still pray in the streets. In this country they're called pedestrians.—**Gloria Pitzer:** Robert Byrne *The Fourth 637 Best Things Anybody Ever Said* (1990)

541. In Washington, the first thing people tell you is what their job is. In Los Angeles you learn their star sign. In Houston you're told how rich they are. And in New York they tell you what their rent is.—**Simon Hoggart:** *America: A User's Guide* (1990)

542. American cities have ever been filled with unfamiliar people, acting in unfamiliar ways, at once terrified and threatening.—**Daniel Patrick Moynihan**, 1927–

Cleveland

543. Two Hobokens back to back.—**Joan Holman:** Laurence J. Peter *Peter's Quotations* (1977)

544. Contest Announcement: First prize— one week in Cleveland. Second prize—two weeks in Cleveland.—**Anonymous:** Laurence J. Peter *Peter's Quotations* (1977)

545. We are now arriving in Cleveland. Set back your watches forty-two minutes.—**Tim McCarver:** Colin Jarman *The Guinness Dictionary of Poisonous Quotes* (1991)

546. The only difference between Cleveland and the *Titanic* is the *Titanic* had better restaurants.—**Barney Nagler:** Colin Jarman *The Guinness Dictionary of More Poisonous Quotes* (1992)

Colorado

547. This state has more sunshine and more bastards than any place on earth.—**Anonymous:** John Gunther *Inside U.S.A.* (1947)

Connecticut

548. In a true democracy everyone can be upper class and live in Connecticut.—**Lisa Birnbach:** *The Official Preppy Handbook* (1980)

549. I've never made the trip to or from Connecticut without its resembling the worst excesses of the French Revolution.—**Pat Buckley:** 1984

Delaware

550. A state that has three counties when the tide is out, and two when it is in.—**John James Ingalls:** speech in the Senate, c. 1885

551. Delaware has fought and bucked, hated, reviled, admired and fawned upon, ignored and courted the Du Ponts, but in the end, it has invariably bowed to Du Pont's benevolent paternalism.—**James Warner Bellah:** *American Panorama: East of the Mississippi* (1960)

552. There are two political parties in Delaware: the DuPonts and the anti–DuPonts, with the proviso that many DuPonts are members of the anti–DuPont family.—**James Phelan** and **Robert Pozen:** *The Company State* (1973)

Detroit

553. The capital of the new planet—the one, I mean, which will kill itself off—is of course Detroit.—**Henry Miller:** *The Air-Conditioned Nightmare* (1945)

554. You can slip up on Detroit in the dead of night, consider it from any standpoint, and it's still hell on wheels.—**George Sessions Perry:** *Cities of America* (1947)

555. Detroit is Cleveland without the glitter.—**Anonymous:** Robert Byrne *The Other 637 Best Things Anybody Ever Said* (1984)

Florida

556. Florida's all right if you can keep from catching a sailfish and going to the expense of having it mounted.—**Kin Hubbard**, 1868–1930: Evan Esar (ed.) *The Dictionary of Humorous Quotations* (1949)

557. The state with the prettiest name, the state that floats in brackish water, held together by mangrove roots. —**Elizabeth Bishop:** *Florida* (1946)

558. I just got wonderful news from my real estate agent in Florida. They found land on my property.—**Milton Berle**, 1908– : H. V. Prochnow, et al. *A Dictionary of Wit, Wisdom & Satire* (1962)

559. God's waiting room.—**Glenn le Grice:** Robert I. Fitzhenry (ed.) *Barnes & Noble Book of Quotations* (1987)

560. I moved to Florida because you don't have to shovel water.—**James Randi:** *Money*, September 1986

561. My parents didn't want to move to Florida, but they turned sixty, and it was the law.—**Jerry Seinfeld:** Robert Byrne *The Fourth 637 Best Things Anybody Ever Said* (1990)

562. Alaska with Jai-alai games.—**Robert Orben,** 1927– : Colin Jarman *The Guinness Dictionary of Poisonous Quotes* (1991)

563. The Florida sun seems not much a single thing overhead but a set of klieg lights that pursue you everywhere with an even white - illumination.—**John Updike:** *Rabbit at Rest* (1990)

Hawaii

564. Paradise for an indolent man.—**Mark Twain:** "The Sandwich Islands," speech, 1866

565. Hawaii is the only place I know where they lay flowers on you while you are alive.—**Will Rogers,** 1879–1935: Alex Ayres *The Wit and Wisdom of Will Rogers* (1993)

566. The *nicest* thing about Hawaii is that when we select a beauty queen at the university we don't have just *one* beauty queen. We have a Polynesian beauty queen, a Chinese beauty queen, a Japanese beauty queen, a Filipino beauty queen, a Portuguese beauty queen, a Puerto Rico beauty queen, a Negro beauty queen, *and* a Caucasian beauty queen. Six, eight beauty queens all in a row. *That's* what I like the best about Hawaii.—**Thomas Hamilton:** Francine du Plessix Gray *Hawaii: The Sugar-Coated Fortress* (1972)

567. Hawaii is not a state of mind, but a state of grace.—**Paul Theroux:** *Observer*, 29 October 1989

Houston

568. A whisky and trombone town.—**J. B. Priestley:** *Journey Down a Rainbow* (1955)

569. This city has been an act of real estate rather than an act of God or man.—**Ada Louise Huxtable:** *New York Times*, 1976

570. Houston is twenty of the most innovative buildings in this country and 2000 rather ordinary gas stations.—**Denis Williams:** *Newsweek*, 1977

571. The economy of Houston is so bad right now that two prostitutes the police arrested turned out to be virgins.—**Bill Abeel:** *San Francisco Chronicle*, 6 May 1986

572. Fish have water, the bushmen of the Kalahari have sand, and Houstonians have interior décor.—**Simon Hoggart:** *America: A User's Guide* (1990)

Hudson River

573. The Hudson River is like old October and tawny Indians in their camping places long ago; it is like long pipes and old tobacco; it is like cool depths and opulence; it is like the shimmer of liquid green on summer days.—**Thomas Wolfe:** *Of Time and the River* (1935)

574. The river of the great 19th-century landscapists, of Cole, Cropsey and Church ... at the end of the summer lies motionless under the haze as under a light coat of varnish.—**Judith Thurman:** *House & Garden*, December 1984

Idaho

575. It is a melancholy strange-looking country, one of fractures and violence and fire.—**John C. Frémont:** 1843

576. Idaho is torn, above all, between two other states, between the pull of Washington in the north, that of Utah in the south. Half of Idaho belongs to Spokane, I heard it said, and the other half to the Mormon church.—**John Gunther:** *Inside U.S.A.* (1947)

Indiana

577. I come from Indiana, the home of more first-rate second-class men than any State in the Union.—**Thomas R. Marshall:** *Recollections* (1925)

Iowa

578. You are brilliant and subtle if you come from Iowa and really strange and you live as you live and you are always very well taken care of if you come from Iowa.—**Gertrude Stein:** *Everybody's Autobiography* (1937)

579. More a demonstration farm than a place; more some cosmic public relations project designed to prove that God's in his heaven and all's right with the world.—**Richard Rhodes:** *The Inland Ground* (1970)

580. Top-choice America, America cut thick and prime.—**Harvey Arden:** *National Geographic*, May 1981

581. They are clean, brave, thrifty, reverent, loyal, honest and able to brush after every meal.—**Donald Kaul:** *Washington Post*, 5 July 1981

582. I had forgotten just how flat and empty it [middle America] is. Stand on two phone books almost anywhere in Iowa and you get a view.—**Bill Bryson:** *The Lost Continent* (1989)

Kansas

583. Kansas had better stop raising corn and begin raising hell.—**Mary Elizabeth Lease:** 1890; E. J. James *Notable American Women 1607–1950* (1971)

584. A kind of gravity point for American democracy.—**John Gunther:** *Inside U.S.A.* (1947)

585. I'm as corny as Kansas in August.—**Oscar Hammerstein II:** "I'm in Love with a Wonderful Guy" (1949)

586. It isn't necessary to have relatives in Kansas City to be unhappy.—**Groucho Marx:** letter to Goodman Ace, 18 January 1951

587. Kansas, by reason of history and location at the heart of our continental power, is a kind of social, political, and cultural barometer for all America.—**Adlai Stevenson:** speech, Wichita, Kansas, 7 October 1954

588. A favorite dish in Kansas is creamed corn on a stick.—**Jeff Harms:** Robert Byrne *The Fourth 637 Best Things Anybody Ever Said* (1990)

Las Vegas

589. The most insidious influence of Las Vegas is its destruction of wonder: The wonder of sex, the wonder of chance, and the wonder of oneself.—**Neil Morgan:** *Westward Tilt—The American West Today* (1963)

590. Las Vegas takes what in other American towns is but a quixotic inflammation of the senses for some poor salary mule in the brief interval between the flagstone rambler and the automatic elevator downtown and magnifies it, foliates it, embellishes it into an institution.—**Tom Wolfe:** *The Kandy-Kolored Tangerine-Flake Streamline Baby* (1965)

591. Vegas is the most extreme and allegorical of American settlements, bizarre and beautiful in its venality and in its devotion to immediate gratification.—**Joan Didion:** *Slouching Towards Bethlehem* (1968)

592. Fear and Loathing in Las Vegas.—**Hunter S. Thompson:** book title, 1972

593. A man-made paradise, the fallen Adam in the arms of a neon serpent.—**Robert Mazzocco:** *New York Review of Books*, 15 September 1977

594. A city both veneer and venereal, dedicated to waste and excess, heartless and without a heart.—**Trevor Fishlock:** *Americans and Nothing Else* (1980)

595. A monument to the Mafia's ability to cater to the lowest form of lust in the souls of the American people; to give the suckers what they want. It's the biggest joke that's ever been played on the people of the United States. —**Thomas Perry:** 1982

596. A natural habitat, where the unnatural runs rampant. —**Robin Finn:** *New York Times*, 29 October 1990

597. The land of the spree and home of the knave. —**Anonymous**

598. It's like a garbage disposal for money. —**Robert Orben,** 1927–

599. Las Vegas exists because it is a perfect reflection of America. —**Steve Wynn:** *Time*, 10 January 1994

600. Las Vegas has always represented the tremendous freedom to do nutty things. —**Steve Wynn:** *Economist*, 20 January 1996

Los Angeles

601. Nineteen suburbs in search of a metropolis. —**H. L. Mencken:** *Americana* (1925)

602. Thought is barred in this City of Dreadful Joy, and conversation is unknown. —**Aldous Huxley:** *Jesting Pilate* (1926)

603. If you tilt the whole country sideways, Los Angeles is the place where everything loose will fall. —**Frank Lloyd Wright,** 1867–1959

604. Los Angeles gives one the feeling of the future more strongly than any city I know of. A bad future, too, like something out of Fritz Lang's feeble imagination. —**Henry Miller:** *The Air-Conditioned Nightmare* (1945)

605. Less a city than a perpetual convention. —**George Sessions Perry:** *Saturday Evening Post*, 15 December 1945

606. A circus without a tent. —**Carey McWilliams:** *Southern California Country* (1946)

607. A city no worse than others, a city rich and vigorous and full of pride, a city lost and beaten and full of emptiness. —**Raymond Chandler,** 1888–1959: Laurence J. Peter (ed.) *Peter's Quotations* (1977)

608. A big hardboiled city with no more personality than a paper cup. —**Raymond Chandler:** *The Little Sister* (1949)

609. The town is like an advertisement for itself; none of its charms are left to the visitor's imagination. —**Christopher Isherwood:** *The Condor and the Cows* (1949)

610. Everything in Los Angeles is too large, too loud and usually banal in concept. The plastic asshole of the world. —**William Faulkner,** 1897–1962

611. Where everybody wears rhinestones on their glasses to show that they own an airplane factory. —**S. J. Perelman:** *The Rising Gorge* (1961)

612. Where the neon lights go when they die. —**Anonymous**

613. There is always something so delightfully real about what is phony here. And something so phony about what is real. A sort of disreputable senility. —**Noël Coward,** 1899–1973

614. In a foreign country people don't expect you to be just like them, but in Los Angeles, which is infiltrating the world, they don't consider that you might be different because they don't recognize any values except their own. And soon there may not be any others. —**Pauline Kael:** *I Lost It at the Movies* (1965)

615. A constellation of plastic. —**Norman Mailer:** 1968

616. A town where you can watch night baseball almost any afternoon. —*Changing Times*

617. Paradise, with a lobotomy. —**Neil Simon,** 1927– : said by Jane Fonda in film *California Suite*

618. Oh to be in L.A. when the polyethyl-vinyl trees are in bloom! —**Herb Gold**

619. A jumble of huts in a jungle somewhere. —**Truman Capote,** 1924–84: Lawrence Grobel (ed.) *Conversations with Truman Capote* (1985)

620. Visitors to Los Angeles, then and now, were put out because the residents of Los Angeles had the inhospitable idea of building a city comfortable to live in, rather than a monument to astonish the eye of jaded travelers. —**Jessamyn West:** *Hide and Seek* (1973)

621. It's redundant to die in L.A.—**Truman Capote:** 1975; Jay Presson Allen *Tru* (1989)

622. You need a car in Los Angeles like you need your liver.—*Transworld Getaway Guide*: (1975–6)

623. A sense of humor is required to savor the special qualities of Los Angeles.—*Transworld Getaway Guide*: (1975–6)

624. I don't wanna live in a city where the only cultural advantage is that you can make a right turn on a red light.—**Woody Allen:** *Annie Hall* (film) 1977

625. The world's most celebrated suburb of nowhere.—*Time*: 4 July 1977

626. When it's 105 in New York City, it's 78 in L.A. When it's 20 below in New York City, it's 78 in L.A. There are 11 million interesting people in New York City and only 78 in L.A.—**Neil Simon:** *Chicago Tribune*, 4 September 1977

627. A kind of post-urban process rather than a city.—**Herb Gold:** 1978

628. The most healthy thing in L.A. is to do nothing.—**James Medlin:** *New West*, 9 October 1978

629. The city's layout is a tangle of circumferences which have lost contact with their centres.—**Clive James:** *Observer*, 10 June 1979

630. Call Los Angeles any dirty name you like—Six Suburbs in Search of a City, Paradise with a Lobotomy, anything—but the fact remains that you are already living in it before you get there.—**Clive James:** *Observer*, 16 June 1979

631. There are two modes of transport in Los Angeles: car and ambulance. Visitors who wish to remain inconspicuous are advised to choose the latter.—**Fran Lebowitz:** *Social Studies* (1981)

632. A large city-like area surrounding the Beverly Hills Hotel.—**Fran Lebowitz:** *Social Studies* (1981)

633. Perhaps there is no life after death … there's just Los Angeles.—**Rich Anderson:** Robert Byrne *The 637 Best Things Anybody Ever Said* (1982)

634. Los Angeles is at the end of America—the last place, the extreme. It has extreme people, extreme buildings, extreme cars.—**Kit Carson:** *Photoplay*, August 1983

635. To qualify for a Los Angelean, you need three things: (a) a driver's licence; (b) your own tennis court; (c) a preference for snorting cocaine.—**Michael Caine:** *Photoplay*, February 1984

636. The city of angels: where every cockroach has a screenplay and even the winos wear roller skates.—**Ian Shoales**

637. If you stay in Beverly Hills too long you become a Mercedes.—**Robert Redford,** 1937– : Jon Winokur (ed.) *The Portable Curmudgeon* (1987)

638. It is in love with its limitless horizontality, as New York may be with its verticality.—**Jean Baudrillard:** *America* (1986)

639. Pick your enemies carefully or you'll never make it in Los Angeles.—**Rona Barrett:** Abby Adams *An Uncommon Scold* (1989)

640. Everybody in Los Angeles lives miles away, not from anywhere, because there isn't actually an anywhere to live away from, but from each other.—**Simon Gray:** *How's That for Telling 'Em, Fat Lady?* (1988)

641. [In Los Angeles] the car is an extension of the self and the self is measured by abdominal tautness.—**David J. Jefferson:** *Wall Street Journal*, 9 February 1989

642. I have a theory about LA architecture. I think all the houses came to a costume party and they all came as other countries.—**Michael O'Donoghue**

643. The chief products of LA are novelisations, salad, game-show hosts, points, muscle tone, mini-series and rewrites. They export all of these items with the twin exceptions of muscle tone and points, neither of which seem to travel well.—**Fran Lebowitz,** 1946– : Colin Jarman *The Guinness Dictionary of Poisonous Quotes* (1991)

644. Double Dubuque.—**H. Allen Smith,** 1907–76

645. It is a geometropolitan predicament rather than a city. You can no more administer it than you could administer the solar system.—**Jonathan Miller,** 1934– : Jon Winokur (ed.) *The Portable Curmudgeon Redux* (1992)

646. A city of several cities, divided by color, culture, and cash.—**Bob McEnery:** CBS-TV, 18 January 1994

Maryland

647. America in miniature.—**Theodor McKelden:** c. 1955; Eugene L. Meyer *Maryland Lost and Found* (1986)

648. The most improbable state in the Union.—**Gerald W. Johnson:** *America-Watching* (1976)

Massachusetts

649. I shall enter on no encomium upon Massachusetts; she needs none. There she is. Behold her, and judge for yourselves.—**Daniel Webster,** 1782–1852: Robert I. Fitzhenry (ed.) *Barnes & Noble Book of Quotations* (1987)

Miami

650. Where neon goes to die.—**Lenny Bruce,** 1923–66: *Saturday Review*, 20 May 1972

651. The famous new skyline, floating between a mangrove swamp and a barrier reef, had a kind of perilous attraction, like a mirage.—**Joan Didion:** *Miami* (1987)

652. [Miami is] not like America anymore. Neither is America.—**David Rieff:** *New York Times*, 23 August 1987

653. We had elected to move voluntarily to Miami. We wanted our child to benefit from the experience of growing up in a community that is constantly being enriched by a diverse and ever-changing infusion of tropical diseases. Also they have roaches down there you could play polo with.—**Dave Barry,** 1948– : Jon

Winokur (ed.) *The Portable Curmudgeon Redux* (1992)

654. Lovers kneading lotions and sun block into one another's flesh like a sort of sexual first aid.—**Stanley Elkin:** on Miami Beach; *Mrs Ted Bliss* (1995)

Michigan

655. The only state in the union boasting a spare part.—**Leonard Lanson Cline:** Ernest H. Gruening (ed.) *These United States* (1924)

656. The Michiganders were a people without identity, without community of purpose or past, without tradition. Then Ford.—**Leonard Lanson Cline:** Ernest H. Gruening (ed.) *These United States* (1924)

657. On the dreary yellow Michigan waste with its gray stains of frozen water, the cars wait like horses at a pond.—**Edmund Wilson:** *New Republics*, 1931

658. Michigan is perhaps the strangest state in the Union, a place where the past, the present, and the future are all tied up together in a hard knot. It is the skyscraper, the mass-production line, and the frantic rush into what the machine will some day make all of us, and at the same time it is golden sand, blue water, green pine trees on empty hills, and a wind that comes down from the cold spaces, scented with the forests that were butchered by hard-handed men in checked flannel shirts and floppy pants.—**Bruce Catton:** *American Panorama* (1960)

659. In Michigan, everybody was still observing the native courting rituals of the North American Caucasian: the parking of the car, the meeting of the mate's parents, the admiring of the father's shotgun collection and stuffed rabbit heads.—**Robin Williams:** *Playboy*, 1982

Midwest

660. Supremely wise. It goes on its own way, hating no man, and fearing no man, and saying, as Shakespeare's Corin said, "The greatest of my pride is to see my ewes graze and my lambs suck."—**A. G. Macodonell:** *A Visit to America* (1935)

661. An Eliot landscape where the spiritual air is "thoroughly small and dry." If I stay here any longer I shall either take to mysticism or buy a library of pornographic books.—**W. H. Auden:** letter to Ursula Niebuhr, 1941; Charles Osborne *W. H. Auden: The Life of a Poet* (1980)

662. The Midwest is exactly what one would expect from a marriage between New England puritanism and *rich* soil.—**John Gunther:** *Inside U.S.A.* (1947)

663. Bland, boring and beige.—**Dan S. Kaercher:** *New York Times*, 27 April 1987

Minneapolis

664. No wonder the streets had seemed so empty. The city had gone somewhere else and cunningly hidden itself inside its own façade. —**Jonathan Raban:** *Old Glory* (1981)

665. May your soul be forever tormented by fire and your bones dug up by dogs and dragged through the streets of Minneapolis.—**Garrison Keillor:** 1982

Minnesota

666. A western Scandinavia where the birds sing in Swedish, the wind sighs its lullabyes in Norwegian, and the snow and rain beat against the windows to the tune of a Danish dirge. —*Journal of the American Medical Association:* c. 1925; H. L. Mencken *Americana* (1925)

667. Minnesotans are different from the rest of us. Minnesotans don't smoke. Minnesotans recycle. Minnesotans return the grocery cart to the store. Minnesotans do not consume butterfat. Minnesotans bike with their helmets on. Minnesotans fasten their seat belts. Minnesotans hold the door for you. Minnesota men

don't leave the toilet seat up. Minnesotans do not blow their horn behind you when the light turns green; they wait for you to notice. Minnesotans are nicer than other people.—**Charles Kuralt:** *Charles Kuralt's America* (1995)

Mississippi

668. When you're in Mississippi, the rest of America doesn't seem real. And when you're in the rest of America, Mississippi doesn't seem real.—**Bob Parris Moses:** c. 1961; Jack Newfield *Bread and Roses Too* (1971)

Mississippi River

669. An enormous ditch ... running liquid mud, six miles an hour.—**Charles Dickens:** *American Notes* (1842)

670. The Mississippi with its paddle boats, ferries and hoot owls, is the most haunted river in the world.—**Cecil Beaton:** *It Gives Me Great Pleasure* (1955)

671. The Mississippi meanders down the spine of America.—**Bob Dodson:** CBS-TV, 26 August 1984

672. The most southern place on earth. —**Anonymous:** on the Mississippi Delta; *Washington Post*, 18 April 1995

Missouri

673. I come from a state that raises corn and cotton and cockleburs and Democrats, and frothy eloquence neither convinces nor satisfies me. I am from Missouri. You have got to show me.—**Willard D. Vandiver:** speech in Philadelphia, 1899, attrib.

674. The catch-words of this state are "Show me," indicative of doubt and mistrust.—**J. Kenneth Ferrier:** *Crooks and Crime* (1928)

675. Be from Missouri, of course; but for God's sake forget it occasionally.—**Elbert Hubbard:** *The Roycroft Dictionary and Book of Epigrams* (1923)

676. A Missourian gets used to Southerners thinking him a Yankee, a Northerner considering him a cracker, a Westerner sneering at his effete Easternness, and the Easterner taking him for a cowhand.—**William Least Heat Moon:** *Blue Highways* (1982)

Missouri River

677. This outlaw hippopotamus, this mud-foaming behemoth of rivers.—**John Gunther:** *Inside U.S.A.* (1947)

678. There's nothin' prettier than the upper Missouri. She's wild and pretty like a virgin woman.—**Dudley Nichols:** *The Big Sky* (1952)

679. A sense comes from it that it does not like or welcome humans.—**John Steinbeck:** *Travels with Charley* (1962)

Nebraska

680. My impression of Nebraska is twin steel rails running dead straight for ever and ever across a dead level plain of dead maize.—**Crosbie Garstin:** *The Dragon and the Lotus* (1928)

681. There is no obstruction but the sky. —**Wright Morris:** *Ceremony in Lone Tree* (1960)

682. Nebraska is proof that Hell is full, and the dead walk the earth.—**Liz Winston:** Robert Byrne *The Fourth 637 Best Things Anybody Ever Said* (1990)

Nevada

683. In Southern Nevada, there is only a screen door between you and hell.—**An early settler**

684. Nevada has no intellectual life. The members of the divorce colony occupy themselves by playing golf, watching the calendar, and practicing adultery.—**H. L. Mencken:** *Americana* (1925)

685. Nevada calls itself, "The Cyclone-Cellar of the Tax-Weary."—**Douglas Reed:** *Far and Wide* (1951)

686. Neon looks good in Nevada. The tawdriness is refined out of it in so much wide black space.—**John McPhee:** *Basin and Range* (1980)

New England

687. New England is the home of all that is good and noble with all her sternness and uncompromising opinions.—**Ellen Henrietta Swallow Richards:** 29 De 1869; Caroline L. Hunt *The Life of Ellen H. Richards* (1912)

688. There is a sumptuous variety about the New England weather that compels the stranger's admiration—and regret. The weather is always doing something there; always attending strictly to business; always getting up new designs and trying them on the people to see how they will go.—**Mark Twain:** speech to New England Society, 22 December 1876; *Speeches* (1910)

689. If you don't like the weather in New England, just wait a few minutes.—**Mark Twain,** 1835–1910: Evan Esar (ed.) *The Dictionary of Humorous Quotations* (1949)

690. Oliver Wendell Holmes says that Yankee Schoolmarms, the cider, and the salt codfish of the Eastern states are responsible for what he calls a nasal accent.—**Rudyard Kipling:** *From Sea to Sea* (1899)

691. I wonder if anybody ever reached the age of thirty-five in New England without wanting to kill himself?—**Barrett Wendell,** 1855–1921: *Barrett Wendell and his Letters* (1924)

692. The New England shopkeepers and theologians never really developed a civilization; all they ever developed was a government.—**H. L. Mencken:** *Prejudices* Second Series (1921)

693. New England isn't mountains and lakes and seashores, but an inhibited and repressed old wretch who is a witch if there ever was one.—**Erskine Caldwell:** c. 1929; Dan B. Miller *Erskine Caldwell* (1995)

694. As for what you're calling hard luck—well, we made New England out of it, that and codfish.—**Stephen Vincent Benét,** 1898–1943: Evan Esar (ed.) *The Dictionary of Humorous Quotations* (1949)

695. New England is a finished place. Its destiny is that of Florence or Venice, not Milan, while the American empire careens onward toward its predicted end. It is the first American section to be finished, to achieve stability in the conditions of its life. It is the first old civilization, the first permanent civilization in America.—**Bernard De Voto:** *New England* (1936)

696. The swaggering underemphasis of New England.—**Heywood Broun:** *Collected Edition* (1941)

697. The most serious charge which can be brought against New England is not Puritanism but February.—**Joseph Wood Krutch:** *The Twelve Seasons* (1949)

698. There is no pleasing New Englanders; their soil is all rocks and their hearts are bloodless absolutes.—**John Updike:** *Buchanan Dying* (1974)

699. The New England conscience does not stop you from doing what you shouldn't—it just stops you from enjoying it.—**Cleveland Amory:** *New York*, 5 May 1980

700. The New England spirit does not seek solutions in a crowd; raw light and solitariness are less dreaded than welcomed as enhancers of our essential selves.—**John Updike:** *Hugging the Shore* (1983)

701. New England likes to think it has a civilization based on character. The South likes to think it has a character based on civilization. A big difference.—**Henry Allen:** *Washington Post Magazine*, 14 July 1991

New Jersey

702. [New Jersey resembles] a beer barrel, tapped at both ends, with all the live beer running into Philadelphia and New York.—**Benjamin Franklin:** attrib. by Abram Browning in an address at the Centennial Exposition in Philadelphia in 1876; Miriam V. Studley *Historic New Jersey Through Visitors' Eyes* (1964)

703. We have always been inconvenienced by New York on the one hand and Philadelphia on the other.—**Woodrow Wilson,** 1856–1924: Federal Writers' Project *New Jersey: A Guide to Its Present and Past* (1939)

704. The cities are indifferent and dingy, the people are seedy and dull, a kind of sloppiness and mediocrity seems to have fallen on the fields themselves, as if Nature had turned slattern and could no longer keep herself dressed.—**Edmund Wilson:** 1924

705. The semi-colon of the Eastern seaboard.—**Irvin S. Cobb:** *Some United States* (1926)

706. Like China, New Jersey absorbs the invader.—**Federal Writers' Project:** *New Jersey: A Guide to Its Present and Past* (1939)

707. New Jersey has always been a useful "no man's land" between the arrogance of New York and the obstinacy of Pennsylvania. The time it takes to traverse it diagonally permits a cooling off, coming or going.—**Struthers Burt:** *Philadelphia: Holy Experiment* (1945)

708. A raucous little state.—**John Gunther:** *Inside U.S.A.* (1947)

709. New Jersey looks like the back of an old radio.—**Josh Greenfeld:** *Time*, 10 April 1978

710. He'd grown up in white New Jersey stringtowns where nobody knew shit about anything and hated anybody who did.—**William Gibson:** *Mona Lisa Overdrive* (1988)

711. Not as bad as you might have imagined.—**Calvin Trillin,** 1935– : motto suggested for New Jersey; Robert Byrne *The Fourth 637 Best Things Anybody Ever Said* (1990)

712. On New Year's Eve, people in New Jersey stay up till midnight and watch their hopes drop.—**Richard Lewis:** Robert Byrne *The Fourth 637 Best Things Anybody Ever Said* (1990)

New Mexico

713. I think New Mexico was the greatest experience from the outside world that I have ever had.—**D.H. Lawrence,** 1885–1930, British author: *Phoenix: The Posthumous Papers of D. H. Lawrence* (1936)

714. It looks rather like Nevada, but is higher, ruggeder, more dramatic. Half the mountains seem to have their tops blown off.—**John Gunther:** *Inside U.S.A.* (1947)

715. New Mexico is old, stupendously old and dry and brown, and wind-worn by the ages. —**Charles Kuralt:** *Charles Kuralt's America* (1995)

New Orleans

716. Arrive at New Orleans, a city of ships, steamers, flatboats, rafts, mud, fog, filth, stench, and a mixture of races and tongues. Cholera, "some." [At] Planters' Hotel. Mem:—Never get caught in a cheap tavern in a strange city.— **Rutherford Birchard Hayes:** *Diary,* 21 December 1848; Charles Richard Williams (ed.) *Diary and Letters of Rutherford Birchard Hayes* vol. I (1922)

717. There is no architecture in New Orleans, except in the cemeteries.—**Mark Twain:** *Life on the Mississippi* (1883)

718. The most cosmopolitan of provincial cities.—**Mark Twain:** *Harper's New Monthly Magazine,* 1887

719. The most congenial city in America ... and it is due to the fact that here at last on this bleak continent the sensual pleasures assume the importance which they deserve. It is the only city in America where, after a lingering meal, accompanied by good wine and good talk, one can still stroll at random through the French quarter and feel like a civilized human being.—**Henry Miller:** *The Air-conditioned Nightmare* (1945)

720. [It] resembles an alluring, party-loving woman who is neither as virtuous as she might be nor as young as she looks.—**George Sessions Perry:** *Cities of America* (1947)

721. It is a town where an architect, a gourmet, or a roué is in hog heaven.—**George Sessions Perry:** *Cities of America* (1947)

722. Hedonistic, complacent, extravagant where amusement is concerned, soft to the point sometimes of insincerity, tolerant to the point sometimes of decadence; but always vivacious, good-natured, well dressed and well mannered.—**Oliver Evans:** *New Orleans* (1959)

723. One of the two most ingrown, self-obsessed little cities in the United States. (The other is San Francisco.)—**Nora Ephron:** *Esquire* (New York), September 1975

724. Every day in New Orleans is like a B-movie.—**Jim Monaghan:** *New Orleans,* January 1976

725. A most peculiar conception of exotic and American ingredients, a gumbo of stray chunks of the south, of Latin and Negro oddments, German and Irish morsels, all swimming in a fairly standard American soup.—**Walker Percy:** *Signposts in a Strange Land* (1991)

726. Same old French Quarter. Still dirty, still loud, still there.—**Robert Sulliva:** *Life,* April 1995

New York

727. The renowned and ancient city of Gotham.—**Washington Irving:** *Salmagundi* (1807–8)

728. New York, like London, seems to be a cloaca of all the depravities of human nature. —**Thomas Jefferson:** letter to William Short, 1823

729. A sucked orange.—**Ralph Waldo Emerson:** *The Conduct of Life* (1860)

730. There is something about this ceaseless buzz, and hurry, and bustle, that keeps a stranger in a state of unwholesome excitement all the time, and makes him restless and uneasy, and saps from him all capacity to enjoy anything or take a strong interest in any matter whatever—a something which impels him to try to do everything, and yet permits him to do nothing. He is a boy in a candy-shop—could choose quickly if there were but one kind of candy, but is hopelessly undetermined in the midst of a hundred kinds. A stranger feels unsatisfied, here, a good part of the time.—**Mark Twain:** 1866–7; *Travels with Mr. Brown* (1940)

731. I would place all the Indians of Nevada on ships in our harbor, take them to New York and land them there as immigrants, that they might be received with open arms … and thus placed beyond the necessity of reservation help.—**Sarah Winnemucca,** c.1842–91, Indian scout and activist: GaeWhimey Canfield *Sarah Winnemucca of the Northern Paiutes* (1983)

732. Appalling, fantastically charmless and elaborately dire.—**Henry James:** letter to W. E. Norris, 15 December 1904

733. A place with no credible possibility of time for history.—**Henry James,** 1843–1916

734. Little old Baghdad-on-the-Subway.—**O. Henry:** *The Trimmed Lamp* (1907)

735. The present in New York is so powerful that the past is lost.—**John Jay Chapman:** letter, 1909

736. The meeting place of the peoples, the only city where you can hardly find a typical American.—**Djuna Barnes:** *Pearson's Magazine*, October 1916

737. A small place when it comes to the part of it that wakes up just as the rest is going to bed.—**P. G. Wodehouse:** *My Man Jeeves* (1919)

738. The posthumous revenge of the Merchant of Venice.—**Elbert Hubbard:** *The Roycroft Dictionary and Book of Epigrams* (1923)

739. The place where all the aspirations of the Western World meet to form one vast master aspiration, as powerful as the suction of a steam dredge. It is the icing on the pie called Christian civilization.—**H. L. Mencken:** *Prejudices Sixth Series* (1927)

740. A 60-story tower in New York evokes a 70-story tower in Chicago [and] a 60-story tower in New York evokes a 70-story tower directly across the street.—**Hugh Ferriss:** *The Metropolis of Tomorrow* (1929)

741. Here I was in New York, city of prose and fantasy, of capitalist automatism, its streets a triumph of cubism, its moral philosophy that of the dollar. New York impressed me tremendously because, more than any other city in the world, it is the fullest expression of our modern age.—**Leon Trotsky:** *My Life* (1930)

742. When an American stays away from New York too long, something happens to him. Perhaps he becomes a little provincial, a little dead, a little afraid.—**Sherwood Anderson,** 1876–1941: Mike Marqusee and Bill Harris *New York* (1985)

743. A harlot amongst cities.—**Bourke Cockran:** Shane Leslie *American Wonderland* (1936)

744. That unnatural city where every one is an exile, none more so than the American.—**Charlotte Perkins Gilman,** 1860–1935: *The Living Perkins Gilman* (1935)

745. This great city has fed my imagination—it has allowed me to dream.—**Thomas Wolfe,** 1900–38: *Thomas Wolfe's Letters to His Mother* (1943)

746. It was a cruel city, but it was a lovely one, a savage city, yet it had such tenderness, a bitter, harsh, and violent catacomb of stone and steel and tunneled rock, slashed savagely with light, and roaring, fighting a constant ceaseless warfare of men and machinery; and yet it was so sweetly and so delicately pulsed, as full of warmth, of passion, and of love, as it was full of hate.—**Thomas Wolfe,** 1900–38: *The Web and the Rock* (1939)

747. One belongs to New York instantly. One belongs to it as much in five minutes as in five years.—**Thomas Wolfe:** *The Web and the Rock* (1939)

748. I love New York, with that powerful love that at times leaves you full of uncertainty and abhorrence: there are times when one needs an exile.—**Albert Camus:** 1946; Herbert R. Lottman *Camus: A Biography* (1979)

749. If Paris is the setting for a romance, New York is the perfect city in which to get over one, to get over anything. Here the lost *douceur de vivre* is forgotten and the intoxication of living takes its place.—**Cyril Connolly:** 1947; *Ideas and Places* (1953)

750. A hundred times I have thought, New York is a catastrophe, and fifty times: it is a beautiful catastrophe.—**Le Corbusier:** *When the Cathedrals Were White* (1947)

751. New York City isn't a melting pot, it's a boiling pot.—**Thomas E. Dewey:** John Gunther *Inside U.S.A.* (1947)

752. An island full of clip joints.—**Anonymous Philadelphian:** John Gunther *Inside U.S.A.* (1947)

753. I particularly like New York on hot summer nights when all the … uh, superfluous people are off the streets.—**Tennessee Williams:** 1948; Gore Vida *Matters of Fact and Fiction* (1977)

754. New Yorkers are nice about giving you street directions; in fact, they seem quite proud of knowing where they are themselves.—**Katharine Brush,** 1902–52: Evan Esar (ed.) *The Dictionary of Humorous Quotations* (1949)

755. There is more sophistication and less sense in New York than anywhere else on the globe.—**Don Herold,** 1889–1966: Evan Esar (ed.) *The Dictionary of Humorous Quotations* (1949)

756. New York is to the nation what the white church spire is to the village—the visible symbol of aspiration and faith, the white plume saying the way is up!—**E. B. White:** *Here is New York* (1949)

757. No one should come to New York to live unless he is willing to be lucky.—**E. B. White:** *Here is New York* (1949)

758. Of all targets, New York has a certain clear priority. In the mind of whatever perverted dreamer might loose the lightning, New York must hold a steady, irresistible charm. —**E. B. White:** *Here is New York* (1949)

759. A haven as cozy as toast, cool as an icebox and safe as skyscrapers.—**Dylan Thomas:** 1950; J. M. Brinnin *Dylan Thomas in America* (1956)

760. New Yorkers are inclined to assume it will never rain, and certainly not on New Yorkers.—**Brooks Atkinson:** *Once Around the Sun* (1951)

761. It looked like a pagan banner planted on a Christian rampart.—**Douglas Reed:** *Far and Wide* (1951)

762. The trouble with New York is it's so convenient to everything I can't afford.—**Jack Barry:** *Reader's Digest*, December 1952

763. More than elsewhere, everybody here wants to be Somebody.—**Sydney J. Harris:** *Strictly Personal* (1953)

764. It is one of the sublime provincialities of New York that its inhabitants lap up trivial gossip about essential nobodies they've never set eyes on, while continuing to boast that they could live somewhere for twenty years without so much as exchanging pleasantries with their neighbors across the hall.—**Louis Kronenberger:** *Company Manners* (1954)

765. This is Red Hook, not Sicily. This is the gullet of New York swallowing the tonnage of the world.—**Arthur Miller:** *A View from the Bridge* (1955)

766. After 20 annual visits, I am still surprised each time to return to see this giant asparagus bed of alabaster and rose and green skyscrapers.—**Cecil Beaton:** on New York City; *It Gives Me Great Pleasure* (1955)

767. Prison towers and modern posters for soap and whisky.—**Frank Lloyd Wright:** *New York Times*, 27 November 1955

768. Everywhere outside New York City is Bridgeport, Connecticut.—**Fred Allen,** 1894–1956: Alistair Cooke *America* (1973)

769. It is ridiculous to set a detective story in New York City. New York City is itself a detective story.—**Agatha Christie:** *Life*, 14 May 1956

770. The nation's thyroid gland.—**Christopher Morley,** 1890–1957: on New York City; *New York Times*, 2 March 1970

771. The biggest mouth in the world. It appears to be prime example of the herd instict, leading the universal urban conspiracy to beguile man from his birthright (the good ground), to hang him by his eyebrows from skyhooks above hard pavement, to crucify him, sell him, or be sold by him. — **Frank Lloyd Wright:** *The Living City* (1958)

772. It [New York City] is a great monument to the power of money and greed … a race for rent. — **Frank Lloyd Wright,** 1867–1959

773. The only credential the city asked was the boldness to dream. For those who did, it unlocked its gates and its treasures, not caring who they were or where they came from. — **Moss Hart:** *Act One* (1959)

774. A city whose living immediacy is so urgent that when I am in it I lose all sense of the past. — **Kenneth Tynan:** 1960; *Tynan Right and Left* (1967)

775. New York is full of people … with a feeling for the tangential adventure, the risky adventure, the interlude that's not likely to end in any double-ring ceremony. — **Joan Didion:** *Mademoiselle* (New York), February 1961

776. Nowhere is [success] pursued more ardently than in the city of New York. — **Stephen Birmingham:** *Holiday*, March 1961

777. The sensual mysticism of entire vertical being. — **E. E. Cummings,** 1894–1962: on New York City; *Architectural Digest*, September 1986

778. He speaks English with the flawless imperfection of a New Yorker. — **Gilbert Millstein:** *Esquire* (New York), January 1962

779. Everybody ought to have a lower East Side in their life. — **Irving Berlin:** *Vogue* (New York), 1 November 1962

780. The faces in New York remind me of people who played a game and lost. — **Lane Adam's daughter:** Murray Kempton *America Comes of Middle Age* (1963)

781. Almost all the people I met in New York were trying to reduce. — **Sylvia Plath:** *The Bell Jar* (1963)

782. Melting pot Harlem — Harlem of honey and chocolate and caramel and rum and vinegar and lemon and lime and gall. Dusky dream Harlem rumbling into a nightmare tunnel where the subway from the Bronx keeps right on downtown. — **Langston Hughes:** *Freedomways*, Summer 1963

783. New York is my Lourdes, where I go for spiritual refreshment … a place where you're least likely to be bitten by a wild goat. — **Brendan Behan,** 1923–64: *New York Post*, 22 March 1964

784. If 1,668,172 people are to be set down in one narrow strip of land between two quiet rivers, you can hardly improve on this solid mass of buildings and the teeming organism of human life that streams through them. — **Brooks Atkinson:** *New York Times*, 17 March 1964

785. One of the few charms that Manhattan has for me is its nearly complete freedom from one of the most annoying of American habits: impertinent curiosity about other people's affairs. — **Denis Brogan:** *Encounter*, June 1964

786. [New York is] humanity in microcosm, reflecting the infinite variety as well as the infinite capacity for good or evil of the human race. — **Diosdado Macapagal:** 1964

787. As only New Yorkers know, if you can get through the twilight, you'll live through the night. — **Dorothy Parker:** *Esquire* (New York), November 1964

788. He lives with his mother and sister in Brooklyn and next week be is bringing Mary Agnes Keely home — in the grand tradition. I expect a delicious kielbasa and a picture of Kosciuszko in the front room. — **Maureen Howard:** *Bridgeport Bus* (1965)

789. The Park Avenue of poodles and polished brass; it is cab country, tip-town, grassville, a window-washer's paradise. — **Gay Talese:** *New York Times*, 23 June 1965

790. Any real New Yorker is a you-name-it-we-have-it-snob. — **Russell Lynes:** *Town & Country*, August 1965

791. [Like] most native New Yorkers I was born out of town, Cedar Rapids, Iowa, to be specific. — **Harry Hershfield:** *New York Times*, 5 December 1965

792. A city where everyone mutinies but no one deserts. — **Harry Hershfield:** *New York Times*, 5 December 1965

793. I love short trips to New York; to me it is the finest three-day town on earth.—**James Cameron:** *Witness* (1966)

794. All its inhabitants ascend to heaven right after their deaths, having served their full term in hell right on Manhattan Island.—*The Barnard Bulletin*: 22 September 1967

795. A city like New York is obsolete. People will no longer concentrate in great urban centers for the purpose of work. New York will become a Disneyland, a pleasure dome.—**Marshall McLuhan,** 1911-80: Tom Wolfe *The Pump House Gang* (1968)

796. Robinson Crusoe, the self-sufficient man, could not have lived in New York City.—**Walter Lippmann:** *Newsweek*, 26 February 1968

797. [New York] isn't like the rest of the country—it's like a nation itself—more tolerant than the rest in a curious way. Littleness gets swallowed up here. All the viciousness that makes other cities vicious is sucked up and absorbed in New York.—**John Steinbeck,** 1902-68: Elaine Steinbeck and Robert Wallsten (eds.) *Steinbeck: A Life in Letters* (1975)

798. A wonderful city.... It is going to be the capital of the world.—**John Steinbeck:** Elaine Steinbeck and Robert Wallsten (eds.) *Steinbeck: A Life in Letters* (1975)

799. It is often said that New York is a city for only the very rich and the very poor. It is less often said that New York is also a city for only the very young.—**Joan Didion:** *Slouching Towards Bethlehem* (1968)

800. Most cumbersome, most restless, most ambitious, most confused, most comical, saddest and coldest and most human of cities.—**Maeve Brennan:** *The Long-Winded Lady* (1969)

801. New York is not the cultural centre of America, but the business and administrative centre of American culture.—**Saul Bellow:** *Listener* (London), 22 May 1969

802. New York makes one think of the collapse of civilization, about Sodom and Gomorrah, the end of the world. The end wouldn't come as a surprise here. Many people already bank on it.—**Saul Bellow:** *Mr. Sammler's Planet* (1970)

803. No place has delicatessen like New York.—**Judy Blume:** *Are you There, God? It's Me, Margaret* (1970)

804. Real estate gone mad.—**Edmund Wilson,** 1895-1972: Nicolas Nabokov *Bagazh* (1975)

805. There's no room for amateurs, even in crossing the streets.—**George Segal:** *Newsweek*, 1972

806. In all my years of New York cab riding I have yet to find the colorful, philosophical cabdriver that keeps popping up on the late movies.—**Jean Shepherd:** *The Ferrari in the Bedroom* (1972)

807. Manhattan cabs are horn old.—**Jean Shepherd:** *The Ferrari in the Bedroom* (1972)

808. That's the New York thing, isn't it? People who seem absolutely crazy going around telling you how crazy they used to be before they had therapy.—**Judith Rossner:** *Any Minute I Can Split* (1972)

809. Fact: Girls who are having a good sex thing stay in New York. The rest want to spend their summer vacations in Europe.—**Gail Parent:** *Europe* (1972)

810. New York was the only city in the United States that did not need a booster organization. In New York we simply assumed that we were the best—in baseball as well as intellect, in brashness and in subtlety, in everything—and it would have been unseemly to remark upon such an obvious fact.—**Michael Harrington:** *Fragments of the Century* (1973)

811. New York, home of the vivisectors of the mind, and of the mentally vivisected still to be reassembled, of those who live intact, habitually wondering about their states of sanity, and home of those whose minds have been dead, bearing the scars of resurrection.—**Muriel Spark:** *The Hothouse by the East River* (1973)

812. [Hell is] New York City with all the escape hatches sealed.—**James R. Frakes:** *New York Times*, 19 May 1974

813. When New Yorkers tell one about the dangers of their city, the muggings, the dinner parties to which no one turns up for fear of being attacked on the way, the traffic snarl-ups, the bland indifference of the city cops, they are unmistakably bragging.—**Jonathan Raban:** *Soft City* (1974)

814. A kind of immense vertical mess set upon a square horizontal order.—**Nicolas Nabokov:** *Bagazh* (1975)

815. If London is a watercolor, New York is an oil painting.—**Peter Shaffer:** *New York Times,* 13 April 1975

816. New York is what Paris was in the twenties ... the center of the art world. And we want to be in the center. It's the greatest place on earth ... I've got a lot of friends here and I even brought my own cash.—**John Lennon,** British rock musician: "The Tomorrow Show," NBC-TV, April 1975

817. Thy name is irreverence and hyperbolic. And grandeur.—**Ada Louise Huxtable:** *New York Times,* 20 July 1975

818. A city that is as heartbreaking in its beauty as it is in its poverty and decay. It is still a city of dreams—promised, built, and broken. —**Ada Louise Huxtable:** *New York Times,* 9 November 1975

819. If there were one city I should pick to live in, it would be New York. It is a city where I walk down the street and feel anything is possible.—**Maria Schell,** 1926– , Austrian actress: Edward F. Murphy *2,715 One-Line Quotations for Speakers, Writers & Raconteurs* (1981)

820. One of the things that amaze me is the amount of energy that's in New York.—**Phil Jackson:** Bill Bradley *Life on the Run* (1976)

821. I like the rough impersonality of New York, where human relations are oiled by jokes, complaints, and confessions—all made with the assumption of never seeing the other person again. I like New York because there are enough competing units to make it still seem a very mobile society. I like New York because it engenders high expectations simply by its pace. —**Bill Bradley:** *Life on the Run* (1976)

822. New York is not Mecca. It just smells like it.—**Neil Simon:** *California Suite* (1976)

823. New York is an arrogant city ... has always wanted to be all things to all people, and a surprising amount of the time it has suc-

ceeded.—**Paul Goldberger:** *The City Observed* (1978)

824. The city of right angles and tough, damaged people.—**Pete Hamill:** *New York Daily News,* 15 November 1978

825. What the New Yorker calls home would seem like a couple of closets to most Americans, yet he manages not only to live there but also to grow trees and cockroaches right on the premises.—**Russell Baker:** *New York Times,* 18 November 1978

826. New York is the only city in the world where you can get deliberately run down on the sidewalk by a pedestrian.—**Russell Baker,** 1925– : Jon Winokur (ed.) *The Portable Curmudgeon* (1987)

827. The perfect model of a city, not the model of a perfect city.—**Lewis Mumford:** *My Work and Days* (1979)

828. Paris is becoming more vulgar, New York more refined.—**G. Y. Dryansky:** *W,* 19 January 1979

829. All of this—the shared apartment in the Village, the illicit relationship, the Friday-night train to a country house—was what he had imagined life in New York to be, and he was intensely happy.—**John Cheever:** *The Stories of John Cheever* (1980)

830. A city of strong flavors, of gasps and not sights. It feeds you on mustard and Tabasco sauce and makes you mainline on adrenalin. It is not possible to be neutral about it. It has a thumping heart.—**Trevor Fishlock:** *Americans and Nothing Else* (1980)

831. Like a disco, but without the music. —**Elaine Stritch:** *Observer,* 17 February 1980

832. It's like living on top of a rotting corpse. —**John Hiatt:** 1982; Colin Jarman *The Guinness Dictionary of More Poisonous Quotes* (1992)

833. The city of Brotherly Shove.—**Anonymous:** Gerald F. Lieberman *3,500 Good Quotes for Speakers* (1983)

834. What is barely hinted at in other American cities is condensed and enlarged in New York.—**Saul Bellow,** 1915– : Mike Marqusee and Bill Harris *New York* (1985)

835. New York is more now than the sum of its people and buildings. It makes sense only as a mechanical intelligence, a transporter system for the daily absorbing and nightly redeploying of the human multitudes whose services it requires.—**Peter Conrad:** *The Art of the City* (1984)

836. The beauty of New York is unintentional; it arose independent of human design, like a stalagmite cavern.—**Milan Kundera:** *The Unbearable Lightness of Being* (1984)

837. New York now leads the world's great cities in the number of people around whom you shouldn't make a sudden move.—**David Letterman:** "Late Night with David Letterman," TV show, 9 February 1984

838. New York is different. It is a very tight little island, not really part of the United States, it belongs to the world. It lives in an abstract world of economics and finance.—**Bruce Graham,** 1984: Charles Knevitt (ed.) *Perspectives* (1986)

839. This muck heaves and palpitates. It is multidirectional and has a mayor.—**Donald Barthelme,** 1931–89

840. I miss the animal buoyancy of New York, the animal vitality. I did not mind that it had no meaning and no depth.—**Anaïs Nin,** 1914–: Robert Andrews *The Concise Columbia Dictionary of Quotations* (1987)

841. If the United States is a melting pot, then New York makes it bubble.—**Anonymous:** *US News & World Report,* 14 April 1986

842. A New Yorker is a person with an almost inordinate interest in mental health, which is only natural considering how much of that it takes to live here.—*New York Times:* 4 October 1986

843. A New Yorker looks to Neil Simon for cheering up, Sigmund Freud for shocks and Sir Thomas More for Utopia.—*New York Times:* editorial mentioning volumes most frequently stolen from New York Public Library, 4 October 1986

844. New York City is filled with the same kind of people I left New Jersey to get away from.—**Fran Lebowitz:** *Rave,* November 1986

845. When you leave New York, you are astonished at how clean the rest of the world is. Clean is not enough.—**Fran Lebowitz,** 1946–

846. In New York—whose subway trains in particular have been "tattooed" with an energy to put our own rude practitioners to shame—not an inch of free space is spared except that of advertisements.—**Gilbert Adair:** *Myths and Memories, Cleaning and Cleansing* (1986)

847. There is no human reason to be here, except for the sheer ecstasy of being crowded together.—**Jean Baudrillard:** *America* (1986)

848. Anytime four New Yorkers get into a cab together without arguing, a bank robbery has just taken place.—**Johnny Carson,** 1925–

849. An exciting town where something is happening all the time, most of it unsolved. —**Johnny Carson:** on his 25th Anniversary Show, 25 September 1986; Robert Byrne *The Fourth 637 Best Things Anybody Ever Said* (1990)

850. New York is just like Kansas—intensified.—**A. J. Carothers:** 1987

851. [There is] a great tango of eye contact between men and women on the streets of New York.—**Joseph Giovannini:** *New York Times,* 18 October 1987

852. A writer in New York is a little bit like a tree falling in a forest. You're never sure if somebody's going to hear you.—**Lucinda Franks:** *New York Times,* 30 January 1988

853. When a cat is dropped, it always lands on its feet, and when toast is dropped, it always lands with the buttered side down. I propose to strap buttered toast to the back of a cat; the two will hover, inches above the ground. With a giant buttered-cat array, a high-speed monorail could easily link New York with Chicago. —**John Frazee**

854. An interesting thing about New York City is that the subways run through the sewers.—**Garrison Keillor:** lecture at College of Marin, Kentfield, California, 12 January 1989; Robert Byrne *The Fourth 637 Best Things Anybody Ever Said* (1990)

855. I like the idea of having to keep eyes in the back of your head all the time.—**John Cale:** *Times,* 27 September 1989

856. I don't have to live in New York. I could live in hell.—**Greta Garbo,** 1905–90

857. A marriage, to be happy, needs an exterior threat. New York provides that threat.—**Garrison Keillor,** 1942–

858. A person who speaks good English in New York sounds like a foreigner.—**Jackie Mason,** 1934– : Robert Byrne *The Fourth 637 Best Things Anybody Ever Said* (1990)

859. [I am] a New York Rican ... an individual that cannot speak English and cannot speak Spanish.—**John Mariotta:** *Too Good to be True* (1990)

860. Living in New York is like being at some terrible late-night party. You're tired, you've had a headache since you arrived, but you can't leave because then you'd miss the party.—**Simon Hoggart,** British journalist: *America: A User's Guide* (1990)

861. The cab driver took her to Times Square, which is like hell without the hygiene.—**Nancy Banks-Smith:** *Guardian*, 8 December 1990

862. New York: the only city where people make radio requests like "This is for Tina—I'm sorry I stabbed you."—**Carol Leifer**

863. New York is of course many cities, and an exile does not return to the one he left.—**John Updike:** *Odd Jobs* (1991)

864. In Manhattan, every flat surface is a potential stage and every inattentive waiter an unemployed, possibly unemployable, actor.—**Quentin Crisp:** TV Channel 4, 6 August 1991

865. New York Taxi Rules: 1) Driver speaks no English. 2) Driver just got here two days ago from someplace like Senegal. 3) Driver hates you.—**Dave Barry,** 1948– : Jon Winokur (ed.) *The Portable Curmudgeon Redux* (1992)

866. The last time anybody made a list of the top hundred character attributes of New Yorkers, common sense snuck in at number 79.—**Douglas Adams:** *Mostly Harmless* (1992)

867. While Paris gets to your heart, London to your mind, and Jerusalem to your soul, New York gets into your veins, a lifeline that becomes part of you more than you become part of it.—**Uri Savir:** *New York Times*, 25 April 1992

868. New York has a life of its own, its own pulse, which beats just a bit faster than that of its inhabitants.—**Uri Savir:** *New York Times*, 25 April 1992

869. I feel about New York as a child whose father is a bank robber ... not perfect, but I still love him.—**Woody Allen:** *New York Times*, 20 August 1992

870. New York was the glamorous town that you only see now in old movies and on Broadway stages. The sky was lit up with dancing neon signs. It was safe to walk out in the streets.—**Art Buchwald:** *Leaving Home: A Memoir* (1993)

871. It is often said that New York is a city for only the very rich and the very poor. It is less often said that New York is also, at least for those of us who came there from somewhere else, a city for only the very young.—**Joan Didion,** 1934– : Phillip Lopate (ed.) *The Art of the Personal Essay* (1994)

872. New York is notoriously inhospitable to the past, disowning it whenever it can.—**John D. Rosenberg:** Connie Robertson (ed.) *The Wordsworth Dictionary of Quotations* (1996)

873. This is New York, and there's no law against being annoying.—**William Kunstler,** lawyer: 1994

874. Anything that's ever happened on the planet can happen in New York City.—**Dick Wolf:** *The New York Times*, 15 August 1995

875. New York City did not corrupt me. I was drawn to it because I had already been corrupted. By the age of six, my sexual horizon was overstimulated by a father who had no control of his fantasies, natural tendencies or criminal urges. Like father, like daughter. Before my teenage years I had already experimented with mescaline, THC, pot, acid, quaaludes, tuinals, valium and angel dust. I was already an experienced pickpocket, shoplifter, short shift hustler. New York was giant candy store, meat market, insane asylum, performance stage. Surrounded by five million other junkies, addicts, alcoholics, rip-off artists, dreamers, schemers and unsuspecting marks, New York afforded me the luxury of anonymity. The devil's playground.—**Lydia Lunch:** *Paradoxia—A Predators Diary* (1997)

876. I walk down the same streets one day and then the next, and they're two totally different streets. The people on them are suddenly different, the attitudes, the colors, the lights, the way the sun is hitting the building. All of a sudden, you go, "Oh my God, I have never seen this building." You look above the second floor, see gargoyles, and go, "Where the hell did those come from?"—**Tom Fontana:** *New York Magazine*, 14 July 1997

877. Susan, like most New Yorkers, has a tendency to speak very fast. We just became more fluent in the English language than others in the rest of the country.—**Guy Molinari:** talking about his daughter Susan; *The New York Post*, 10 September 1997

878. The main thing I like about New Yorkers is that they understand that their lives are a relentless circus of horrors, ending in death. As New Yorkers, we realize this, we resign ourselves to our fate, and we make sure that everyone else is as miserable as we are. Good town. —**Kyle Baker:** *Why I Hate Saturn* (1998)

879. The weird mix of self-loathing and arrogance that has been so often marked in the New York identity—"I live in a tough, rotten city, so I must be better than you"—simply does not hold up at a time when many visitors say that New York has grown almost, well, *nice.*—**Kirk Johnson,** and **Marjorie Connelly:** *The New York Times*, 13 March 1998

880. It's sort of destroying and corrupting the character of the city that people have loved to hate.—**Sian Foulkes:** *New York Times*, 13 March 1998

Niagara Falls

881. I was disappointed with Niagara—most people must be disappointed with Niagara. Every American bride is taken there, and the sight of the stupendous waterfall must be one of the earliest, if not the keenest disappointments in American married life.—**Oscar Wilde:** *Impressions of America* (1883)

882. On seeing Niagara Falls, Mahler ex-

claimed: "Fortissimo at last!"—**Gustav Mahler:** 1908; K. Blaukopf *Gustav Mahler* (1969)

883. Niagara is really some waterfall. It falls over like a great noisy beard made of cotton wool, veiled by spray and spanned by rainbows. —**Harold Nicolson:** *Diary*, 31 January 1933

884. A traveller's first duty in America is to visit Niagara, and his second is to record impressions as fleeting as the waters.—**Shane Leslie:** *American Wonderland* (1936)

885. The roar of Niagara is the Delphian voice of the great spaces of North America.—**Osbert Sitwell:** *The Four Continents* (1954)

886. It's like a large version of the old Bond sign on Times Square. I'm very glad I saw it, because from now on if I am asked whether I have seen Niagara Falls I can say yes.—**John Steinbeck:** *Travels with Charley* (1962)

North Carolina

887. A valley of humility between two mountains of conceits.—**Anonymous:** Suzy Platt (ed.) *Respectfully Quoted* (1989); the so-called mountains are the states of Virginia and South Carolina

888. North Carolina begins with the brightness of sea sands and ends with the loneliness of the Smokies reaching in chill and cloud to the sky.—**Ovid William Pierce:** Richard Walser *The North Carolina Miscellany* (1962)

889. If indeed there exists a physical heaven, I hope it is patterned after North Carolina between the summer hours of 6 and 8 am.—**Ted McLaurin:** *Keeper of the Moon* (1992)

North Dakota

890. Freely admitted is the rural character of the States, and there is seldom an attempt to cover native crudities with a veneer of eastern culture.—**Federal Writers' Project:** *North Dakota* (1938)

891. I like the democracy of North Dakota, the state without a millionaire and with the fewest paupers. A radical is not so radical nor a conservative so conservative in this rather free-and-easy non-eastern state.—**Mart Connolly:** Elwyn B. Robinson *History of North Dakota* (1966)

892. To grow up in a North Dakota town is an experience so radical—in the original meaning of that word, "root"—that it is more than a clue to the character of anyone who has survived. —**Raymond A. Schroth:** *The American Journey of Eric Sevareid* (1995)

Oakland

893. The trouble with Oakland is that when you get there, there is no there there.—**Gertrude Stein:** *Everybody's Autobiography* (1937)

894. The trouble with Oakland is that when you get there, it's there!—**Herb Caen,** 1916– : Laurence J. Peter *Peter's Quotations* (1977)

Oregon

895. Oregon is seldom heard of. Its people believe in the Bible, and hold that all radicals should be lynched. It has no poets and no statesmen.—**H. L. Mencken:** *Americana* (1925)

896. Oregon is only an idea. It is in no scientific way a reality.—**Philip Wylie:** *Generation of Vipers* (1942)

897. Welcome to Oregon. While you're here I want to you to enjoy yourselves. Travel, visit, drink in the beauty of our state. But for God's sake, don't move here.—**Tom McCall:** Neal R. Pierce *The Pacific States of America* (1972)

898. The green damp England of Oregon. —**Alistair Cooke:** *America* (1973)

Pennsylvania

899. There is no part of America where the people and the soil fit as they seem to do in Pennsylvania.—**Wallace Nutting:** *Pennsylvania Beautiful* (1924)

900. Pennsylvanians tend to take the fascinating form of clouds. If the Middle Atlantic states have a psycho-history, it is that Puritanism skipped over them on its way west.—**John Updike:** *Picked Up Pieces* (1976)

901. The state that has produced two great men: Benjamin Franklin of Massachusetts, and Albert Gallatin of Switzerland.—**John James Ingalls:** Robert I. Fitzhenry (ed.) *Barnes & Noble Book of Quotations* (1987)

Philadelphia

902. A great, flat, overbaked brick-field.— **Alexander Mackay:** *The Western World* (1849)

903. Philadelphians are every whit as mediocre as their neighbors, but they seldom encourage each other in mediocrity by giving it a more agreeable name.—**Agnes Repplier:** *Philadelphia: The Place and the People* (1898)

904. Philadelphia has always been one of the most Pecksniffian of American cities, and thus probably leads the world.—**H. L. Mencken:** *The American Language* (1919)

905. On the whole I'd rather be in Philadelphia.—**W. C. Fields,** 1879–1946: attrib.

906. I once spent a year in Philadelphia. I think it was on a Sunday.—**W. C. Fields:** Gerald F. Lieberman *3,500 Good Quotes for Speakers* (1983)

907. Last week, I went to Philadelphia, but it was closed.—**W. C. Fields:** Richard J. Anobile *Godfrey Daniels* (1975)

908. The City of Bleak November Afternoons. —**S. J. Perelman:** *Westward Ha!* (1948)

909. An old wino sleeping it off in the doorway littered with busted dreams. Its teams are doomed to lose and its fans are cruel and crabbed.—**Jimmy Cannon,** 1910–73

910. Philadelphia is not a town, it's a jungle. They don't have gyms there, they have zoos. They don't have sparring session, they have wars.—**Angelo Dundee**

911. The streets are safe in Philadelphia, it's only the people who make them unsafe.—**Frank Rizzo**

912. In Philadelphia, Philadelphians feel, the Right Thing is more natural and more firmly bred in [them] than anywhere else.—**Stephen Birmingham:** *The Golden Dream* (1978)

913. This old city is full of joiners. There's a club on every corner. Nowhere does the outsider feel as far outside as in Philadelphia. —**Charles Kuralt:** *Dateline America* (1979)

914. All the filth and corruption of a big city; all the pettiness and insularity of a small town. —**Howard Ogden:** Jon Winokur (ed.) *The Portable Curmudgeon* (1987)

915. They have Easter egg hunts in Philadelphia, and if the kids don't find the eggs, they get booed.—**Bob Uecker:** Jon Winokur (ed.) *The Portable Curmudgeon Redux* (1992)

Pittsburgh

916. Hell with the lid off.—**Charles Dickens,** 1812–70

917. They call it a shot-and-beer town. Hardworking guys with stumpy legs. A team with mean-looking black uniforms. Nothing squeaky-clean about Pittsburgh. It's good boys versus bad guys.—**Rocky Blier:** *New York Post*, 20 January 1979

918. The Lazarus of American cities.—**John Huey:** *Fortune*, 4 November 1991

San Diego

919. San Diego is as close to Utopia as any American city of metropolitan size is likely to come.—**Jack Smith:** Laurence J. Peter *Peter's Quotations* (1977)

920. San Diego didn't look like the kind of town where people get born.—**Steve Ellman:** Laurence J. Peter *Peter's Quotations* (1977)

San Francisco

921. A mad city—inhabited by perfectly insane people.—**Rudyard Kipling:** *From Sea to Sea* (1889)

922. The coldest winter I ever spent was a summer in San Francisco.—**Mark Twain,** 1835–1910: attrib.; *Chronicle of Higher Education*, 4 September 1991

923. That moral penal colony of the world. —**Ambrose Bierce:** letter, 25 June 1907

924. The city that never was a town.—**Will Rogers,** 1879–1935: Fred Metcalf *The Penguin Dictionary of Modern Humorous Quotations* (1986)

925. Perhaps the most European of all American cities.—**Cecil Beaton:** *It Gives Me Great Pleasure* (1955)

926. I went to San Francisco,
I saw the bridges high,
Spun across the water,
Like cobwebs in the sky.
—**Langston Hughes:** *The Langston Hughes Reader* (1958)

927. San Francisco was where the social hemorrhaging was showing up. San Francisco was where the missing children were gathering and calling themselves "hippies."—**Joan Didion:** *Slouching Towards Bethlehem* (1968)

928. San Francisco is not a part of America. —**Bill Graham:** *Chicago Daily News Panorama*, 22 January 1977

929. San Francisco rock, San Francisco writing, its always real lightweight, ephemeral stuff. Nothing *important* has ever come out of San Francisco, Rice-A-Roni aside.—**Michael O'Donoghue:** *Playboy*, 1983

930. Dames with hard-luck stories usually come from San Francisco.—**Damon Runyon,** 1884–1946: Bob Chieger *Was It Good for You, Too?* (1983)

931. San Francisco is like granola: Take away the fruits and the nuts, and all you have are the flakes.—**Anonymous:** Robert Byrne *The Other 637 Best Things Anybody Ever Said* (1984)

932. In San Francisco, Halloween is redundant.—**Will Durst:** Robert Byrne *The Other 637 Best Things Anybody Ever Said* (1984)

933. At times this town is like one big closet with a revolving door.—**Herb Caen:** 1983; Bob Chieger *Was It Good for You, Too?* (1983)

934. The poor man's paradise.—**Anonymous**

935. Such a beautiful city, people have to make excuses for not living here.—**Garrison Keillor:** broadcast from San Francisco, 15 December 1990

The South

936. The palavery kind of Southerner; all that slushy gush on the surface, and no sensibilities whatever: a race without consonants and without delicacy.—**Willa Cather:** 1926; Colin Jarman *The Guinness Dictionary of Poisonous Quotes* (1991)

937. The beaten, ignorant, Bible-ridden, white South.—**Sherwood Anderson,** 1876–1941: Arthur M. Schlesinger, Jr. *The Politics of Upheaval* (1960)

938. Southerners can never resist a losing cause.—**Margaret Mitchell:** *Gone with the Wind* (1936)

939. A mythological people. Lost by choice in dreaming of high days gone and big house burned, now we cannot even wish to escape. —**Jonathan Daniels:** *A Southerner Discovers the South* (1938)

940. Being Southerners, it was a source of shame to some members of the family that we had no recorded ancestors on either side of the Battle of Hastings.—**Harper Lee:** *To Kill a Mockingbird* (1960)

941. Isn't it fantastic that George Washington Carver found over 300 uses for the lowly peanut—but the South never had any use for George Washington Carver?—**Dick Gregory:** *From the Back of the Bus* (1962)

942. The old South which the Southerner idealized, which he may still be found idealizing today and which the Northerner has come to idealize, too, was mostly located in time in the eighteenth century; and in geography especially in eastern Virginia, colonial, and post–Revolutionary, that powerful and wealthy society, self-confident and self-contained and ruled by a few hundred families who were themselves pretty nearly autonomous.—**Edmund Wilson:** *Patriotic Gore* (1962)

943. While the South is hardly Christ-centered, it is most certainly Christ-haunted. —**Flannery O'Connor:** 1960; *Cluster Review*, 1965

944. The South has preaching and shouting, the South has grits, the South has country songs, old mimosa traditions, clay dust, Old Bigots, New Liberals—and all of it, all of that old mental cholesterol, is confined to the Sunday radio.—**Tom Wolfe:** *The Kandy-Colored Tangerine-Flake Streamline Baby* (1965)

945. The South is memories. Some of the memories are extraordinary well-packaged, but when a place has been reduced in its own estimation no amount of artful packaging can hide the gloom.—**Larry McMurtry:** *In a Narrow Grave* (1968)

946. The South is the land of the sustained sibilant. Everywhere, the letter "s" insinuates itself in the scene: in the sound of sea and sand, in the singing shell, in the beat of sun and sky, in the sultriness of the gentle hours, in the siesta, in the stir of birds and insects.—**E. B. White,** 1899–1985: Phillip Lopate (ed.) *The Art of the Personal Essay* (1994)

947. The thing you have to remember about Southerners is that we're always generous and forgiving—with our friends.—**Hidding Carter III:** *New York*, 26 July 1976

948. Southerners say that their speech is so measured that before a southern girl can explain that she won't, she already has.—**Trevor Fishlock:** *Americans and Nothing Else* (1980)

949. Storytelling and copulation are the two chief forms of amusement in the South. They're inexpensive and easy to procure.—**Robert Penn Warren:** *Newsweek*, 25 August 1980

950. What is the difference between the South and the rest of America? It was a while before

I figured out there isn't any. The South *is* America. The South is what we started out with in this bizarre, slightly troubling, basically wonderful country—fun, danger, friendliness, energy, enthusiasm and brave, crazy, tough people. After all, America is where the wildest humans on the planet came to do anything they damn pleased.—**P. J. O'Rourke:** *Rolling Stone*, 1982

951. The South may be the last place where dying is still sometimes a community project. —**Shirley Abbott:** *Womenfolks: Growing Up Down South* (1983)

952. This curious sense of separateness is one of the most stubbornly preserved Southern attitudes. The South, its historians say, stands apart from other American regions because of its peculiar history. History has been cruel to Southerners, has persistently dealt them deuces. —**Shirley Abbott:** *Womenfolks: Growing Up Down South* (1983)

953. In the South, Sunday morning sex is accompanied by church bells.—**Florence King:** *Confessions of a Failed Southern Lady* (1985)

954. Southerners are probably not more hospitable than New Englanders are; they are simply more willing to remind you of the fact that they are being hospitable.—**Ray L. Birdwhistell:** Jon Winokur (ed.) *The Portable Curmudgeon* (1987)

955. The South is one of those kingdoms of the mind, like India or Scotland, that are neat and understandable only to people who have never been there.—**Alistair Cooke:** *America Observed* (1988)

956. The average Southerner has the speech patterns of someone slipping in and out of consciousness. I can change my shoes and socks faster than most people in Mississippi can speak a sentence.—**Bill Bryson:** *The Lost Continent* (1989)

957. Next to fried foods, the South has suffered most from oratory.—**Brooks Hays**

958. You can't be Southern without being black, and you can't be a black Southerner without being white.—**Ralph Ellison:** *New York Times*, 31 July 1994

South Carolina

959. Too small for a republic and too large for a lunatic asylum.—**James Louis Petigru:** 1860, attrib.

960. The South Carolinian has fire in his head, comfort in his middle, and a little lead in his feet.—**Federal Writers' Project:** *South Carolina: A Guide to the Palmetto State* (1941)

961. South Carolinians are among the rare folk in the South who have no secret envy of Virginians.—**Federal Writers' Project:** *South Carolina: A Guide to the Palmetto State* (1941)

962. We were taught to be South Carolinians, Ca-ro-li-ni-ans, mind you, and not, please God, the Tarheel slur, Calinians.—**William Francis Guess:** Eric Larrabee (ed.) *American Panorama: East of the Mississippi* (1960)

South Dakota

963. A part of hell with the fires burnt out.— **General Custer:** Colin Jarman *The Guinness Dictionary of Poisonous Quotes* (1991)

964. I learnt more about politics during one South Dakota dust storm than in seven years at the university.—**Hubert H. Humphrey,** 1911–78

965. You could shoot a cue ball from the southern boundary of the state all the way to Canada and halfway to the North Pole.—**Holger Cahill:** *The Shadow of My Hand* (1956)

966. The physical and cultural remoteness compels everyone to memorize almost every South Dakotan who has left the state and achieved some recognition.—**Tom Brokaw:** John Milton *South Dakota* (1977)

Tennessee

967. Tennessee summer days were not made for work: in fact, many a resident had doubted that they were made at all, but that they sprang to life from the cauldrons of hell.—**Carl Rowan:** *South of Freedom* (1952)

968. What you need for breakfast, they say in East Tennessee, is a jug of good corn liquor, a thick beefsteak, and a hound dog. Then you feed the beefsteak to the hound dog.—**Charles Kuralt:** *Dateline America* (1979)

Texas

969. If I owned Texas and Hell, I would rent out Texas and live in Hell.—**General Phillip P. Sheridan:** at Fort Clark Texas, 1855

970. The place where there are the most cows and the least milk and the most rivers and least water in them, and where you can look the farthest and see the least.—**H. L. Mencken,** 1880–1956

971. Other states were carved or born,
Texas grew from hide to horn.
—**Berta Hart Nance:** c. 1930

972. Texas seemed to be half Mexico already—and half Will Rogers.—**Graham Greene:** *The Lawless Roads* (1939)

973. Texas could wear Rhode Island as a watch fob.—**Pat Neff:** John Gunther *Inside U.S.A.* (1947)

974. If a man's from Texas, he'll tell you. If he's not, why embarrass him by asking?—**Joke:** John Gunther *Inside U.S.A.* (1947)

975. We know about champagne and caviar but we talk hog and hominy.—**Edna Ferber:** *Giant* (1952)

976. Take Texas the way Texas takes bourbon. Straight. It goes down easier.—**Edna Ferber:** *Giant* (1952)

977. I just mean that here in Texas maybe we've got into the habit of confusing bigness with greatness.—**Edna Ferber:** *Giant* (1952)

978. Texas, in the eyes of its inhabitants and in maps supplied to visitors, occupies all of the North American continent but a fraction set aside for the United States, Canada, and Mex-ico.—**Lord Kinross:** *The Innocents at Home* (1959)

979. The Texan turned out to be good-natured, generous and likable. In three days no one could stand him.—**Joseph Heller:** *Catch-22* (1961)

980. Texas is a state of mind. Texas is an obsession. Above all, Texas is a nation in every sense of the word. A Texan outside of Texas is a foreigner.—**John Steinbeck:** *Travels with Charley* (1962)

981. Once you are in Texas it seems to take forever to get out, and some people never make it.—**John Steinbeck:** *Travels with Charley* (1962)

982. Many people have believed that they were Chosen, but none more badly than the Texans.—**Edward Hoagland:** *Sports Illustrated* (New York), 14 January 1974

983. Texas is the third most urbanized state (behind New York and California) with all the tangles, stench, random violence, architectural rape, historical pillage, neon blight, pollution and ecological imbalance the term implies.—**Larry King:** 1975

984. Texas is sort of an opera.—**John S. Samuels:** *New York Times*, 21 January 1979

985. To be from Texas will always have a kind of gusto to it.—**Ronnie Dugger:** *New York Times*, 15 October 1979

986. For most Northerners, Texas is the home of real men. The cowboys, the rednecks, the outspoken self-made right-wing millionaires strike us as either the best or worst examples of American manliness.—**Edmund White:** *States of Desire* (1980)

987. If God had meant for Texans to ski, He would have made bullshit white.—**Anonymous:** *Texas Observer*, 19 September 1980

988. Most Texans think Hanukkah is some sort of duck call.—**Richard Lewis:** "Late Night with David Letterman," TV show, 6 January 1984

989. It is considerably smaller than Australia and British Smaliland put together. As things stand at present there is nothing much the Texans can do about this, and they are inclined to shy away from the subject in ordinary conversation, muttering defensively about the size of the oranges.—**Alex Atkinson,** British humorous writer: Robert Andrews *The Concise Columbia Dictionary of Quotations* (1987)

990. Parts of Texas look like Kansas with a goiter.—**Anonymous:** Robert Byrne *The Third and Possibly the Best 637 Best Things Anybody Ever Said* (1986)

991. A Texan virgin is a girl who can run faster than her brother.—**Anonymous**

992. San Antonio is just about the only city in Texas that anybody has ever accused of being charming.—**Calvin Trillin,** 1935–

993. New England may have culture, but Texas has crass.—**J. H. Goldfuss**

994. You can always tell a Texan, but not much.—**Anonymous:** Robert Byrne *The Fourth 637 Best Things Anybody Ever Said* (1990)

995. Texans are proof that the world was populated by aliens.—**Cynthia Nelms:** Robert Byrne *The Fourth 637 Best Things Anybody Ever Said* (1990)

996. Humanism is not alive and well in Texas. Different colors and types of Texans do not like one another, nor do they pretend to.—**Molly Ivins:** *Molly Ivins Can't Say That, Can She?* (1991)

Town and Country

See also CULTURE AND MEDIA: Architecture; NATURE: Nature

997. The essence of the United States is to be found in its small towns. This cannot be said of any other country. The American village is a small edition of the whole country, in its civil government, its press, its schools, its banks, its town hall, its census, its spirit, and its appearance.—**Domingo Faustino Sarmiento:** *Travels in the United States in 1847,* tr. Michael A. Rockland (1970)

998. For any American who had the great and priceless privilege of being raised in a small town there always remains with him nostalgic memories.... And the older he grows the more he senses what he owed to the simple honesty and neighborliness, the integrity that he saw all around him in those days.—**Dwight D. Eisenhower,** 1890–1969

999. When a village ceases to be a community, it becomes oppressive in its narrow conformity. So one becomes an individual and migrates to the city. There, finding others likeminded, one re-establishes a village community. Nowadays only New Yorkers are yokels.—**Paul Goodman:** *Five Years* (1966)

1000. The United States was born in the country and moved to the city in the nineteenth century.—**Anonymous:** Robert I. Fitzhenry *Barnes & Noble Book of Quotations* (1986)

1001. This is a dream as old as America itself: give me a piece of land to call my own, a little town where everyone knows my name.—**Faith Popcorn:** *The Popcorn Report* (1991)

Travel

See also THE AMERICAN PEOPLE: Americans Abroad

1002. I always think that the most delightful thing about traveling is to always be running into Americans and to always feel at home.—**Anita Loos:** *Gentlemen Prefer Blondes* (1925)

1003. In America there are two classes of travel—first class and with children.—**Robert Benchley:** *Pluck and Luck* (1925)

1004. The way to see America is from a lower berth about two in the morning [with] nothing but the irrational universe with you in the center trying to reason it out.—**Jacques Barzun:** *God's Country and Mine* (1954)

1005. In the USA "First" and "Second" class can't be painted on railroad cars, for all passengers, being Americans, are equal and it would be "un-American." But paint "Pullman" on a car and everyone is satisfied.—**Owen Wister**

1006. Movement is the magic which keeps expectations high in America.—**James Oliver Robertson:** *American Myth, American Reality* (1980)

1007. There are two classes of travel in America: Steerage and Steerage with Free Drinks. You pay a great deal extra for the free drinks, of course.—**Judith Martin (Miss Manners)**

1008. Motels are among the distinctive artifacts of American civilization.—**Lance Morrow:** *Civilization,* Nov-Dec 1994

Vermont

1009. Vermonters are really something quite special and unique. This state bows to nothing: the first legislative measure it ever passed was "to adopt the laws of God ... until there is time to frame better."—**John Gunther:** *Inside U.S.A.* (1947)

1010. There is no cure for Vermont weather. It is consistent only in its inconsistency.—**Noel Perrin:** *Third Person Rural* (1983)

1011. As Maine goes, so goes Vermont.—**James A. Farley:** Jon Winokur (ed.) *The Portable Curmudgeon Redux* (1992)

1012. They deliberately chose Vermont, and a hard-working, old-fashioned life. I hear this attitude of Vermonters described as "preventing the future."—**Charles Kuralt:** *Charles Kuralt's America* (1995)

Washington, D.C.

1013. There is something good and motherly about Washington, the grand old benevolent National Asylum for the helpless.—**Mark Twain:** *The Gilded Age* (1873)

1014. A plantation of public edifices amid a rather unkempt growth of streets.—**Arnold Bennett:** *Journal,* 17 October 1911

1015. The only place where sound travels faster than light.—**C. V. R. Thompson:** *Reader's Digest,* 1949

1016. The District of Columbia is a territory hounded on all sides by the USA.—**Irving D. Tressler:** *Reader's Digest,* 1949

1017. Washington isn't a city, it's an abstraction.—**Dylan Thomas:** 1950; John Malcolm Brinnin *Dylan Thomas in America* (1956)

1018. Washington is like a self-sealing tank on a military aircraft. When a bullet passes through, it closes up.—**Dean Acheson,** 1893–1971: Walter Isaacson and Evan Thomas *The Wise Men* (1986)

1019. All over Washington today, the politicians and the power brokers are happy. In fact, if you listen closely, you can hear the sound of champagne corks popping.—**Paul Jacob:** *Term Limits Executive Director*

1020. There's nothing so permanent as a temporary job in Washington.—**George Allen,** 1894–1957: Fred Metcalf *The Penguin Dictionary of Modern Humorous Quotations* (1986)

1021. There are a number of things wrong with Washington. One of them is that everyone has been too long away from home.—**Dwight D. Eisenhower:** press conference, 11 May 1955

1022. The more I observed Washington, the more frequently I visited it, and the more people I interviewed there, the more I understood how prophetic L'Enfant was when he laid it out as a city that goes around in circles.—**John Mason Brown:** *Through These Men* (1956)

1023. A city of Southern efficiency and Northern charm.—**John F. Kennedy,** 1917–63: William Manchester *Portrait of a President* (1962)

1024. New York has total depth in every area. Washington has only politics; after that, the second biggest thing is white marble.—**John V. Lindsay:** 1963

1025. People only leave [Washington] by way of the box—ballot or coffin.—**Senator Claiborne Pell:** on Washington life; *Vogue,* 1 August 1963

1026. I love Washington, but it *is* a self-important town.—**Lady Bird Johnson:** *A White House Diary* (1970)

1027. A very easy city for you to forget where you came from and why you got there in the first place.—**Harry S Truman,** 1884–1972: Merle Miller *Plain Speaking: Conversations with Harry S Truman* (1973)

1028. The cocktail party remains a vital Washington institution, the official intelligence system. —**Barbara Howar:** *Laughing All the Way* (1973)

1029. Washington is, for one thing, the news capital of the world. And for another, it is a company town. Most of the interesting people in Washington either work for the government or write about it. —**Sally Quinn:** *We're Going to Make You a Star* (1975)

1030. A place where men praise courage and act on elaborate personal cost-benefit calculations. —**John Kenneth Galbraith,** 1908– : Robert I. Fitzhenry *Barnes & Noble Book of Quotations* (1986)

1031. There was no other city in the world where rumor fed upon itself so virulently. Whispers wiped out careers just as cholera destroyed its human victims. —**Evelyn Anthony:** *The Avenue of the Dead* (1982)

1032. A city of cocker spaniels. A city of people who are more interested in being petted and admired, loved, than rendering the exercise of power. —**Elliot L. Richardson:** *New York Times*, 13 July 1982

1033. Too small to be a state but too large to be an asylum for the mentally deranged. —**Anne Gorsuch Burford:** speech, 27 July 1984

1034. An endless series of mock palaces clearly built for clerks. —**Ada Louise Huxtable:** Abby Adams *An Uncommon Scold* (1989)

1035. Outside of the killings, Washington has one of the lowest crime rates in the country. —**Marion S. Barry,** 1936– , Mayor of Washington, D.C.

1036. In Washington it is an honor to be disgraced … you have to have *been* somebody to fall. —**Meg Greenfield:** *Newsweek*, 1986

1037. A town where more people contemplate writing a book than finish reading one. —**Ann Geracimos:** *Washington Times*, 29 March 1989

1038. In Washington, success is just a training course for failure. —**Simon Hoggart:** *America: A User's Guide* (1990)

1039. Washington has lots of those Greek- and Roman-style buildings that practically make you feel like a senator just walking up the steps of them. Senators, in particular, are fond of this feeling, and this is one reason official Washington escaped the worst effects of modern architecture. —**P. J. O'Rourke:** *Parliament of Whores* (1991)

1040. Washington is awash in post-war testosterone. —**Patricia S. Schroeder:** *New York Times*, 30 June 1991

1041. A steering wheel that's not connected to the engine. —**Richard N. Goodwin,** 1931– : Peter McWilliams *Ain't Nobody's Business if You Do* (1993)

1042. Lively, but on the whole it wasn't called Ground Zero for nothing. —**Joseph Brodsky:** *Washington Post*, 31 May 1992

1043. Washington is a resigning town. Nothing else holds the special excitement of a rumored resignation. —**George P. Shultz:** *Turmoil and Triumph* (1993)

The West

1044. The West may be called the most distinctively American part of America because the points in which it differs from the East are the points in which America as a whole differs from Europe. —**James Bryce:** *The American Commonwealth* (1888)

1045. West of the Mississippi it's a little more look, see, act. A little less rationalize, comment, talk. —**F. Scott Fitzgerald:** letter to Andrew Turnbull, Summer 1934

1046. Ahead, north to Canada and west to the Coast lay what to me is the most exciting stretch of land in America. Despite its rudeness, newness, rawness, it is not worn out, not yet filled, not yet exhausted. —**Larry McMurtry:** *In a Narrow Grave* (1968)

1047. In the West the past is very close. In many places, it still believes it's the present. —**John Masters:** *Pilgrim Son* (1971)

1048. It's no surprise that user-friendliness is a concept developed on the West Coast. The guy who invented the Smiley face is running for mayor of Seattle—for real. —**Douglas Coupland:** *Microserfs* (1995)

Wyoming

1049. A land of great open spaces with plenty of elbow room. There are sections of the state where it is said you can look farther and see less than any other place in the world.—**Federal Writers' Project:** *Wyoming: A Guide to Its History, Highways, and People* (1941)

1050. Here is America high, naked, and exposed.—**John Gunther:** *Inside U.S.A.* (1947)

1051. One of my favorite states—of existence.—**Vladimir Nabokov:** 1964

1052. If anything is endemic to Wyoming it is wind. This big room of space is swept out daily, leaving a bone yard of fossils, agates, and carcasses in every stage of decay. Though it was water that initially shaped the state, wind is the meticulous gardener, raising dust and pruning the stage.—**Gretel Ehrlich:** *The Solace of Open Spaces* (1985)

1053. Things happen suddenly in Wyoming, the change of seasons and weather; for people, the violent swings in and out of isolation. But good-naturedness is concomitant with severity.—**Gretel Ehrlich:** *The Solace of Open Spaces* (1985)

NATURE

Environment

1054. Oh beautiful, for smoggy skies, o'er insecticide waves of grain, and strip-mined mountain's majesty, above the asphalt plains! America, America, man sheds his waste on thee! And hides the pines, with billboard signs, from sea to oily sea!—**George Carlin**

1055. It isn't pollution that's harming the environment. It's the impurities in our air and water that are doing it.—**Dan Quayle,** 1947–

1056. An American is a person who demonstrates against a new power plant, then goes home and flips on all the lights, turns up the air conditioner, puts a tape in the stereo, opens the refrigerator door, plugs in the coffee maker and sits down to see if the television cameras caught him protesting.—**Wendell Trogdon**

1057. I love the environment, but I'm cheap on the environment.—**Newt Gingrich,** 1943–

1058. We cannot permit the extreme in the environmental movement to shut down the United States. We cannot shut down the lives of many Americans by going to the extreme on the environment.—**George Bush:** speech, California, 30 May 1992

Nature

See also PLACES: Town and Country

1059. In America nature is autocratic, saying, "I am not arguing, I am telling you."—**Erik H. Erikson:** *Childhood and Society* (1950)

1060. Kitsch is the daily art of our time, as the vase or the hymn was for earlier generations. For the sensibility it has that arbitrariness and importance which works take on when they are no longer noticeable elements of the environment. In America kitsch is Nature. The Rocky

Mountains have resembled fake art for a century.—**Harold Rosenberg:** *The Tradition of the New* (1960)

1061. There are dangers in sentimentalizing nature. Most sentimental ideas imply, at bottom, a deep if unacknowledged disrespect. It is no accident that we Americans, probably the world's champion sentimentalizers about nature, are at one and the same time probably the world's most voracious and disrespectful destroyers of wild and rural countryside.—**Jane Jacobs:** *The Death and Life of Great American Cities* (1961)

1062. Nature in America has always been suspect, on the defensive, cannibalized by progress. In America, every specimen becomes a relic.—**Susan Sontag:** *On Photography* (1977)

1063. To an American, land is solidity, goodness, and hope. American history is about land. —**A North Carolinian:** William Least Heat Moon *Blue Highways* (1982)

1064. The human landscape of the New World shows a conquest of nature by an intelligence that does not love it.—**Northrop Frye,** 1912–91: Robert I. Fitzhenry *Barnes & Noble Book of Quotations* (1986)

1065. Unfortunately, the balance of nature decrees that a super-abundance of dreams is paid for by a growing potential for nightmares. —**Peter Ustinov:** *Independent,* 25 February 1989

1066. Nature is very un–American. Nature never hurries.—**William George Jordan**

Weather

1067. Summer is drawn blinds in Louisiana, long winds in Wyoming, shades of elms and maples in New England.—**Archibald MacLeish:** *Collier's,* 8 July 1955

1068. Autumn is the American season. In Europe the leaves turn yellow or brown, and fall. Here they take fire on the trees and hang there flaming.—**Archibald MacLeish,** 1892–1982

1069. Americans are weather junkies. They monitor it the way a hypochondriac listens to his own breathing and heartbeat in the middle of the night.—**Lance Morrow:** *Fishing in the Tiber* (1988)

MIND

Creativity and Talent

See also INDIVIDUAL: Success and Failure; HUMAN RELATIONS: Loneliness; CULTURE AND MEDIA: Intellectuals

1070. The dearth of genius in America is owing to the continual teasing of mosquitoes.

—**Edgar Allan Poe,** 1809–49: Evan Esar (ed.) *The Dictionary of Humorous Quotations* (1949)

1071. The American Way is so restlessly creative as to be essentially destructive; the American way is to carry common sense almost to the point of madness.—**Louis Kronenberger:** *Company Manners* (1954)

1072. In this country we encourage "creativity" among the mediocre, but real bursting creativity appalls us. We put it down as undisciplined, as somehow "too much."—**Pauline Kael:** 1965; *Newsweek*, 1991

1073. Americans worship creativity the way they worship physical beauty—as a way of enjoying elitism without guilt: God did it.—**Florence King:** *Reflections in a Jaundiced Eye* (1989)

1074. Americans respect talent only insofar as it leads to fame, and we reserve our most fervent administration for famous people who destroy their lives as well as their talent. The fatal flaws of Elvis, Judy, and Marilyn register much higher on our national applause meter than their living achievements. In America, talent is merely a tool for becoming famous in life so you can become more famous in death—where all are equal.—**Florence King:** *Lump It or Leave It* (1990)

Fear

See also SOCIAL LIFE: Tragedy

1075. An American who can make money, invoke God, and be no better than his neighbor, has nothing to fear but truth itself.—**Marya Mannes:** *More in Anger* (1958)

1076. The people of the United States are at the present time dominated and driven by two kinds of officially propagated fear: fear of the Soviet Union and fear of the income tax.—**Edmund Wilson:** *The Cold War and the Income Tax* (1963)

1077. There is an almost paranoid fear eating at the guts of all Americans. Black–White, Male–Female, Young–Old represent schisms between us. Racial Polarization, the Generation Gap and Virginia Slims are all brand names for products that may become lethal.—**Shirley Chisholm:** speech, Church Women United, Massachusetts, 21 August 1969

1078. America fears the unshaven legs, the unshaven men's cheeks, the aroma of perspiration, and the limp prick. Above all it fears the limp prick.—**Walter Abish:** *In the Future Perfect* (1975)

1079. Americans' great and secret fear is that America may turn out to be a phenomenon rather than a civilization.—**Shirley Hazzard,** 1931–

Happiness

See also INDIVIDUAL: Life; RELIGION AND BELIEF: Materialism and Spirituality

1080. The pursuit of happiness, which American citizens are obliged to undertake, tends to involve them in trying to perpetuate the moods, tastes and attitudes of youth.—**Malcolm Muggeridge:** *The Most of Malcolm Muggeridge* (1966)

1081. Here we are the way politics ought to be in America, the politics of happiness, the politics of purpose and the politics of joy. —**Hubert H. Humphrey,** Democrat politician: speech in Washington, 27 April 1968; *New York Times*, 28 April 1968

1082. America is a vast conspiracy to make you happy.—**John Updike:** *Problems* (1980)

1083. I always say I don't think everyone has the right to happiness or to be loved. Even the Americans have written into their constitution that you have the right to the "pursuit of happiness." You have the right to try but that is all.—**Clair Rayner,** 1931–   : G. Kinnock and F. Miller (eds.) *By Faith and Daring* (1993)

Humor

1084. That joke was lost on the foreigner—guides cannot master the subtleties of the American joke.—**Mark Twain:** *The Innocents Abroad* (1869)

1085. The saving grace of America lies in the fact that the overwhelming majority of Americans are possessed of two great qualities—a sense of humor and a sense of proportion.—**Franklin D. Roosevelt:** address in Savannah, Georgia, 18 November 1933

1086. The hallmark of American humor is its pose of illiteracy.—**Ronald Knox,** 1888–1957: Ted Goodman (ed.) *The Forbes Book of Business Quotations* (1997)

1087. America is a nation of comics and comedians; nevertheless, humor has no stature and is accepted only after the death of the perpetrator.—**E. B. White:** *New Yorker,* 27 September 1952

1088. Whatever else an American believes or disbelieves about himself, he is absolutely sure he has a sense of humor.—**E. B. White:** *The Second Tree From the Corner* (1954)

1089. We are a nation that has always gone in for the loud laugh, the wow, the belly laugh and the dozen other labels for the roll-'em-in-the-aisles of gagerissimo.—**James Thurber:** *New York Times,* 21 February 1960

1090. Humor, a good sense of it, is to Americans what manhood is to Spaniards. Nobody wants to be left holding the joke.—**Garrison Keillor:** *We Are Still Married* (1989)

1091. The difference between English and American humor is $150 a minute.—**Eric Idle:** *Film Yearbook* (1990)

1092. Although every American has a sense of humor—it is his birthright and encoded somewhere in the Constitution—few Americans have ever been able to cope with wit or irony, and even the simplest jokes often cause unease, especially today when every phrase must be examined for covert sexism, racism, ageism.—**Gore Vidal:** *Nation,* 26 August 1991

1093. In America today, we have Woody Allen, whose humor has become so sophisticated that nobody gets it any more except Mia Farrow.—**Dave Barry,** 1948–   : *Why Humor Is Funny*

Insult

1094. No one can be as calculatedly rude as the British, which mazes Americans, who do not understand studied insult and can only offer abuse as a substitute.—**Paul Gallico:** *New York Times,* 14 January 1962

Intelligence

See also CULTURE AND MEDIA: Intellectuals

1095. No one ever went broke underestimating the intelligence of the American people. —**H. L. Mencken,** 1880–1956: attrib.; Nigel Rees *A Dictionary of Twentieth Century Quotations* (1987)

1096. In our society to admit inferiority is to be a fool, and to admit superiority is to be an outcast. Those who are in reality superior in intelligence can be accepted by their fellows only if they pretend they are not.—**Marya Mannes,** American writer: *More in Anger* (1958)

1097. Americans have always had an ambivalent attitude toward intelligence. When they feel threatened, they want a lot of it, and when they don't they regard the whole thing as somewhat immoral.—**Vernon A. Walters:** *Silent Missions* (1978)

Optimism

1098. The voice of America has no undertones or overtones in it. It repeats its optimistic catchwords in a tireless monologue that has the slightly metallic sound of a gramophone. —**Vance Palmer:** 1923; H. P. Heseltine (ed.) *Intimate Portraits* (1969)

1099. The thing that impresses me most about this country [America] is its hopefulness. It is this which distinguishes it from Europe, where there is hopeless depression and fear.—**Aldous Huxley,** 1894–1963

1100. Americans have always assumed, subconsciously, that all problems can be solved; that every story has a happy ending; that the application of enough energy and good will can make everything come out right. In view of our history, this assumption is natural enough. As a people, we have never encountered any obstacle that we could not over-come.—**Adlai Stevenson:** *Call to Greatness* (1954)

1101. The happy ending is our national belief.
—**Mary McCarthy:** *On the Contrary* (1961)

Pessimism

1102. In the United States today, we have more than our share of the nattering nabobs of negativism.—**Spiro T. Agnew,** vice president: speech in San Diego, 11 September 1970

1103. Pessimism is as American as apple pie— frozen apple pie with a slice of processed cheese. —**George F. Will:** 1982

Psychology

1104. Psychoanalysis is for hysterical pathological cases, not for silly rich American women who should be learning to darn socks.—**Sigmund Freud:** interview with Dorothy Thompson, 1925

1105. Therapy has become what I think of as the tenth American muse.—**Jacob Bronowski,** 1908–74: *Radio Times*

1106. A well-known psychiatric joke declares that the cure for severe depression has been discovered: it is to fly to the United States, where you will be diagnosed instead as a schizophrenic.—**Peter Sedgewick:** *Sunday Times,* 27 January 1980

1107. Sigmund Freud was a half-baked Viennese quack. Our literature, culture, and the films of Woody Allen would be better today if Freud had never written a word.—**Ian Shoales:** Jon Winokur (ed.) *The Portable Curmudgeon* (1987)

1108. The pursuit of the Inner Child has taken over just at the moment when Americans ought to be figuring out where their Inner Adult is. —**Robert Hughes:** *Culture of Conservatives* (1993)

1109. The statistics on sanity are that one out of every four Americans is suffering from some form of mental illness. Think of your three best friends. If they're okay, then it's you.—**Rita Mae Brown,** 1944–

1110. This is really America in therapy, people trying to get themselves together and be whole.—**Dr. David Viscott**

Thinking

See also CULTURE AND MEDIA: Intellectuals

1111. Americans seem sometimes to believe that if you are a thinker you must be a frowning bore, because thinking is so damn serious. —**Jacques Maritain:** *Reflections on America* (1958)

1112. Something is wrong with America. I wonder sometimes what people are thinking about or if they're thinking at all.—**Bob Dole**

Wrath

1113. The American people are slow to wrath, but when their wrath is once kindled it burns like a consuming flame.—**Theodore Roosevelt:** First Annual Address to Congress, 3 December 1901

THE INDIVIDUAL

Aging

1114. Safety razors make it hard to grow beards in America: America would be a better place if there were a few bearded, savage, terrible old men.—**Lewis Mumford:** *Findings and Keepings* (1957)

1115. No American is prepared to attend his own funeral without the services of highly skilled cosmeticians. Part of the American dream, after all, is to live long and die young. —**Edgar Z. Friedenberg:** *The Vanishing Adolescent* (1959)

1116. Gracious dying is a huge, macabre and expensive joke on the American public.—**Jessica Mitford:** *The American Way of Death* (1963)

1117. An important antidote to American democracy is American gerontocracy. The positions of eminence and authority in Congress are allotted in accordance with length of service, regardless of quality. Superficial observers have long criticized the United States for making a fetish of youth. This is unfair. Uniquely among modern organs of public and private administration, its national legislature rewards senility.—**John Kenneth Galbraith:** *New York,* 15 November 1971

1118. America's lifestyle prepares us well … but it prepares us not at all for old age.—**J. Merrill Foster:** *New York Times,* 31 January 1988

1119. You don't have to be old in America to say of a world you lived in: That world is gone. —**Peggy Noonan:** *What I Saw at the Revolution* (1990)

1120. On getting old in America—best to do it somewhere else.—**Tama Janowitz**

Children

1121. I was never allowed to read the popular American children's books of my day because, as my mother said, the children spoke bad English *without the author's knowing it.*—**Edith Wharton,** 1862–1937, American novelist: Abby Adams *An Uncommon Scold* (1989)

1122. There are probably few children in America who haven't been lied to magnificently about birth and sex.—**Margaret Mead:** "An Anthropologist Looks at the Kinsey Report" (1948)

1123. You Americans do not rear children, you *incite* them; you give them food and shelter and applause.—**Randall Jarrell:** *Pictures from an Institution* (1954)

1124. The lack of emotional security of our American young people is due to their isolation from the larger family unit. No two people—no mere father and mother—are enough to provide emotional security for a child. He needs to feel himself one in a world of kinfolk, persons of variety in age and temperament, and yet allied to himself by an indissoluble bond which he cannot break if he could, for nature has welded him into it before he was born.—**Pearl S. Buck,** 1892–1973

1125. What the vast majority of American children needs is to stop being pampered, stop being indulged, stop being chauffeured, stop being catered to. In the final analysis it is not what you do for your children but what you have taught them to do for themselves that will make them successful human beings.—**Ann Landers:** *Ann Landers Says Truth is Stranger* (1968)

1126. Americans, indeed, often seem to be so

overwhelmed by their children that they'll do anything for them except stay married to the co-producer.—**Katharine Whitehorn**: *Observations* (1970)

1127. America is not a democracy, it's an absolute monarchy ruled by King Kid. In a nation of immigrants, the child is automatically more of an American than his parents. Americans regard children as what Mr. Hudson in "Upstairs, Downstairs" called "betters." Aping their betters, American adults do their best to turn themselves into children. Puerility exercises *droit de seigneur* everywhere.—**Florence King**: *Reflections in a Jaundiced Eye* (1989)

1128. America's gross national product.—**Florence King**, 1936– : Jon Winokur (ed.) *The Portable Curmudgeon Redux* (1992)

1129. Contemporary American children, if they are old enough to grasp the concept of Santa Claus by Thanksgiving, are able to see through it by December 15th.—**Roy Blount, Jr.**

1130. The typical American boy would love to go to the moon, but hates to go to the supermarket for his mother.—**Anonymous**

Commitment

1131. One of the best-kept secrets in America is that people are aching to make a commitment—if they only had the freedom and environment in which to do so.—**John Naisbitt** and **Patricia Aburdene**: *Re-inventing the Corporation* (1985)

House and Home

See also CULTURE AND MEDIA: Architecture

1132. A man builds a house in England with the expectation of living in it and leaving it to his children; while we shed our houses in America as easily as a snail does his shell.—**Harriet Beecher Stowe**, 1811–96: Cathrene P. Gilbertson *Harriet Beecher Stowe* (1937)

1133. The Americans do not build walls around their houses. The humblest pedestrian going afoot through the suburbs of Philadelphia, Indianapolis, or any other city, sees not only the houses hut anything in the way of a view which lies beyond them.—**James Hanney**: *From Dublin to Chicago* (1914)

1134. The bungalow had more to do with how Americans live today than any other building that has gone remotely by the name of architecture in our history.—**Russell Lynes**: *The Domesticated Americans* (1963)

1135. In America a man's home is not his castle but merely a gigantic listening device with a mortgage.—**Anonymous**: Tom Wolfe *Mauve Gloves and Madmen, Clutter and Vine* (1976)

1136. I don't know exactly why the notion of homeownership has such a grasp on the American imagination. Perhaps as descendants of landless immigrants we turn our plots into symbols of stability.—**Ellen Goodman**: *Close to Home* (1979)

1137. To be an American is to aspire to a room of one's own.—*New York Times*: 19 April 1987

1138. Owning your home is America's unique recipe for avoiding revolution and promoting pseudo-equality at the same time.—**Florence King**: *Reflections in a Jaundiced Eye* (1989)

Individualism

See also HUMAN RELATIONS: Friendship and Friendliness; HUMAN RELATIONS: Loneliness; HUMAN RELATIONS: Privacy; RELIGION AND BELIEF: Humanism

1139. The American system of rugged individualism.—**Herbert Hoover**: speech in New York City, 22 October 1928

1140. So much of learning to be an American is learning not to let your individuality become a nuisance.—**Edgar Z. Friedenberg**: *The Vanishing Adolescent* (1959)

1141. I don't believe in quotas. America was founded on a philosophy of individual rights, not group rights.—**Clarence Thomas**

1142. American individualism, much celebrated and cherished, has developed without its essential corrective, which is belonging.— **Wallace Stegner:** *When the Bluebird Sings in the Lemonade Springs* (1992)

1143. Individualism and mobility are at the core of American identity.— **Deborah Tall:** *From Where We Stand* (1993)

Life

See also MIND: Happiness; HUMAN RELATIONS; RELIGION AND BELIEF; SOCIAL LIFE; INTERNATIONAL RELATIONS: Europe

1144. In this realm of Mammon and Moloch everything has a value-except human life. —**Count Vay de Vaya Und Zu Luskod:** *Inner Life of the United States* (1908)

1145. The most amazing feature of American life is its boundless publicity. Everybody has to meet everybody, and they even seem to enjoy this enormity. To a central European such as I am, this American publicity of life, the lack of distance between people, the absence of hedges or fences round the gardens, the belief in popularity, the gossip columns of the newspapers, the open doors in the houses, the defencelessness of the individual against the onslaught of the press, all this is more than disgusting, it is positively terrifying.—**C. G. Jung:** *The Complications of American Psychology* (1930)

1146. There are no second acts in American lives.— **F. Scott Fitzgerald:** 1937–40; *The Last Tycoon* (1941)

1147. The American lives even more for his goals, for the future, than the European. Life for him is always becoming, never being.—**Albert Einstein,** 1875–1955: *Ideas & Opinions* (1954)

1148. There is a need for heroism in American life today.— **Vicki Baum,** 1888–1960

1149. In America, life also ebbs away in the effort to survive.—**Simone de Beauvoir:** *America Day by Day* (1953)

1150. The trouble with us in America isn't that the poetry of life has turned to prose, but that it has turned to advertising copy.—**Louis Kronenberger:** *Company Manners* (1954)

1151. There is a rowdy strain in American life, living close to the surface but running very deep. Like an ape behind a mask, it can display itself suddenly with terrifying effect.—**Bruce Catton:** *This Hallowed Ground* (1956)

1152. Life for the European is a career; for the American, it is a hazard.—**Mary McCarthy:** *On the Contrary* (1961)

1153. The quality of American life is an insult to the possibilities of human growth ... the pollution of American space, with gadgetry and cars and TV and box architecture, brutalizes the senses, making gray neurotics of most us, and perverse spiritual athletes and strident self-transcenders of the best of us.—**Susan Sontag:** *Partisan Review*, Winter 1967

1154. American civilization is a bloodless extrapolation of a satisfying life.—**J. B. Priestley:** *New Statesman*, 1971

1155. Like a good American Robert Johnson lived for the moment and died for the past. —**Greil Marcus:** *Mystery Train* (1975)

1156. The true mark of American society is an informality which itself forms its own patterns and codes. Although the outsider at first cannot detect it, there is a rhythm to American life. This rhythm is a constant improvisation, a flexibility that will accommodate the wishes and whims of every member of a group. No voice in an American family takes precedence over the rest.—**Henry Fairlie:** *Manchester Guardian Weekly*, 1 August 1976

1157. Conspicuous waste beyond the imagination of Thorstein Veblen has become the mark of American life. As a nation we find ourselves overbuilt, if not overhoused; overfed, although millions of poor people are undernourished; overtransported in overpowered cars; and also ... overdefended or overdefensed. —**Eugene J. McCarthy:** *America Revisited* (1978)

1158. Part of the American dream is to live long and die young.—**Edgar Z. Friedenberg,** 1921– : Robert I. Fitzhenry (ed.) *Barnes & Noble Book of Quotations* (1987)

1159. I loved the audacity of that American principle which says: "When life gets tainted or goes stale, junk it! Leave it behind! Go West!"—**Jonathan Raban:** *Old Glory* (1982)

Men

See also HUMAN RELATIONS

1160. I really think that American gentlemen are the best after all, because kissing your hand may make you feel very very good but a diamond and safire [*sic*] bracelet lasts forever.—**Anita Loos:** *Gentlemen Prefer Blondes* (1925)

1161. American husbands are the best in the world; no other husbands are so generous to their wives, or can be so easily divorced.—**Elinor Glyn,** 1864–1943, English novelist: Evan Esar (ed.) *20,000 Quips and Quotes* (1968)

1162. Perhaps you have to be born an Englishwoman to realize how much attention American men shower on women and how tremendously considerate all the nice ones among them are of a woman's wishes.—**Gertrude Lawrence:** *A Star Danced* (1945)

1163. Maleness in America is not absolutely defined; it has to be kept and re-earned every day, and one essential element in the definition is beating women in every game that both sexes play.—**Margaret Mead:** *Male and Female* (1948)

1164. If American men are obsessed with money, American women are obsessed with weight. The men talk of gain, the women talk of loss, and I do not know which talk is the more boring.—**Marya Mannes:** *More in Anger* (1958)

1165. America is a land of boys who refuse to grow up.—**Salvador de Madariaga y Rogo:** *The Perpetual Pessimist* (1958)

1166. Because there is very little honor left in American life, there is a certain built-in tendency to destroy masculinity in American men. —**Norman Mailer:** 1962–63; *Cannibals and Christians* (1966)

1167. The American male doesn't mature until he has exhausted all other possibilities.—**Wilfrid Sheed:** *Office Politics* (1966)

1168. When an American heiress wants to buy a man, she at once crosses the Atlantic.—**Mary McCarthy,** 1912–89: Abby Adams (ed.) *An Uncommon Scold* (1989)

1169. Eternal boyhood is the dream of a depressing percentage of American males, and the locker room is the temple where they worship arrested development.—**Russell Baker,** 1925–   : Jon Winokur (ed.) *The Portable Curmudgeon Redux* (1992)

1170. The American male is the world's fattest and softest; this might explain why he also loves guns—you can always get your revolver up.—**Gore Vidal:** *Matters of Fact and Fiction* (1977)

1171. I think that if most guys in America could somehow get their fave-rave poster girl in bed and have total license to do whatever they wanted with this legendary body for one afternoon, at least 75 percent of the guys in the country would elect to beat her up.—**Lester Bangs,** 1948–82: Simon Frith *Sound Effects* (1979)

1172. Eighty percent of American men cheat in America—the rest cheat in Europe.—**Jackie Mason:** 1981; Bob Chieger *Was It Good for You, Too?* (1983)

1173. In the past, it was easy to be a Real Man. All you had to do was abuse women, steal land from Indians, and find some place to dump the toxic waste.—**Bruce Feistein:** *Real Men Don't Eat Quiche* (1982)

1174. The iconic myth surrounding him is built on American notions of heroism: the index of a man's value as measured in *physical courage*. Such ideas have perverted manliness into a self-absorbed race for cheap thrills.—**Gretel Ehrlich:** *The Solace of Open Spaces* (1985)

1175. All American males are failed athletes. —**Pete Gent:** *Weekend Guardian*, 8 July 1989

1176. In the United States adherence to the values of the masculine mystique makes intimate, self-revealing, deep friendships between men unusual.—**Myriam Miedzian:** *Boys Will Be Boys* (1991)

1177. [For American men] maintaining one's lawn is more important than maintaining one's friendships.—**Larry Letich:** *Utne Reader*, May 1991

1178. Years ago, manhood was an opportunity for achievement, and now it is a problem to be overcome.—**Garrison Keillor,** American humorous writer: *The Book of Guys* (1994)

Names

See also PLACES: Cities

1179. I have fallen in love with American names,
The sharp, gaunt names that never get fat.
—**Stephen Benét:** "American Names" (1927)

1180. "My first name is Esmé. I don't think I shall tell you my full name, for the moment. I have a title and you may just be impressed by titles. Americans are, you know."—**J. D. Salinger:** *Nine Stories by J. D. Salinger* (1953)

1181. It was an odious, alien, distasteful name, that just did not inspire confidence. It was not at all like such clean, crisp, honest, American names as Cathcart, Peckem and Dreedle.—**Joseph Heller:** *Catch-22* (1961)

1182. Avoid naming your child for a celebrity. You will never find an Elvis dining at the Harvard Club.—**Quentin Crisp** and **Donald Carroll:** *Doing It with Style* (1981)

1183. Remember, they only name things after you when you're dead or really old.—**Barbara Bush,** former First Lady: as CIA headquarters was renamed after her husband George Bush; *Time*, 10 May 1999

Success and Failure

See also MIND: Creativity and Talent; BUSINESS AND ECONOMY: Money; SOCIAL LIFE: Poverty and Wealth; SOCIAL LIFE: Progress

1184. The only way to success in American public life lies in flattering and kowtowing to the mob.—**H. L. Mencken,** 1880–1956

1185. Success is commonly regarded as an exclusively American product, and it is advertised on matchbook covers and in the back pages of adventure magazines, accessible by way of a high-school education or a new truss.—**Stephen Birmingham:** *Holiday*, March 1961

1186. Success, instead of giving freedom of choice, becomes a way of life. There's no country I've been to where people, when you come into a room and sit down with them, so often ask you, "What do you do?" And, being American, many's the time I've almost asked that question, then realized it's good for my soul not to know. For a while! Just to let the evening wear on and see what I think of this person without knowing what he does and how successful he is, or what a failure. We're ranking everybody every minute of the day.—**Arthur Miller,** 1915–

1187. The story of Americans is the story of arrested metamorphoses. Those who achieve success come to a halt and accept themselves as they are. Those who fail become resigned and accept themselves as they are.—**Harold Rosenberg:** *Discovering the Present* (1973)

1188. America, where overnight success is both a legend and a major industry.—**John Leggett:** *Ross and Tom* (1974)

1189. No failure in America, whether of love or money, is ever simple; it is always a kind of betrayal, of a mass of shadowy, shared hopes.—**Greil Marcus:** *Mystery Train* (1975)

1190. Losing is the great American sin.—**John Tunis:** *New York Times*, 1977

1191. You don't die in the United States, you underachieve.—**Jerzy Kosinski,** 1933–91: Robert I. Fitzhenry *Barnes & Noble Book of Quotations* (1986)

1192. Americans have mastered the art of being prosperous though broke.—**Billy Boy Franklin**

1193. Success is somebody else's failure. Success is the American Dream we can keep dreaming because most people in most places, including thirty million of ourselves, live wide awake in the terrible reality of poverty.—**Ursula K. Le Guin:** 1983; *Dancing at the Edge of the World* (1989)

1194. In the United States there's a Puritan ethic and a mythology of success. He who is successful is good. In Latin countries, a successful person is a sinner.—**Umberto Eco:** *International Herald Tribune*, 14 December 1988

1195. I think the greatest taboos in America are faith and failure.—**Michael Malone:** *Guardian*, 7 July 1989

1196. The only country where failure to promote yourself is widely considered as arrogant.—**Garry Trudeau:** *Newsweek*, 15 October 1990

Women

See also HUMAN RELATIONS

1197. I have no hesitation in saying that although the American woman never leaves her domestic sphere and is in some respects very dependent within it, nowhere does she enjoy a higher station. And if anyone asks me what I think the chief cause of the extraordinary prosperity and growing power of this nation, I should answer that it is due to the superiority of their women.—**Alexis de Tocqueville,** 1805–59

1198. I esteem it a chief felicity of this country that it excels in women.—**Ralph Waldo Emerson:** *Essays* Second Series (1844)

1199. American women expect to find in their husbands a perfection that English women only hope to find in their butlers.—**W. Somerset Maugham:** *A Writer's Notebook* (1896)

1200. There a woman takes to the telephone as women in more decadent lands take to morphia.—**Arnold Bennett:** *Those United States* (1912)

1201. American women shoot the hippopotamus with eyebrows made of platinum.—**E. M. Forster:** *Abinger Harvest* (1936)

1202. Every American woman has two souls to call her own, the other being her husband's.—**James Agate:** *Diary*, 15 May 1937

1203. My advice to the women's clubs of America is to raise more hell and fewer dahlias.—**William Allen White,** 1868–1944: Evan Esar (ed.) *The Dictionary of Humorous Quotations* (1949)

1204. American female energy is increased enormously by the fact that they don't mind being middle aged.—**Freya Stark:** letter, 23 December 1943; *Dust in the Lion's Paw* (1961)

1205. "She happens to belong to a type [of American woman] I frequently met—it goes to lectures. And entertains afterwards.... Amazing, their energy," he went on. "They're perfectly capable of having three or four children, running a house, keeping abreast of art, literature and music—superficially of course, but good lord, that's something—and holding down a job into the bargain. Some of them get through two or three husbands as well, just to avoid stagnation."—**Dodie Smith:** *I Capture the Castle* (1948)

1206. The dream of the American male is for a female who has an essential languor which is not laziness, who is unaccompanied except by himself, and who does not let him down. He desires a beautiful, but comprehensible creature who does not destroy a perfect situation by forming a complete sentence.—**E. B. White:** *The Second Tree from the Corner* (1953)

1207. No woman has ever stepped on Little America—and we have found it to be the most silent and peaceful place in the world.—**Richard E. Byrd,** 1888–1957: Jon Winokur (ed.) *The Portable Curmudgeon* (1987)

1208. All the American women had purple noses and gray lips and their faces were chalk white from terrible powder. I recognized that the United States could be my life's work.—**Helena Rubinstein,** 1870–1965, American cosmetician: recalled her arrival in America on a cold day in 1914; *Time*, 9 April 1965

1209. In Europe, when a rich woman has an affair with a conductor, they have a baby. In America, she endows an orchestra for him.—**Edgar Varèse,** 1885–1965: Herman G. Weinberg *Saint Cinema* (1970)

1210. The American girl makes a servant of her husband and then finds him contemptible for being a servant.—**John Steinbeck,** 1902–68: Elaine Steinbeck and Robert Wallsten (eds.) *Steinbeck: A Life in Letters* (1975)

1211. The impulse of the American woman to geld her husband and castrate her son is very strong.—**John Steinbeck:** Elaine Steinbeck and Robert Wallsten (eds.) *Steinbeck: A Life in Letters* (1975)

1212. An interviewer asked me what book I thought best represented the modern American Woman. All I could think of to answer was: *Madame Bovary.*—**Mary McCarthy:** *On the Contrary* (1961)

1213. American women no longer know who they are.—**Betty Friedan:** *The Feminine Mystique* (1963)

1214. The feminine mystique has succeeded in burying millions of American women alive.—**Betty Friedan:** *The Feminine Mystique* (1963)

1215. American Women: How they mortify the flesh in order to make it appetizing! Their beauty is a vast industry, their enduring allure a discipline which nuns or athletes might find excessive.—**Malcolm Muggeridge:** *The Most of Malcolm Muggeridge* (1966)

1216. The most wasteful "brain drain" in America today is the drain in the kitchen sink.—**Elizabeth Gould Davis:** *First Sex* (1971)

1217. The single most impressive fact about the attempt by American women to obtain the right to vote is how long it took.—**Alice Schaerr Rossi:** *The Feminist Papers* (1973)

1218. A definition of capitalism … the process whereby American girls turn into American women.—**Christopher Hampton:** *Savages* (1974)

1219. Growing up female in America. What a liability! You grew up with your ears full of cosmetic ads, love songs, advice columns, whoreoscopes, Hollywood gossip, and moral dilemmas on the level of TV soap operas. What litanies the advertisers of the good life chanted at you! What curious catechisms!—**Erica Jong:** *Fear of Flying* (1974)

1220. American girls are like horses, very independent. They have never been controlled by anybody. But if you can break them in, they are very grateful.—**Michael Caine:** 1974; David Olive *GenderBabble* (1993)

1221. If I told you, for example that Playboy, in its 22 years, was one of the major things that contributed to the women's movement, you might find it a mindboggler, but it happens to be true.—**Hugh M. Hefner:** *Chicago Tribune*, 3 May 1976

1222. The prostitute is the only honest woman left in America.—**Ti-Grace Atkinson,** 1938–   , American feminist: Bob Chieger *Was It Good for You, Too?* (1983)

1223. In those days, it didn't matter: you could be a Wimbeldon champion, Phi Beta Kappa, Miss America, Nobel Peace Prize winner, but if they asked you about marriage and you didn't at least have a hot prospect ready to get down on one knee, you knew you were considered to be no more than half a woman.—**Billie Jean King:** *Billie Jean* (1982)

1224. The American girl. I've always felt sympathetic toward her. She was raised on promises.—**Tom Petty:** *Playboy*, 1982

1225. The truth is that women's income, on average, will always be a fraction of men's, so long as America remains free.—**Patrick Buchanan:** 1984; David Olive *GenderBabble* (1993)

1226. American women like quiet men: they think they're listening.—**Anonymous**

1227. Heaven is an American salary, a Chinese cook, an English house, and a Japanese wife. Hell is having a Chinese salary, an English cook, a Japanese house, and an American wife.—**James H. Kabbler III:** *Parade*, 1 January 1989

1228. For any woman to succeed in American life she must first do two things: Prepare herself for a profession, and marry a man who wants her to succeed as much as she does.—**Cathleen Douglas**

1229. Viscount Waldorf Astor owned Britain's two most influential newspapers, *The Times* and the *Observer*, but his American wife, Nancy, had a wider circulation than both papers put together.—**Emery Kellen:** Jon Winokur (ed.) *A Curmudgeon's Garden of Love* (1989)

1230. American women are fools because they

try to be everything to everybody.—**Viva:** Jon Winokur (ed.) *A Curmudgeon's Garden of Love* (1989)

1231. When a woman reaches twenty-six in America, she's on the slide. It's downhill all the way from then on. It doesn't give you a tremendous feeling of confidence and well-being.—**Lauren Bacall,** 1924– : Abby Adams (ed.) *An Uncommon Scold* (1989)

1232. The witty woman is a tragic figure in American life. Wit destroys eroticism and eroticism destroys wit, so women must choose between taking lovers and taking no prisoners. —**Florence King:** *Reflections in a Jaundiced Eye* (1989)

1233. Mr. President, I don't know why it took 200 years for one of us to get the job [of ambassador].—**Shirley Temple Black,** 1928– : Carolyn Warner *The Last Word* (1992)

1234. The American woman has not yet slipped into a cocoon, but she has tumbled down a rabbit hole into sudden isolation.—**Susan Faludi:** *Backlash* (1991)

1235. It is capitalist American that produced the modern independent woman. Never in history have women had more freedom of choice in regard to dress, behavior, career, and sexual orientation.—**Camille Paglia:** *Philadelphia Enquirer*, 12 May 1991

1236. In America, first you get the sugar, then you get the power, then you get the women! —**Homer Simpson**

1237. Gloria Steinem's marriage is proof of the emotional desperation of aging feminists who for over 30 years worshiped the steely career woman and trashed stay-at-home moms. —**Camille Paglia:** *Time*, 18 September 2000

Youth

See also PAST AND FUTURE: Generation

1238. In America the young are always ready to give to those who are older than themselves the full benefits of their inexperience.—**Oscar Wilde:** *Court and Society Review* (London), 23 March 1887

1239. The youth of America is their oldest tradition. It has been going on now for three hundred years.—**Oscar Wilde:** *A Woman of No Importance* (1893)

1240. The American ideal is youth—handsome, empty youth.—**Henry Miller:** *The Wisdom of the Heart* (1941)

1241. Americans began by loving youth, and now, out of adult self-pity, they worship it. —**Jacques Barzun:** *The House of Intellect* (1959)

1242. American youth attributes much more importance to arriving at driver's-license age than at voting age.—**Marshall McLuhan:** *Understanding Media* (1964)

1243. The pursuit of happiness, which American citizens are obliged to undertake, tends to involve them in trying to perpetuate the moods, tastes and aptitudes of youth.—**Malcolm Muggeridge:** *The Most of Malcolm Muggeridge* (1966)

1244. Perhaps without knowing all the reasons, they were ahead of many others in seeing that something was missing in modern life.—**Warren Earl Burger:** on American youth of the '60s; *Washington Post*, 29 May 1976

1245. You're going to learn that one of the most brutal things in the world is your average nineteen-year-old American boy.—**Philip Joseph Caputo:** *A Rumor of War* (1977)

HUMAN RELATIONS

Conversation

1246. An American cannot converse, but he can discuss, and his talk falls into a dissertation. He speaks to you as if he was addressing a meeting; and if he should chance to become warm in the discussion, he will say " Gentlemen" to the person with whom he is conversing.—**Alexis de Tocqueville:** *Democracy in America* (1835)

1247. In America, people talk either to say or to listen to *memorable* things—but there is no atmosphere.—**John Butler Yeats:** letter to Ruth Hart, 3 July 1912

1248. The Americans have invented so wide a range of pithy and hackneyed phrases that they can carry on an amusing and animated conversation without giving a moment's reflection to what they are saying and so leave their minds free to consider the more important matters of big business and fornication.—**W. Somerset Maugham:** *Cakes and Ale* (1930)

1249. We do not talk—we bludgeon one another with facts and theories gleaned from cursory readings of newspapers, magazines, and digests.—**Henry Miller:** *The Air-Conditioned Nightmare* (1945)

1250. The Americans are violently oral. That's why in America the mother is all-important and the father has no position at all—isn't respected in the least. Even the American passion for laxatives can be explained as an oral manifestation. They want to get rid of any unpleasantness taken in through the mouth. —**W. H. Auden:** 1947; Nicholas Jenkins (ed.) *The Table Talk of W. H. Auden* (1990)

1251. Americans cannot realize how many chances for mental improvement they lose by their inveterate habit of keeping six conversations when there are twelve in the room.—**Ernest Dimnet,** 1866–1954, French cleric: Sidney Madwed *Poor Man's University* (1994)

Divorce

1252. A New York divorce is in itself a diploma of virtue.—**Edith Wharton:** *The Descent of Man* (1904)

1253. France may claim the happiest marriages in the world, but the happiest divorces in the world are "made in America."—**Helen Rowland:** *A Guide to Men* (1922)

1254. I have heard earnest American sociologists say that American children have a *right* to the divorce experience as an enriching element of an advanced civilization.—**Anthony Burgess:** *You've Had Your Time* (1990)

Family

See also INDIVIDUAL

1255. The family is the ultimate American fascism.—**Paul Goodman,** 1911–72: Jon Winokur (ed.) *The Portable Curmudgeon* (1987)

1256. To my way of thinking, the American family started to decline when parents began to communicate with their children. When we began to "rap," "feed into one another," "let things hang out" that mother didn't know about and would rather not.—**Erma Bombeck:** *If Life Is a Bowl of Cherries, What Am I Doing in the Pits?* (1978)

1257. You hear a lot of dialogue on the death of the American family. Families aren't dying. They're merging into big conglomerates.—**Erma Bombeck:** *San Francisco Examiner*, 1 October 1978

1258. I know that family life in America is a minefield, an economic trap for women, a study in disappointment for both sexes.—**Anne Roiphe:** *Lovingkindness* (1987)

1259. The proliferation of support groups suggests to me that too many Americans are growing up in homes that do not contain a grandmother. A home without a grandmother is like an egg without salt and Helpists know it. They have jumped into the void left by the disappearance of morbid old ladies from the bosom of the American family.—**Florence King:** *Reflections in a Jaundiced Eye* (1989)

Friendship and Friendliness

See also INDIVIDUAL: Individualism; RELIGION AND BELIEF: Humanism; RELIGION AND BELIEF: Materialism and Spirituality

1260. There is no part of the world perhaps, where you have more difficulty in obtaining permission to be alone, and indulge in a reverie, than in America. The Americans are as gregarious as school-boys and think it an incivility to leave you by yourself.—**Frederick Marryat:** *Diary in America with Remarks on Its Institutions* (1839)

1261. The American has dwindled into an Odd Fellow—one who may be known by the development of his organ of gregariousness. —**Henry David Thoreau:** *Civil Disobedience* (1849)

1262. Americans are very friendly and very suspicious, that is what Americans are and that is what always upsets the foreigner, who deals with them, they are so friendly how can they be so suspicious they are so suspicious how can they be so friendly but they are.—**Gertrude Stein:** *New York Herald Tribune*, 9 March 1935

1263. In America every woman has her set of girl-friends; some are cousins, the rest are gained at school. These form a permanent committee who sit on each other's affairs, who "come out" together, marry and divorce together, and who end as those groups of bustling, heartless well-informed club-women who govern society. Against them the Couple of Ehepaar is helpless and Man in their eyes but a biological interlude.—**Cyril Connolly:** *The Unquiet Grave* (1944)

1264. That impersonal insensitive friendliness which takes the place of ceremony in that land of waifs and strays.—**Evelyn Waugh:** *The Loved One* (1948)

1265. America is so terribly grim in spite of all that material prosperity. Compassion and the old neighborliness are gone, people stand by and do nothing when friends and neighbors are attacked, libeled and ruined.—**Charlie Chaplin:** 1953; Lois and Alan Gordon *American Chronicle* (1987)

1266. In general, American social life constitutes an evasion of talking to people. Most Americans don't, in any vital sense, get together; they only do things together.—**Louis Kronenberger:** *Company Manners* (1954)

1267. I'm not against friendliness, she said, I'm not even against Americans.—**Grace Paley:** *Enormous Changes at the Last Minute* (1974)

1268. If a stranger taps you on the ass and says, "How's the little lady today!" you will probably cringe. But if he's an American, he's only being friendly.—**Margaret Atwood:** *Malahat Review*, No. 41, 1977

1269. Since the earliest days of our frontier irreverence has been one of the signs of our affection.—**Dean Rusk,** 1909–94: Robert Andrews *The Concise Columbia Dictionary of Quotations* (1987)

Homosexuality

1270. I'm always amazed at the American practice of allowing one party to a homosexual act to remain passive—it's so undemocratic. Sex must be mutual.—**W. H. Auden:** 20 October 1947; Alan Ansen (comp.) *The Table Talk of W. H. Auden* (1990)

1271. America, I'm putting my queer shoulder to the wheel.—**Allen Ginsberg:** *America* (1956)

1272. [When asked by a US immigration official if he was a practicing homosexual] Practising? Certainly not. I'm absolutely perfect. —**Quentin Crisp,** 1908–99: *Sunday Times,* 20 January 1980

1273. For a woman to be a lesbian in a male-supremacist, capitalist, misogynist, racist, homophobic, imperialist culture, such as that of North America, is an act of resistance.—**Cheryl Clarke:** Cherríe Moraga and Gloria Anzaldúa (eds.) *This Bridge Called My Back* (1983)

1274. I'd rather be black than gay because when you're black you don't have to tell your mother. —**Charles Pierce,** 1926–99: Fred Metcalf *The Penguin Dictionary of Modern Humorous Quotations* (1986)

1275. If you removed all of the homosexuals and homosexual influence from what is generally regarded as American culture, you would be pretty much left with *Let's Make a Deal.* —**Fran Lebowitz,** 1946– : Leigh W. Rutledge *Unnatural Quotations* (1988)

1276. For men who want to flee Family Man America and never come back, there is a guaranteed solution: homosexuality is the new French Foreign Legion.—**Florence King:** *Reflections in a Jaundiced Eye* (1989)

1277. Gay men have followed a very dramatic itinerary ... repressed in the 50s, liberated in the 60s, exalted in the 70s and wiped out in the 80s. —**Edmund White:** *AIDS Quarterly,* Fall 1990

1278. Being gay was worse than being Communist.—**Donald Spoto:** on Hollywood of the 1950s; *A Passion for Life* (1995)

Loneliness

See also INDIVIDUAL: Individualism

1279. All men are lonely. But sometimes it seems to me that we Americans are the loneliest of all. Our hunger for foreign places and new ways has been with us almost like a national disease. Our literature is stamped with a quality of longing and unrest, and our writers have been great wanderers.—**Carson McCullers:** *Vogue* (New York), 1 December 1940

1280. When you become used to never being alone, you may consider yourself Americanized. —**André Maurois,** 1885–1967: Evan Esar (ed.) *The Dictionary of Humorous Quotations* (1949)

1281. One of the greatest necessities in America is to discover creative solitude.—**Carl Sandburg,** 1878–1967: Laurence J. Peter (ed.) *Peter's Quotations* (1977)

1282. The great omission in American life is solitude ... that zone of time and space, free from the outside pressures, which is the incinerator of the spirit.—**Marya Mannes**

1283. Loneliness: It is a continual, almost palpable quality which the country gives off like a heat shimmer.—**A. Alvarez:** *Encounter,* June 1965

1284. Solitude is un–American.—**Erica Jong:** *Fear of Flying* (1973)

1285. North Americans have a peculiar bias. They go outside to be alone and they go home to be social.—**Marshall McLuhan:** *Sunday Times Magazine,* 26 March 1978

1286. Loneliness seems to have become the great American disease.—**John Corry:** *New York Times,* 25 April 1984

1287. She had figured out that the most pervasive American disease was loneliness, and that even people at the top often suffered from it, and that they could be surprisingly responsive to attractive strangers who were friendly. —**Kurt Vonnegut:** *Bluebeard* (1987)

1288. Americans become unhappy and vicious because their preoccupation with amassing possessions obliterates their loneliness. This is why production in America seems to be on such an endless upward spiral: every time we buy something we deepen our emotional deprivation and hence our need to buy something. —**Philip Saltier**

Love

See also INDIVIDUAL: Men; INDIVIDUAL: Women

1289. If there is any country on earth where the course of true love may be expected to run smooth, it is America.—**Harriet Martineau:** *Society in America* (1837)

1290. The Americans, like the English, probably make love worse than any other race. —**Walt Whitman**, 1819–92: Evan Esar (ed.) *The Dictionary of Humorous Quotations* (1949)

1291. From seeing *The Petrified Forest*, I gathered that Americans often made love under tables while gangster bullets whizzed through the air.—**Jessica Mitford:** *Daughters and Rebels* (1960)

1292. In France quarrels strengthen a love affair, in America they end it.—**Ned Rorem:** *The Paris Diary of Ned Rorem* (1966)

1293. American men say "I love you" as part of the conversation.—**Liv Ullmann:** *Changing* (1976)

1294. [Americans are] better at having a love affair that lasts ten minutes than any other people in the world.—**Stephen Spender:** *New York Post*, 1975

1295. A society where mistresses are rare, expensive, and difficult.—**Nicholas von Hoffman:** *Spectator*, 21 September 1978

1296. In Europe we tend to see marital love as an eternity which encompasses hate and also indifference: when we promise to love we really mean that we promise to honour a contract. Americans, seeming to take marriage with not enough seriousness, are really taking love and sex with too much.—**Anthony Burgess:** *You've Had Your Time* (1990)

Marriage

See also INDIVIDUAL: Men; INDIVIDUAL: Women

1297. Marrying is like enlisting in a war or being sentenced to a form of penal servitude

that makes the average American husband into a slave.—**H. L. Mencken**, 1880–1956: Jon Winokur (ed.) *A Curmudgeon's Garden of Love* (1989)

1298. Marriage still remained the most holy of institutions in America; even the rising rate of divorce seemed chiefly to be for the purpose of remarriage.—**Andrew Sinclair:** *The Better Half* (1965)

1299. Like so many substantial Americans, he had married young and kept on marrying, springing from blonde to blonde like the chamois of the Alps leaping from crag to crag. —**P. G. Wodehouse**, 1881–1975: Richard Usborne *Wodehouse at Work to the End* (1977)

1300. American girls often marry someone they can't stand to spite someone they can.—**James Thurber**, 1894–1961: Bob Chieger *Was It Good for You, Too?* (1983)

1301. The American woman's concept of marriage is a clearly etched picture of something uninflated on the floor. A sleeping-bag without air, a beanbag without beans, a padded bra without pads. To work on it, you start pumping— what the magazines call "breathing life into your marriage." Do enough of this and the marriage becomes a kind of Banquo's ghost, a quasi-living entity.—**Florence King:** *Reflections in a Jaundiced Eye* (1989)

1302. American couples have gone to such lengths to avoid the interference of in-laws that they have to pay marriage counselors to interfere between them.—**Florence King:** *Reflections in a Jaundiced Eye* (1989)

1303. Modern American marriage is like a wire fence. The woman's the wire—the posts are the husband's.—**Langdon Mitchell:** Robert I. Fitzhenry *The Harper Book of Quotations* (1993)

Parents

See also INDIVIDUAL

1304. In England every man you meet is some man's son; in America, he may be some man's father.—**Ralph Waldo Emerson**, 1803–82

1305. The thing that impresses me most about America is the way parents obey their children. —**Duke of Windsor (Edward VIII):** *Look,* 5 March 1957

1306. Only in America do these peasants, our mothers, get their hair dyed platinum at the age of sixty, and walk up and down Collins Avenue in Florida in pedal-pushers and mink stoles— and with opinions on every subject under the sun. It isn't their fault they were given a gift like speech—look, if cows could talk, they would say things just as idiotic. —**Philip Roth:** *Portnoy's Complaint* (1967)

1307. Most American children suffer too much mother and too little father. —**Gloria Steinem:** *New York Times,* 26 August 1971

1308. If the new American father feels bewildered and even defeated, let him take comfort from the fact that whatever he does in any fathering situation has a fifty percent chance of being right. —**Bill Cosby,** 1937–

1309. No culture on earth outside of mid-century suburban America has ever deployed one woman per child without simultaneously assigning her such major productive activities as weaving, farming, gathering, temple maintenance, and tent-building. The reason is that full-time, one-on-one child-raising is not good for women *or* children. —**Barbara Ehrenreich:** *The Worst Years of Our Lives* (1989)

Privacy

See also INDIVIDUAL: Individualism

1310. The most amazing feature of American life is its boundless publicity. Everybody has to meet everybody, and they even seem to enjoy this enormity. —**C. G. Jung:** *The Complications of American Psychology* (1930)

1311. There are only two occasions when Americans respect privacy, especially in presidents. Those are prayer and fishing. —**Herbert Hoover:** *New York Herald Tribune,* 19 May 1947

1312. Privacy is a reservation of civilized life which Americans do not cherish. —**Ashley Montagu:** *The American Way of Life* (1967)

Sex

See also INDIVIDUAL: Men; INDIVIDUAL: Women

1313. Sex. In America an obsession. In other parts of the world a fact. —**Marlene Dietrich:** *Marlene Dietrich's ABC* (1962)

1314. Instead of fulfilling the promise of orgiastic bliss, sex in America of the feminine mystique is becoming a strangely joyless national compulsion, if not a contemptuous mockery. —**Betty Friedan:** *The Feminine Mystique* (1963)

1315. We do not understand these Americans who, like adolescents, always speak of sex, and who, like adolescents, all of a sudden have discovered that sex is good not only for procreating children. —**Oriana Fallaci,** Italian journalist and author: *The Egotists* (1963)

1316. That our popular art forms have become so obsessed with sex has turned the USA into a nation of hobbledehoys; as if grown people don't have more vital concerns, such as taxes, inflation, dirty politics, earning a living, getting an education, or keeping out of jail. —**Anita Loos:** *Kiss Hollywood Good-by* (1974)

1317. American eroticism has always been of a different provenance and complexion than the European variety, an enjoyment both furtive and bland that is closer to a blushing cartoon than a sensual celebration. —**Molly Haskell:** *From Reverence to Rape* (1974)

1318. Fifty percent of the women in this country are not having orgasms. If that were true of the male population, it would be declared a national emergency. —**Margo St. James:** *San Francisco Bay Guardian,* 1978

1319. That's the national pastime in this country, at least for the lonely man: masturbation. It is the biggest sport in town. Bigger than pro football. —**Gay Talese:** *Playboy,* 1980

1320. For most Americans, the sexual revolution was not a vast national orgy of swingers. There was never widespread approval of adultery or promiscuity. The revolution—evolution is a better word—appeared rather a massive questioning of the double standard and the sexual constraints we grew up with.—**Ellen Goodman:** *Washington Post*, October 1980

1321. [By the mid 1920s the typical American town] was in full sexual bloom. The change came with erotic fashions, literature and movies, and an unsuspected sexual aid, the automobile.—**John Leo:** *Time*, 9 April 1984

1322. Another American conspiracy of recent vintage holds that women are as highly sexed as men. This is the insane side of equality ... the female sex drive is sixty per cent vanity,

thirty per cent curiosity, and ten per cent physical.—**Florence King,** 1936– : Jon Winokur (ed.) *The Portable Curmudgeon* (1987)

1323. According to the latest research, 60% of American couples are now screwing dog fashion—so both parties can watch television in bed.—**Billy Wilder,** 1906– : Jon Winokur (ed.) *A Curmudgeon's Garden of Love* (1989)

1324. The seven million impotent American males who emerged as customers for Viagra were almost certainly the product of a changing relationship between the sexes, whereby the woman is nowadays accepted as the more important member of a partnership, being more intelligent, more opinionated and the better judge of moral or political correctness.—**Auberon Waugh:** *Sunday Telegraph*, 27 September 1998

SOCIAL LIFE

Cars

See also BUSINESS AND ECONOMY: General Motors

1325. The slogan of progress is changing from the full dinner pail to the full garage.—**Herbert Hoover:** speech in New York, 22 October 1928

1326. To have the license number of one's automobile as low as possible is a social advantage in America.—**André Maurois,** 1885–1967: Evan Esar (ed.) *The Dictionary of Humorous Quotations* (1949)

1327. The moving van is a symbol of more than our restlessness, it is the most conclusive

possible evidence of our progress.—**Louis Kronenberger:** 1951

1328. Stepping into his new Buick convertible he [the American] knows that he would gladly do without it, but imagines that to his neighbor, who is just backing *his* out of the driveway, this car is the motor of life.—**Mary McCarthy:** *On the Contrary* (1961)

1329. Except the American woman, nothing interests the eye of American man more than the automobile, or seems so important to him as an object of esthetic appreciation.—**Alfred H. Barr, Jr.:** *News Summaries*, 31 December 1963

1330. As hand-to-hand combat has gradually disappeared from our civilization, even in wartime, and competition has become more and more sophisticated and abstract, Americans have turned to the automobile to satisfy their love of direct aggression.—**Tom Wolfe:** *The Kandy-Kolored Tangerine-Flake Streamline Baby* (1965)

1331. Storing your car in New York is safer than entering it in a demolition derby. But not much.—**Dan Greenberg:** *New York*, 25 January 1971

1332. This country developed in a particular way because of the automobile, and you can't just push a button and change it.—**Henry Ford II:** *Time*, 10 February 1975

1333. The improved American highway system isolated the American-in-transit. On his speedway he had no contact with the towns which he by-passed. If he stopped for food or gas, he was served no local fare or local fuel, but had one of Howard Johnson's nationally branded ice cream flavors, and so many gallons of Exxon. This vast ocean of superhighways was nearly as free of culture as the sea traversed by the *Mayflower* Pilgrims.—**Daniel J. Boorstin:** Reith Lectures, October 1975; *America and the World Experience* (1976)

1334. Mass transportation is doomed to failure in North America because a person's car is the only place where he can be alone and think.—**Marshall McLuhan,** 1911–80: Louis E. Boone (ed.) *Quotable Business* (1992)

1335. Americans are broad-minded people. They'll accept the fact that a person can be an alcoholic, a dope fiend, a wife beater, and even a newspaperman; but if a man doesn't drive there's something wrong with him.—**Art Buchwald,** 1925– : Ted Goodman (ed.) *The Forbes Book of Business Quotations* (1997)

1336. Americans will put up with anything provided it doesn't block traffic.—**Dan Rather,** 1931–

1337. If all the cars in the United States were placed end to end, it would probably be Labor Day Weekend.—**Doug Larson:** Robert Byrne *The Fourth 637 Best Things Anybody Ever Said* (1990)

1338. All American cars are basically Chevrolets.—**Herb Caen,** 1916– : Jon Winokur (ed.) *The Portable Curmudgeon Redux* (1992)

1339. Natives who beat drums to drive off evil spirits are objects of scorn to smart Americans who blow horns to break up traffic jams.—**Mary Ellen Kelly:** Carolyn Warner *The Last Word* (1992)

1340. Americans are the only people in the world known to me whose status anxiety prompts them to advertise their college and university affiliations in the rear window of their automobiles.—**Paul Fussell**

1341. America is the only country in the world where the poor have a parking problem. —**Anonymous**

Christmas

1342. In the United States, Christmas has become the rape of an idea.—**Richard Bach:** *Jonathan Livingston Seagull* (1970)

Classes

See also PLACES: Cities; PAST AND FUTURE: Revolution

1343. The Americans never use the word *peasant*, because they have no idea of the class which that term denotes; the ignorance of more remote ages, the simplicity of rural life, and the rusticity of the villager have not been preserved among them; and they are alike unacquainted with the virtues, the vices, the coarse habits, and the simple graces of an early stage of civilization.—**Alexis de Tocqueville:** *Democracy in America* vol. 1 (1835)

1344. That which in England we call the Middle Classes is in America virtually the nation. —**Matthew Arnold:** *A Word About America* (1882)

1345. I can hire one half of the working class to kill the other half.—**Jay Gould,** American financier: 1886

1346. The American race seems to have developed two classes, and only two, the upper-middle, and the lower-middle.—**Rupert Brooke:** *Letters from America* (1916)

1347. Perhaps the rarest bit of irony in American history is the later custodianship of democracy by the middle class.—**Vernon Louis Parrington,** 1871-1929

1348. Americans, while willing, even eager, to be serfs, have always been obstinate about being peasantry.—**F. Scott Fitzgerald:** *The Great Gatsby* (1926)

1349. There is a crisis in American leadership in the middle of the twentieth century that is partly due to the declining authority of an establishment which is now based on an increasingly castelike White-Anglo Saxon-Protestant (WASP) upper class.—**E. Digby Baltzell:** *The Protestant Establishment,* 1964

1350. NQOCD (not quite our class, darling) is an American joke. You might say "He's a bit ordinaire."—**Peter York** and **Ann Barr:** *The Official Sloane Ranger's Handbook* (1982)

1351. Americans are notoriously hard to divide along class lines. With the exception of professors of sociology (who know exactly where in the upper middle class they fit) and a few billionaires—who hope they are upper-class, but have a horrible fear there may be a real aristocracy hiding somewhere in Boston or Philadelphia—most of us have only the vaguest idea what class we belong to.—**Noel Perrin:** *Third Person Rural* (1983)

Education

See also INDIVIDUAL: Youth; BUSINESS AND ECONOMY: Technology

1352. [Princeton University:] A quaint ceremonious village of puny demigods on stilts.—**Albert Einstein:** letter to the Queen of Belgium, 20 November 1933

1353. America is the best half-educated country in the world.—**Nicholas Murray Butler,** 1862-1947: Laurence J. Peter (ed.) *Peter's Quotations* (1977)

1354. One might say that the American trend of education is to reduce the senses almost to nil.—**Isadora Duncan:** *My Life* (1942)

1355. America is the only country left where we teach languages so that no pupil can speak them.—**John Erskine,** 1879-1951: Laurence J. Peter *Peter's Quotations* (1977)

1356. It is our American habit if we find the foundations of our educational structure unsatisfactory to add another story or wing. We find it easier to add a new study or course or kind of school than to recognize existing conditions so as to meet the need.—**John Dewey,** 1859-1952

1357. The business of the American teacher is to liberate American citizens to think apart and act together.—**Stephen S. Wise:** *New York Times Magazine,* 22 March 1953

1358. I find that the three major administrative problems on campus are sex for the students, athletics for the alumni, and parking for the faculty.—**Clark Kerr,** head of the University of California: speech at the University of Washington; *Time,* 17 November 1958

1359. It has been said that we have not had the three R's in America, we had the six R's: remedial readin', remedial 'ritin' and remedial 'rithmetic.—**Robert M. Hutchins,** 1899-1977: Jon Winokur (ed.) *The Portable Curmudgeon Redux* (1992)

1360. October is a fine and dangerous season in America, a wonderful time to begin anything at all. You go to college, and every course in the catalogue looks wonderful.—**Thomas Merton,** 1915-68

1361. Education has in America's whole history been the major hope for improving the individual and society.—**Gunnar Myrdal,** 1898-1987: Laurence J. Peter *Peter's Quotations* (1977)

1362. High school is closer to the core of the American experience than anything else I can think of.—**Kurt Vonnegut,** 1922- : John Birmingham (ed.) *Our Times Is Now: Notes from the High School Underground* (1970)

1363. One trouble: to be a professional anything in the United States is to think of oneself as an expert and one's ideas as semisacred, and to treat others in a certain way—professionally.—**Marge Piercy,** 1936–   : Robin Morgan *Sisterhood Is Powerful* (1970)

1364. I read in the newspapers they are going to have 30 minutes of intellectual stuff on television every Monday from 7:30 to 8 ... to educate America. They couldn't educate America if they started at 6:30.—**Groucho Marx,** 1895–1977

1365. American education needs training for character.—**Seymour Cohen:** *Affirming Life* (1987)

1366. We're going to have the best-educated American people in the world.—**Dan Quayle:** 21 September 1988

1367. Palm Springs University—more than one hundred degrees available.—**Anonymous:** Robert Byrne *The Fourth 637 Best Things Anybody Ever Said* (1990)

1368. On many American campuses the only qualification for admission was the ability actually to find the campus and then discover a parking space.—**Malcolm Bradbury,** 1932–   : Robert I. Fitzhenry *The Harper Book of Quotations* (1993)

1369. A serious problem in America is the gap between academe and the mass media, which is our culture. Professors of humanities, with all their leftist fantasies, have little direct knowledge of American life and no impact whatever on public policy.—**Camille Paglia:** *Sex, Art, and American Culture* (1992)

1370. Education is the established church of the United States. It is one of the religions that Americans believe in. It has its own orthodoxy, its pontiffs and its noble buildings.—**Michael Sadler**

1371. Everyone has a right to a university degree in America, even if it's in Hamburger Technology.—**Clive James,** 1939–

1372. There are two major products that come out of Berkeley: LSD and UNIX. We don't believe this to be a coincidence.—**Jeremy S. Anderson**

Health Care

1373. It is strange indeed that the more we learn about how to build health, the less healthy Americans become.—**Adelle Davis:** *Let's Have Healthy Children* (1951)

1374. The American ideal of a doctor was essentially a nurse.—**Lucille Joel:** on sentimental recollections of the kindly, caring, reassuring physician; *Newsweek,* 23 May 1988

1375. America's health care system is neither healthy, caring, nor a system.—**Walter Cronkite:** PBS-TV, 17 December 1990

1376. What we have in the United States is not so much a health-care system as a disease-care system.—**Edward M. Kennedy,** 1932–   , American politician

Information and Learning

See also CULTURE AND MEDIA: Journalism; RELIGION AND BELIEF: Lies and Truth; RELIGION AND BELIEF: Reality

1377. The greatest American superstition is belief in facts.—**Hermann A. Keyserling:** John Gunther *Inside U.S.A.* (1947)

1378. America is full of a violent desire to learn.—**Le Corbusier:** *When Cathedrals Were White* (1947)

1379. One of the things that is wrong with America is that everybody who has done anything at all in his own field is expected to be an authority on every subject under the sun. **Davis Elmer Holmes,** 1890–1958

1380. America has always been a country of amateurs where the professional, that is to say, the man who claims authority as a member of an élite which knows the law in some field or other, is an object of distrust and resentment. —**W. H. Auden:** *Faber Book of Modern American Verse* (1956)

1381. Among all the world's races, Americans are the most prone to misinformation. This is not a consequence of any special preference for mendacity. It is rather that so much of what they themselves believe is wrong.—**John Kenneth Galbraith**, 1908–

1382. The American vice is explanation. —**Gore Vidal:** *The Second American Revolution and Other Essays* (1982)

1383. The problem with America today is that too many people know too much about not enough.—**Anonymous**

Leisure

See also MIND: Happiness; INDIVIDUAL: Life

1384. The superficiality of the American is the result of his hustling. It needs leisure to think things out; it needs leisure to mature. People in a hurry cannot think, cannot grow, nor can they decay. They are preserved in a state of perpetual puerility.—**Eric Hoffer:** *The Passionate State of Mind* (1955)

1385. It takes application, a fine sense of value, and a powerful community-spirit for a people to have serious leisure, and this has not been the genius of the Americans.—**Paul Goodman:** *Growing Up Absurd* (1960)

1386. Leisure does not automatically develop the soul. And this is a real dilemma of Americans.—**Margaret Mead:** *Life*, 23 August 1968

1387. The multi-billion-dollar entertainment and leisure industries notwithstanding, Americans have not learned how to use large amounts of leisure in noncompulsive, personally satisfying ways.—**Janet Saltzman Chafetz:** *Masculine/Feminine or Human?* (1974)

Poverty and Wealth

See also INDIVIDUAL: Success and Failure; RELIGION AND BELIEF: Humanism; RELIGION AND BELIEF: Materialism and Spirituality; BUSINESS AND ECONOMY: Money

1388. We have two American flags always; one for the rich and one for the poor. When the rich fly it it means that things are under control; when the poor fly it it means danger, revolution, anarchy.—**Henry Miller:** *The Air-Conditioned Nightmare* (1945)

1389. The big majority of Americans, who are comparatively well off, have developed an ability to have enclaves of people living in the greatest misery without almost noticing them. —**Gunnar Myrdal**, 1898–1987

1390. No one in the United States has the right to own millions of acres of American land, I don't care how they came by it.—**Edna Ferber:** *Giant* (1952)

1391. A poor American feels guilty at being poor, but less guilty than an American *rentier* who has inherited wealth but is doing nothing to increase it; what can the latter do but take to drink and psychoanalysis?—**W. H. Auden:** *The Dyer's Hand* (1962)

1392. Clothes make the poor invisible.... America has the best-dressed poverty the world has ever known.—**Michael Harrington:** *The Other America* (1962)

1393. The other America, the America of poverty, is hidden today in a way that it never was before. Its millions are socially invisible to the rest of us. The very development of American society is creating a new kind of blindness about poverty. The poor are increasingly slipping out of the very experience and consciousness of the nation.—**Michael Harrington:** *The Other America* (1962)

1394. Look what can happen in this country, they'd say. A girl lives in some out-of-the-way town for nineteen years, so poor she can't afford a magazine, and then she gets a scholarship to college and wins a prize here and a prize there and ends up steering New York like her own private car.—**Sylvia Plath:** *The Bell Jar* (1963)

1395. Every morning, I get up and look through the *Forbes* list of the richest people in America. If I'm not there, I go to work. —**Robert Orben**, 1927– , American editor and writer: Louis E. Boone (ed.) *Quotable Business* (1992)

1396. Prior to the Reagan era, the newly rich aped the old rich. But that isn't true any longer. Donald Trump is making no effort to behave like Eleanor Roosevelt as far as I can see.—**Fran Lebowitz,** 1946–

1397. Americans are like a rich father who wishes he knew how to give his son the hardships that made him rich.—**Robert Frost:** 1874–1963

1398. We were poor when I was young, but the difference then was the government didn't come around telling you you were poor.—**Ronald Reagan:** *Time,* 7 July 1986

1399. Ninety-eight of 100 of the rich men in America are honest. That is why they are rich. —**Russell Herman Conwell**

1400. America is still a place where most people react to seeing a man in a Ferrari by redoubling their own efforts to be able to afford one, rather than by trying to let down his tires. —*Economist*: 3 January 1998

Progress

See also THE NATION: The Dream and the Ideal; INDIVIDUAL: Success and Failure; CULTURE AND MEDIA: Architecture; CULTURE AND MEDIA: Culture and Civilization; PAST AND FUTURE: Change; PAST AND FUTURE: Future

1401. I claim that this country has been built by speculation, and further progress must be made in that line.—**Richard Whitney:** statement to the Senate Banking Committee, c.1932

1402. America has believed that in differentiation, not in uniformity, lies the path of progress. It acted on this belief; it has advanced human happiness, and it has prospered.—**Louis D. Brandeis,** 1856–1941

1403. It is possible to believe in progress as a fact without believing in progress as an ethical principle; but in the catechism of many Americans, the one goes with the other.—**Norbert Wiener:** *The Human Use of Human Beings* (1954)

1404. The United States has to move very fast to even stand still.—**John F. Kennedy:** *Observer,* 21 July 1963

1405. The American: a titan enamored of progress, a fanatical giant who worships "getting things done" but never asks himself what he is doing nor why he is doing it.—**Octavio Paz:** *Alternating Current* (1973)

1406. For most Americans, progress means accepting what is new because it is new, and discarding what is old because it is old.—**Lewis Mumford,** 1895–1990: Laurence J. Peter *Peter's Quotations* (1977)

1407. We Americans are tempted to distinguish ourselves from other current and former inhabitants of this planet by assuming that we are ruled by "progress."—**Michael Dorris:** *Paper Trail* (1994)

Society

See also PLACES: Cities; INDIVIDUAL: Individualism; CULTURE AMD MEDIA: Culture and Civilization; POLITICS AND GOVERNMENT: Government; POLITICS AND GOVERNMENT: Politics; POLITICS AND GOVERNMENT: Power; PAST AND FUTURE: Revolution; BUSINESS AND ECONOMY: Economy; BUSINESS AND ECONOMY: Money

1408. Inequality is as dear to the American heart as liberty itself.—**William Dean Howells:** *Impressions and Experiences* (1896)

1409. American society is a sort of flat, freshwater pond which absorbs silently, without reaction, anything which is thrown into it. —**Henry Brooks Adams:** letter to Royal Cortissox, 20 September 1911

1410. The great social adventure of America is no longer the conquest of the wilderness but the absorption of fifty different peoples.—**Walter Lippmann:** *A Preface to Politics* (1914)

1411. No man has a right in America to treat any other man tolerantly, for tolerance is the assumption of superiority.—**Wendell Lewis Willkie,** 1892–1944: Laurence J. Peter (ed.) *Peter's Quotations* (1977)

1412. In America everybody is of the opinion that he has no social superiors, since all men are equal, but he does not admit that he has no social inferiors, for, from the time of Jefferson onward, the doctrine that all men are equal applies only upwards, not downwards.—**Bertrand Russell:** *Unpopular Essays* (1950)

1413. It would seem that Americans have a kind of resistance to looking closely at society. —**Lionel Trilling:** *The Liberal Imagination* (1950)

1414. The organization of American society is an interlocking system of semi-monopolies notoriously venal, an electorate notoriously unenlightened, misled by a mass media notoriously phony.—**Paul Goodman:** *The Community of Scholars'* (1962)

1415. In your time we have the opportunity to move not only toward the rich society and the powerful society but upward to the Great Society.—**Lyndon B. Johnson:** speech, University of Michigan, May 1964

1416. Our society is not a community, but merely a collection of isolated family units. —**Valerie Solanas:** *The SCUM Manifesto* (1968)

1417. The mayor is perhaps the most important single social force for good or evil in America.—**Richard Lee:** Laurence J. Peter (ed.) *Peter's Quotations* (1977)

1418. Today Americans are overcome not by the sense of endless possibility but by the banality of the social order they have erected against it.—**Christopher Lasch:** *The Culture of Narcissism* (1978)

1419. No country has washed more dirty laundry in public than we have.—**Shirley Temple Black,** 1928–   : Esther Stineman *American Political Women* (1980)

1420. It was not their irritating assumption of equality that annoyed Nicholai so much as their cultural confusions. The Americans seemed to confuse standard of living with quality of life, equal opportunity with institutionalized mediocrity, bravery with courage, machismo with manhood, liberty with freedom, wordiness with articulation, fun with pleasure—in short, all of the misconceptions common to those who assume that justice implies equality for all, rather than equality for equals.—**Trevanian:** *Shibumi* (1979)

1421. More than ever before, Americans are suffering from back problems—back taxes, back rent, back auto payments.—**Robert Orben,** 1927–   : Lloyd Cory (comp.) *Quotable Quotations* (1985)

1422. Deep down, the US, with its space, its technological refinement, its bluff good conscience, even in those spaces which it opens up for simulation, is the *only remaining primitive society.*—**Jean Baudrillard:** *America* (1986)

1423. I think the greatest curse of American society has been the idea of an easy millennialism—that some new drug, or the next election or the latest in social engineering will solve everything.—**Robert Penn Warren,** 1905–89: *The Ultimate Success Quotations Library* (1997)

1424. Modernization is Americanization. It is the American way of organizing society that is prevailing in the world.—**Rupert Murdoch:** lecture, Manhattan Institute, New York, 9 November 1989; William Shawcross *Rupert Murdoch* (1992)

1425. No society can survive, no civilization can survive, with 12-year-olds having babies, with 15-year-olds killing each other, with 17-year-olds dying of AIDS, with 18-year-olds getting diplomas they can't read.—**Newton Gingrich:** December 1994; *Times,* 9 February 1995

Sport

1426. The Americans never walk. In winter, too cold; in summer, too hot.—**W. B. Yeats,** 1865–1939: Louis E. Boone (ed.) *Quotable Business* (1992)

1427. Spectator sports found lodgement in American society earlier than did those in which participation is the price of enjoyment.—**Frederic L. Paxson,** 1877–1948

1428. If I were to indicate today that element of American life, which is most characteristic of our nationality, my finger would unerringly point to our athletic escutcheon.—**Douglas MacArthur,** 1880–1964

1429. Whoever wants to know the heart and mind of America had better learn baseball. —**Jacques Barzun:** *God's Country and Mine* (1954)

1430. Baseball is an allegorical play about America, a poetic, complex and subtle play of courage, fear, good luck, mistakes, patience about fate and sober self-esteem (batting average). It is impossible to understand America without a thorough knowledge of baseball. —**Saul Steinberg:** 1954; Harold Rosenberg *Saul Steinberg* (1978)

1431. If baseball goes for pay television, shouldn't the viewers be given a bonus for watching a ball game between Baltimore and Kansas City?—**Jimmy Cannon:** *New York Post,* 1954

1432. Walking is an-American activity. —**Lord Kinross:** *The Innocents at Home* (1959)

1433. Baseball gives every American boy a chance to excel, not just to be as good as someone else but to be better than someone else. —**Ted Williams:** *Sports Illustrated,* 8 August 1966

1434. In America, it is sport that is the opiate of the masses.—**Russell Baker:** *New York Times,* 3 October 1967

1435. Anyone who will tear down sports will tear down America. Sports and religion have made America what it is today.—**Woody Hayes,** 1913– : Bill Bradley *Life on the Run* (1976)

1436. In this country, when you finish second, no one knows your name.—**Frank McGuire:** James A. Michener *Sports in America* (1976)

1437. Americans are experts at winning, but still amateurs at losing.—**Edward Walsh:** 1977

1438. Whether we view sports as a reflection of the mores of American life or as the promoter of these mores, it is a sobering analysis to consider that they may represent the end result of American pragmatism.—**Arnold R. Beisser:** 1977

1439. The concepts and language of sports are so familiar and pervasive that they are used as metaphors to clarify other aspects of American life.—**Arnold R. Beisser:** 1977

1440. Football is a metaphor for America's sinfulness.—**George F. Will:** *The Pursuit of Happiness and Other Sobering Thoughts* (1978)

1441. Black people exist in perpetual struggle with mainstream America about the nature of reality. And nowhere is this more evident than in sports.—**Harry Edwards:** *The New York Times,* 6 May 1979

1442. Football is about the only unifying force left in America today.—**Woody Hayes:** *Life,* December 1979

1443. America has been erased like a blackboard, only to be rebuilt and erased again. But baseball has marked time while America has rolled by like a procession of steamrollers. —**W. P. Kinsella:** *Shoeless Joe* (1982)

1444. Americans are sportophiles.—**Steve Miller:** *USA Today,* November 1984

1445. It is a curious fact that you can give an American man some kind of ball and he will be thoroughly content.—**Judson P. Philips**

1446. We have to have impact, and action, and instant reward, and punishment. Soccer is too subtle for most Americans.—**Anonymous**

1447. Football combines the two worst things about America: it is violence punctuated by committee meetings.—**George F. Will:** *International Herald Tribune* (Paris), 7 May 1990

1448. Boxing has become America's tragic theater.—**Joyce Carol Oates,** 1938–

1449. I think there are only three things America will be known for 2,000 years from now when they study this civilization: the Constitution, jazz music, and baseball.—**Gerald Early:** *Baseball Documentary* (1994)

Thanksgiving

1450. 'T was founded be th' Puritans to give thanks f'r bein' presarved fr'm th' Indyans, an' ... we keep it to give thanks we are presarved fr'm th' Puritans.—**Finley Peter Dunne:** *Mr. Dooley's Opinions* (1901)

1451. The only truly indigenous American inventions are Thanksgiving turkey and finger-fucking.—**Lyndon B. Johnson,** 1908–73

1452. Thanksgiving is a typically *American* holiday. In spite of its religious form (giving thanks to God for a good harvest), its essential, secular meaning is a *celebration of successful production*. It is a producers' holiday. The lavish meal is a symbol of the fact that abundant consumption is the result and reward of production.—**Ayn Rand:** *The Ayn Rand Letter* (1971)

1453. Thanksgiving dinners take eighteen hours to prepare. They are consumed in twelve minutes. Half-times take twelve minutes. This is not coincidence.—**Erma Bombeck,** 1927–

1454. Most turkeys taste better the day after; my mother's tasted better the day before.—**Rita Rudner**

1455. On Thanksgiving Day, all over America, families sit down to dinner at the same moment—halftime.—**Anonymous:** Henry O. Dormann *The Speaker's Book of Quotations* (1987)

1456. Thanksgiving comes *after* Christmas for people over thirty.—**Peter Kreeft:** J. Bryan *Hodgepodge Two* (1989)

1457. Thanksgiving is so called because we are all so thankful that it comes only once a year.—**P. J. O'Rourke,** 1947–

Time

1458. In America, an hour is 40 minutes.—**German proverb:** H. L. Mencken *A New Dictionary of Quotations* (1942)

1459. Americans have more timesaving devices and less time than any other people in the world.—**Duncan Cladwell,** 1874–1965: Laurence J. Peter *The Peter Pyramid* (1986)

1460. Speed is scarcely the noblest virtue of graphic composition, but it has its curious rewards. There is a sense of getting somewhere fast, which satisfies a native American urge.—**James Thurber:** *A Thurber Garland* (1955)

1461. American time has stretched around the world. It has become the dominant tempo of modern history, especially of the history of Europe.—**Harold Rosenberg:** *The Tradition of the New* (1960)

1462. Americans will pay a big price for an invention that will help them save time they don't know what to do with.—**Anonymous**

Tragedy

See also MIND: Happiness

1463. I suspect tragedy in the American countryside because all the people capable of it move to the big towns at twenty.—**F. Scott Fitzgerald,** 1896–1940: Andrew Turnbull *The Letters of F. Scott Fitzgerald* (1963)

1464. Nothing is more difficult for Americans to understand than the possibility of tragedy.—**Henry Kissinger:** *New York Times,* 1973

Work

1465. On their side the workers had only the Constitution. The other side had bayonets.—**Mother Jones,** 1830–1930, American labor leader: Linda Atkinson *Mother Jones* (1978)

1466. In an English ship, they say, it is poor grub, poor pay, and easy work; in an American ship, good grub, good pay, and hard work.—**Jack London:** *The People of the Abyss* (1903)

1467. Work in the United States is everything, and everything has become work.—**Count Vay de Vaya Und Zu Luskod:** *Inner Life of the United States* (1908)

1468. There is no right to strike against the public safety by anybody, anywhere, anytime.—**Calvin Coolidge:** telegram to president of American Federation of Labor, 14 September 1919

1469. We'll never recognize the United Auto Workers Union or any other union.—**Henry**

Ford: 1937; Lois and Alan Gordon *American Chronicle* (1987)

1470. A tremendous number of people in America work very hard at something that bores them. Even a rich man thinks he has to go down to the office everyday. Not because he likes it but because he can't think of anything else to do.—**W. H. Auden:** 16 November 1946; Alan Ansen (comp.) *The Table Talk of W. H. Auden* (1990)

1471. Anyone who is honestly seeking a job and can't find it, deserves the attention of the United States government, and the people. —**John F. Kennedy,** 1917–63: Connie Robertson (ed.) *The Wordsworth Dictionary of Quotations* (1996)

1472. Injustice was as common as streetcars. When men walked into their jobs, they left their dignity, their citizenship and their humanity outside.—**Walter Reuther,** 1907–70: on working life in America before the Wagner Act, attrib.

1473. Consider the history of labor in a country [USA] in which, spiritually speaking, there are no workers, only candidates for the hand of the boss's daughter.—**James Baldwin:** *The Fire Next Time* (1963)

1474. On my visits to America I discovered that the old Marxist dictum "From each according to his abilities, to each according to his needs," was probably more in force in America, that holy of holies of capitalism, than in any other country in the world.—**Felix Houphouet-Boigny:** *Newsweek,* 9 August 1965

1475. The terrible newly-imported American doctrine that everyone ought to do something. —**Sir Osbert Sitwell,** 1892–1969: Laurence J. Peter (ed.) *Peter's Quotations* (1977)

1476. Work is the only kind of property many people have in America.—**Eugene J. McCarthy:** *Center Report,* December 1975

1477. Farmer, laborer, clerk: That's a brief history of the United States.—**John Naisbitt:** *Megatrends* (1984)

1478. I suspect that American workers have come to lack a work ethic. They do not live by the sweat of their brow.—**Kiichi Miyazawa,** Japan's prime minister: *Daily Telegraph* (London), 5 February 1992

CULTURE AND MEDIA

Architecture

See also PLACES: Cities; INDIVIDUAL: House and Home

1479. The American sign of civic progress is to tear down the familiar and erect the monstrous.—**Shane Leslie:** *American Wonderland* (1936)

1480. America's poetry is not in literature, but in architecture.—**Oliver St. John Gogarty:** *As I Was Going Down Sackville Street* (1937)

1481. Our national flower is the concrete cloverleaf.—**Lewis Mumford,** 1895–1990: *Quote,* 8 October 1961

1482. In Hollywood's heyday the films were only celluloid, but the cinemas that showed them were marbled citadels of fantasy and opulence.—*Time*: 5 May 1980

1483. While American interiors are often designed to provide an idealized picture of their owner's circumstances, English interiors tend to tell the truth about the people who live in them.—**John Richardson:** *New York Times*, 29 July 1984

1484. [Capitol:] the most recognizable building in America.—**Kenneth L. Burns:** "The Congress," PBS-TV, 4 July 1990; it designed by an Englishman, inspired by a Russian church, decorated by Italian craftsmen and built in part by slaves

1485. [White House:] no other single building is so much a part of the American consciousness.—**Barbara Bush,** First Lady: *Washington Times*, 24 January 1992

1486. America is a much newer experiment in human living, one with moral concerns at its core. In this respect it differs from Europe, which has preferred sophistication and worldly wisdom to "righteousness," and resembles China, which saw the universe itself as essentially a moral order. However materialistic Americans may be in their economic pursuits, their ceremonies emphasize the material far less than European societies have. America has imposing official architecture. Washington, D.C., boasts a radial baroque stateliness. Yet one of its most important buildings, the White House, is a modest dwelling, its scale far smaller than that of the palaces of Europe and Asia.—**Yi-Fu Tuan:** *Passing Strange and Wonderful: Aesthetics, Nature, and Culture* (1993)

1487. To Americans, the dome is the architectural symbol of democracy.—**William Seale:** *Washington Post*, 21 October 1995

Art

1488. The only works of art produced by America are its plumbing and its bridges.—**Marcel Duchamp:** 1917

1489. When a man paints the El, a 1740 house or a miner's shack, he is likely to be called by his critics, American. The American painter is supposed to paint as though he had never seen another painting.—**Arthur G. Dove,** 1880–1946: Frederick S. Wight *Arthur G. Dove* (1958)

1490. All the arts in America are a gigantic racket run by unscrupulous men for unhealthy women.—**Thomas Beecham,** 1879–1961: *Observer*, 5 May 1946

1491. America is no place for an artist: to be an artist is to be a moral leper, an economic misfit, a social liability.—**Henry Miller:** *The Air-Conditioned Nightmare* (1945)

1492. [The American artist:] the unwanted cockroach in the kitchen of a frontier society.—**John Sloan,** 1871–1951: Barbara Rose *American Art since 1900* (1967)

1493. Art, for most Americans, is a very queer fish—it can't be reasoned with, it can't be bribed, it can't be doped out or duplicated; above all, it can't be cashed in on.—**Louis Kronenberger:** *Company Manners* (1954)

1494. America is an orgy of color, noise, smartness, and multitudinous legs.—**Augustus John,** 1878–1961

1495. I feel that America is essentially against the artist, that the enemy of America is the artist, because he stands for individuality and creativeness, and that's *un*-American somehow.—**Henry Miller:** *Paris Review*, No. 28, 1962

1496. [The USA] a chaos of ugliness.—**Edward Hopper,** 1882–1967: Barbara Rose *American Art since 1900* (1967)

1497. Pop art is an American phenomenon that departs from the cliché of big, bold, raw America that became current when Abstract Expressionism triumphed internationally.—**Lucy Lippard:** *Pop Art* (1966)

1498. One of the big problems of American painting is that it is American.—**Emile de Antonio:** *Painters Painting* (1972)

1499. A fog-horn chorus of blah.—**Forbes Watson**

1500. The smallest ham sandwich ever wrapped at the world's biggest and noisiest banquet.—**Edwin Avery Park**

1501. I never can pass by the Metropolitan Museum of art in New York without thinking of it not as a gallery of living portraits but as a cemetery of tax-deductible wealth. —**Lewis H. Lapham:** *Money and Class in America* (1988)

Chaplin, Charlie (1889–1977), actor and filmmaker

1502. The son of a bitch is a ballet dancer. —**W. C. Fields,** 1879–1946

1503. Somehow importing to the peeling of a banana the elegant nonchalance of a duke drawing a monogrammed cigarette from a platinum case. —**Alexander Woolcott:** *While Rome Burns* (1934)

1504. He always portrays one and the same figure ... himself as he was in his early, dismal youth. —**Sigmund Freud,** 1856–1939: *Time,* 8 June 1998

1505. The Zulus know Chaplin better than Arkansas knows Garbro. —**Will Rogers,** 1879–1935: *Atlantic Monthly,* August 1939

1506. The one genius created by the cinema. —**George Bernard Shaw,** 1856–1950: *Time,* 2 January 1978

1507. I am for people. I can't help it. —**Charlie Chaplin:** *Observer,* 28 September 1952

1508. I remain just one thing, and one thing only—and that is a clown. It places me on a far higher plane than any politician. —**Charlie Chaplin:** *Observer,* 17 June 1960

1509. Chaplin is no business man—all he knows is that he can't take anything less. —**Samuel Goldwyn,** 1882–1974: Charlie Chaplin *My Autobiography* (1964)

1510. All I need to make a comedy is a park, a policeman and a pretty girl. —**Charlie Chaplin:** *My Autobiography* (1964)

1511. When he discarded the little tramp, the little tramp turned around and killed him. —**Mary Pickford:** *New York Times,* 28 March 1971

1512. I have no further use for America. I wouldn't go back there if Jesus Christ was president. —**Charlie Chaplin:** Leslie Halliwell *Halliwell's Filmgoer's Companion* (1984)

1513. He has no sense of humor, particularly about himself. —**Lita Grey Chaplin,** Charlie's second wife: radio interview, 1974; Richard Lamparski *Whatever Became Of* Eighth Series (1982)

1514. When Chaplin found a voice to say what was on his mind, he was like a child of eight writing lyrics for Beethoven's Ninth. —**Billy Wilder,** 1906–

Culture and Civilization

See also THE NATION: The Dream and the Ideal; SOCIAL LIFE: Progress; SOCIAL LIFE: Society

1515. America is the only nation in history which, miraculously, has gone directly from barbarism to degeneration without the usual interval of civilization. —**Georges Clemenceau,** 1841–1929: attrib.; *Saturday Review of Literature* (New York), 1 December 1945

1516. A few suits of clothes, some money in the bank, and a new kind of fear constitute the main differences between the average American today and the hairy men with clubs who accompanied Attila to the city of Rome. —**Philip Wylie:** *Generation of Vipers* (1942)

1517. The weakness of American civilization, and perhaps the chief reason why it creates so much discontent, is that it is so curiously abstract. It is a bloodless extrapolation of a satisfying life. You dine off the advertisers "sizzling" and not the meat of the steak. —**J. B. Priestley:** *New Statesman,* 10 December 1971

1518. What a filthy brutal dirty culture you have in North America—with of course its obverse sentimentality. —**Lawrence Durrell,** Indian-born British poet and novelist: letter to Henry Miller, January 1979

1519. American cultural traditions define personality, achievement, and the purpose of human life in ways that leave the individual suspended in glorious, but terrifying, isolation. These are limitations of our culture, of the categories and ways of thinking we have inherited, not limitations of individuals who inhabit this culture. —**Robert Bellah,** et al: *Habits of the Heart* (1985)

1520. The microwave, the waste disposal, the orgasmic elasticity of the carpets, this soft resort-style civilization irresistibly evokes the end of the world. —**Jean Baudrillard:** *America* (1986)

1521. Here in the U.S., culture is not that delicious panacea which we Europeans consume in a sacramental mental space and which has its own special columns in the newspapers— and in people's minds. Culture is space, speed, cinema, technology. —**Jean Baudrillard:** *America* (1986)

1522. When I was a graduate student at Harvard, I learned about showers and central heating. Ten years later, I learned about breakfast meetings. These are America's three contributions to civilization. —**Mervin A. King:** *New York Times,* 4 March 1987

1523. We are being swallowed up by the popular culture of the United States, but then the Americans are being swallowed up by it too. It's just as much a threat to American culture as it is to ours. —**Northrop Frye,** 1912–91, Canadian literary critic: Connie Robertson (ed.) *The Wordsworth Dictionary of Quotations* (1996)

Dance

1524. The real American type can never be a ballet dancer. The legs are too long, the body too supple and the spirit too free for this school of affected grace and toe walking. —**Isadora Duncan:** *My Life* (1927)

1525. America does not concern itself now with Impressionism. We own no involved philosophy. The psyche of the land is to be found in its movement. It is to be felt as a dramatic force of energy and vitality. We move; we do not stand still. We have not yet arrived at the

stocktaking stage. —**Martha Graham,** 1894– 1991, American dancer and choreographer: Virginia Stewart (ed.) *Modern Dance* (1935)

1526. We look at the dance to impart the sensation of living in an affirmation of life, to energize the spectator into keener awareness of the vigor, the mystery, the humor, the variety, and the wonder of life. This is the function of the American dance. —**Martha Graham:** Virginia Stewart (ed.) *Modern Dance* (1935)

Dylan, Bob (1941–   ), singer and songwriter

1527. Bob freed your mind in the way Elvis freed your body. —**Bruce Springsteen:** speech, New York City, 20 January 1988

1528. In writing songs I've learned as much from Cézanne as I have from Woody Guthrie. —**Bob Dylan:** Clinton Heylin *Dylan: Behind the Shades* (1991)

1529. All those songs were great lyrically. Dylan's gobbledygook and his cluttered poetry was very appealing. —**Paul McCartney:** *Time,* 8 June 1998

1530. He's always on to the next thing. It's as though it's a compulsion, and in a sense, it serves him. It serves his art. —**Joan Baez:** *Time,* 8 June 1998

1531. He makes William Shakespeare look like Billy Joel. —**George Harrison,** 1943–   : Robert Andrews *The New Penguin Dictionary of Modern Quotations* (2001)

Fashion

1532. The jean! The jean is the destructor! It is a dictator! It is destroying creativity. The jean must be stopped! —**Pierre Cardin:** *People,* 28 June 1976

1533. The midi was un-American, it was subversive, it was against the best instincts and the finest qualities of this great nation.—**James Brady:** Bob Chieger *Was It Good for You, Too?* (1983)

1534. Rich white Protestant men have held on to some measure of power in America almost solely by getting women, blacks, and other disadvantaged groups to wear crippling foot fashions. This keeps them too busy with corns and bunions to compete in the job market.—**P. J. O'Rourke:** *Modern Manners* (1988)

Fonda, Jane (1937–   ), actress

1535. I am not a do-gooder. I am a revolutionary. A revolutionary woman.—**Jane Fonda:** 1972; *Los Angeles Weekly*, 28 November 1980

1536. Jane Fonda—exasperating at times, inspiring at times—is a modern-day version of the mythical bird, the phoenix, rising constantly from the ashes.—**Bill Davidson:** *Jane Fonda: An Intimate Biography* (1990)

1537. Today I'd be a dyed blonde, a numb and dumb pill-popping star, if I hadn't taken a cause. I could very well be dead like Marilyn. Not through drugs but dead just the same.—**Jane Fonda:** *Daily Mail*, 14 April 1980

1538. She didn't get that terrific body from exercise. She got it from lifting all that money.—**Joan Rivers:** 1987

Hellman, Lillian (1905–84), playwright

1539. Hellman has chosen to write on a Tennessee Williams theme in an Agatha Christie style.—*Times:* on *Toys in the Attic* (1960)

1540. It is curious how incest, impotence, nymphomania, religious mania and real estate speculation can be so dull.—**Richard Findlater:** *Time and Tide* (1961); on *Toys in the Attic*

1541. Every word she writes is a lie, including

"and" and "the."—**Mary McCarthy:** January 1980; *New York Times*, 16 February 1980

1542. Much has been written about her enemies. She picked them with care, and God knows they deserved her.—**Jules Feiffer,** 1929–: graveside eulogy; Peter Feibleman *Lilly: Reminiscences of Lillian Hellman* (1988)

1543. The biggest difference between Lillian as a grown-up and Lillian as a child was that she was taller.—**Peter Feibleman:** *Lilly: Reminiscences of Lillian Hellman* (1988)

1544. There's a place where everybody wants to be insulted, and Lilly knew where it was.—**Peter Feibleman:** *New Yorker*, 21 June 1993

1545. Anger was Hellman's oxygen.—**John Lahr:** *New Yorker*, 21 June 1993

Hollywood

1546. They know only one word of more than one syllable here, and that is *fillum*.—**Louis Sherwin:** c.1920; H. L. Mencken *A New Dictionary of Quotations* (1942)

1547. A trip through a sewer in a glass-bottomed boat.—**Wilson Mizner,** 1876–1933: Alva Johnston *The Legendary Mizners* (1953)

1548. A place where the inmates are in charge of the asylum.—**Laurence Stallings:** c. 1930; H. L. Mencken *A New Dictionary of Quotations* (1942)

1549. I'm not very keen on Hollywood. I'd rather have a nice cup of cocoa really.—**Noël Coward:** letter to his mother, 1931; Cole Lesley *The Life of Noël Coward* (1976)

1550. The people are unreal. The flowers are unreal, they don't smell. The fruit is unreal, it doesn't taste of anything. The whole place is a glaring, gaudy, nightmarish set, built up in the desert.—**Ethel Barrymore,** American actress: on first arriving in Hollywood, 1932

1551. What I like about Hollywood is that one can get along by knowing two words of English—*swell* and *lousy*.—**Vicki Baum:** c. 1933, attrib.; H. L. Mencken *A New Dictionary of Quotations* (1942)

1552. Bankers, nepotists, contracts and talkies: on four fingers one may count the leeches which have sucked a young and vigorous industry into paresis.—**Dalton Trumbo:** *North American Review*, August 1933

1553. I'm not a little girl from a little town making good in a big town. I'm a big girl from a big town making good in a little town.—**Mae West,** 1892–1980: arriving in Hollywood; Abby Adams *An Uncommon Scold* (1989)

1554. We [Hollywood people] are the croupiers in a crooked gambling house.—**Samuel Hoffenstein,** 1890–1947: Lillian Ross *Picture* (1952)

1555. Isn't Hollywood a dump—in the human sense of the word. A hideous town, pointed up by the insulting gardens of its rich, full of the human spirit at a new low of debasement.—**F. Scott Fitzgerald:** letter, 29 Jul 1940; Andrew Turnbull (ed.) *The Letters of F. Scott Fitzgerald* (1963)

1556. It's a mining town in lotus land.—**F. Scott Fitzgerald,** 1896–1940: *The Last Tycoon* (1941)

1557. A place where people from Iowa mistake each other for movie stars.—**Fred Allen,** 1894–1956: Evan Esar (ed.) *The Dictionary of Humorous Quotations* (1949)

1558. You can take all the sincerity in Hollywood, place it in the navel of a fruit fly and still have room enough for three caraway seeds and a producer's heart.—**Fred Allen:** John Robert Colombo *Popcorn in Paradise* (1980)

1559. Some are able and humane men and some are low-grade individuals with the morals of a goat, the artistic integrity of a slot machine, and the manners of a floorwalker with delusions of grandeur.—**Raymond Chandler:** on movie producers; *Atlantic Monthly*, November 1945

1560. A world with all the personality of a paper cup.—**Raymond Chandler,** 1888–1959: attrib.; Nigel Rees *A Dictionary of Twentieth Century Quotations* (1987)

1561. If my books had been worse I should not have been invited to Hollywood, and if they had been any better I should not have come. —**Raymond Chandler:** F. MacShane *The Life of Raymond Chandler* (1976)

1562. I came out here with one suit and everybody said I looked like a bum. Twenty years later Marlon Brando came out with only a sweatshirt and the town drooled over him. That shows how much Hollywood has progressed.—**Humphrey Bogart,** 1899–1957

1563. The only place in the world where a man can get stabbed in the back while climbing a ladder.—**William Faulkner,** 1897–1962: John Robert Colombo (ed.) *Colombo's Hollywood* (1979)

1564. The only "ism" Hollywood believes in is plagiarism.—**Dorothy Parker,** 1893–1967: Evan Esar (ed.) *The Dictionary of Humorous Quotations* (1949)

1565. To survive there, you need the ambition of a Latin-American revolutionary, the ego of a grand opera tenor, and the physical stamina of a cow pony.—**Billie Burke:** *With a Feather on My Nose* (1949)

1566. Everybody liked Bill Shannon, even in Hollywood, where nobody likes anybody.—**P. G. Wodehouse:** *The Old Reliable* (1951)

1567. Hollywood's like Egypt, full of crumbled pyramids. It' ll never come back. It'll just keep on crumbling until finally the wind blows the last studio prop across the sands.—**David O. Selznick:** 1951; Ben Hecht *A Child of the Century* (1954)

1568. A trip through a sewer in a glass-bottomed boat.—**Wilson Mizner:** *The Incredible Mizners* (1953)

1569. The average Hollywood film star's ambition is to be admired by an American, courted by an Italian, married to an Englishman and have a French boyfriend.—**Katharine Hepburn:** *New York Journal-American*, 22 February 1954

1570. Where there is no definition of your worth earlier than your last picture.—**Murray Kempton:** 1955

1571. Hollywood money isn't money. It's congealed snow, melts in your hand, and there you are.—**Dorothy Parker:** *Paris Review*, Summer 1956

1572. The honors Hollywood has for the writer are as dubious as tissue-paper cufflinks.—**Ben Hecht:** *Charlie* (1957)

1573. I went out there for a thousand a week, and I worked Monday, and I got fired Wednesday. The guy that hired me was out of town Tuesday.—**Nelson Algren,** 1909–81: Malcolm Cowley (ed.) *Writers at Work* First Series (1958)

1574. The most beautiful slave-quarters in the world.—**Moss Hart,** 1904–61: attrib.

1575. A place where they'll pay you a thousand dollars for a kiss, and fifty cents for your soul.—**Marilyn Monroe,** 1926–62: *Marilyn Monroe in Her Own Words* (1990)

1576. [Hollywood] is filled with people who make adventure pictures and who have never left this place … religious pictures and they haven't been in a church or synagogue for years … pictures about love and they have never been in love—ever.—**Richard Brooks:** *New York Post,* 7 December 1960

1577. With a mental equipment which allows me to tell the difference between hot and cold, I stand out in this community like a modern-day Cicero.—**Anita Loos:** *No Mother to Guide Her* (1961)

1578. Too many freeways, too much sun, abnormality taken normally, pink stucco houses and pink stucco consciences.—**Clancy Sigal:** *Going Away* (1962)

1579. The place where they take an author's steak-tartare and make cheeseburgers out of it.—**Fletcher Knebel:** *Look,* 19 November 1963

1580. No one has a closest ffiend in Hollywood.—**Sheilah Graham:** *The Rest of the Story* (1964)

1581. Lunch Hollywood-style—a hot dog and vintage wine.—**Harry Kurnitz,** 1907–68: Max Wilk *The Wit and Wisdom of Hollywood* (1971)

1582. A dreary industrial town controlled by hoodlums of enormous wealth.—**S. J. Perelman:** *Paris Review,* Spring 1964

1583. Strip away the phony tinsel of Hollywood and you find the real tinsel underneath. —**Oscar Levant:** *Inquisition in Eden* (1965)

1584. A cultural boneyard.—**Marlon Brando:** *Daily Express,* 3 February 1966

1585. Hollywood is like Picasso's bathroom. —**Candice Bergen:** *New York Post,* 14 February 1967

1586. To survive there, you need the ambition of a Latin-American revolutionary, the ego of a grand opera tenor, and the physical stamina of a cow pony.—**Billie Burke,** 1885–1970, American stage and screen actor: Leslie Halliwell *Filmgoer's Companion* (1984)

1587. The Mont Saint Michel of tit and tale. —**Gabrielle "Coco" Chanel,** 1883–1971: Paul Morand *L'Allure de Chanel* (1976)

1588. Deep below the glitter, it's all solid tinsel.—**Samuel Goldwyn,** 1882–1974: attrib.; *Guardian,* 11 April 1984

1589. Hollywood brides keep the bouquets and throw away the grooms.—**Groucho Marx,** 1895–1977: Jon Winokur (ed.) *The Portable Curmudgeon* (1987)

1590. A golden suburb for golf addicts, gardeners, men of mediocrity and satisfied stars. —**Orson Welles:** *Observer,* 1969

1591. The convictions of Hollywood and television are made of boiled money.—**Lillian Hellman:** *An Unfinished Woman* (1969)

1592. Living in Hollywood is like living in a lit cigar butt.—**Phyllis Diller:** 1970; Abby Adams *Uncommon Scold* (1989)

1593. A carnival where there are no concessions.—**Wilson Mizner:** *The Wit and Wisdom of Hollywood* (1971)

1594. One giant, self-contained orgy farm … with every male in the business on the make. —**Veronica Lake:** *Veronica* (1971)

1595. Hollywood is like being nowhere and talking to nobody about nothing.—**Michelangelo Antonioni:** *Sunday Times,* 1971

1596. Hollywood is bounded on the north, south, east, and west by agents.—**William Fadiman:** *Hollywood Now* (1972)

1597. The propaganda arm of the American Dream machine.—**Molly Haskell:** *From Reverence to Rape* (1973)

1598. The most flourishing factory of popular mythology since the Greeks.—**Alistair Cooke:** *America* (1973)

1599. If we have to tell Hollywood good-by, it may be with one of those tender, old-fashioned, seven-second kisses exchanged between two people of the *opposite* sex, with all their clothes on.—**Anita Loos:** *Kiss Hollywood Good-by* (1974)

1600. Hollywood always had a streak of the totalitarian in just about everything it did.—**Shirley MacLaine:** *You Can Get There from Here* (1975)

1601. In Beverly Hills they don't throw their garbage away. They make it into television shows.—**Woody Allen:** *Annie Hall* (film), 1977

1602. Every country gets the circus it deserves. Spain gets bullfights. Italy gets the Catholic Church. America gets Hollywood.—**Erica Jong:** *How To Save Your Own Life* (1977)

1603. Where is Hollywood located? Chiefly between the ears. In that part of the American brain lately vacated by God.—**Erica Jong:** *How To Save Your Own Life* (1977)

1604. The land of the definite maybe.—**Norman Lear:** *US*, 14 June 1977

1605. The sinkhole of Los Angeles.—**Jack Hines, Jr.:** *Time*, 15 August 1977

1606. Hollywood is like Harvard. Once you're accepted, you can't flunk out.—**Brandon Tartikoff:** *New Times*, 9 January 1978

1607. In Hollywood, all marriages are happy. It's trying to live together afterward that causes the problems.—**Shelley Winters:** *Rolling Stone*, 1978

1608. Pearl is a disease of oysters. Levant is a disease of Hollywood.—**Kenneth Tynan,** 1927–80

1609. Hollywood is the only industry, even taking in soup companies, which does not have laboratories for the purpose of experimentation.—**Orson Welles,** 1915–85: Frank Brady *Citizen Welles* (1989)

1610. Hollywood has always been a cage … a cage to catch our dreams.—**John Huston,** 1906–87, American filmmaker: *Sunday Times* (London), 27 December 1987

1611. In some countries being president is just an honorary position—like being a husband in Hollywood.—**Earl Wilson,** 1907– : Bob Chieger *Was It Good for You, Too?* (1983)

1612. In Europe an actor is an artist. In Hollywood, if he isn't working, he's a bum.—**Anthony Quinn,** 1915–2001: Leslie Halliwell *Filmgoer's Companion* (1984)

1613. There are basically two types of exercise in Hollywood these days: jogging and helping a recently divorced friend move.—**Robert Wagner:** 1982; Bob Chieger *Was It Good for You, Too?* (1983)

1614. Nobody knows anything.—**William Goldman:** *Adventures in the Screen Trade* (1983)

1615. Studio executives are intelligent, brutally overworked men and women who share one thing in common with baseball managers: they wake up every morning of the world with the knowledge that sooner or later they're going to get fired.—**William Goldman:** *Adventures in the Screen Trade* (1983)

1616. In Hollywood you don't have happiness, you send out for it.—**Rex Reed:** *Chicago Tribune*, 16 October 1983

1617. I'm not bitter about Hollywood's treatment of me—but of its treatment of Griffith, von Sternberg, Buster Keaton and a hundred others.—**Orson Welles,** 1915–85: French TV, 1985

1618. It's the place where the sky is always blue and so are the screenwriters. Where the story line is accepted on Monday by the twenty-four-year-old head of a studio, and rejected on the Thursday by his sixteen-year-old replacement.—**Maureen Lipman:** *How Was It for You?* (1985)

1619. They are often glowing with the effusive sentimentality to be found only among those who have stolen each other's ideas, deals and live-in companions.—**Frederic Raphael:** *New York Times*, 6 January 1985

1620. Fame is no sanctuary from the passing of youth … suicide is much easier and more acceptable in Hollywood than growing old gracefully.—**Julie Burchill:** *Girls on Film* (1986)

1621. We Americans have always considered Hollywood, at best, a sinkhole of depraved venality. And, of course, it is. It is not a Protective Monastery of Aesthetic Truth. It is a place where everything is incredibly expensive.—**David Mamet:** *Writing in Restaurants* (1986)

1622. Born schizophrenic... for 75 years it has been both a town and a state of mind, an industry and an art form.—**Richard Corliss:** *Time*, 3 February 1986

1623. Only three things you need if you want to make it in Hollywood. Learn how to make your own salad. Learn how to fall in slow motion. And learn to cry.—**Gary Busey:** *Film Yearbook* (1987)

1624. I think people need something to look up to, and Hollywood was the only Royalty that America ever had.—**Bette Davis:** *Sunday Times*, 20 September 1987

1625. Through the thirties, Hollywood was a combination kosher deli and El Dorado.—**Marion Meade:** *Dorothy Parker* (1988)

1626. If New York is the Big Apple, tonight Hollywood is the Big Nipple.—**Bernardo Bertolucci,** Italian filmmaker: said at Oscar presentation ceremony; *Guardian*, 13 April 1988

1627. When I first went into the movies Lionel Barrymore played my grandfather. Later he played my father and finally he played my husband. If he had lived, I'm sure I would have played his mother. That's the way it is in Hollywood. The men get younger and the women get older.—**Lillian Gish,** 1896– : Abby Adams *An Uncommon Scold* (1989)

1628. An emotional Detroit.—**Lillian Gish:** Abby Adams *An Uncommon Scold* (1989)

1629. Just like those other black holes from outer space, Hollywood is postmodern to this extent: it has no center, only a spreading dead zone of exhaustion, inertia, and brilliant decay.—**Arthur Kroker:** Marilouise Kroker and David Cook *Panic Encyclopedia* (1989)

1630. It is said that life begins when the fetus can exist apart from its mother. By this definition, many people in Hollywood are legally dead.—**Jay Leno,** 1950– : Robert Byrne *The Fourth 637 Best Things Anybody Ever Said* (1990)

1631. In Hollywood now when people die they don't say, "Did he leave a will?" but "Did he leave a diary?"—**Liza Minnelli:** *Observer*, 13 August 1989

1632. In Hollywood if you don't sing or dance, you end up as an after-dinner speaker.—**Ronald Reagan:** *An American Life* (1990)

1633. I'm a product of Hollywood. Fantasy is not unnatural to me: it's my reality. Hollywood people are like everyone else, only more so. They depict reality as opposed to living it.—**Carrie Fisher:** *Weekend Guardian*, 12 January 1991

1634. The Academy Awards—Hollywood's annual orgy of self-congratulations.—**Harry Smith:** "Good Morning America," ABC-TV, 26 March 1991

1635. Hollywood is a place that attracts people with massive holes in their souls.—**Julia Phillips:** *Times*, 3 April 1991

1636. In Hollywood, writers are considered only the first drafts of human beings.—**Frank Deford,** 1938–   : Eileen Mason *Great Book of Funny Quotes* (1993)

1637. If you have a vagina *and* an attitude in this town, then that's a lethal combination.—**Sharon Stone:** *Empire* (London), June 1992

1638. The only reason I'm in Hollywood is that I don't have the moral courage to refuse the money.—**Marlon Brando,** 1924–

1639. Loneliness beside the swimming pool.—**Liv Ullmann,** 1938–

1640. Hollywood was itself a collage, importing not movies by movie makers and actors, internalizing Germany as Marlene Dietrich, France as Charles Boyer, Hungary as Peter Lorre.—**Geoffrey O'Brien:** *The Phantom Empire* (1993)

1641. There's a big trend in Hollywood of taking very good European films and turning them into very bad American films.—**Roddy Doyle:** *Independent on Sunday* (London), 1 May 1994

1642. Giving your book to Hollywood is like turning your daughter into a pimp.—**Tom Clancy,** novelist: *Guardian Weekly*, 25 December 1994

1643. Hollywood is significantly responsible for the infantilisation of America.—**Leon Wieseltier:** *Time*, 1 September 1997

1644. Hollywood loves roles in which women deteriorate in front of their very own eyes and end up either in the gutter or dead.—**Glenn Close,** actress: *Time,* 4 December 2000

Intellectuals

See also MIND: Intelligence; MIND: Thinking; POLITICS AND GOVERNMENT: Dissent

1645. American life is a powerful solvent. It seems to neutralize every intellectual element, however tough and alien it may be, and to fuse it in the native good will, complacency, thoughtlessness, and optimism.—**George Santayana:** *Character and Opinion in the United States* (1920)

1646. The trouble with me is, I belong to a vanishing race. I'm one of the intellectuals. —**Robert E. Sherwood,** American writer and dramatist: *The Petrified Forest* (1934)

1647. Most Americans want to be ... only comfortably cultivated. They dabble with the intellectual just enough to avoid being lowbrow and escape being highbrow.—**Alan C. Valentine:** *The Age of Conformity* (1954)

1648. It is ironic that the United States should have been founded by intellectuals, for throughout most of our political history, the intellectual has been for the most part either an outsider, a servant or a scapegoat.—**Richard Hofstadter:** *Anti-Intellectualism in American Life* (1963)

1649. A spirit of national masochism prevails, encouraged by an effete corps of impudent snobs who characterize themselves as intellectuals.—**Spiro T. Agnew,** Republican vice-president: speech, New Orleans, 19 October 1969; *Frankly Speaking* (1970)

1650. The courage we inherit from our Jeffersons and Lincolns and others is not the Solzhenitsyn courage of the true believer, but the courage to doubt.—**Daniel J. Boorstin:** *Time,* 26 June 1978

1651. I don't want people running around saying Gwen Brooks's work is intellectual. That makes people think instantly about obscurity. It shouldn't have to mean that, but it often seems to.—**Gwendolyn Brooks,** 1917– : Claudia Tate (ed.) *Black Women Writers at Work* (1983)

Journalism

See also SOCIAL LIFE: Information

1652. In America, the majority raises formidable barriers around the liberty of opinion: within these barriers, an author may write what he pleases; but woe to him if he goes beyond them.—**Alexis de Tocqueville:** *Democracy in America* vol. 1 (1835)

1653. In America the president reigns for four years, and journalism governs for ever and ever. —**Oscar Wilde:** *The Soul of Man under Socialism* (1891)

1654. There is no such thing as an independent press in America. I am paid for keeping my honest opinions out of the paper I am connected with.—**John Swinton,** editor of *New York Sub*: Twilight Club, New York City, 12 April 1893

1655. All the news that's fit to print.—**Adolph S. Ochs:** motto of the *New York Times,* from 1896

1656. When a tabloid prints it, that's smut. When the [*New York*] *Times* prints it, that's sociology.—**Adolph S. Ochs,** 1858–1935: *Time,* 15 August 1977

1657. Your newspapers are too big, and your lavatory paper's too small.—**Ernest Bevin:** on his first visit to the USA in 1915, when asked for his views on America by newsmen; Alistair Horne *Canada and the Canadians* (1961)

1658. In America the press rules the country; it rules its politics, its religion, its social practices.—**E. W. Scripps,** 1854–1926: *Damned Old Crank* (1951)

1659. The *Chicago Tribune* has come out against syphilis. Bet you 8 to 5 syphilis will win.—**Anonymous:** 1940

1660. Germany was the cause of Hitler as much as Chicago is responsible for the *Chicago Tribune.*—**Alexander Woollcott:** 1943

1661. Read *the New Yorker*, trust in God; And take short views.
—**W. H. Auden**: "On the Circuit"; *Collected Poems: 1939–1947*

1662. Trying to be a first-rate reporter on the average American newspaper is like trying to play Bach's "St. Matthew's Passion" on a ukelele.—**Bagdikian's** Observation

1663. The tabloid newspaper actually means to the typical American what the Bible is popularly supposed to have meant to the typical Pilgrim Father: a very present help in time of trouble, plus a means of keeping out of trouble via harmless, since vicarious, indulgence in the pomps and vanities of this wicked world.
—**E. E. Cummings**, 1894–1962

1664. The *New York Times* is deliberately pitched to the liberal point of view.—**Herman Dismore,** foreign editor of the *New York Times* from 1950 to 1960

1665. I thought it was *Time's* job to make people unhappy and *Life's* job to make them happy.
—**Henry R. Luce,** 1898–1967, co-founder and publisher of *Time*: *Esquire*, January 1978

1666. In America, journalism is apt to be regarded as an extension of history; in Britain, as an extension of conversation.—**Anthony Sampson:** *Anatomy of Britain Today* (1965)

1667. Europe has a press that stresses opinions; America a press, radio, and television that emphasize news.—**James B. Reston:** *The Artillery of the Press* (1966)

1668. The *New York Times* is the best and the worst newspaper on earth, a daily monument to the sloppy and extravagant simplification of the overdone.—**James Cameron,** British journalist: *Point of Departure* (1967)

1669. When something happens in America, the media cover every detail of the event: a Mafia scandal in New Jersey, with political implications; illegal betting on football games; the financial wheeling and dealing of a former secretary to the Senate Majority. There is never any "Mr. X." Names are given, and photographs, and details about the crime, and the amounts of money involved.—**Jean-François Revel:** *Without Marx or Jesus* (1970)

1670. It is impossible for any objective newspaperman to be a friend of a president.—**Walter Lippmann,** 1899–1974: Wesley D. Camp *What a Piece of Work Is Man!* (1990)

1671. The *New York Times Book Review* is alive with the sound of axes grinding.—**Gore Vidal,** 1925–

1672. I handled the first presidential bowel movement in the history of the *New York Times.*—**Russell Baker:** *Esquire* (New York), April 1976

1673. I understand the function of American media. Essentially, they exist to please their advertisers.—**Justin Charles Ravitz:** *Mother Jones* Sep–Oct 1977

1674. In this country, when you attack the Establishment, they don't put you in jail or a mental institution. They do something worse. They make you a member of the Establishment.—**Art Buchwald:** *Time*, 5 December 1977

1675. The First Amendment gives newspapermen a status and a mandate, an honored place in society, that cannot be matched in England, much less on the European continent.—**Isidor Feinstein Stone:** *Chicago Tribune*, 26 January 1978

1676. When news is concerned, nobody in the press is a friend—they are all enemies.—**Richard M. Nixon:** *Time*, 17 April 1978

1677. Viewing with dismay the conditions in somebody else's backyard is the speciality of the *New York Times.*—**John Crosby,** 1912– : Jonathon Green (ed.) *A Dictionary of Contemporary Quotations* (1982)

1678. In modern America, anyone who attempts to write satirically about the events of the day finds it difficult to concoct a situation so bizarre that it may not actually come to pass while his article is still on the presses.—**Calvin Trillin:** *Uncivil Liberties* (1982)

1679. More than illness or death, the American journalist fears standing alone against the whim of his owners or the prejudices of his audience. Deprive William Safire of the insignia of the *New York Times*, and he would have a hard time selling his truths to a weekly broadsheet in suburban Duluth.—**Lewis H. Lapham:** *Money and Class in America* (1988)

1680. My Watergate reporting was very important for the country and for journalism and for subduing this rightist movement in American, tramping it down and saying, "Whoa!"—**Bob Woodward:** *Wall Street Journal*, 3 January 1988

Marx, Groucho (1895–1977), actor

1681. The man was a major comedian, which is to say that he had the compassion of an icicle, the effrontery of a carnival shill and the generosity of a pawnbroker.—**S. J. Perelman,** 1904–79: Robert Andrews *The New Penguin Dictionary of Modern Quotations* (2001)

1682. What Groucho preached was a life without a script.—**Ronald Blythe:** *Listener*, 1979

Monroe, Marilyn (1926–62), actress

1683. Young lady, I think you're a case of arrested development. With your development, somebody's bound to get arrested.—**Groucho Marx:** on the *Love Happy* set 1949; *Playboy*, May 1979

1684. If I'm going to be a symbol of something I'd rather have it sex than some other things we've got symbols of.—**Marilyn Monroe:** *Time*, 14 June 1999

1685. She's something different to each man, blending somehow the thing she seems to require most.—**Clark Gable,** 1901–60: *Playboy*, 1986

1686. She is a phenomenon of nature, like Niagara Falls or the Grand Canyon. You can't talk to it. It can't talk to you. All you can do is stand back and be awed by it.—**Nunnally Johnson,** 1897–1977: Peter Harry Brown and Patte B. Barham *Marilyn, the Last Take* (1990)

1687. There's a broad with her future behind her.—**Constance Bennett,** 1904–65: Jonathon

Green (ed.) *The Pan Dictionary of Contemporary Quotations* (1989)

1688. I've never met anyone as utterly mean as Marilyn Monroe. Nor as utterly fabulous on the screen.—**Billy Wilder:** *Los Angeles Times*, 1968

1689. I remember her on the screen, huge as a colossus doll. Mincing and whispering and simply hoping her way into total vulnerability.—**Gloria Steinem:** *Ms.* (New York), August 1972

1690. So we think of Marilyn who was every man's love affair with America, Marilyn Monroe who was blonde and beautiful and had a sweet little rinky-drink of a voice and all the cleanliness of all the clean American backyards. She was our angel, the sweet angel of sex, and the sugar of sex came up from her like a resonance of sound in the clearest grain of a violin.—**Norman Mailer:** *Marilyn* (1973)

1691. Next to her, Lucrezia Borgia was a pussycat.—**David Hall:** *Sunday Times*, 9 September 1973

1692. Kissing Marilyn was like kissing Hitler—sure, I said that. It wasn't *that* bad. But you can see through that line: there was this woman, beautifully endowed, treating all men like shit. Why did I have to take that?—**Tony Curtis:** *Game*, September 1975

1693. She was good at playing abstract confusion in the same way that a midget is good at being short.—**Clive James:** *Visions before Midnight* (1977)

1694. Monroe, the consummate sexual doll, is empowered to act but afraid to act, perhaps because no amount of acting, however inspired, can convince the actor herself that her ideal female life is not a dreadful form of dying.—**Andrea Dworkin:** *Right-Wing Women* (1978)

1695. A vacuum with nipples.—**Otto Preminger,** 1906–86: Jonathon Green (ed.) *The Pan Dictionary of Contemporary Quotations* (1989)

1696. She was the victim of ballyhoo and sensation—exploited beyond anyone's means.—**Laurence Olivier,** 1907–89: *Observer*, 3 May 1987

Movies

1697. [D. W. Griffith's film *Birth of a Nation*] is like writing history with lightning and my only regret is that it is all so terribly true. —**President Woodrow Wilson**, 1856–1924: Daniel J. Boorstin *The Image* (1962)

1698. Movies are one of the bad habits that corrupted our century. They have slapped into the American mind more misinformation in one evening than the Dark Ages could muster in a decade. —**Ben Hecht:** *A Child of the Century* (1954)

1699. In Westerns you were permitted to kiss your horse but never your girl. —**Gary Cooper:** *Saturday Evening Post*, 17 March 1958

1700. I was born at the age of twelve on a Metro-Goldwyn-Mayer lot. —**Judy Garland,** 1922–69: Abby Adams *An Uncommon Scold* (1989)

1701. American motion pictures are written by the half-educated for the half-witted. —**St John Ervine:** *New York Mirror*, 6 June 1963

1702. It's the movies that have really been running things in America ever since they were invented. They show you what to do, how to do it, when to do it, how to feel about it, and how to look how you feel about it. Everybody has their own America, and then they have the pieces of a fantasy America that they think is out there but they can't see. —**Andy Warhol,** 1928–87, American pop artist: Victor Bokris *Warhol* (1989)

1703. In this business we make movies, American movies. Leave the films to the French. —**Sam Shepard,** American playwright and screenwriter: *True West* (1980)

1704. All Americans born between 1890 and 1945 wanted to be movie stars. —**Gore Vidal:** *New York Review of Books*, 1 May 1980

1705. If Americans didn't speak English, we'd have no problem. —**Leon Clore,** British film producer: on marketing British films in America; *New York Times*, 13 July 1980

1706. Americans don't like sexual movies—they like sexy movies. —**Jack Nicholson:** *Rolling Stone*, March 1984

1707. All of the books in the world contain no more information than is broadcast as video in a single large American city in a single year. Not all bits have equal value. —**Carl Sagan,** 1934–

1708. If it weren't for the Japanese and Germans, we wouldn't have any good war movies. —**Stanley Ralph Ross:** Robert Byrne *The Fourth 637 Best Things Anybody Ever Said* (1990)

Music

1709. The future music of this country must be founded on what are called the Negro melodies. —**Antonin Dvorák,** 1841–1904: *New York Herald*

1710. I am trying to do something for the future of American music, which today has no class whatsoever and is mere barbaric mouthing. —**Jerome Kern:** *New York Times*, 1920

1711. Jazz came to America three hundred years ago in chains. —**Paul Whiteman:** *Jazz* (1926)

1712. It is from the blues that all that may be called American music derives its most distinctive character. —**James Weldon Johnson:** *Black Manhattan* (1930)

1713. Jazz I regard as an American folk music; not the only one, but a very powerful one which is probably in the blood and feeling of the American people more than any other style of folk music. —**George Gershwin:** *The Relation of Jazz to American Music* (1933)

1714. Jazz is the result of the energy stored up in America. —**George Gershwin,** 1898–1937: Sam Morgenstern *Composers on Music* (1956)

1715. If there is a national American form of song it is the blues. —**Russell Ames:** *The Story of American Folk Song* (1955)

1716. Jazz may be thought of as a current that bubbled forth from a spring in the slums of New Orleans to become the main spring of the twentieth century.—**Henry Pleasants:** *News Summarise*, 30 December 1955

1717. The way to write American music is simple. All you have to do is be an American and then write any kind of music you wish. —**Virgil Thomson,** 1896–1989: Joseph Machlis *Introduction to Contemporary Music* (1961)

1718. Jazz to me is one of the inherent expressions of Negro life in America: the eternal tom-tom beating in the Negro soul—the tom-tom of revolt against weariness in a white world, a world of subway trains, and work, work, work; the tom-tom of joy and laughter, and pain swallowed in a smile.—**Langston Hughes,** 1902–67

1719. English music is literary, while American music is painterly.—**Morton Feldman:** lecture, 29 April 1966

1720. Syncopation is in the soul of every true American.—**Irving Berlin,** 1888–1989: Ian Whitcomb *After the Ball* (1973)

1721. In Vienna people listen and know about style—in America they listen with their heart. —**Ljuba Welitsch,** 1913– : Robert Jacobson *Reverberations* (1974)

1722. We are not an aria country. We are a song country.—**Alan Jay Lerner,** 1918–86: Tony Palmer *All You Need Is Love* (1976)

1723. Country music belongs to America. —**Bill Monroe,** 1920–96, American musician: Criswell Freeman (ed.) *The Book of Country Music Wisdom* (1994)

1724. Young singers ask me, "Do I have to live in New York?" I say, "You can live wherever you want—as long as people *think* you live in New York."—**Benita Valente:** *New York Times,* 3 February 1985

1725. Jazz is music that really deals with what it means to be an American. The irony is when they wrote the Declaration of Independence and the United States Constitution, they didn't even think of a Black man. Yet Louis Armstrong, the grandson of a slave, is the one more than anybody else [who] could translate into music that feeling of what it is to be an American.—**Wynton Marsalis:** *Ebony,* February 1986

1726. The manner in which Americans "consume" music has a lot to do with leaving it on their coffee tables, or using it as wallpaper for their lifestyles, like the score of a movie—it's consumed that way without any regard for how and why it's made.—**Frank Zappa:** *Real Frank Zappa Book* (1989)

1727. I mean jazz. I don't mean rock and roll. I mean the never-the-same-way-twice music the American black people gave the world. —**Kurt Vonnegut:** *Hocus Pocus* (1990)

Presley, Elvis (1935–77), singer

1728. I don't know anything about music—in my line you don't have to.—**Elvis Presley:** attrib.

1729. I was very lucky. The people were looking for something different and I came along just in time.—**Elvis Presley:** Mick Farren *Elvis in His Own Words* (1977)

1730. Elvis Presley, the Hillbilly Cat, Swivel-Hips, the King of Rock and Roll, the King of Bebop, the King of Country Music, simply, the King.—**Michal Bane:** *Country Music,* December 1977

1731. Everything starts and ends with him. —**Bruce Springsteen,** 1949– : Robert Andrews *The New Penguin Dictionary of Modern Quotations* (2001)

1732. Commercial to the core, Elvis was the kind of singer dear to the heart of the music business. For him to sing a song was to sell a song. His G clef was a dollar sign.—**Albert Goldman:** *Elvis* (1981)

1733. Elvis was as big as the whole country itself, as big as the whole dream. He just embodied the essence of it and he was in mortal combat with the thing. It was horrible and at the same time, it was fantastic. Nothing will ever take the place of that guy.—**Bruce Springsteen:** Jonathon Green *The Book of Rock Quotes* (1982)

1734. When I first heard Elvis's voice I just knew that I wasn't going to work for anybody and nobody was gonna be my boss. Hearing him for the first time was like busting out of jail.—**Bob Dylan:** *US*, August 1987

Sinatra, Frank (1915–98), singer and actor

1735. Frank walks like America. Cocksure. —**Sonny Bono:** Robert Andrews *The New Penguin Dictionary of Modern Quotations* (2001)

1736. James Brown and Frank Sinatra are two different quantities in the universe. They represent two different experiences of the world. —**Imamu Amiri Baraka:** interview, David Frost *The Americans* (1970)

1737. It was my idea to make my voice work in the same way as a trombone or violin—not sounding like them, but "playing" the voice like those instruments.—**Frank Sinatra:** John Shepherd *Tin Pan Alley* (1982)

1738. I wish Frank Sinatra would just shut up and sing.—**Lauren Bacall,** 1924– : Abby Adams *An Uncommon Scold* (1989)

1739. I could go on stage and make a pizza and they'd still come to see me.—**Frank Sinatra:** *Independent on Sunday*, 31 May 1992

1740. Just a very old-fashioned Italian man. —**Nancy Reagan:** *Time*, 8 June 1998

Spielberg, Steven (1947–), filmmaker

1741. When I grow up I still want to be a director.—**Steven Spielberg:** *Time*, 15 July 1985

1742. Steven must be making a movie, physically shooting something at some point during the course of the year—or he'd go mad. —**Kathleen Kennedy:** Deauville, 14 September 1985

1743. A master of imagination, a master of spontaneity and a master of necessity.—**George Lucas:** *Time*, 8 June 1998

1744. Once a month the sky falls on my head, I come to, and I see another movie I want to make.—**Steven Spielberg:** *Time*, 8 June 1998

1745. When he was growing up, I didn't know he was a genius. Frankly, I didn't know what the hell he was.—**Leah Adler,** Spielberg's mother: *Time*, 8 June 1998

1746. The Puccini of the cinema, a little too sweet for some tastes, but what melodies, what orchestrations, what catherdrals of emotion. —**J. G. Ballard,** 1930– : Robert Andrews *The New Penguin Dictionary of Modern Quotations* (2001)

Television

1747. American TV must raise its ceiling by some method other than lowering the floor. —**Jack Gould:** *New York Times*, 1966

1748. In America, television can make so much money doing its worst, it cannot afford to do it best.—**Fred Friendly:** 1967

1749. Television has changed the American child from in irresistable force into an immovable object.—**Laurence J. Peter,** 1919–

1750. Most American television stations reproduce all night long what only a Roman could have seen in the Coliseum during the reign of Nero.—**George Faludy:** Laurence J. Peter *Peter's Quotations* (1977)

1751. Disparagement of television is second only to watching television as an American pastime.—**George F. Will:** *The Pursuit of Happiness and Other Sobering Thoughts* (1978)

1752. Television is the national campfire around which we spend our time.—**Bill Moyers:** *Los Angeles Times*, 25 December 1981

1753. If we may say that the Age of Andrew Jackson took political life out of the hands of aristocrats and turned it over to the masses, then we may say, with equal justification, that the Age of Television has taken politics away from the adult mind altogether.—**Neil Postman:** *The Disappearance of Childhood* (1982)

1754. As the age of television progresses the Reagans will be the rule, not the exception. To be perfect for television is all a president has to be these days.—**Gore Vidal:** *Observer*, 7 February 1982

1755. In America you watch TV and think that's totally unreal, then you step outside and it's just the same.—**Joan Armatrading**

1756. Television has made places look alike, and it has transformed the way we see. A whole generation of Americans, maybe two, has grown up looking at the world through a lens.—**Ronald Steel**

1757. Thank God we're living in a country where the sky's the limit, the stores are open late and you can shop in bed thanks to television.—**Joan Rivers,** 1937–

1758. Modern politics today requires a mastery of television. I've never really warmed up to television and, in fairness to television, it's never warmed up to me.—**Walter F. Mondale,** 1928–

1759. I can get a better grasp of what is going on in the world from one good Washington dinner party than from all the background information NBC piles on my desk.—**Barbara Walters,** 1931– : Robert I. Fitzhenry *The Harper Book of Quotations* (1993)

1760. You aren't anybody in America if you're not on TV. In short, you don't exist unless you're on TV.—**Buck Henry:** *New York Times*, 10 October 1995

1761. In order to grow as an artist, I feel it's important to do the same crap over at CBS. —**David Letterman**

1762. It always makes me laugh when people ask why anyone would want to do a sitcom in America. If it runs five years, you never have to work again.—**Twiggy:** *Independent*, 4 October 1997

1763. If an Afghan village is bombed and CNN is not there to film it, did it really happen? —**Mike Hynek:** 18 January 2002

Theater

1764. When you are away from old Broadway you are only camping out.—**George M. Cohan,** 1878–1942: Fred J. Ringel *America as Americans See It* (1932)

1765. If you really want to help the American theater, don't be an actress, darling. Be an audience.—**Tallulah Bankhead,** actress: *News Summaries*, 31 December 1952

1766. The most alarming thing about the contemporary American theater is the absolute regularity of its march toward extinction. —**Walter Kerr:** *How to Write a Play* (1955)

1767. The American theater is the aspirin of the middle classes.—**Wolcott Gibbs:** *More in Sorrow* (1958)

1768. Surely no other American institution is so bound around and tightened up by rules, strictures, adages, and superstitions as the Broadway theater.—**James Thurber,** 1894–1961: *Collecting Himself* (1989)

1769. Theater people are always pining and agonizing because they're afraid that they'll be forgotten. And in America they're quite right. They will be.—**Agnes De Mille:** *Life*, 15 November 1963

1770. In New York people don't go to the theater—they go to see hits.—**Louis Jourdan:** attrib.

1771. I'm the end of the line; absurd and appalling as it may seem, serious New York theater has died in my lifetime.—**Arthur Miller:** *Times*, 11 January 1989

Warhol, Andy (1928–87), artist and filmmaker

1772. He's a sphinx without a secret.—**Truman Capote:** *People Weekly*, 10 May 1976

1773. The man whose heart is as warm as a hanky soaked in ethyl chloride.—**Edmund White:** *States of Desire* (1980)

1774. A genius with the IQ of a moron.—**Gore Vidal**, 1925–   : Robert Andrews *The New Penguin Dictionary of Modern Quotations* (2001)

1775. Ultimately Warhol's private moral reference was to the supreme kitsch of the Catholic church.—**Allen Ginsberg**: *Andy Warhol* (1986)

1776. He was the person who created Attitude. Before Warhol, in artistic circles, there was Ideology—you took a stance against the crassness of American life. Andy Warhol turned that on its head, and created an attitude. And that attitude was "It's so awful, it's wonderful. It's so tacky, let's wallow in it."—**Tom Wolfe**: *Rolling Stone*, 9 April 1987

Welles, Orson (1915–85), director and actor

1777. He knew that he was precisely what he himself would have chosen to be had God consulted him on the subject of his birth; he fully appreciated and approved what had been bestowed, and realized that he couldn't have done the job better himself, in fact he would not have changed a single item.—**Micheál MacLiammóir**: *All For Hecuba* (1947)

1778. A giant with the look of a child, a lazy activeness, a mad wisdom, a solitude encompassing the world.—**Jean Cocteau**, 1889–1963: *New York Times*, 11 October 1985

1779. A bravura personality.—**Kenneth Tynan**, 1927–80: Robert Andrews *The New Penguin Dictionary of Modern Quotations* (2001)

1780. Everybody denies I am a genius, but nobody ever called me one!—**Orson Welles**: Robert Andrews *The New Penguin Dictionary of Modern Quotations* (2001)

1781. *Citizen Kane* seems as fresh as the day it opened. It may seem even fresher.—**Pauline Kael**: *The Citizen Kane* (1971)

1782. I started at the top and worked my way down.—**Orson Welles**: Leslie Halliwell *The Filmgoer's Book of Quotes* (1973)

1783. There, but for the grace of God, goes God.—**Herman Mankiewicz**: *American Film*, February 1979

1784. I'm just in love with making movies. Not very fond of movies—I don't go to them much. I think it's very harmful for movie-makers to see movies, because you either imitate them or worry about not imitating them. —**Orson Welles**: *Listener*, 17 October 1985

West, Mae (1892–1980), actress

1785. A plumber's idea of Cleopatra.—**W. C. Fields**, 1879–1946

1786. I used to be Snow White ... but I drifted.—**Mae West**: Joseph Weintraub (ed.) *The Wit and Wisdom of Mae West* (1967)

1787. She stole everything but cameras.—**George Raft**, 1895–1980: attrib.

1788. In a non-permissive age, she made remarkable inroads against the taboos of her day, and did so without even lowering her neckline.—**Leslie Halliwell**: *The Filmgoer's Book of Quotes* (1973)

LITERATURE AND LANGUAGE

Capote, Truman (1924–84), author

1789. At his worst Capote has less to say than any good writer I know.—**Norman Mailer:** 1959

1790. He is a sweetly vicious old lady.—**Tennessee Williams,** 1911–83

1791. I always said Little Truman had a voice so high it could only be detected by a bat. —**Tennessee Williams**

1792. He thinks he is a very rich Society Lady, and spends a great deal of money.—**Gore Vidal,** 1925–

1793. Capote should be heard, not read. —**Gore Vidal**

1794. Capote has made lying an art. A *minor* art.—**Gore Vidal:** Robert Andrews *The New Penguin Dictionary of Modern Quotations* (2001)

1795. Without question, the greatest jewel, the greatest zircon in the diadem of American literature.—**Gore Vidal:** on the death of Capote; *Palimpsest* (1995)

Dreiser, Theodore (1871–1945), novelist

1796. His style is atrocious, his sentences are chaotic, his grammar and syntax faulty; he has no feeling for words, no sense of diction. His wordiness and his repetitions are unbearable, his cacophonies incredible.—**Thomas K. Whipple:** *Spokesman* (1928)

1797. Dreiser's English is bum, yet it has a peculiar beauty and excellence. You feel you're reading a rather inadequate translation of a very great foreign novel—Russian, probably. —**James Agee:** *Letters of James Agee to Father Flye* (1962)

1798. [He] lacked everything but genius. —**Mark Van Doren,** 1894–1972: Richard Lingeman *Theodore Dreiser* (1990)

Faulkner, William (1897–1962), novelist

1799. I gave the world what it wanted—guts and genitals.—**William Faulkner:** *True*, December 1975

1800. Faulkner is interested in making your mind rather than your flesh creep.—**Clifton Fadiman:** *New Yorker*, 21 April 1934

1801. Poor Faulkner. Does he really think big emotions come from big words? He thinks I don't know the ten-dollar words. I know them all right. But there are older and simpler and better words, and those are the ones I use. —**Ernest Hemingway,** 1899–1961: A. E. Hotchner *Papa Hemingway* (1966)

1802. He uses a lot of big words, and his sentences are from here back to the airport.—**Carolyn Chute:** *New York Times*, 1985

Fitzgerald, F. Scott (1896–1940), author

1803. I talk with the authority of failure—Ernest [Hemingway] with the authority of success.—**F. Scott Fitzgerald:** *Time*, 3 April 1978

1804. The first of the last generation.—**Gertrude Stein,** 1874–1946

1805. Scott took LITERATURE so solemnly. He never understood that it was just writing as well as you can and finishing what you start. —**Ernest Hemingway:** letter to Arthur Mizner, 12 May 1950; Carlos Baker (ed.) *Selected Letters* (1981)

1806. The first American to formulate his own philosophy of the absurd.—**Wright Morris,** 1910–

1807. He couldn't distinguish between innocence and social climbing.—**Saul Bellow,** 1915–

1808. Although he would write a bad story, he could not write badly.—**Dorothy Parker:** *Daily Telegraph*, 2 December 1979

1809. An alcoholic, a spendthrift and a superstar playboy possessed of a beauty and a glamour that only a Byron could support without artistic ruination.—**Anthony Burgess:** *Observer*, 7 February 1982

Hemingway, Ernest (1898–1961), author

1810. He has a capacity for enjoyment so vast that he gives away great chunks to those about him, and never even misses them. He can take you to a bicycle race and make it raise your hair.—**Dorothy Parker:** *New Yorker*, 30 November 1929

1811. Hemingway, Remarks are not literature. —**Gertrude Stein:** *The Autobiography of Alice B. Toklas* (1933)

1812. It is of course a commonplace that Hemingway lacks the serene confidence that he is a full-sized man.—**Max Eastman:** *New Republic*, 1933

1813. Hemingway's words strike you, each one, as if they were pebbles fetched fresh from a brook.—**Ford Madox Ford,** 1873–1939: Robert Andrews *The New Penguin Dictionary of Modern Quotations* (2001)

1814. He has never been known to use a word that might send the reader to the dictionary. —**William Faulkner,** 1897–1962: attrib.

1815. I think Hemingway's [book] titles should be awarded first prize in any contest. Each of them is a poem, and their mysterious power over readers contributes to Hemingway's success. His titles have a life of their own, and they have enriched the American vocabulary.—**Sylvia Beach:** *Shakespeare and Company* (1956)

1816. He is the bully on the Left Bank, always ready to twist the milksop's arm.—**Cyril Connolly:** *Observer*, 24 May 1964

1817. Each day was a challenge of enjoyment, and he would plan it out as a field general plans a campaign.—**A.E. Hotchner:** *Papa Hemingway* (1966)

1818. I read him for the first time in the early 40's, something about bells, balls, and bulls, and loathed it.—**Vladimir Nabokov:** recalled on Nabokov's death, 7 July 1977

1819. Hemingway knew in advance, with a fine sense of timing, that he would have to campaign for himself, that the best tactic to hide the lockjaw of his shrinking genius was to become the personality of our time.—**Norman Mailer:** *Time*, 3 April 1978

James, Henry (1843–1916), author

1820. Mr. Henry James writes fiction as if it were a painful duty.—**Oscar Wilde,** 1856–1900: Laurence J. Peter *Peter's Quotations* (1977)

1821. Henry James chews more than he bites off.—**Mrs. Henry James:** Abby Adams *An Uncommon Scold* (1989)

1822. A magnificent but painful hippopotamus resolved at any cost upon picking up a pea.—**H. G. Wells:** *Boon* (1915)

1823. The work of Henry James has always seemed divisible by a simple dynastic arrangement into three reigns. James I, James II, and the Old Pretender.—**Philip Guedalla:** *Supers and Supermen* (1920)

1824. Poor Henry, he's spending eternity wandering round and round a stately park and the fence is just too high for him to peep over and they're having tea just too far away for him to hear what the countess is saying.—**W. Somerset Maugham:** *Cakes and Ale* (1930)

1825. That courtly, worldly, sentimental old gentleman [who] can still make us afraid of the dark.—**Virginia Woolf,** 1882–1941: Robert Andrews *The New Penguin Dictionary of Modern Quotations* (2001)

1826. I am reading Henry James … and feel myself as one entombed in a block of smooth amber.—**Virginia Woolf:** Abby Adams *An Uncommon Scold* (1989)

1827. An idiot, and a Boston idiot, to boot, than which there is nothing lower in the world.—**H. L. Mencken,** 1880–1956: *H. L. Mencken: The American Scene* (1965)

1828. One of the nicest old ladies I ever met.—**William Faulkner,** 1897–1962: Laurence J. Peter *Peter's Quotations* (1977)

1829. Henry James had a mind so fine that no idea could violate it.—**T. S. Eliot,** 1888–1965: Laurence J. Peter *Peter's Quotations* (1977)

Language

See also INTERNATIONAL RELATIONS: England

1830. The word Americanism, which I have coined is exactly similar in its formation and signification to the word Scotticism.—**John Witherspoon:** *Pennsylvania Journal and Weekly Advertiser,* 9 May 1781

1831. Let us then seize the present moment, and establish a *national language,* as well as a national government.—**Noah Webster,** American lexicographer: 1789

1832. The common faults of American language are an ambition of effect, a want of simplicity, and a turgid abuse of terms.—**James Fenimore Cooper:** *The American Democrat* (1838)

1833. We have really everything in common with America nowadays, except, of course, language.—**Oscar Wilde:** *Court and Society Review* (London), 23 February 1887

1834. Bismarck, when asked what was the most important fact in modern history, replied: "The fact that North America speaks English." —**Gurney Benham:** *Benham's Book of Quotations* (1948)

1835. We have room but for one Language here and that is the English Language, for we intend to see that the crucible turns our people out as Americans of American nationality and not as dwellers in a polyglot boarding-house.—**Theodore Roosevelt,** 1858–1919

1836. He spoke and wrote trade-English—a toothsome amalgam of Americanisms and epigrams.—**Rudyard Kipling:** 1917

1837. The American has no language. He has dialect, slang, provincialism, accent, and so forth.—**Rudyard Kipling,** 1865–1936

1838. English was good enough for Jesus Christ and it's good enough for the children of Texas.—**Miriam "Ma" Ferguson,** Governor of Texas: 1924

1839. The American language differs from English in that it seeks the top of expression while English seeks its lowly valleys.—**Salvador de Madariaga:** *Americans* (1930)

1840. It [American slang] is one part "natural growth" and nine parts a nervous disorder. It is St. Vitus's Talk.—**A. P. Herbert:** *What a Word!* (1935)

1841. When the American people get through with the English language, it will look as if it had been run over by a musical comedy.—**Finley Peter Dunne,** 1867–1936: *Mr. Dooley at His Best* (1938)

1842. I haven't been abroad in so long that I almost speak English without an accent. — **Robert Benchley,** 1889–1945, American humorist and critic: *Inside Benchley* (1942)

1843. England and America are two countries separated by the same language. — **George Bernard Shaw,** 1856–1950: attrib.; *Reader's Digest,* November 1942

1844. America is the only country left where we teach languages so that no pupil can speak them. — **John Erskine,** 1879–1951: Laurence J. Peter (ed.) *Peter's Quotations* (1977)

1845. Things on the whole move much faster in America; people don't *stand for election,* they *run for office.* If a person says he's *sick,* it doesn't mean regurgitating; it means *ill. Mad* means angry, not *insane.* Don't ask for the *left-luggage;* it's called a *check-room.* A *nice joint* means a good pub, not roast meat. — **Jessica Mitford:** *Daughters and Rebels* (1960)

1846. The American language is in a state of flux based on the survival of the unfittest. — **Cyril Connolly:** *Sunday Times,* 1966

1847. Will America be the death of English? I'm glad I asked me that. My well-thought-out mature judgment is that it will. — **Edwin Newman:** *Strictly Speaking* (1974)

1848. Many Americans feel themselves inferior in the presence of anyone with an English accent, which is why an English accent has become fashionable in television commercials; it is thought to sound authoritative. — **Edwin Newman:** *Strictly Speaking* (1974)

1849. The varieties of spoken American could not be counted, and most of them were incomprehensible to me, used as I was to the clean-cut pronunciation of Italian. — **Luigi Barzini:** *O America* (1977)

1850. We [the English] have evolved a language that always means more than it says, both emotionally and imaginatively. With Americans it is the reverse: they mean and feel far less than they have the habit of saying. — **John Robert Fowles:** 1977

1851. Americans … generally think of language as some arcane disease of the throat. — **Peter Ackroyd:** *Spectator,* 1 October 1977

1852. I am sure that the two main forms of English, American English and British English, separated geographically from the beginning and severed politically since 1776, are continuing to move apart, and that existing elements of linguistic dissimilarity between them will intensify as time goes on, notwithstanding the power of the cinema, TV, *Time Magazine,* and other two-way gluing and fuelling devices. — **Robert Burchfield:** *Unlocking the English Language* (1989)

1853. Perhaps more than anyone else in the world, Americans are devoted to hyperbole. — **Fred Washofsky:** *The Chip Wars* (1989)

1854. American is the language in which people say what they mean as Italian is the language in which they say what they feel. English is the language in which what a character means or feels has to be deduced from what he or she says, which may be quite the opposite. — **John Mortimer:** *Mail on Sunday,* 26 March 1989

Literature

1855. America is about the last place in which life will be endurable at all for an inspired writer. — **Samuel Butler,** 1835–1902: James Charlton *The Writer's Quotation Book* (1991)

1856. When a young American writer seems mad, it is usually because an old one drives him crazy. — **Frank Moore Colby,** 1865–1925: Evan Esar (ed.) *The Dictionary of Humorous Quotations* (1949)

1857. Our American professors like their literature clear and cold and pure and very dead. — **Sinclair Lewis:** Nobel Prize Address, 12 December 1930

1858. American writers never have a second act. — **F. Scott Fitzgerald,** 1896–1940

1859. Our hunger for foreign places and new ways has been with us [Americans] almost like a national disease. Our literature is stamped with a quality of longing and unrest, and our writers have been great wanderers. — **Carson McCullers:** *Vogue,* 1 December 1940

1860. Modern American literature was born in protest, born in rebellion, born out of the sense of loss and indirection which was imposed upon the new generations out of the realization that the old formal culture—the "New England idea"—could no longer serve.—**Alfred Kazin:** *On Native Ground* (1942)

1861. [Moving from England to New York in 1939] has taught me the kind of writer I am—an introvert who can only develop by obeying his introversion. All Americans are introverts.—**W. H. Auden,** 1907–73

1862. There is no way of being a creative writer in America without being a loser.—**Nelson Algren,** 1909–81

1863. Some American writers who have known each other for years, have never met in the daytime or when both were sober.—**James Thurber,** 1894–1961: Fred Metcalf *The Penguin Dictionary of Modern Humorous Quotations* (1986)

1864. What this country needs is a great poem … something simple enough for a child to spout in school on Fridays.—**Herbert Hoover:** *Saturday Review Treasury*, 1957

1865. Nothing could be more inappropriate to American literature than its English source since the Americans are not British in sensibility.—**Wallace Stevens:** *Opus Posthumous* (1959)

1866. Most Americans do not like poetry. We may respect it, but we do not enjoy it.—**Gilbert Highet:** *The Powers of Poetry* (1960)

1867. It is a sad fact about our culture that a poet can earn much more money writing or talking about his art than he can by practicing it.—**W. H. Auden:** *The Dyer's Hand* (1962)

1868. The task of an American writer is not to describe the misgivings of a woman taken in adultery as she looks out of a window at the rain but to describe four hundred people under the lights reaching for a foul ball. This is ceremony.—**John Cheever:** 1963; Robert Gottlieb (ed.) *John Cheever: The Journals* (1991)

1869. The novel being dead, there is no point to writing made-up stories. Look at the French who will not and the Americans who cannot.—**Gore Vidal:** *Myra Breckinridge* (1968)

1870. American writers want to be not good but great; and so are neither.—**Gore Vidal:** *Two Sisters* (1970)

1871. Of the creative spirits that flourished in Concord, Massachusetts, during the middle of the nineteenth century, it might be said that Hawthorne loved men but felt estranged from them, Emerson loved ideas even more than men, and Thoreau loved himself.—**Leon Edel:** *University of Minnesota Pamphlets on American Writers* (1970)

1872. The country is crawling with angry young men, in sociology, in politics, in biology. But I am looking for the angry men in literature. I am waiting for a strong spiritual man who would bang his fist on the table and say, "Enough of this nonsense!"—**Isaac Bashevis Singer:** *Atlantic Monthly*, July 1970

1873. It is rarely that you see an American writer who is not hopelessly sane.—**Margaret Anderson,** 1891–1973: Carolyn Warner *The Last Word* (1992)

1874. Most contemporary novelists, especially the American and the French, are too subjective, mesmerized by private demons; they're enraptured by their navels and confined by a view that ends with their own toes.—**Truman Capote,** 1924–84

1875. Poets have to dream, and dreaming in America is no cinch.—**Saul Bellow,** 1915–

1876. It is one of the paradoxes of American literature that our writers are forever looking back with love and nostalgia at lives they couldn't wait to leave.—**Anatole Broyard:** *Times*, 16 March 1973

1877. American writers were the first to intuit … that the catchall web of the vernacular reflected the mind at its conscious level. This new melodious tongue shaped the writer to a greater extent than he shaped the language.—**Wright Morris:** *About Fiction* (1975)

1878. Teaching has ruined more American novelists than drink.—**Gore Vidal:** *Oui magazine*, April 1975

1879. Hemingway described literary New York as a bottle full of tapeworms trying to feed on each other.—**John Updike:** *Picked Up Pieces* (1976)

1880. Most American writers I find phony, but it's a phony country.—**Gore Vidal:** *Bookviews*, June 1978

1881. We are all desperately afraid of sounding like Carrie Nation. I must take the risk. Any writer who wants to do his best against a deadline should stick to Coca-Cola.—**John Kenneth Galbraith:** *Annals of an Abiding Liberal* (1979)

1882. It's hard to get to the top in America, but it's even harder to stay there.—**Norman Mailer:** *Time*, 2 April 1979

1883. Authors don't have any respect at all in terms of a profession in America—and this is quite a good and stimulating thing.—**J. P. Donleavy:** *Newsweek*, 22 October 1979

1884. The American novel is a conquest of the frontier; as it describes experience it creates it.—**Ralph Ellison,** 1914–94: Jon Winokur *Writers on Writing* (1990)

1885. In America the race goes to the loud, the solemn, the hustler. If you think you're a great writer, you must say that you are.—**Gore Vidal,** 1925– : George Plimpton (ed.) *Writers at Work* Fifth Series (1981)

1886. The great American novel has not only already been written, it has already been rejected.—**Frank Dane:** Gerald F. Lieberman *3,500 Good Quotes for Speakers* (1983)

1887. [It] spoke to me of New York, sophistication, amusing adult misery, carefree creativity ... nervous quiggles given permanence and celebrity by the intervening miracle of printer's ink ... a super way to live, to be behind such a book.—**John Updike:** on James Thurber's *Men, Women and Dogs* (1943), as the book that most influenced Updike to become a writer; *Hugging the Shore* (1983)

1888. In the Soviet Union a writer who is critical, as we know, is taken to a lunatic asylum. In the United States, he's taken to a talk show. —**Carlos Fuentes:** *Writers at Work* Sixth Series (1984)

1889. Today Americans seem to want their writers to reveal all their weaknesses, their meannesses, to celebrate their very confusions. And they want it in the most direct possible way—they want it served up neat, as it were, without the filtering and generalizing power of fiction.—**Saul Bellow,** 1915– : Robert I. Fitzhenry (ed.) *Barnes & Noble Book of Quotations* (1987)

1890. In America they make too much fuss of poets; in London they make too little. —**Caitlin Thomas:** *Caitlin: A Warring Absence* (1986)

1891. One classic American landscape haunts all of American literature. It is a picture of Eden, perceived at the instant of history when corruption has just begun to set it. The serpent has shown his scaly head in the undergrowth. The apple gleams on the tree. The old drama of the Fall is ready to start all over again. —**Jonathan Raban:** *For Love and Money* (1987)

1892. I miss the spirit of social activism in American literature of the '20 and '30s. In your novels I learn a lot about universities and teachers. They are well written, but they bore me.—**Günter Grass,** 1927– : Jon Winokur *Writers on Writing* (1990)

1893. Writing a novel about this astonishing metropolis, a big novel, cramming as much of New York City between covers as you could, was the most tempting, the most challenging, and the most obvious idea an American writer could possibly have.—**Tom Wolfe:** *Harper's*, November 1989

1894. America is not overrun by great literary critics.—**Fran Lebowitz,** 1946– : interview with William A. Gordon

1895. Poe played on one key-bank of a church organ, Whittier on a meeting-house melodeon, Walt Whitman on a Salvation Army bass drum.—**Austin O'Malley:** Colin Jarman *The Guinness Dictionary of Poisonous Quotes* (1991)

1896. Americans say what they think whereas with the English you have to deduce what they think from what they say.—**John Mortimer:** NPR, 7 January 1993

Mailer, Norman (1923–), author

1897. If only he would take his eyes from the world's genital glands.—**William F. Buckley, Jr.**: *Rumbles* (1963)

1898. Norman Mailer is one of the leading spectator sports in America.—**Merv Griffin:** May 1968; Jack Newfield *Bread and Roses Too* (1971)

1899. Mailer decocts matters of the first philosophical magnitude from an examination of his own ordure, and I am not talking about books. —**William F. Buckley, Jr.**: *National Review*, 1968

1900. Mailer's sexual journalism reads like the sporting news grafted onto a series of war dispatches.—**Kate Millet**: *Washington Post*, 30 July 1970

1901. A clown with the bite of a ferret.—**Calder Willingham**: recalled on Willingham's death, *London Times*, 22 February 1995

1902. If he has a taste for transcribing banalities, he also has a talent for it.—*New Republic*

1903. He is now what he wanted to be: the patron saint of bad journalism.—**Gore Vidal,** 1925– : Robert Andrews *The New Penguin Dictionary of Modern Quotations* (2001)

Miller, Henry (1891–1980), author

1904. It is true I swim in a perpetual sea of sex but the actual excursions are fairly limited. —**Henry Miller:** letter to Anaïs Nin, 1 February 1932

1905. At last, an unprintable book that's read-able.—**Ezra Pound**, 1885–1972: on *Tropic of Capricorn* (1934)

1906. Last week I went up to London to meet Henry Miller who is a dear, mad, mild man, bald and fifty, with great enthusiasm for commonplaces.—**Dylan Thomas**, 1914–53: letter to Vernon Watkins

1907. He is fiddling while Rome is burning, and, unlike the enormous majority of people who do this, fiddling with his face towards the flames.—**George Orwell:** *Inside the Whale and Other Essays* (1949)

1908. A gadfly with delusions of grandeur. —*Time*: 1962; on *Tropic of Capricorn* (1934)

1909. I don't think he has read a pornographic book in his life. Pornography puts him to sleep, he has told me time and again.—**Alfred Perles:** *My Friend Henry Miller* (1955)

1910. I went back to intuition when I turned to Henry, who represents the non-rational. The very fact that he is all paradox and contraries, unresolved and without care, is like life itself. —**Anaïs Nin:** *Diaries* vol. 2 (1967)

1911. I never liked the language of Miller. I don't think pornography has added to our sensual life.—**Anaïs Nin:** *Times*, 1 June 1970

1912. Miller does have something highly important to tell us; his virulent sexism is beyond question an honest contribution to social and psychological understanding which we can hardly afford to ignore. But to confuse this neurotic hostility, this frank abuse, with sanity, is pitiable. To confuse it with freedom were vicious, were it not so very sad.—**Kate Millett:** *Sexual Politics* (1970)

1913. I owe everything to the French. I am more close to France than America even though I lived there only 10 years, from 1929 to 1939. Those years in France meant everything to me and formed my whole career.—**Henry Miller:** *New York Times*, 23 November 1976

1914. Miller is not really a writer but a nonstop talker to whom someone has given a typewriter.—**Gerald Brenan:** *Thoughts in a Dry Season* (1978)

Parker, Dorothy (1893-1967), humorous writer

1915. A combination of Little Nell and Lady Macbeth.—**Alexander Woollcott:** *While Rome Burns* (1934)

1916. She has put into what she has written a voice, a state of mind, an era, a few moments of human experience that nobody else has conveyed.—**Edmund Wilson,** 1895–1972: attrib.

1917. Ducking for apples—change a letter and it's the story of my life.—**Dorothy Parker**

1918. She looked like a vulnerable, deceptively incapable child who had gone to sleep and awakened 40 years later with puffy eyes, false teeth, and whiskey on her breath.—**Truman Capote,** 1924–84: *Answered Prayers* (1987)

Poe, Edgar Allan (1809-49), poet and writer

1919. A kind of Hawthorne with delirium tremens.—**Leslie Stephen:** *Hours in a Library* (1879)

1920. Three-fifths of him genius and two-fifths sheer fudge.—**James Russell Lowell,** 1819–91: *A Fable for Critics*

1921. I've an idea that if Poe had been an exemplary, conventional, tax-oppressed citizen, like Longfellow, his few poems, as striking as they are, would not have made so great a stir. —**Thomas Bailey Aldrich:** letter to E. C. Stedman, 15 November 1900

1922. He was an adventurer into the vaults and cellars and horrible underground passages of the human soul. He sounded the horror and the warning of his own doom.—**D. H. Lawrence:** *Studies in Classic American Literature* (1923)

1923. The substance of Poe is refined; it is the form that is vulgar. He is, as it were, one of Nature's gentlemen, unhappily cursed with incorrigible bad taste.—**Aldous Huxley,** 1894–1963: Robert Regan (ed.) *Vulgarity in Literature* (1930)

1924. Perhaps the first great nonstop literary drinker of the American nineteenth century. He made the indulgences of Coleridge and De Quincey seem like a bit of mischief in the kitchen with the cooking sherry.—**James Thurber:** *Alarms and Diversions* (1957)

1925. That Poe had a powerful intellect is undeniable, but it seems to me the intellect of a highly gifted young person before puberty. The forms which his lively curiosity takes are those in which a pre-adolescent delights; wonders of nature and mechanics and the supernatural, cryptograms and cyphers, puzzles and labyrinths, mechanical chessplayers and wild flights of speculation.—**T. S. Eliot,** 1888–1965: *Collected Essays*

1926. An unmanly sort of man whose love-life seems to have been largely confined to crying in laps and playing mouse.—**W. H. Auden,** 1907–73

Pound, Ezra (1885-1972), poet and critic

1927. He was a village explainer, excellent if you were a village, but if you were not, not. —**Gertrude Stein:** *The Autobiography of Alice B. Toklas* (1933)

1928. Ezra was right half the time, and when he was wrong, he was so wrong you were never in any doubt about it.—**Ernest Hemingway:** *New Republic*, 11 November 1936

1929. I confess I am seldom interested in what he is saying, but only in the way he says it. —**T. S. Eliot,** 1888–1965: *The Dial*

1930. Pound's crazy. All poets are. They have to be.—**Ernest Hemingway:** *New York Post*, 24 January 1957

1931. To me Pound remains the exquisite showman minus the show.—**Ben Hecht,** 1893–1964: *Pounding Ezra*

1932. To cite passages is to pull one quill from a pocupine.—**Marianne Moore,** 1887–1972: Patricia C. Willis (ed.) *The Complete Prose of Marianne Moore* (1986)

Publishing and Publishers

1933. Zuckerman, sucker though he was for seriousness, was still not going to be drawn into a discussion about agents and editors. If ever there was a reason for an American writer to seek asylum in Red China, it would be to put ten thousand miles between himself and those discussions.—**Philiph Roth:** *Zuckerman Unbound* (1981)

1934. The Englishman loves to roll his tongue around the word, "extraordinary." It so pleases him that he is reluctant to finish the sound which goes on into harmonics and overtones. The American publisher is likewise inclined.—**Robert I. Fitzhenry:** Connie Robertson (ed.) *The Wordsworth Dictionary of Quotations* (1996)

Reading

1935. I have every sympathy with the American who was so horrified by what he had read of the effects of smoking that he gave up reading.—**Henry G. Strauss,** 1892–1974

1936. Americans like fat books and thin women.—**Russell Baker,** 1925– : James Charlton *The Writer's Quotation Book* (1991)

1937. I can't wait to run against a president who owns more tuxedos than books.—**Senator Gary Hart,** 1936– : James Charlton *The Writer's Quotation Book* (1991)

1938. American men do not read novels because they feel guilty when they read books which do not have facts in them.—**Gore Vidal:** *Saturday Review,* 18 June 1984

1939. The British say, "Jolly good story!" The Canadians ask, "Can it happen here?" And the Americans say, "How much time have we got?" —**Margaret Atwood,** 1939– , Canadian novelist: commenting on the critical comments in three countries on her novel *The Handmaid's Tale*; Sheldon Teitelbaum *Cinefantastique* (1990)

1940. Americans will listen, but they do not care to read. *War and Peace* must wait for the leisure of retirement, which never really comes: meanwhile it helps to furnish the living room. —**Anthony Burgess:** *You've Had Your Time* (1990)

1941. Blockbusting fiction is bought as furniture. Unread, it maintains its value. Read, it looks like money wasted. Cunningly, Americans know that books contain a person, and they want the person, not the book.—**Anthony Burgess:** *You've Had Your Time* (1990)

1942. A lot of them don't read, a lot of them don't read English and a lot of them can't read. —**Terry Prachett,** British science-fiction writer: *Time,* 25 May 1998

Sandburg, Carl (1878–1967), poet and author

1943. He is submerged in adolescence. Give Sandburg a mind, and you perhaps destroy him.—**Sherwood Anderson:** 1919

1944. I've written some poetry I don't understand myself.—**Carl Sandburg:** George Plimpton *The Writer's Chapbook* (1989)

1945. It's a book about a man whose mother could not sign her name, written by a man whose father could not sign his. Perhaps that could happen only in America.—**Carl Sandburg:** on completing his study of Lincoln; recalled on Sandburg's death, 22 July 1967

1946. Under close scrutiny Sandburg's verse reminds us of the blobs of livingly jelly or plankton brought up by deep-sea dredging; it is a kind of protoplasmic poetry, lacking higher organization.—**George F. Whicher,** 1889-1954: *The Twentieth Century*

1947. The poet lariat of Chicago.—**Richard Daley:** 1960

1948. The cruelest thing that has happened to Lincoln since he was shot by Booth has been to fall into the hands of Carl Sandburg.—**Edmund Wilson:** *Time,* 1972

Stein, Gertrude (1874–1946), author

1949. You would be surprised to know just how altogether American I found you.—**Sherwood Anderson,** 1876-1941: letter to Gertrude Stein

1950. What an old covered wagon she is.—**F. Scott Fitzgerald,** 1896-1940

1951. The mama of dada.—**Clifton Fadiman:** *Party of One* (1955)

1952. Stein was masterly in making nothing happen very slowly.—**Clifton Fadiman:** *Puzzlements*

1953. Stein's prose song is a cold, black suet-pudding. We can represent it as a cold suet roll of fabulously reptilian length. Cut it at any point, it is the same thing; the same heavy, sticky, opaque mass all through and all along … it is mournful and monstrous, composed of dead and inaimate material.—**Percy W. Lewis:** John Malcolm Brinnin *The Third Rose* (1959)

1954. While she believed that most writers failed to allow writing to express all that it could, in her own practice she scrupulously saw to it that writing expressed less than it would. —**John Malcolm Brinnin:** *The Third Rose* (1959)

1955. She has outdistanced any of the symbolists in using words for pure purposes of suggestion—she has gone so far that she no longer even suggests.—**Edmund Wilson,** 1895-1972: B. L. Reid *Art by Subtraction* (1958)

1956. Reading Stein at length is not unlike making one's way through an interminable and badly printed game book.—**Richard Bridgman:** *Gertrude Stein in Pieces* (1970)

Thurber, James (1894–1961), humorist

1957. Thurber wrote the way a child skips rope, the way a mouse waltzes.—**E. B. White:** *New Yorker,* 1961

1958. The greatest unlistener I know.—**Harold Ross,** 1892-1951: James Thurber *The Years with Ross* (1959)

1959. A tall, thin, spectacled man with the face of a harassed rat.—**Russell Maloney:** *Saturday Review*

Twain, Mark (1835–1910), author

1960. The average American loves his family. If he has any love left over for some other persons, he generally selects Mark Twain. —**Thomas Edison,** 1847-1931: attrib.

1961. Mark Twain and I are in the same position. We have to put things in such a way as to make people, who would otherwise hang us, believe that we are joking.—**George Bernard Shaw,** 1856-1950: attrib.

1962. All modern American literature comes from one book by Mark Twain called *Huckleberry Finn.*—**Ernest Hemingway:** *The Green Hills of Africa* (1935)

1963. A hack writer who would not have been considered fourth rate in Europe, who tried out a few of the old proven "sure-fire" literary skeletons with sufficient local color to intrigue the superficial and the lazy.—**William Faulkner,** 1897-1962

1964. He combined syntactical elegance with tobacco-spitting raciness, and an exquisite ear with a healthy Philistinism which rejected Jane Austen, Scott, George Eliot and Henry James. —**Anthony Burgess:** *Observer*, 4 July 1982

1965. He had vanity that makes Donald Trump look like a nun. —**Garrison Keillor:** American Public Radio, 1 December 1990

1966. The face of American literature has freckles. —*US News & World Report*: on the influence of *Huckleberry Finn*, 22 April 1991

1967. [Of the opening of Chapter 19 of *Huckleberry Finn*] the most beautiful prose paragraph yet written by any American. —**Harold Bloom:** *The Western Canon* (1994)

Updike, John (1932–), author and critic

1968. [John Updike] left the self-conscious literary *demimonde* of New York for the quiet infidelities of New England. —**John Heilpern:** *Observer* (London), 25 May 1979

1969. Had Updike done more dramatising and less editorising he might have created a series that would outlives its period. But the book's bogged down in opinion, and opinion is a poor substitute for appetite. —**James Wolcott:** *Observer*, on *Rabbit at Rest* (1990)

Whitman, Walt (1819–92), poet

1970. Well, he looks like a man. —**Abraham Lincoln,** 1809–65: on catching sight of Whitman, attrib.

1971. He is a factor in the heroic and spiritual evolution of the human being. If Poetry has passed him by, Philosophy will take note of him. —**Oscar Wilde:** *Pall Mall Gazette* (London), 25 January 1889

1972. He is a writer of something occasionally like English, and a man of something occasionally like genius. —**Algernon Charles Swinburne,** 1837–1909: *Whitmania*

1973. Under the dirty clumsy paws of a harper whose plectrum is a muck-rake, any tune will become a chaos of dischords.... Mr Whitman's Eve is a drunken apple-woman, indecently sprawling in the slush and garbage of the gutter amid the rotten refuse of her overturned fruit-stall: but Mr Whitman's Venus is a Hottentot wench under the influence of catharides and adulterated rum. —**Algernon Charles Swinburne**

1974. A boorish, awkward *poseur.* —**Rebecca Harding Davis:** *Bits of Gossip* (1904)

1975. Whitman is like a human document, or a wonderful treatise in human self revelation. It is neither art nor religion nor truth: Just a self revelation of a man who could not live, and so had to write himself. —**D. H. Lawrence:** letter, 22 December 1913; George J. Zytaruk and James T. Boulton *The Letters of D. H. Lawrence* (1981)

1976. This awful Whitman. This post-mortem poet. This poet with the private soul leaking out of him all the time. All his privacy leaking out in a sort of dribble, oozing into the universe. —**D. H. Lawrence:** *Studies in Classic American Literature* (1923)

1977. Not for a moment, beautiful aged Walt Whitman, have I failed to see your beard full of butterflies. —**Federico García Lorca,** 1899–1936: *Oda a Walt Whitman* (1959)

1978. Walt Whitman who laid end to end words never seen in each other's company before outside of a dictionary. —**David Lodge:** *Changing Places* (1975)

1979. He was John the Baptist to Lincoln's Christ. —**Daniel Barshay:** Radio Station WETA, Washington, 30 May 1991

Wilson, Edmund (1895–1972), critic

1980. A penumbra of somber dignity. —**James Atlas:** *New York Times*, 28 July 1985

1981. To read Wilson is to be instructed and amused in the highest sense—that is, be educated.—**James Atlas:** *New York Times,* 28 July 1985

1982. A grateful, exuberant diner at life's feast.—**John Updike:** *New Yorker,* 29 November 1993

Wolfe, Thomas (1900–38), author

1983. He tried to do the greatest of the impossible—to reduce all human experience to literature.—**William Faulkner,** 1897–1962: Robert Andrews *The New Penguin Dictionary of Modern Quotations* (2001)

1984. Thomas Wolfe has always seemed to me the most overrated, longwinded and boring of reputable American novelists.—**Edith Oliver:** Laurence J. Peter *Peter's Quotations* (1977)

1985. The greatest five-year-old who ever lived.—**Norman Mailer:** *New York Times Book Review,* 2 December 1979

1986. Anybody that admires Thomas Wolfe can be expected to like good fiction only by accident.—**Flannery O'Connor:** *New York Times Book Review,* 2 December 1979

1987. Long untrimmed essays grew up in the window boxes of his prose.—**James Thurber,** 1894–1961: Michael Rosen (ed.) *James Thurber Collecting Himself* (1989)

Wolfe, Tom (1931–   ), author and journalist

1988. One wants to say to Mr. Wolfe; you're so clever, you can write so well, tell us something interesting.—*Saturday Review:* 1965; on *The Kandy-Kolored Tangerine-Flake Streamline Baby* (1965)

RELIGION AND BELIEF

Humanism

See also THE INDIVIDUAL: Individualism; THE INDIVIDUAL: Life; HUMAN RELATIONS: Friendship and Friendliness

1989. We are a nation of twenty million bathrooms, with a humanist in every tub.—**Mary McCarthy:** *On the Contrary* (1961)

1990. Humanism, it seems, is almost impossible in America where material progress is part of the national romance whereas in Europe such progress is relished because it feels nice.—**Paul West:** *The Wine of Absurdity* (1966)

Jews

1991. An American is either a Jew, or an anti-Semite, unless he is both at the same time.—**Jean-Paul Sartre:** *Les Séquestrés d'Altona* (1959)

1992. Since my daughter is only half–Jewish, could she go in the water up to her knees? —**Groucho Marx,** 1895–1977: when excluded from a beach club on racial grounds; *Observer,* 21 August 1977

1993. It's time to say that America is a better place to be a Jew than Jerusalem. If there ever was a promised land, we Jewish Americans are living in it. —**Rabbi Jacob Neusner:** 1987

Lies and Truth

See also SOCIAL LIFE: Information; POLITICS AND GOVERNMENT: Lincoln

1994. Everybody in America is soft, and hates conflict. The cure for this, both in politics and social life, is the same—hardihood. Give them raw truth. —**John Jay Chapman:** *Practical Agitation* (1898)

1995. Americans detest all lies except lies spoken in public or printed lies. —**Edgar Watson Howe:** *Ventures in Common Sense* (1919)

1996. The men the American people admire most extravagantly are the most daring liars; the men they detest the most violently are those who try to tell the truth. —**H. L. Mencken,** 1880–1956: Alistair Cooke (ed.) *The Vintage Mencken* (1955)

1997. To [William Jennings] Bryan, truth lay only in holy scripture, and scripture comprised two books: the Bible and the Constitution of the United States. —**Alistair Cooke:** *America* (1973)

1998. Truth is still more effective than money in America. But it takes persistence. —**Thomas M. Devine,** 1927– : Henry O. Dormann *The Speaker's Book of Quotations* (1987)

Materialism and Spirituality

1999. I remember somebody once saying to me a long time ago, that the Americans had at-tained to luxury by jumping over comfort. I think this is true. —**Maurice Baring:** *Round the World in Any Number of Days* (1913)

2000. The materialistic idealism that governs American life, that on the one hand makes a chariot of every grocery wagon, and an the other a mere hitching post of every star, lets every man lead a very enticing double life. —**Louis Kronenberger:** *Company Manners* (1954)

2001. Americans are not materialistic in the money sense: they are too generous and wasteful, too idealistic for that. Yet their idealism is sometimes curiously lacking in the spiritual values. They have an abiding belief in their ability to control reality by purely spiritual means. —**Cecil Beaton:** *It Gives Me Great Pleasure* (1955)

2002. Every generation of Americans has wanted more material wealth, more luxury for the next generation. In my opinion the time has come when we must hope our children and their children ad infinitum will want from life more than material success. They must have enough of that to ensure a roof, clothing, food and some recreation, but, if we are to survive for another two hundred years, we must change our way of life. —**India Edwards:** *Pulling No Punches* (1977)

2003. I question whether I want to be integrated into America as it stands now, with its complacency and materialism, its soullessness. —**Paule Marshall:** *Reena and Other Stories* (1983)

2004. Greed is good! Greed is right! Greed works! Greed will save the U.S.A.! —**Oliver Stone:** *Wall Street* (screenplay), 1987

2005. America has abandoned the strong woman of spirituality and is shacking up with the harlot of materialism. —**Joseph Losery:** c. 1989; Deirdre Mullane *Words to Make My Dream Children Live* (1995)

2006. America is a consumer culture, and when we change what we buy—and how we buy it—we'll change who we are. —**Faith Popcorn:** *The Popcorn Report* (1991)

Morality and Ethics

2007. We are an obsessively moral people, but our morality is a team morality.—**Edgar Z. Friedenberg:** *The Vanishing Adolescent* (1959)

2008. There is much cant in American moralism and not a little inconsistency.—**J. William Fulbright:** speech to the Senate, 25 March 1964

2009. It is a depressing fact that Americans tend to confuse morality and art (to the detriment of both) and that, among the educated, morality tends to mean social consciousness. —**Pauline Kael:** *I Lost It at the Movies* (1965)

2010. America will tolerate the taking of human life without giving it a second thought. But don't misuse a household pet.—**Dick Gregory:** *The Shadow That Scares Me* (1968)

2011. Post-Watergate morality, by which anything left private is taken as presumptive evidence of wrongdoing.—**Charles Krauthammer:** *Time*, 10 September 1984

2012. We [Americans] all try to be virtuous. It's our national pastime.—**Carlos Fuentes:** *The Old Gringo* (1985)

Reality

See also SOCIAL LIFE: Information

2013. The unreal is natural, so natural that it makes of unreality the most natural of anything natural. That is what America does, and that is what America is.—**Gertrude Stein:** *Cosmopolitan*, February 1936

2014. In the American metaphysic, reality is always material reality, hard, resistant, unformed, impenetrable, and unpleasant.—**Lionel Trilling:** *Nation*, 20 April 1946

2015. Americans have an abiding belief in their ability to control reality by purely material means … airline insurance replaces the fear of death with the comforting prospect of cash. —**Cecil Beaton:** *It Gives Me Great Pleasure* (1955)

2016. We [Americans] suffer primarily not from our vices or our weaknesses, but from our illusions. We are haunted, not by reality, but by those images we have put in place of reality. —**Daniel J. Boorstin:** *The Image* (1962)

2017. Everybody is in analysis. It's the dominant mode for the American interpretation of reality.—**A. Alvarez:** *Encounter*, February 1965

Religion

2018. The Inhabitants seem very Religious, showing many outward and visible Signs of an inward and Spiritual Grace: But tho' they wear in their Faces the Innocence of Doves, you will find them in their Dealings, as Subtile as Serpents. Interest is their Faith, Money their God, and Large Possessions the only Heaven they covet.—**Edward Ward:** *A Trip to New-England* (1699); Ward is thought to have based this book on the experiences of others. He probably never visited America.

2019. The religion most prevalent in our northern colonies is a refinement on the principles of resistance: it is the dissidence of dissent, and the Protestantism of the Protestant religion. —**Edmund Burke,** 1729–97: Speech on Conciliation with America, 1774-5; *Works* vol. 2

2020. Believing with you that religion is a matter which lies solely between man and his God, that he owes account to none other for his faith or his worship, that the legislative powers of government reach actions only, and not opinions, I contemplate with sovereign reverence that act of the whole American people which declared that their legislature should "make no law respecting an establishment of religion, or prohibiting the free exercise thereof," thus building a wall of separation between Church and State.—**Thomas Jefferson,** 1743–1826: letter to Connecticut Baptists

2021. America owes most of its social prejudices to the exaggerated religious opinions of the different sects which were so instrumental in establishing the colonies.—**James Fenimore Cooper:** *The American Democrat* (1838)

2022. An American Religion: Work, play, breathe, bathe, study, live, laugh, and love. —**Elbert Hubbard:** *The Roycroft Dictionary and Book of Epigrams* (1923)

2023. In Europe art has to a large degree taken the place of religion. In America it seems rather to be science.—**Johan Huizinga**, 1872–1945, Dutch historian: an observation made on a visit to America in the 20s; *Life and Thought in America* (1972)

2024. When the American poor turn to religion, as most of them do, they turn not to faith in revolution, but to a more radical revolt against faith in their fellow man.—**Herbert Wallace Schneider:** *Religion in the 20th Century* (1952)

2025. Some of us worship in churches, some in synagogues, some on golf courses.—**Adlai Stevenson:** 1952; Lois and Alan Gordon *American Chronicle* (1987)

2026. The American idea of religion is that religion is very much this-worldly; that it is less a philosophical picture, it is a view of your duty here and now … of good works … of service.—**Denis William Brogan**, 1900–74: Arthur Goodfriend *What Is America?* (1954)

2027. I am waiting for them to prove that God is really American.—**Lawrence Ferlinghetti:** *A Coney Island of the Mind* (1958)

2028. Ultimately, America's answer to the intolerant man is diversity, the very diversity which our heritage of religious freedom has inspired.—**Robert F. Kennedy:** *The Pursuit of Justice* (1964)

2029. Politics in America is the binding secular religion.—**Theodore H. White:** *Firing Line*, 26 July 1975

2030. We are now in the Me Decade—seeing the upward roll of … the third great religious wave in American history.—**Tom Wolfe:** *Mauve Gloves and Madmen* (1976)

2031. The Catholic Church with its foreshortened American history and tangled puritanical roots was as inviolate to my mother and father as it was to the last-ditch aristocrats of Evelyn Waugh.—**Maureen Howard:** *Facts of Life* (1978)

2032. Our church is, I believe, the first split-level church in America. It has five rooms and two baths downstairs. There is a small worship area at one end.—**Peter De Vries:** *The Mackerel Plaza* (1984)

2033. But then the country is our religion. The true religion of America has always been America.—**Norman Mailer:** *Time Out*, 27 September 1984

2034. No Western nation is as religion-soaked as ours. The varieties of religions that have grown on American soil: Christian Science, Seventh-day Adventism, Jehovah's Witnesses, Pentecostalism, the varieties of New Age and African-American beliefs, Mormons and Southern Baptists.—**Harold Bloom:** *The American Religion* (1992)

2035. My ancestors were Puritans from England. They arrived here in 1648 in the hope of finding greater restrictions than were permissible under English law at that time.—**Garrison Keillor**, American writer: 1993, attrib.

2036. Prayer of the modern American: "Dear God, I pray for patience. And I want it right now."—**Oren Arnold**

Secret Societies

2037. [They] became Knights of Pythia, Odd Fellows, Red Men, Nobles of the Mystic Shrine, Knights Templar, Patriarchs Militant, Elks, Moose, Woodmen of the World, Foresters, Hoo-Hoos, Ku Kluxzers.—**H. L. Mencken**, 1880–1956: on American fondness for secret societies; Alistair Cook (ed.) *The Vintage Mencken* (1955)

2038. They [Ku Klux Klan] wear white sheets and their hats have a point—which is more than can be said for their beliefs.—**David Frost** and **Michael Shea:** *A Mid-Atlantic Companion* (1986)

2039. The Klan will never return … with the robes and the rallies and the cross lightings and parades, everything that made the Klan the Klan, the mysticism, what we called Klankraft.—**Robert Shelton**, Imperial Wizard, Ku Klux Klan: *Washington Times*, 21 December 1994

Sunday

2040. Sunday: A day given over by Americans to wishing that they themselves were dead and in Heaven, and that their neighbors were dead and in Hell.—**H. L. Mencken:** *A Book of Burlesques* (1916)

2041. The eleven o'clock hour on Sunday is the most segregated hour in American life. —**James A. Pike:** *U.S. News & World Report*, 16 May 1960

PAST AND FUTURE

Change

See also SOCIAL LIFE: Progress; HISTORY: History

2042. We started from scratch, every American an immigrant who came because he wanted change. *Why are we now afraid to change?*— **Eleanor Roosevelt,** 1884–1962: *Tomorrow Is Now* (1963)

2043. Most Americans have never seen the ignorance, degradation, hunger, sickness, and futility in which many other Americans live. They won't become involved in economic or political change until something brings the seriousness of the situation home to them. —**Shirley Chisholm:** *Unbought and Unbossed* (1970)

2044. America is the civilization of people engaged in transforming themselves. In the past, the stars of the performance were the pioneer and the immigrant. Today, it is youth and the Black.—**Harold Rosenberg:** *Discovering the Present* (1973)

2045. Americans always seem to be looking for change. Car is old after two years, a dress no longer in style, so you pitch them away.

Same thing wid house, work, family, and love. —**Joseph Olshan:** *Clara's Heart* (1985)

Future

See also THE NATION: The Dream and the Ideal; SOCIAL LIFE: Progress; HISTORY: History

2046. America, which has the most glorious present still existing in the world today, hardly stops to enjoy it, in her insatiable appetite for the future.—**Anne Morrow Lindbergh:** *Gift From the Sea* (1955)

2047. Not a future. At least not in Europe. America's different, of course, but America's really only a kind of Russia. You've no idea how pleasant it is not to have any future. It's like having a totally efficient contraceptive.—**Anthony Burgess:** *Honey for the Bears* (1963)

2048. Americans are, so to speak, canted toward the future.—**Frances Fitzgerald:** *Fire in the Lake* (1972)

2049. This nation's impulse is toward the future, and tradition seems more of a shackle to it than an inspiration.—**Allan Bloom:** *The Closing of the American Mind* (1987)

Generations

2050. The future of America is based on one generation sacrificing for the next.—**Alex Mayhew**

2051. Remember the battle between the generations twenty-some years ago. Well, our parents won. They're out there living the American dream on some damned golf course, and we're stuck with the jobs and haircuts.—**P. J. O'Rourke:** *Parliament of Whores* (1991)

2052. In America, a nation that believes it transcends history, each generation can be a world of its own.—**Richard Reeves:** *Time*, 22 November 1993

Memory

See also HISTORY: History

2053. We have no national memory.—**Lillian Hellman:** *Time*, 23 April 1979

2054. Memory in America suffers amnesia.—**Meridel Le Sueur:** *A Woman's Notebook* (1980)

2055. Americans are impatient with memory.—**Jamaica Kincaid:** "Alien Soil"; *New Yorker*, 21 June 1993

The Past

See also HISTORY: History

2056. It is a peculiar business, the American attitude to Antiquity. Of all the citizens of the world there is no one so alive as the American to the values of modernity, so fertile in experiment, so feverish in the search for something new. There is nothing, from Architecture to Contract Bridge, from the Immortality of the Soul to the Ventilation of Railroad-Cars, from Golf to God that he does not pounce upon and examine critically to see if it cannot be im-

proved. And then, having pulled it to pieces, mastered its fundamental theory, and reassembled it in a novel and efficient design, he laments bitterly because it is not old.—**A. G. Magdonell:** *A Visit to America* (1935)

2057. We are afraid to be either proud of our ancestors or ashamed of them.—**Dorothy Day:** *The Long Loneliness* (1952)

2058. We are a people who do not want to keep much of the past in our heads. It is considered unhealthy in America to remember mistakes, neurotic to think about them, psychotic to dwell on them.—**Lillian Hellman:** *Scoundrel Time* (1976)

2059. Everyone who lives in an industrialized society is obliged gradually to give up the past, but in certain countries, such as the United States, the break with the past has been particularly traumatic.—**Susan Sontag:** *On Photography* (1977)

Revolution

See also WAR AND THE MILITARY: American Revolution

2060. The right of revolution does not exist in America. We had a revolution 140 years ago which made it unnecessary to have any other revolution in this country. One of the many meanings of democracy is that it is a form of government in which the right of revolution has been lost.—**State manual for elementary schools:** Robert S. Lynd and Helen Merrell Lynd *Middletown* (1921)

2061. "There won't be any revolution in America," said Isadore. Niktin agreed. "The people are all too clean. They spend all their time changing their shirts and washing themselves. You can't feel fierce and revolutionary in a bathroom."—**Eric Linklater:** *Juan in America* (1931)

2062. America was born of revolt, flourished in dissent, became great through experimentation.—**Henry Steele Commager:** 1954

2063. Our own revolution has ended the need for revolution forever.—**William C. West-**

moreland: speech to Daughters of the American Revolution; Daniel Berrigan *America is Hard to Find* (1972)

2064. We are revolutionaries, we Americans—although we abhor revolutions which are not made by our rules.—**James Oliver Robertson:** *American Myth, American Reality* (1980)

2065. America is at that awkward stage. It's too late to work within the system, but too early to shoot the bastards.—**Claire Wolfe**

2066. The land of the permanent revolution.—**Ted Morgan**

Tradition

See also SOCIAL LIFE: Progress; HISTORY: History

2067. America delights in tradition, and destroys it as she goes. She hates the thing she respects, burns the god that she worships.—**W. L. George:** *Hail Columbia!* (1921)

2068. Nothing can last in America more than ten years.—**Philip Rahv:** *Time*, 15 August 1977

2069. America has a way of inventing tradition each morning and erasing the past by nightfall, and the hold of ancient custom is endangered by a thousand circumstances.—**Israel Shenker:** *Coat of Many Colors* (1985)

2070. In America nothing dies easier than tradition.—**Russell Baker:** *New York Times*, 14 May 1991

Twentieth Century

2071. America's present need is not heroics, but healing; not nostrums but normalcy; not revolution, but restoration.—**Warren G. Harding,** Republican: on 1920s; speech, Boston, 14 May 1920

2072. The twentieth century is only the nine-

teenth speaking with a slightly American accent.—**Philip Guedalla,** 1889–1944: Evan Esar (ed.) *The Dictionary of Humorous Quotations* (1949)

2073. If anything characterizes the cultural life of the seventies in America, it is an insistence on preventing failures of communication.—**Richard Dean Rosen:** *Psychobabble* (1977)

2074. All over the world people were in love with the life of the American teenager. It was so much freer than it was anywhere else. Anything the young wanted to do they could do in an automobile. On Saturday nights the drive-in was the automobile meeting ground where carloads of boys and girls would go to do anything from picking up each other to picking a fight.—**Tom Wolfe:** on 1950s; Peter Lewis *The Fifties* (1978)

2075. The seventies was the disease decade, when Americans learned their destiny was to be medical patients.—**Nicholas von Hoffman:** *Spectator*, 5 January 1980

2076. The age of masturbation.—**Bob Dylan:** on 1980s; interview, 1985

2077. During the 1960s people forgot what emotions were supposed to be. And I don't think they've ever remembered.—**Andy Warhol:** *Newsweek*, 9 March 1987

2078. The worst feature of the 50s is that they were pregnant with the 60s.—**George F. Will:** *Newsweek*, 4 July 1988

2079. In economics, we borrowed from the Bourbons; in foreign policy, we drew on themes fashioned by the nomad warriors of the Eurasian steppes. In spiritual matters, we emulated the braying intolerance of our archenemies, the Shi'ite fundamentalists.—**Barbara Ehrenreich:** on 1980s; *The Worst Years of Our Lives* (1991)

2080. We can safely abandon the doctrine of the eighties, namely that the rich were not working because they had too little money, the poor because they had much.—**John Kenneth Galbraith:** on 1980s; *Guardian*, 20 November 1991

2081. In the 1950s, America was at the wheel of the world and Americans were at the wheel of two-toned (and sometimes even more-toned) cars, tail-finned, high-powered, soft-spring rolling sofas.—**George F. Will,** 1941– : Ken Burns and Geoffrey C. Ward (eds.) *Baseball* (1994)

Twenty-first Century

2082. The American century—and the European half millennium—is coming to an end. The world century is beginning.—**Rosabeth Moss Kanter:** *World Class* (1995)

HISTORY

Confederacy

See also WAR AND THE MILITARY: American Civil War; WAR AND THE MILITARY: American Revolution; POLITICS AND GOVERNMENT: States

2083. The Confederacy has been done to death by politicians.—**Mary Chesnut:** 1863; Ken Burns *The Civil War* (documentary), 1989

2084. If the Confederacy fails, there should be written on its tombstone: *Died of a Theory.* —**Jefferson Davis,** president of the Confederacy: 1865; Geoffrey C. Ward *The Civil War* (1991)

Declaration of Independence

See also WAR AND THE MILITARY: American Revolution

2085. We must indeed all hang together, or, most assuredly, we shall all hang separately. —**Benjamin Franklin:** at the signing of the Declaration, 4 July 1776; P. M. Zall *Ben Franklin* (1980)

2086. A more impudent, false, and atrocious Proclamation was never fabricated by the hands of man.—**Ambrose Serle:** c. 1776; George F. Scheer and Hugh Rankin *Rebels and Redcoats* (1957)

2087. The Declaration of Independence I always considered as a theatrical show. Jefferson ran away with all the stage effect of that … and all the glory of it.—**John Adams:** letter to Benjamin Rush, 1811

2088. Its constitution the glittering and sounding generalities of natural right which make up the Declaration of Independence.—**Rufus Choate:** letter to the Maine Whig State Central Committee, 9 August 1856

2089. Jefferson's Declaration of Independence is a practical document for the use of practical men. It is not a thesis for philosophers, but a whip for tyrants; it is not a theory of government, but a program of action.—**Woodrow Wilson:** speech at Indianapolis Indiana, 13 April 1911

2090. The Americans believe they answered all first questions in 1776: since then they've

just been hammering out the practical details.
—**Ray Smith:** Robert I. Fitzhenry *Barnes & Noble Book of Quotations* (1986)

Discovery

See also THE AMERICAN PEOPLE: Immigrants;
THE AMERICAN PEOPLE: Indians

2091. What a blessing this smoking is! Perhaps the greatest that we owe to the discovery of America.—**Arthur Helps,** English historian: *Friends in Council* New Series (1859)

2092. Columbus discovered no isle or key so lonely as himself.—**Ralph Waldo Emerson,** 1803–82: *The Ultimate Success Quotations Library* (1997)

2093. Perhaps, after all, America never has been discovered. I myself would say that it had merely been detected.—**Oscar Wilde:** *The Picture of Dorian Gray* (1891)

2094. America has been discovered before, but it has always been hushed up.—**Oscar Wilde,** 1856–1900: Robert Byrne (ed.) *1,911 Best Things Anybody Ever Said* (1988)

2095. America was too big to have been discovered all at one time. It would have been better for the graces if it had been discovered in pieces of about the size of France or Germany at a time.—**Samuel Butler,** 1835–1902, British author: *Samuel Butler's Notebooks* (1951)

2096. Christopher Columbus, as everyone knows, is honoured by posterity because he was the last to discover America.—**James Joyce:** *Piccolo della Sera* (Trieste), 5 September 1912

2097. The true America is the Middle West, and Columbus discovered nothing at all except another Europe.—**W. L. George,** 1882–1926: Connie Robertson (ed.) *The Wordsworth Dictionary of Quotations* (1996)

2098. I am not belittling the brave pioneer men but the sunbonnet as well as the sombrero has helped to settle this glorious land of ours.
—**Edna Ferber:** *Cimarron* (1929)

2099. What a pity, when Christopher Colum-

bus discovered America, that he ever mentioned it.—**Margot Asquith,** 1864–1945

2100. So Columbus said, somebody show me the sunset and somebody did and he set sail for it. And he discovered America and they put him in jail for it. And the fetters gave him welts. And they named America after somebody else.
—**Ogden Nash,** 1902–71

2101. America is not a young land: it is old and dirty and evil before the settlers, before the Indians. The evil is there waiting.—**William S. Burroughs:** *The Naked Lunch* (1959)

2102. Who stole America?—**Lawrence Ferlinghetti:** *Starting from San Francisco* (1961)

2103. And furthermore did you know that behind the discovery of America there was a Jewish financier?—**Mordecai Richler:** *Cocksure* (1968)

2104. What I admire in Columbus is not his having discovered a world but his having gone to search for it on the faith of an opinion.
—**Robert Turgot,** c. 1910–87: *Readers' Digest,* October 1992

2105. Columbus did not seek a new route to the Indies in response to a majority directive.
—**Milton Friedman,** 1912–   : *Reader's Digest,* 1 June 1978

2106. Thank God for single people. America would never have been discovered if Columbus had been married: "You're going where? With whom? To find what? And I suppose she's giving you those three ships for nothing?"—**Richard Chamberlain:** 1982; Bob Chieger *Was It Good for You, Too?* (1983)

2107. What did the Indians call America before the white man came? Ours.—**Anonymous:** Stuart Turner *The Public Speaker's Bible* (1988)

2108. Columbus only discovered that he was in some new place. He didn't discover America.—**Louise Erdrich,** 1954–   : Bill Moyers *A World of Ideas* (1989)

2109. Everybody in fifteenth-century Spain was wrong about where China was and as a result, Columbus discovered Caribbean vacations.—**P. J. O'Rourke:** *Parliament of Whores* (1991)

Heroes

2110. The Americans are certainly hero-worshippers, and always take their heroes from the criminal classes.—**Oscar Wilde:** letter to Norman Forbes-Robertson, 19 April 1882

2111. Nowhere in the world is superiority more easily attained, or more eagerly admitted. The chief business of the nation, as a nation, is the setting up of heroes, mainly bogus.—**H. L. Mencken:** *Prejudices* Third Series (1923)

2112. The more characteristic American hero in the earlier day, and the more beloved type at all times, was not the hustler but the whittler.—**Mark Sullivan:** *Our Times: The United States, 1900–1925* vol. 3 (1930)

2113. Europe makes heroes of the scrapped. America scraps her heroes.—**Shane Leslie:** *American Wonderland* (1936)

2114. America has enjoyed the doubtful blessing of a single-track mind. We are able to accommodate, at a time, only one national hero; and we demand that that hero shall be uniform and invincible. As a literate people we are preoccupied, neither with the race nor the individual, but with the type. Yesterday, we romanticized the "tough guy;" today, we are romanticizing the underprivileged, tough or tender; tomorrow, we shall begin to romanticize the pure primitive.—**Ellen Glasgow:** 1937; *The Woman Within* (1954)

2115. There is a hate layer of opinion and emotion in America. There will be other McCarthys to come who will be hailed as its heroes.—**Max Lerner:** *New York Post*, 5 April 1950

2116. To be a celebrity in America is to be forgiven everything.—**Mary McGrory,** 1918– : Abby Adams *An Uncommon Scold* (1989)

2117. Heroes are pretty well all washed up in America these days.—**Russell Baker:** *New York Times Book Review*, 14 October 1990

History

See also PAST AND FUTURE; WAR AND THE MILITARY: War and Peace

2118. America was thus clearly top nation, and History came to a.—**W. C. Sellar** and R. **J. Yeatman:** *1066 and All That* (1930)

2119. There was even a recurrent idea in America about an education that would leave out history and the past, that should be a sort of equipment for aerial adventure, weighed down by none of the stowaways of inheritance or tradition.—**F. Scott Fitzgerald,** 1896–1940: *The Crack-Up* (1945)

2120. American history is longer, larger, more various, more beautiful, and more terrible than anything anyone has ever said about it.—**James Baldwin:** 16 October 1963; *The Price of the Ticket* (1985)

2121. English history is all about men liking their fathers, and American history is all about men hating their fathers and trying to burn down everything they ever did.—**Malcolm Bradbury:** *Stepping Westward* (1965)

2122. The central fact of North American history is that there were fifteen British Colonies before 1776. Thirteen rebelled and two did not.—**June Callwood:** Robert I. Fitzhenry *Barnes & Noble Book of Quotations* (1986)

2123. Americans, more than most people, believe that history is the result of individual decisions to implement conscious intentions. For Americans, more than most people, history has been that…. This sense of openness, of possibility and autonomy, has been a national asset as precious as the topsoil of the Middle West. But like topsoil, it is subject to erosion; it requires tending. And it is not bad for Americans to come to terms with the fact that for them too, history is a story of inertia and the unforeseen.—**George F. Will:** *Statecraft as Soulcraft* (1984)

2124. Once a president gets to the White House, the only audience that is left that really matters is history.—**Doris Kearns Goodwin:** *New York Times*, 1985

2125. American history is essentially different from the history of other nations in that the people were ahead of the government. That is, they arrived in places where there was no government, whether the place was Plymouth, or Ohio, or Utah. America is a much more grass-roots-created continent than Europe; it was made by the many and not by the few, by Native Americans and slaves and squatters as much as by statesmen. —**Ted Morgan:** *Wilderness at Dawn* (1993)

Myth

2126. Myths and legends die hard in America. We love them for the extra dimension they provide, the illusion of near-infinite possibility to erase the narrow confines of most men's reality. —**Hunter S. Thompson:** *Pageant*, September 1969

2127. To be an American (unlike being English or French or whatever) is precisely to *imagine* a destiny rather than to inherit one; since we have always been, insofar as we are Americans at all, inhabitants of myth rather than

history. —**Leslie Fiedler:** *Playboy*, December 1969

2128. The American myth is of free will in its simple, primary sense. One can choose oneself and will oneself; and this absurdly optimistic assumption so dominates the republic that it has bred all its gross social injustices. —**John Fowles:** *Daniel Martin* (1977)

2129. America is the world's living myth. There's no sense of wrong when you kill an American or blame America for some local disaster. This is our function, to be character types, to embody recurring themes that people can use to comfort themselves, justify themselves and so on. We're here to accommodate. Whatever people need we provide. A myth is a useful thing. —**Don Delillo:** *The Names* (1982)

2130. He is our myth, the American myth. —**David Newman,** screenwriter: on Superman; *Time*, 14 March 1988

WAR AND THE MILITARY

American Civil War (1861–5)

See also HISTORY: Confederacy

2131. Universal suffrage, furloughs and whiskey have ruined us. —**General Braxton Bragg:** after the battle of Shiloh, 6–7 April 1862

2132. A rich man's war and a poor man's fight. —**Slogan:** used during the conscription riots

in New York City, July 1863; anyone who was drafted could hire a volunteer to take his place

2133. My opinion is that the Northern States will manage somehow to muddle through. —**John Bright:** said during the Civil War; Justin McCarthy *Reminiscences* vol.1 (1899)

2134. Let's have the Union restored as it was, if we can; but if we can't, *I'm in favor of the Union as it wasn't.* —**Artemus Ward:** *Artemus Ward: His Travels* (1865)

2135. The war is over—the rebels are our countrymen again.—**Ulysses S. Grant:** 9 April 1865

2136. Strange, (is it not?) that battles, martyrs, blood, even assassination, should so condense— perhaps only really, lastingly condense—a Nationality.—**Walt Whitman,** 1819–92: Geoffrey C. Ward *The Civil War* (1991)

2137. In the South, the war is what A.D. is elsewhere: they date from it.—**Mark Twain:** *Life on the Mississippi* (1883)

2138. Had the South had a people as numerous as it was warlike, and a navy commensurate with its other resources as a sea power, the great extent of its sea-coast and its numerous inlets would have been elements of great strength.—**Alfred Thayer Mahan:** *The Influence of Sea Power Upon History* (1890)

2139. It [the Civil War] created what had never existed before—a national consciousness. It was not the salvation of the Union, it was the rebirth of the Union.—**Woodrow Wilson:** Memorial Day address, Arlington National Cemetery, 31 May 1915

2140. The only war in modern times as to which we can be sure, first, that no skill and patience of diplomacy could have avoided it, and second, that preservation of the American Union and abolition of Negro slavery were two vast triumphs of good by which even the inferno of war was justified.—**Lord Morley:** Stephen Crane *Red Badge of Courage* (1951)

2141. There will never be anything in America more interesting than the Civil War.—**Gertrude Stein:** *Everybody's Autobiography* (1937)

2142. I see no results of this great conflict which justify the tremendous sacrifices which we as a nation were required to make.—**Henry Miller:** *The Air-Conditioned Nightmare* (1945)

2143. The first of the unlimited industrial wars was the Civil War in America. It was the first great conflict of the steam age, and the aim of the Northern, or Federal, States was unconditional surrender—that is, total victory. Its character was, therefore, that of a crusade, and because of this, as well as because it put to the test the military developments of the Industrial Revolution, it opened a radically new chapter in the history of war.—**J. F. C. Fuller:** *The Decisive Battles of the Western World* (1954–56)

2144. It was the railroad and the river steamboat which robbed the great battlefield victories of finality. It was these devices, managed by telegraphic communications, which made it possible promptly to repair the terrible casualties of the major battles.—**Walter Millis:** *Arms and Men* (1958)

2145. The transcending facts of the American Civil War are the military genius of Robert E. Lee and the naval superiority of the North. Lee's tactical opponent was the Army of the Potomac, but his strategic rival was the Union Navy. —**John D. Hayed:** *Sea Power in the Civil War* (1961)

2146. The war ended only by the extinction of the military power of the South and its occupation.—**Correlli Barnet:** *Britain and Her Army* (1970)

2147. The men of 1860-61 allowed an academic argument about an "imaginary Negro in an impossible place" to end in a bloody Civil War. —**Peter J. Parish:** *The American Civil War* (1975)

2148. War had become a matter of management and organization more than individual heroism or feats of derring-do. It was all summed up in a few words written in 1863 by one of the organization men of the new warfare, Quartermaster-General Meigs: "It is exhaustion of men and money that finally terminates all modern wars."—**Peter J. Parish:** *The American Civil War* (1975)

2149. The Civil War had been a war of the people, miscellaneously armed, shoddily clad, often unwillingly conscripted and corruptly officered, ragged in step, clumsy in drill, uncertain and sometimes panic-stricken in the face of the enemy—blue or grey.—**John Keegan:** *Six Armies in Normandy* (1982)

American Revolution (1775–83)

See also HISTORY: Declaration of Independence

2150. What a glorious morning is this.—**Samuel Adams:** on hearing gunfire at Lexington, 19 April 1775

2151. Men, you are all marksmen—don't one of you fire until you see the white of their eyes. —**Israel Putman:** at Bunker Hill, 1775

2152. If every nerve is not strained to recruit the new army with all proper expedience, I think the game the game is pretty near up. —**General George Washington:** letter to his brother, 1776

2153. It is a common observation here [Paris] that our cause is *the cause of all mankind*, and that we are fighting for their liberty in defending our own.—**Benjamin Franklin:** letter to Samuel Cooper, 1777

2154. If I were an American, as I am an Englishman, while a foreign troop was landed in my country, I would never lay down my arms— never, never, never! You cannot conquer America.—**William Pitt the Elder:** speech in the House of Lords, 18 November 1777

2155. If there was ever a just war since the world began, it is this in which America is now engaged.—**Thomas Paine:** *The American Crisis* No. 5, 21 March 1778

2156. The British officers in general behaved like boys who had been whipped at school. Some bit their lips, some pouted, others cried. Their round, broad-rimmed hats were well adapted to the occasion, hiding those faces they were ashamed to show.—**Anonymous American officer:** after the surrender of Yorktown, 1781; Esmond Wright (ed.) *The Fire of Liberty* (1984)

2157. It is a most accursed, wicked, barbarous, cruel, unnatural, unjust, and diabolical war. —**William Pitt the Younger,** British statesman: 1781

2158. The Revolution was effected before the War commenced. The Revolution was in the minds and hearts of the people.—**John Adams:** letter to Hezekiah Niles, 13 February 1818

2159. [The American Revolution] was a vindication of liberties inherited and possessed. It was a conservative revolution.—**William E. Gladstone:** *North American Review*, September 1878

2160. The American Revolution was a beginning, not a consummation.—**Woodrow Wilson,** 1856–1924: Laurence J. Peter (ed.) *Peter's Quotations* (1977)

2161. It was a blameless insurrection, founded on equity and quotations from Blackstone, a sedate rebellion, a sedition of the highest principles.—**Philip Guedalla:** *Fathers of the Revolution* (1926)

2162. Most American heroes of the Revolutionary period are by now two men, the actual man and the romantic image. Some are even three men—the actual man, the image, and the debunked remains.—**Esther Forbes:** *Paul Revere* (1942)

2163. The British had captured the hill, but the Americans had won the glory.—**Winston Churchill:** on the Battle of Bunker Hill 1775; *A History of the English Speaking Peoples* vol. 2 (1957)

2164. The American case is different: it is not a question of the Old Man transforming himself into the New, but of the New Man becoming alive to the fact that he is new, that he has been transformed already without his having realized it.—**W. H. Auden:** *The Dyer's Hand* (1962)

2165. If the American Revolution had produced nothing but the Declaration of Independence, it would have been worth while. —**Samuel Eliot Morison:** *The Oxford History of the American People* (1965)

2166. Make no mistake; the American Revolution was not fought to *obtain* freedom, but to *preserve* the liberties that Americans already had as colonials. Independence was no conscious goal, secretly nurtured in cellars or jungle by bearded conspirators, but a reluctant last resort, to preserve "life, liberty, and the pursuit of happiness."—**Samuel Eliot Morison:** *The Oxford History of the American People* (1965)

2167. One of the peculiarities of the American Revolution was that its leaders pinned their hopes on the organization of decision-making units, the structuring of their incentives, and the counterbalancing of the units against one another, rather than on the more usual (and more exciting) principle of substituting "the good guys" for "the bad guys."—**Thomas Sowell**

Korean War (1950–53)

2168. You're not here to die for your country. You're here to make those fucking die for theirs. —**John H. Michaels,** American general: to 27th Infantry (Wolfhound) regiment during the Korean War, attrib.; Nigel Rees *A Dictionary of Twentieth Century Quotations* (1987)

2169. Here we fight Europe's war with arms while the diplomats there still fight with words. —**General Douglas MacArthur:** letter to Joseph Martin, 6 April 1951

2170. This strategy would involve us in the wrong war, at the wrong place, at the wrong time, and with the wrong enemy.—**Omar N. Bradley:** to the Senate Committee on Armed Services and Foreign Relations, contemplating conflict with China, 15 May 1951

2171. This Korean War is a Truman War. —**Robert A. Taft:** speech at Milwaukee, 1951

2172. I shall go to Korea and try to end the war.—**Dwight D. Eisenhower:** campaign promise, speech in Detroit, 24 October 1952

2173. The Korean War began in a way in which wars often begin. A potential aggressor miscalculated.—**John Foster Dulles:** speech at St. Louise, 1953

2174. I was the first American commander to put his signature on a paper ending a war when we did not win it.—**General Mark W. Clark:** *New York Herald Tribune*, 21 October 1953

2175. It was the five-paragraph war, because that's all history gives it.—**Colonel William Webber**

2176. Truman lost his temper, MacArthur lost his job, Acheson lost his war, a million and a half people lost their lives, and Stalin didn't even lose a night's sleep.—*New York Herald Tribune*: 6 April 1964

2177. [Guerrilla warfare was] as fast as rabbits and cautious as virgins.—**Anonymous:** Vicki Goldberg *Margaret Bourke-White* (1986)

2178. Korea put the CIA on the map.—**Max Hastings:** *The Korean War* (1987)

MacArthur, General Douglas (1880–1964)

2179. I studied dramatics under him for twelve years.—**Dwight D. Eisenhower,** 1890–1969: Robert Andrews *The New Penguin Dictionary of Modern Quotations* (2001)

2180. The best and the worst things you hear about him are quite true.—**Thomas Blamey,** 1884–1951: John A. Hetherington *Blamey* (1954)

2181. Like the old soldier of the ballad, I now close my military career and just fade away, an old soldier who tried to do his duty as God gave him the light to see that duty. Goodbye. —**Douglas MacArthur:** farewell address to Congress, 19 April 1951

2182. There wasn't a dry eye on the Democratic side of the House, nor a dry seat on the Republican side.—**Joseph Martin,** American congressman: on MacArthur's farewell's address, April 1951

2183. We heard God speak here today. God in the flesh, the voice of God.—**Dewey Short,** American congressman: on MacArthur's farewell's address, April 1951

2184. I fired him because he wouldn't respect the authority of the president. I didn't fire him because he was a dumb son of a bitch, although he was, but that's not against the law for generals. If it was, half to three-quarters of them would be in jail.—**Harry S Truman,** 1884–1972: Merle Miller *Plain Speaking* (1974)

2185. He doesn't have a staff, he has a court. —**Harry S Truman:** *Newsweek*, 12 May 1975

2186. His twenty-two medals—thirteen of them for heroism—probably exceeded those of any other figure in American history. He seemed to seek death on battlefields.—**William Manchester:** *American Caesar* (1978)

2187. His own heroes were Lincoln and Washington, and in some ways he resembled them. —**William Manchester:** *American Caesar* (1978)

2188. He was a great thundering paradox of a man, noble and ignoble, inspiring and outrageous, arrogant and shy, the best of men and the worst of men, the most protean, most ridiculous, and most sublime.—**William Manchester:** *American Caesar* (1978)

means in a wholly realistic way. Don't slide in, don't mislead yourself.—**Colin Powell,** American general: speech at the National Press Club luncheon, 28 September 1993; *National Interest*, Spring 1994

The Military

2189. In the first place the genius of this nation is not in the least to be compared with that of the Prussians, Austrians, or French. You say to your soldier, "Do this," and he doeth it. But I am obliged to say, "This is the reason why you ought to do that," and then he does it. —**Friedrich Wilhelm von Steuben,** 1730–94: letter to a Prussian officer; J. Lawton Collins *War in Peacetime: The History and Lessons of Korea* (1969)

2190. If there is one basic element in our Constitution, it is civilian control of the military. —**Harry S Truman:** *Memoirs* vol. 2 (1955)

2191. In the United States, we go to considerable trouble to keep soldiers out of politics, and even more to keep politics out of soldiers. —**Samuel Blair Griffith:** "Introduction" to Mao Tsetung *Guerilla Warfare* (1961)

2192. In setting our military goals we need first of all to recognize that most of the world's most basic woes do not lend themselves to purely military solutions.—**Matthew B. Ridgway,** American general: *The Korean War* (1967)

2193. A nation that continues year after year to spend more money on military defense than on programs of social uplift is approaching spiritual death.—**Martin Luther King, Jr.:** *Where Do We Go From Here?* (1967)

2194. One of the problems we're going to have to solve is to make the Armed Forces so popular, everyone wants to get in.—**General Lewis B. Hershey,** 1893– : Laurence J. Peter (ed.) *Peter's Quotations* (1977)

2195. There has been a strong tradition in this country that it is not the function of the military to educate the public on political issues. —**J. William Fulbright,** 1905–95, American senator

2196. My philosophy in all this is rather simple: match political expectations to military

NATO

2197. NATO exists for three reasons—to keep the Russians out, the Americans in and the Germans down.—**Hastings Lionel Ismay,** British general and first Secretary-General of Nato: 1949

2198. I bear solemn witness to the fact that NATO heads of state and of government meet only to go through the tedious motions of reading speeches, drafted by others, with the principal activity of not rocking the boat.—**Pierre Elliot Trudeau,** 1919– , Canadian politician: Colin Jarman *The Guinness Dictionary of More Poisonous Quotes* (1992)

2199. I guess that these letters N-A-T-O may stand for Navies, Aircraft, Tanks, Obsolete. —**Mikhail Gorbachev:** *New York Times,* 4 June 1990

2200. Six countries in search of an enemy. —**Peter Ustinov,** 1921–

2201. NATO is now a biological monstrosity— an organ without a function.—**Denis Healey,** 1917–

Pentagon

2202. That immense monument to modern man's subservience to the desk.—**Oliver Franks:** *Observer,* 30 November 1952

2203. A place where costs are always rounded to the nearest tenth of a billion dollars.—**C. Merton Tyrrell:** 1970

2204. A log going down the river with 25,000 ants on it, each thinking he's steering.—**Anonymous Assistant Secretary of State**

2205. The Pentagon has five sides on every issue.—**Anonymous Russian**

Persian Gulf War (1991)

2206. If Kuwait grew carrots we wouldn't give a damn.—**Lawrence Korb,** American politician: *International Herald Tribune,* 21 August 1990

2207. The specter of Vietnam has been buried forever in the desert sands of the Arabian Peninsula.—**George Bush:** Radio address to American troops, 2 March 1991

2208. We've kicked the Vietnam syndrome once and for all!—**George Bush:** *Newsweek,* 11 March 1991

2209. The Gulf War was like teenage sex. We got in too soon and out too soon.—**Tom Harkin,** American senator: *Independent on Sunday,* 29 September 1991

2210. I bit the bullet, and he bit his nails. —**George Bush:** on Bill Clinton's views on the war; 1992

2211. Our leaders had the audacity to say the Gulf War made America feel good again. How morally corrupt are we that we need a war to feel good about ourselves?—**Tim Robbins:** *Independent on Sunday,* 10 September 1992

Spanish-American War (1898)

2212. I should welcome any war. The country needs one.—**Theodore Roosevelt,** Assistant Secretary of the Navy: one year before the war, 1897; *American Heritage,* July 1969

2213. You furnish the pictures and I'll furnish the war.—**William Randolph Hearst:** cable to Frederic Remington, in Cuba, March 1898

2214. It has been a splendid little war, begun with the highest motives, carried on with magnificent intelligence and spirit, favored by that fortune which loves the brave.—**John Hay:** letter to Theodore Roosevelt, 27 July 1898

2215. While we are conducting war, and until its conclusion, we must keep all we get; when the war is over we must keep what we want. —**William McKinley:** memorandum, 1898

2216. The Spanish-American War was not a great war. A large number of our troops took the hazard of watermelons in Georgia and Florida, and fought the malaria and mosquitoes, but very few Spanish.—**James L. Slayden:** in the House of Representatives, 1906

Vietnam War (1961–75)

See also POLITICS AND GOVERNMENT: Johnson, Lyndon B.

2217. Now we have a problem in making our power credible, and Vietnam is the place.—**John F. Kennedy:** remark to James Reston, June 1961; Stanley Karnow *Vietnam: A History* (1983)

2218. Anyone who isn't confused doesn't really understand the situation.—**Ed Murrow,** 1908–65, American broadcaster and journalist: Walter Bryan *The Improbable Irish* (1969)

2219. I don't object to it being called "McNamara's war." It is a very important war and I am pleased to be identified with it and do whatever I can to win it.—**Robert S. McNamara,** Secretary of Defense: *New York Times,* 25 April 1964

2220. Tell the Vietnamese they've got to draw in their horns or we're going to bomb them back into the Stone Age.—**General Curtis LeMay,** American air-force officer: May 1964; *Mission with LeMay* (1965)

2221. We are not going to send American boys nine or ten thousand miles away from home to do what Asian boys ought to be doing for themselves.—**Lyndon B. Johnson:** speech at Akron University, 21 October 1964

2222. We should declare war on North Vietnam.... We could pave the whole country and put parking strips on it, and still be home by Christmas.—**Ronald Reagan:** *Fresno Bee*, 10 October 1965

2223. I'd rather see America save her soul than her face.—**Norman Thomas,** American Presbyterian minister and writer: speech, Washington DC, 27 November 1965

2224. All the noises of this war have an unaccountably Texan ring.—**Nicholas Tomalin:** *Sunday Times*, 1966

2225. Declare the United States the winner and begin de-escalation.—**George Aiken,** Vermont's senator: speech, the Senate, 19 October 1966

2226. Characteristically, the world at large believes that if JFK were alive there would be no war in Vietnam. The myth-makers have obscured the fact that it was JFK who began our active participation in the war when, 1n 1961, he added to the six hundred American observers the first of a gradual build-up of American troops, which reached twenty thousand at the time of his assassination. And there is no evidence that he would not have persisted in that war, for, as he said to a friend shortly before he died, "I have to go all the way with this one." He could not suffer a second Cuba and hope to maintain the appearance of Defender of the Free World at the ballot box in 1964.—**Gore Vidal:** *Esquire* (New York), April 1967

2227. The war in Vietnam … [is] of questionable loyalty and constitutionality … diplomatically indefensible … even in military terms … [and] morally wrong.—**Senator Eugene J. McCarthy:** Conference of Concerned Democrats, 2 December 1967

2228. You let a bully come into your front yard, the next day he'll be on your porch.—**Lyndon B. Johnson,** 1908–73: *Time*, 15 April 1984

2229. I never felt I was fighting for any particular cause. I fought to stay alive and I killed to keep from being killed.—**David Parks:** *GI Diary* (1968)

2230. To win in Vietnam, we will have to exterminate a nation.—**Benjamin Spock:** *Dr Spock on Vietnam* (1968)

2231. It is our will and not our strength that is being tried.—**Lyndon B. Johnson:** State of the Union, 17 January 1968

2232. It became necessary to destroy the town to save it.—**Anonymous US Army Major:** on the bombing of the town of Ben Tre; Associated Press, 8 February 1968

2233. The war in Vietnam is mainly unpopular because it is a war with limited aims, a police action, and Americans do not identify with the police.—**Frederick A. Pottle:** 1968; George A. Panichas *Promise of Greatness* (1968)

2234. The war against Vietnam is only the ghastliest manifestation of what I'd call imperial provincialism, which afflicts America's whole culture—aware only of its own history, insensible to everything which isn't part of the local atmosphere.—**Stephen Vizinczey:** *Times Saturday Review* (London), 21 September 1968

2235. The war is simply an obscenity, a depraved act by weak and miserable men, including all of us who have allowed it to go on and on with endless fury and destruction—all of us who would have remained silent had stability and order been secured. It is not pleasant to use such words, but candor permits no less.—**Noam Chomsky:** *American Power and the New Mandarins* (1969)

2236. The conventional army loses if it does not win, the guerilla wins if he does not lose.—**Henry Kissinger:** *Foreign Affairs*, January 1969

2237. Let us understand: North Vietnam cannot defeat or humiliate the United States. Only Americans can do that.—**Richard M. Nixon:** television broadcast, 3 November 1969

2238. I'm not going to be the first American president to lose a war.—**Richard M. Nixon:** October 1969

2239. We flattened cities in Germany and Japan in World War II. I don't know what's so sacred about Hanoi. Let world opinion go fly a kite.—**Mendel Rivers:** Laurence J. Peter (ed.) *Peter's Quotations* (1977)

2240. It's worse than immoral, it's a mistake.—**Dean Acheson,** 1893–1971

2241. This war has already stretched the generation gap so wide that it threatens to pull the country apart.—**Senator Frank Church:** May 1970

2242. Yippies, hippies, yahoos, Black Panthers, lions and tigers alike—I would swap the whole damn zoo for the kind of young Americans I saw in Vietnam.—**Spiro T. Agnew,** 1918–96: Laurence J. Peter (ed.) *Peter's Quotations* (1977)

2243. The war the soldiers tried to stop.—**John F. Kerry:** speech at antiwar rally, Washington, D.C., 26 April 1971

2244. When someone asked him [Lyndon B. Johnson] later why he had not involved the public more in the question of Vietnam, he was told: "If you have a mother-in-law with only one eye and she has it in the center of her forehead, you don't keep her in the living-room." —**David Halberstam:** *The Best and the Brightest* (1972)

2245. By intervening in the Vietnamese struggle the United States was attempting to fit its global strategies into a world of hillocks and hamlets, to reduce its majestic concerns for the containment of communism and the security of the Free World to a dimension where governments rose and fell as a result of arguments between two colonels' wives.—**Frances Fitzgerald:** *Fire in the Lake* (1972)

2246. Think big.—**President Richard Nixon:** in a conversation with Henry Kissinger in 1972; Nixon considered but rejected using nuclear weapons; *Newsweek,* 11 March 2002

2247. This is a war run to show the world, and particularly the Third World, where exactly it stands in relation to our technology.—**Daniel Berrigan,** American anti–Vietnam War activist: 1973, attrib.

2248. The last crusade.—**Chester Cooper:** *Daily Telegraph,* 4 April 1975

2249. Today, America can regain the sense of pride that existed before Vietnam. These events, tragic as they are, portend neither the end of the world nor of America's leadership in the world.—**Gerald R. Ford:** April 1975

2250. Television brought the brutality of war into the comfort of the living room. Vietnam was lost in the living rooms of America—not on the battlefields of Vietnam.—**Marshall McLuhan:** *Montreal Gazette,* 16 May 1975

2251. As I look back, what I regret most was that I wasn't able to influence Johnson to abandon the war in Vietnam. Too see that war go on, to find him listening to people with such a completely wrong point of view. Every day there were those whispering in his ear, "No president ever lost a war." That was red meat for a Texan.—**W. Averell Harriman:** *Washington Post,* 7 December 1975

2252. Our mission was not to win terrain, or seize positions, but simply to kill: to kill Communists and to kill as many of them as possible. Stack 'em like cordwood. Victory was a high body-count, defeat a low kill-ratio, war a matter of arithmetic.—**Philip Joseph Caputo:** *A Rumor of War* (1977)

2253. Vietnam was what we had instead of happy childhoods.—**Michael Herr:** *Dispatches* (1977)

2254. Vietnam was as much a laboratory experiment as a war.—**John Pilger:** "Do You Remember Vietnam?" ATV Network production, 3 October 1978

2255. I used to see Vietnam as a war rather than a country.—**John Pilger:** "Do You Remember Vietnam?" ATV Network production, 3 October 1978

2256. The important point was that whatever errors America had made "we are so powerful [according to Secretary Kissinger] that Hanoi is simply unable to defeat us militarily" and must therefore eventually be forced to compromise.—**William Shawcross:** *Sideshow* (1979)

2257. Some of the critics viewed Vietnam as a morality play in which the wicked must be punished before the final curtain and where any attempt to salvage self-respect from the outcome compounded the wrong. I viewed it as a genuine tragedy. No one had a monopoly on anguish.—**Henry Kissinger:** *The White House Years* (1979)

2258. Kissinger brought peace to Vietnam the same way Napoleon brought peace to Europe: by losing.—**Joseph Heller:** *Good as Gold* (1979)

2259. I love the smell of napalm in the morning. It smells like victory.—**Francis Ford Coppola:** *Apocalypse Now* (1979 film, with John Milius)

2260. Vietnam presumably taught us that the United States could not serve as the world's policeman; it should also have taught us the dangers of trying to be the world's midwife to democracy when the birth is scheduled to take place under conditions of guerrilla war.—**Jeane Kirkpatrick:** *Commentary* (New York), November 1979

2261. It's time that we recognized that ours was in truth a noble cause.—**Ronald Reagan:** October 1980

2262. One of the hardest things for me to really adjust to in my mind was to step off an air-conditioned plane where I'd just watched a first-run movie and hear this stewardess say: "Have a nice war."—**James Webb:** Michael Maclear *Vietnam: The Ten Thousand Day War* (1981)

2263. There is the guilt all soldiers feel for having broken the taboo against killing, a guilt as old as war itself. Add to this the soldier's sense of shame for having fought in actions that resulted, indirectly or directly, in the deaths of civilians. Then pile on top of that an attitude of social opprobrium, an attitude that made the fighting man feel personally morally responsible for the war, and you get your proverbial walking time bomb.—**Philip Caputo:** 1982

2264. Vietnam was the first war ever fought without any censorship.—**William C. Westmoreland:** *Time*, 5 April 1982

2265. If he had "lost" Vietnam, he [Lyndon B. Johnson] told Doris Kearns years later, "there would be Robert Kennedy out in front leading the fight against me, telling everybody that I had betrayed John Kennedy's commitment to South Vietnam. That I had let a democracy fall into the hands of the Communists. That I was a coward. An unmanly man. A man without a spine. Oh, I could see it coming all right. Every night when I fell asleep I would see myself tied to the ground in the middle of a long, open space. In the distance I could hear the voices of thousands of people. They were all shouting and running toward me: 'Coward! Traitor! Weakling!'"—**Stanley Karnow:** *Vietnam: A History* (1983)

2266. Above all, Vietnam was a war that asked everything of a few and nothing of most in America.—**Myra Macpherson:** *Long Time Passing* (1984)

2267. No event in American history is more misunderstood than the Vietnam War. It was misreported then, and it is misremembered now.—**Richard M. Nixon:** *New York Times*, 28 March 1985

2268. Saigon was an addicted city, and we were the drug: the corruption of children, the mutilation of young men, the prostitution of women, the humiliation of the old, the division of the family, the division of the country—it had all been done in our name.... The French city ... had represented the opium stage of the addiction. With the Americans had begun the heroin phase.—**James Fenton:** *Granta* no 15, 1985

2269. The war was won on both sides: by the Vietnamese on the ground, by the Americans in the electronic mental space. And if the one side won an ideological and political victory, the other made *Apocalypse Now* and that has gone right around the world.—**Jean Baudrillard:** *America* (1986)

2270. I was proud of the youths who opposed the war in Vietnam because they were my babies.—**Benjamin Spock,** American pediatrician: *Times*, 2 May 1988

2271. All the wrong people remember Vietnam. I think all the people who remember it should forget it, and all the people who forgot it should remember it.—**Michael Herr,** American journalist: *Observer*, 15 January 1989

2272. In Vietnam, you went anywhere nerve or foolishness would take you.—**Tony Clifton,** foreign correspondent: on non-restrictive freedom to cover the war; *Newsweek*, 11 February 1991

2273. We acted according to what we thought were the principles and traditions of this nation.... We were wrong. We were terribly wrong.—**Robert S. McNamara:** speaking in Washington, April 1995

War and Peace

See also THE NATION: Patriotism; HISTORY: History; POLITICS AND GOVERNMENT: Foreign Policy

2274. The United States is not a nation to which peace is a necessity.—**President Grover**

Cleveland: Annual Message to Congress, 7 December 1896

2275. What the Spanish War began the World War accomplished: America became the world's banker and ceased to be the world's pioneer. —**Anna Louise Strong:** *I Change Worlds* (1935)

2276. The combination of a hatred of war and militarism with an innocent delight in playing soldiers is one of apparent contradictions of American life that one has to accept. —**Denis W. Brogan:** *The American Character* (1944)

2277. For Americans war is almost all of the time a nuisance, and military skill is a luxury like Mah-Jongg. But when the issue is brought home to them, war becomes as important, for the necessary period, as business or sport. And it is hard to decide which is likely to be the more ominous for the Axis, an American decision that this is sport, or that it is business. —**Denis W. Brogan:** *The American Character* (1944)

2278. We must be patient—making peace is harder than making war. —**Adlai Stevenson:** speech to Chicago Council on Foreign Relations, 21 March 1946

2279. When at peace they [Americans] are reluctant to think of the possibility of war. When at war they concentrate solely on winning the war, as if it were a grim football match, and refuse to worry about the peace which is the goal of war. —**Philip E. Mosely:** *Negotiating with the Russians* (1951)

2280. God and politicians willing, the United States can declare peace on the world, and win it. —**Ely Culbertson,** 1891–1955, American bridge player: Henry O. Dormann *The Speaker's Book of Quotations* (1987)

2281. Frankly, I'd like to see the government get out of war altogether and leave the whole field to private industry. —**Joseph Heller,** American novelist: *Catch-22* (1955)

2282. I think that Lincoln, Wilson, and F.D.R. were all carried into war by the power drive behind them—though they all must have had moments, Woodrow Wilson especially, when they hoped that it might be avoided. I don't believe that it is possible to be president and not be willing to lead the country into war. Nobody can get to be president who has not himself a

strong drive to power. —**Edmund Wilson:** letter to Barbara Deming, 11 April 1962; *Letters on Literature and Politics, 1912–1972* (1977)

2283. No country has suffered so much from the ruins of war while being at peace as the American. —**Edward Dahlberg:** *Alms for Oblivion* (1964)

2284. A European soldier, [Europeans complained in World War II] when he steals, will steal a package or even a carton of cigarettes. But Americans, nothing but a whole train and all of its contents will do! —**Ashley Montagu:** *The American Way of Life* (1967)

2285. All this stuff you heard about America not wanting to fight, wanting to stay out of the war, is a lot of horse dung. Americans, traditionally, love to fight. All real Americans love the sting of battle … Americans play to win all the time. I wouldn't give a hoot in hell for a man who lost and laughed. That's why Americans have never lost—and will never lose—a war, because the very thought of losing is hateful to Americans. —**George C. Scott:** as General George S. Patton, Jr., *Patton* (film, 1970)

2286. Very little is known about the War of 1812 because the Americans lost it. —**Eric Nicol:** Laurence J. Peter (ed.) *Peter's Quotations* (1977)

2287. Of the four wars in my lifetime, none came about because the US was too strong. —**Ronald Reagan:** *Observer*, 29 June 1980

2288. American boys should not be seen dying on the nightly news. Wars should be over in three days or less, or before Congress invokes the War Powers Resolution. Victory must be assured in advance. And the American public must be all for it from the outset. —**Evan Thomas:** *Time*, 7 April 1986

2289. To be a great president, you have to have a war. All the great presidents have had their wars. —**Admiral James Crowe:** 1990

2290. If America cannot win a war in a week, it begins negotiating with itself. —**William Safire:** *The New York Times*, 10 August 1990

2291. What makes war interesting for Americans is that we don't fight war on our soil, we don't have direct experience of it, so there's an openness about the meanings we give it.

—**Robert Dallek:** *New York Times*, 24 February 1991

2292. War for us is like a tabula rasa, a black slate which we can use to turn into a moral crusade, and that's what's happening now, particularly as a healing experience in relation to Vietnam.—**Robert Dallek:** *New York Times*, 24 February 1991

2293. America is addicted to wars of distraction.—**Barbara Ehrenreich:** *Times*, 22 April 1991

2294. The American approach to war is that it's like football, only with guns.—**David Evans:** *Chicago Tribune*, 9 June 1991

World War I (1914–18)

2295. We're going to try to get the boys out of the trenches before Christmas. I've chartered a ship, and some of us are going to Europe.—**Henry Ford:** statement, 1915

2296. Great War Ends Christmas Day. Ford To Stop It.—*New York Tribune:* 1915

2297. Wake up America!—**Augustus P. Gardner:** speech, 16 October 1916

2298. It must be a peace without victory.—**Woodrow Wilson:** speech, Senate, 22 January 1917

2299. The world must be made safe for democracy.—**Woodrow Wilson:** speech to the Congress asking for a declaration of war, 2 April 1917

2300. It is a war against all nations.—**Woodrow Wilson:** speech to the Congress asking for a declaration of war, 2 April 1917

2301. America has at one bound become a world-power in a sense she never was before.—**David Lloyd-George:** message to the American people on the signing of the war resolution, 6 Apr 1917

2302. The government will ... go on in the highly democratic method of conscripting American manhood for European slaughter.—**Emma Goldman,** American anarchist: *Mother Earth*, July 1917

2303. America is the prize amateur nation of the world. Germany is the prize professional nation.—**Woodrow Wilson:** speech to Officers of the Fleet, August 1917; John Dos Passos *Mr Wilson's War* (1962)

2304. We're here because we're here because we're here because we're here.—**Anonymous:** American song of World War I

2305. Once lead the American people into war, and they'll forget there ever was such a thing as tolerance. To fight you must be brutal and ruthless, and the spirit of ruthless brutality will enter into every fiber of our national life.—**Woodrow Wilson,** 1856–1924

2306. The war was won by the American spirit. You know what one of our American wits said, that it took only half as long to train an American army as any other, because you only had to train them to go one way.—**Woodrow Wilson:** speech, Kansas City, 6 September 1919

2307. All of you young people who served in the war. You are a lost generation. You have no respect for anything. You drink yourselves to death.—**Gertrude Stein,** 1874–1946, American author: remark to Ernest Hemingway; Ernest Hemingway *A Moveable Feast* (1964)

2308. If the Allies lost the war, the American loans would be lost also. In the last resort, the United States went to war so that America could remain prosperous and rich Americans could grow richer.—**A. J. P. Taylor:** *The First World War* (1963)

2309. It was said in the First World War that the French fought for their country, the British fought for freedom of the seas, and the Americans fought for souvenirs.—**Harry S Truman:** Margaret Truman *Harry S Truman* (1973)

World War II (1939–45)

2310. As long as Europe prepares for war, America must prepare for neutrality.—**Walter Lippmann:** *New York Herald Tribune*, 17 May 1934

2311. And while I am talking to you mothers and fathers, I give you one more assurance. I have said this before, but I shall say it again and again and again: Your boys are not going to be sent into any foreign wars.—**Franklin D. Roosevelt:** speech in Boston, 30 October 1940

2312. The best immediate defence of the United States is the success of Great Britain defending itself.—**Franklin D. Roosevelt:** press conference, 17 December 1940

2313. If we see that Germany is winning the war we ought to help Russia, and if Russia is winning we ought to help Germany, and in that way let them kill as many as possible.—**Harry S Truman:** when Russia was invaded by Germany; *New York Times*, 24 July 1941

2314. Never before have we had so little time in which to do so much.—**Franklin D. Roosevelt:** radio broadcast, 22 February 1942

2315. Americans love to fight. All real Americans love the sting of battle.—**George S. Patton,** American General: speech, Third Army, England, July 1944

2316. Overpaid, overfed, oversexed, and over here.—**Tommy Trinder,** British comedian: of American troops in Britain during World War II

2317. The two most serious miscalculations of the Second World War both concerned the Soviet Union: Hitler's miscalculations of Russia's military strength and Roosevelt's miscalculation of Russia's political ambition.—**Chester Wilmot:** *The Struggle for Europe* (1952)

2318. In the last war, United States soldiers were known as the most homesick army in the world.—**Frederick Martin:** Arthur Goodfriend *What Is America* (1954)

2319. In private the British and American commanders despised each other for lack of drive, attacking in insufficient strength and lack of appetite for combat.—**Dominick Graham** and **Shelford Bidwell:** *Tug of War: The Battle for Italy 1943–1945* (1986)

2320. American commanders were overtly romantic about the capability of their men and covertly disgusted at their actual achievements. —**Dominick Graham** and **Shelford Bidwell:** *Tug of War: The Battle for Italy 1943–1945* (1986)

2321. No one ever mentioned it, but thousands of men welcomed World War II as a way to escape their humdrum lives rather than a chance to fight for God and country.—**Art Buchwald:** *Leaving Home: A Memoir* (1993)

INTERNATIONAL RELATIONS

Canada

2322. If Canada did not exist it would be to the interest of the United States to invent her.

—**James Bryce,** 1838–1922: H. A. L. Fisher *An Unfinished Autobiography* (1940)

2323. Canada is a live country—live, but not, like the States, kicking.—**Rupert Brooke,** 1887–1915

2324. Saskatchewan is much like Texas—except it's more friendly to the United States. —**Adlai Stevenson,** 1900–65

2325. Geography has made us [America and Canada] neighbors. History has made us friends. Economics has made us partners. And necessity has made us allies. Those whom nature hath so joined together, let no man put asunder.—**John F. Kennedy:** Address to Canadian Parliament, Ottawa, 17 May 1961

2326. We are always watching Big Brother to see what trouble he might get us in—while at the same time protesting the fact that Big Brother is not watching us.—**Lester Pearson,** Prime Minister of Canada: commencement address at Notre Dame University; *New York Times,* 10 June 1963

2327. Americans assume Canada to be bestowed as a right and accept this bounty, as they do air, without thought or appreciation.—**Dean Acheson,** 1893–1971

2328. Canada was supposed to get British government, French culture, and American know-how. Instead it got French government, American culture, and British know-how. —**Lester Pearson,** 1897–1972, Canadian prime minister: *Economist,* 27 July 1991

2329. We tended to imagine Canada as a kind of vast hunting preserve convenient to the United States.—**Edmund Wilson:** *O Canada* (1965)

2330. A few Americans know Canada well, but many do not know it even a little. This irks us. Indeed a major irritant in our relations with the United States is the tendency of some Americans simply to take Canadians for granted. —**Lester Pearson:** *Foreign Affairs,* January 1965

2331. Canadians look down on the United States and consider it Hell. They are right to do so. Canada is to the United States what, in Dante's scheme, Limbo is to Hell.—**Irving Layton:** *The Whole Bloody Bird* (1969)

2332. Living next to you is like sleeping with an elephant. No matter how friendly and even-tempered the beast, one is affected by every twitch and grunt.—**Pierre Elliott Trudeau:** speech, 25 March 1969; *New York Times,* 26 March 1969

2333. Americans are benevolently ignorant about Canada, while Canadians are malevolently well informed about the United States. —**J. Bartlet Brebner**

2334. Perhaps the most striking thing about Canada is that it is not part of the United States.—**J. Bartlet Brebner**

2335. A Canadian is a fellow who has become a North American without becoming an American.—**Arthur L. Phelps**

2336. John Kenneth Galbraith and Marshall McLuhan are the two greatest modern Canadians the United States has produced.—**Anthony Burgess,** 1917–

2337. The Americans are our best friends, whether we like it or not.—**Robert Thompson:** Peter C. Newman *Home Country* (1973)

2338. A sentry between the United States and Canada would be about as appropriate as a fire extinguisher on top of the Great Pyramid. —**Vincent Massey**

2339. Canadians are generally indistinguishable from Americans, and the surest way of telling the two apart is to make the observation to a Canadian.—**Richard Staines**

2340. Canadians are Americans with no Disneyland.—**Margaret Mahy:** *The Changeover* (1984)

2341. If Canada invented the wheel, it would drag it on a sled to be marketed in the United States.—**Denzil Doyle:** *Globe & Mail's Report on Business* (Toronto), November 1985

2342. When times get tough, we [Canadians] get terribly pro–American and cost-conscious. When times get better, we get a little more uppity with the U.S.—**Professor Morton,** University of Toronto: *Forbes,* 16 May 1986

2343. Canadians shouldn't come down to Southern California and take jobs away from our Mexicans.—**Stanley Ralph Ross:** Robert Byrne *The Fourth 637 Best Things Anybody Ever Said* (1990)

2344. Historically, a Canadian is an American who rejects the Revolution.—**Northrop Frye,** 1912–91, Canadian literary critic: Connie Robertson (ed.) *The Wordsworth Dictionary of Quotations* (1996)

2345. Canadians are more polite when they are being rude than Americans are when they are being friendly. — **Edgar Z. Friedenberg,** 1921–

2346. If the general attitude of Canadians toward their mighty neighbor to the south could be distilled into a single phrase, that phrase would probably be "Oh, shut up." The Americans talked too much, mainly about themselves. Their torrid love affair with their own history and legend exceeded — painfully — the quasi-British Canadian idea of modesty and self-restraint. They were forever busting their buttons in spasms of insufferable yahoo pride or all too publicly agonizing over their crises. — **Bruce McCall:** *Thin Ice: Coming of Age in Canada* (1997)

2347. God Bless America, but God help Canada to put up with them! — **Anonymous**

Cuba

See also POLITICS AND GOVERNMENT: Cuban Missile Crisis

2348. Castro is without any question a remarkable man. I think it is important for Americans to understand that individuals who go into the mountains to lead a revolution are not motivated be economic considerations. If they were, they would be bank presidents and not revolutionaries. — **Henry Kissinger:** TV interview, May 1975

2349. The Cubans may be hostile to America, but they love Americans. — **Howard K. Smith:** *TV Guide*, 26 February 1977

2350. Castro couldn't even go to the bathroom unless the Soviet Union put the nickel in the toilet. — **Richard M. Nixon:** September 1980; Robert Sam Anson *Exile* (1984)

2351. Everything was blamed on Castro. Mudslides in California. The fact that you can't buy a decent tomato anymore. Was there an exceptionally high pollen count in Massapequa, Long Island, one day? It was Castro, exporting sneezes. — **Calvin Trillin:** syndicated column, 18 May 1986

England

See also LITERATURE AND LANGUAGE: Language; CULTURE AND MEDIA: Journalism

2352. The American is only the continuation of the English genius into new conditions, more or less propitious. — **Ralph Waldo Emerson:** *English Traits* (1856)

2353. An American whether he be embarked in politics, in literature, or in commerce, desires English admiration, English appreciation of his energy, and English encouragement. — **Anthony Trollope:** *North America* (1862)

2354. America's hatred of England is the hoop round the forty-four staves of the Union. — **John Hay:** 1890s; Rudyard Kipling *Something of Myself* (1937)

2355. An Englishman is a person who does things because they have been done before. An American is a person who does things because they haven't been done before. — **Mark Twain,** 1835–1910: Alex Ayers (ed.) *The Wit and Wisdom of Mark Twain* (1987)

2356. American hospitality will explain the difference between watermelon, honeydew, and casaba, while English hospitality consists of letting the lunch lie about for you to eat if you like. — **W. L. George:** *Hail Columbia!* (1921)

2357. I am American bred,
I have seen much to hate here — much to forgive,
But in a world where England is finished and dead,
I do not wish to live.
— **Alice Duer Miller,** American writer: *The White Cliffs* (1940)

2358. In England, is something goes wrong — say, if one finds a skunk in the garden — he writes to the family solicitor, who proceeds to take the proper measures; whereas in America, you telephone the fire department. Each satisfies a characteristic need; in the English, love of order, and legalistic procedure; and here in America what you like is something vivid, and red, and swift. — **Alfred North Whitehead:** 30 August 1941; Lucien Price (ed.) *Dialogues of A. N. Whitehead* (1954)

2359. Who am I now? An American? No, a New Yorker who opens his *Times* at the obit page.—**W. H. Auden,** 1907–73, British-born poet emigrated to America in 1939: "Prologue at 60," Edward Mendelston (ed.) *W. H. Auden: Collected Poems* (1991)

2360. You know there are no secrets in America. It's quite different in England, where people think of a secret as a shared relation between two people.—**W. H. Auden:** 16 March 1948; Alan Ansen (comp.) *The Table Talk of W. H. Auden* (1990)

2361. To Americans, English manners are far more frightening than none at all.—**Randall Jarrell:** *Pictures from an Institution* (1954)

2362. The Englishman wants to be recognized as a gentleman, or as some other suitable species of human being; the American wants to be considered a "good guy."—**Louis Kronenberger:** *Company Manners* (1954)

2363. The American mind, unlike the English, is not formed by books, but, as Carl Sandburg once said to me, by newspapers and the Bible.—**Van Wyck Brooks:** *Nation*, 14 August 1954

2364. Americans relate all effort, all work, and all of life itself to the dollar. Their talk is of nothing but dollars. The English seldom sit happily chatting for hours on end about pounds. In England, public business is its own reward, nobody would go into Parliament in order to become rich, neither do riches bring public appointments.—**Nancy Mitford:** *Noblesse Oblige* (1956)

2365. I did a picture in England one winter and it was so cold I almost got married.—**Shelley Winters,** American actress: *New York Times*, 29 April 1956

2366. England was the friend whose policy stood like a bulwark against Continental animosity to the ambitions of the American republic.—**Margaret Leech:** 1959

2367. We are American at puberty. We die French.—**Evelyn Waugh:** 18 July 1961; *The Diaries of Evelyn Waugh* (1976)

2368. England is my wife, America my mistress. It is very good sometimes to get away from one's wife.—**Cedric Hardwicke,** English actor: 1964

2369. The English are polite by telling lies. The Americans are polite by telling the truth. —**Malcolm Bradbury:** *Stepping Westward* (1965)

2370. Americans are taught that they won the war of 1812. British children are taught the opposite. Each nation believes that the other fired the first shot at Lexington. For many Americans the First World War really began in 1917 and was quickly won by American troops. The British, on the other hand, believe that they won the war almost single-handed.—*Times* (London): 10 February 1966

2371. America is a land whose center is nowhere; England one whose center is everywhere.—**John Updike:** 1969; *Picked Up Pieces* (1976)

2372. The Englishman is under no constitutional abligation to believe that all men are created equal. The American agony is therefore scarcely intelligible, like a saint's self-flagellation viewed by an atheist.—**John Updike,** 1932– : Connie Robertson (ed.) *The Wordsworth Dictionary of Quotations* (1996)

2373. We, my dear Mr. [Richard] Crossman, are Greeks in the Roman Empire. You will find the Americans much as the Greeks found the Romans—a great big, vulgar, bustling people, more vigorous than we are, but also more idle, with more unspoilt virtues but also more corrupt.—**Harold Macmillan,** 1894–1986: obituary, *Times*, 30 December 1986

2374. I've discovered that what we in England call drafts you in America call cross-ventilation. —**Hermione Gingold,** 1897–1987

2375. Among the virtues and vices that make up the British character, we have one vice, at least, that Americans ought to view with sympathy. For they appear to be the only people who share it with us. I mean our worship of the antique. I do not refer to beauty or even historical association. I refer to age, to a quantity of years.—**William Golding,** 1911–93, British author

2376. As always, the British especially shudder at the latest American vulgarity, and then they embrace it with enthusiasm two years later.—**Alistair Cooke:** *American Way*, March 1975

2377. People in America, when listening to radio, like to lean forward. People in Britain like to lean back.—**Alistair Cooke**, 1908–

2378. Why is it, do you suppose, that an Englishman is unhappy until he has explained America?—**E. B. White:** 1977

2379. Americans are a nation of salesmen just as the English are a nation of small shopkeepers.—**Ruth Rendell:** 1981

2380. Trousers—it's such a stumbling word. It epitomizes the British bumbling and inability to be streamlined and coherent. In the States they have pants and jeans, but in England we still have trousers.—**Roger Ruskin Spear**

2381. It seems that in the United States, Englishmen are regarded as pets, like budgies, that can almost speak American.—**Quentin Crisp**, 1908–99: Guy Kettelhack *The Wit and Wisdom of Quentin Crisp* (1984)

2382. Americans want to be loved; the English want to be obeyed.—**Quentin Crisp**

2383. In England, the system is benign and the people are hostile. In America, the people are friendly—and the system is brutal!—**Quentin Crisp:** *Guardian*, 23 October 1985

2384. Different cultures. You [the British] are too modest—in a very vain way. We [the Americans] are too busy—in a very humble way. —**Gore Vidal:** *Observer Magazine*, 15 November 1987

2385. Britain may imagine itself a new Greece to America's Rome.—**Alan Brinkley:** Christopher Hitchens *Blood, Class, and Nostalgia* (1990)

2386. That's the main trouble with the two nations: bad Brits are snobs, bad Americans are slobs.—**Peter Shaffer:** *Whom Do I Have the Honour of Addressing?* (1990)

2387. The sea was the beginning of English journeys; it was the end of American ones. —**Jonathan Raban:** *The Oxford Book of the Sea* (1992)

2388. Kipling is our first American writer. —**V. S. Pritchett,** 1900–97 English writer: obituary, *Independent*, 22 March 1997

2389. I do *detest* the Americans. They expect everyone to go to the devil at the same hectic pace as themselves. It takes hundreds of years to do it properly. Look at us [the English]. —**John Le Carré:** *The Tailor of Panama* (1996)

Europe

See also INDIVIDUAL: Life; WAR AND THE MILITARY: World War I; WAR AND THE MILITARY: World War II; POLITICS AND GOVERNMENT: Foreign Policy

2390. I called the New World into existence, to redress the balance of the Old.—**George Canning,** British Tory statesman: in the House of Commons, 12 December 1826; *The King's Message*

2391. People nowadays have such high hopes of America and the political conditions obtaining there that one might say the desires, at least the secret desires, of all enlightened Europeans are deflected to the west, like our magnetic needles.—**G. C. Lichtenberg,** 1765–99, German physicist and philosopher: R. J. Hollingdale (tr.) *Aphorisms* (1990)

2392. Let Americans disdain to be the instruments of European greatness.—**Alexander Hamilton:** November 1787

2393. It is the sincere wish of United America to have nothing to do with the political intrigues, or the squabbles of European nations. —**George Washington:** April 1793

2394. Europe has a set of primary interests, which to us have none, or a very remote relation. Hence, she must be engaged in frequent controversies, the causes of which are essentially foreign to our concerns.—**George Washington:** farewell address, 17 September 1796

2395. America is a fortunate country. She grows by the follies of our European nations. —**Napoleon Bonaparte,** 1769–1821

2396. I have ever deemed it fundamental for the United States never to take active part in the quarrels of Europe. Their political interests are entirely distinct from ours. Their mutual jealousies, their balance of power, their complicated alliances, their forms and principles of government, are all foreign to us. They are nations of eternal war.—**Thomas Jefferson:** letter to Pres. James Monroe, 11 June 1823

2397. Our first and fundamental maxim should be never to entangle ourselves in the broils of Europe. Our second, never to suffer Europe to intermeddle with cis–Atlantic affairs.—**Thomas Jefferson:** October 1823

2398. The American continents are henceforth not to be considered as subjects for future colonization by any European powers. In the wars of the European powers in matters relating to themselves we have never taken any part, nor does it comport with our policy so to do.—**James Monroe:** annual message to Congress, 2 December 1823

2399. One day we will cast out the passion for Europe, by the passion for America.—**Ralph Waldo Emerson:** *The Conduct of Life* (1860)

2400. We go to Europe to be Americanized. —**Ralph Waldo Emerson:** *The Conduct of Life* (1860)

2401. Can we never extract the tapeworm of Europe from the brain of our countrymen? —**Ralph Waldo Emerson:** *The Conduct of Life* (1860)

2402. Both the French and Italians dislike the Americans, and call them a *nation mal élevée.* —**Matthew Arnold:** letter to his sister, 21 June 1865

2403. For some reason or other, the European has rarely been able to see America except in caricature.—**James Russell Lowell:** 1869

2404. It's a complex fate, being an American, and one of the responsibilities it entails is fighting against a superstitious valuation of Europe. —**Henry James:** letter to Charles Eliot Norton, 4 February 1872; Leon Edel (ed.) *Henry James Letters* vol. 1 (1974)

2405. America has never quite forgiven Europe for having been discovered somewhat earlier in history than itself.—**Oscar Wilde:** *Court and Society Review* (London), April 1887

2406. Life in America is in most ways pleasanter, easier, simpler than in Europe.—**James Bryce:** *The American Commonwealth* (1888)

2407. As a rule we develop a borrowed European idea forward, and Europe develops a borrowed American idea backwards.—**Mark Twain, 1835–1910:** Charles Neider (ed.) *Complete Essays* (1963)

2408. In Europe life is histrionic and dramatized, and in America, except when it is trying to be European, it is direct and sincere.—**William Dean Howells:** *Harper's* (New York), September 1899

2409. The action of America upon the nerves and emotions of Europe is that of a power whose strength is known, but whose future course can only be guessed at. In a flash, she has expanded from a stay-at-home republic into a venturesome empire.—**Sydney Brooks:** *Atlantic Monthly*, November 1901

2410. Europe, the great American sedative. —**Henry James:** 1902

2411. It seems the natural thing for us to listen whilst the Europeans talk.—**William James:** *The Varieties of Religious Experience* (1902)

2412. In European Thought in general, as contrasted with American, vigor, life and originality have a kind of easy, professional utterance. American—on the other hand, is expressed in an eager amateurish way. A European gives a sense of scope, of survey, of consideration. An American is strained, sensational. One is artistic gold; the other is bullion.—**Wallace Stevens:** letter, 9 April 1906; Holly Stevens (ed.) *Letters of Wallace Stevens* (1967)

2413. Every time Europe looks across the Atlantic to see the American eagle, it observes only the rear end of an ostrich.—**H. G. Wells:** *America* (1907)

2414. America is God's Crucible, the great Melting-Pot where all the races of Europe are melting and re-forming.—**Israel Zangwill:** *The Melting Pot* (1908)

2415. Europe's the mayonnaise, but America supplies the good old lobster.—**D. H. Lawrence, 1885–1930:** *The Lovely Lady* (1933)

2416. When the war closed we were challenged with a peace-time choice between the American system of rugged individualism and a European philosophy of diametrically opposed doctrines—doctrines of paternalism and state socialism.—**Herbert Hoover:** speech in New York City, 22 October 1928

2417. The United States is the greatest single achievement of European civilization.—**Robert Balmain Mowat:** *The United States of America* (1938)

2418. The American lives even more for his goals, for the future, than the European.—**Albert Einstein,** 1879–1955

2419. The sorrows and disasters of Europe always brought fortune to America.—**Stephen Leacock,** 1869–1944

2420. The American character looks always as if it had just had a rather bad haircut, which gives it, in our eyes at any rate, a greater humanity than the European, which even among its beggars has an all too professional air.—**Mary McCarthy:** *Commentary* (New York), September 1947

2421. The immense popularity of American movies abroad demonstrates that Europe is the unfinished negative of which America is the proof.—**Mary McCarthy:** *Commentary,* September 1947

2422. It is the first time in history that a great power, instead of basing its policy on ruling by dividing, has consistently and resolutely backed the creation of a large Community uniting peoples previously apart.—**Jean Monnet:** of American foreign policy in relation to European Community, 1953; Francois Duchêne *Jean Monnet* (1994)

2423. I decided that Europeans and Americans are like men and women: they understand each other worse, and it matters less, than either of them suppose.—**Randall Jarrell:** *Pictures from an Institution* (1954)

2424. The economic vice of Europeans is avarice, while that of Americans is waste.—**Wystan Hugh Auden,** 1907–73: *Time,* 31 March 1980

2425. Until now when we have started to talk about the uniqueness of America we have almost always ended by comparing ourselves to Europe. Toward her we have felt all the attraction and repulsions of Oedipus.—**Daniel J. Boorstin:** *America and the Image of Europe* (1960)

2426. Europe has what we do not have yet, a sense of the mysterious and inexorable limits of life, a sense of tragedy. And we [Americans] have what they sorely need: a sense of life's possibilities.—**James Baldwin:** *Nobody Knows My Name* (1961)

2427. Somebody said that I am the last American living the tragedy of Europe.—**Ezra Pound,** 1885–1972, American poet: George Plimpton (ed.) *Writers at Work* Second Series (1963)

2428. The mediocre American is possessed by the Present, and the mediocre European is possessed by the Past.—**Wystan Hugh Auden:** *The Dyer's Hand and the Other Essays* (1963)

2429. The civilization whose absence drove Henry James to Europe.—**Gore Vidal:** *Two Sisters* (1970)

2430. After one week [visiting Austria] I couldn't wait to go back to the United States. Everything was much more pleasant in the United States, because of the mentality of being open-minded, always positive. Everything you want to do in Europe is just, "No way. No one has ever done it." They haven't any more the desire to go out to conquer and achieve; I realized that I had much more the American spirit.—**Arnold Schwarzenegger**

2431. It was his optimism that Freud bequeathed to America and it was the optimism of our youthfulness, our freedom from the sterner, sadder tradition of Europe which enabled us to seize his gift.—**Karl A. Menninger,** 1893–

2432. I met a lot of people in Europe. I even encountered myself.—**James Baldwin,** 1924–87

2433. There are a whole group of people in Europe who are constantly anti–American, who have never forgiven us for the Marshall Plan.—**General Vernon A. Walters,** 1917–

2434. Europeans are aware of the difficulties of constructing a constitutional republic and keeping it going through assassinations, civil wars, world wars. So they do appreciate what the United States is and what it means to the rest of the world. We [Americans] have embodied the democratic ideal in a living complex, heterogenous society.—**William Lee Miller:** 1975

2435. The Yanks have colonized our subconscious.—**Wim Wenders,** German filmmaker: *Kings of the Road* (film), 1976

2436. From the moment of its discovery ... America has been, sometimes quite literally, the creation of European wishful thinking.—**J. Martin Evans:** *America: The View From Europe* (1976)

2437. Time passes in America and Asia; in Europe, history occurs.—**John Updike:** 1976

2438. It's interesting that more European communities have managed to survive in a pure form in America, and not in Europe.—**Ruth Prawer Jhabvala:** *Times,* 13 July 1978

2439. Europe was created by history. America was created by philosophy.—**Margaret Thatcher,** 1925–

2440. Europeans used to say Americans were puritanical. Then they discovered that we were not puritans. So now they say we are obsessed with sex.—**Mary McCarthy,** 1912–89: Abby Adams *An Uncommon Scold* (1989)

2441. I've come to think of Europe as a hardcover book, America as the paperback version.—**Don Delillo:** *The Names* (1982)

2442. Europe and the U.K. are yesterday's world. Tomorrow is in the United States.—**Tiny Rowland:** *Observer,* 16 January 1983

2443. In America everything goes and nothing matters, while in Europe nothing goes and everything matters.—**Philip Roth:** *Time,* November 1983

2444. Dress impressively like the French, speak with authority like the Germans, have blond hair like the Scandinavians and speak of no American presidents except Lincoln, Roosevelt and Kennedy.—**Sylvaine Rouy Neves:** on how to gain respect while traveling in Europe; *New York Times,* 30 September 1984

2445. Americans are uneasy with their possessions, guilty about power, all of which is difficult for Europeans to perceive because they are themselves so truly materialistic, so versed in the use of power.—**Joan Didion,** 1934– : Robert Andrews *The Concise Columbia Dictionary of Quotations* (1987)

2446. Most Americans live in small towns and

think Europe is fully of dirty despicable foreigners, which is ironic because America is a land of foreigners.—**Bernard Falk:** BBC-TV, April 1986; *Travel Weekly,* 1 May 1986

2447. Europeans are in love with the American dream. It's like one hundred years ago, but the cowboys have motorcycles and Cadillacs.—**Philippe Cotton:** explaining why Europeans are opening restaurants in America in the 1980s; Henry O. Dormann *The Speaker's Book of Quotations* (1987)

2448. The confrontation between America and Europe reveals not so much a rapprochement as a distortion, an unbridgeable rift. There isn't just a gap between us, but a whole chasm of modernity.—**Jean Baudrillard,** French semiologist: *America* (1986)

2449. America and its demons, Europe and its ghosts.—*Le Monde:* Robert I. Fitzhenry *The Harper Book of Quotations* (1993)

2450. In my lifetime Europe has been the source of our problems, not the source of our solutions. It's America and Britain that saved the world.—**Margaret Thatcher:** *Saga Magazine,* September 1998

2451. Every president is a caricature in Europe until his first trip.—**Andrew Card,** White House chief of staff: acknowledging George W. Bush's uncertain reputation among European leaders; *Time,* 25 June 2001

France

2452. Far less envy in America than in France, and far less wit.—**Stendhal:** *Love* (1822)

2453. Good Americans, when they die, go to Paris.—**Thomas Gold Appleton,** 1812–84: Oliver Wendell Holmes, Sr., *The Autocrat of the Breakfast-Table* (1858)

2454. A joke in Chicago is a riddle in Paris.—**Mark Twain,** 1835–1910: E. Fisher *Abroad with Mark Twain and Eugene Field* (1922)

2455. DEJEUNER, n. The breakfast of an American who has been in Paris. Variously pronounced.—**Ambrose Bierce:** *The Devil's Dictionary* (1911)

2456. The best of America drifts to Paris. The American in Paris is the best American. It is more fun for an intelligent person to live in an intelligent country. France has the only two things toward which we drift as we grow older—intelligence and good manners.—**F. Scott Fitzgerald:** *New York World*, 3 April 1927

2457. America is my country and Paris is my home town.—**Gertrude Stein:** *An American and France* (1936)

2458. The American arrives in Paris with a few French phrases he has culled from a conversational guide or picked up from a friend who owns a beret.—**Fred Allen**, 1894–1956: Art Buchwald *Paris After Dark* (1954)

2459. Paris seems to be full of American girls who are hiding from their mothers.—**James Thurber**, 1894–1961: *Credits and Curios* (1962)

2460. One becomes aware in France, after having lived in America, that sex pervades the air. It's there all around you, like a fluid.—**Henry Miller:** *Paris Review*, Summer 1961

2461. We are all Americans at puberty; we die French.—**Evelyn Waugh**, English writer: *Diary*, July 1961

2462. Paris is where the American tourist speaks French and then explains it in English.—**Anonymous:** Evan Esar (ed.) *20,000 Quips & Quotes* (1968)

2463. Every French town has an Avenue Victor Hugo. We [in America] never have Mark Twain Street.—**Barbara Tuchman:** *New York Times*, 28 February 1979

2464. The ten Frenchmen journeyed to America despite warnings from their mothers that they would be mugged within five minutes of their arrival in New York and mowed down by gangsters in Chicago—provided, of course, that they were not scalped by Indians along the way [or captured by] crowds of American women waiting at the airport to get their hands on a Frenchman.—**William E. Geist:** *New York Times*, 20 April 1985

2465. The American goes to Paris, always has, and comes back and tells his neighbor, always does, how exorbitant and inhospitable it is, how rapacious and selfish and unaccommodating and unresponsive it is, how dirty and noisy it is—and the next summer his neighbor goes to Paris.—**Milton Mayer:** *New York Times*, 9 June 1985

2466. To be an American is an ideal, while to be a Frenchman is a fact.—**Carl Friedrich:** *Time*, 9 November 1987

2467. How do the French see America? As an attractive, animated drawing that trends to be simplistic, just like any image that one people conjures up about another. Pell-mell you would doubtless see the landing of the GIs in Normandy, Roosevelt, Ike, and Kennedy, Wall Street, cavalcades of Indians in the Far West, Al Capone, Marilyn Monroe, Marlon Brando, Muhammad Ali, pretty majorettes, *West Side Story*, bourbon and Coca-Cola, man's first steps on the moon—with a musical background of Louis Armstrong and Duke Ellington.—**Valéry Giscard d'Estaing**, 1926– , French politician: Louis E. Boone (ed.) *Quotable Business* (1992)

2468. Frenchmen have a peculiar sense of humor; Americans find this out when they try to talk to them in French.—**Anonymous**

2469. Face-to-face is better than fax to fax … and nowhere is it more true than dealings between the French and ourselves.—**Pamela Harriman,** US ambassador to France: *Vanity Fair*, February 1994

Mexico

2470. Poor Mexico! So far from God and so close to the United States.—**Porfirio Díaz,** 1830–1915: attrib.; John S. D. Eisenhower *The U.S. War with Mexico 1846–1848* (1989)

2471. Mexicans have always asked themselves why a people so close to God should be so near the United States.—**Carlos Fuentes:** *W*, 29 October 1976

2472. The U.S.–Mexican border *es una herida abierta* where the Third World grates against the first and bleeds. And before a scab forms it hemorrhages again, the lifeblood of two worlds merging to form a third country—a border culture.—**Gloria Anzaldúa:** *Borderlands/La Frontera: The New Mestiza* (1987)

Panama

2473. It's not like they make or grow anything. The whole country is based on international banking and a canal the United States can take back any time it wants with one troop of Boy Scouts.—**P. J. O'Rourke,** 1947–   : Jon Winokur (ed.) *The Portable Curmudgeon Redux* (1992)

Russia

See also POLITICS AND GOVERNMENT: Cold War; POLITICS AND GOVERNMENT: Cuban Missile Crisis; POLITICS AND GOVERNMENT: Foreign Policy

2474. To American productivity, without which this war would have been lost.—**Joseph Stalin:** toast, Teheran, Iran, 1943; Lois and Alan Gordon *American Chronicle* (1987)

2475. What we ought to do is to send up a flight of a thousand B-29s and drop a million Sears, Roebuck catalogs all over Russia.—**Bruce Barton,** American advertising tycoon: late 1940s; Alistair Cook *America* (1973)

2476. I have always liked Americans, and the sort of man that likes Americans is liable to like Russians.—**Claud Cockburn:** *Crossing the Line* (1958)

2477. We have beaten you to the moon, but you have beaten us in sausage making.—**Nikita Khrushchev:** Des Moines, Iowa, 1959; Lois and Alan Gordon *American Chronicle* (1987)

2478. The Russians can give you arms, but only the United States can give you a selection.—**Anwar El-Sadat:** *Newsweek,* 13 January 1975

2479. One of the most serious problems in planning against American doctrine is that the Americans do not read their manuals nor do they feel any obligations to follow their doctrine.—**From a Russian document**

2480. The dollar is Russia's national currency now, the rouble is just a sweetie paper. We've handed our sword to America.—**Alexander Rutskoi,** Russian politician: *Newsweek,* 1994

2481. My analysis of modern history shows that when Republicans were heading the U.S. administration, U.S.–Soviet relations were not harmed.—**Vladimir Putin,** Russian president: *Time,* 8 January 2001

2482. Our countries have stopped hating each other.—**Vladimir Putin:** *Newsweek,* 26 November 2001

World

See also THE AMERICAN PEOPLE: Americans Abroad; WAR AND THE MILITARY: World War I; WAR AND THE MILITARY: World War II; POLITICS AND GOVERNMENT: Cold War; POLITICS AND GOVERNMENT: Foreign Policy

2483. We are the pioneers of the world; the advance guard sent on through the wilderness of untried things to break a new path in the New World that is ours. In our youth is our strength; in our inexperience, our wisdom.—**Herman Melville:** *White-Jacket* (1850)

2484. The less America looks abroad, the grander its promise.—**Ralph Waldo Emerson,** 1803–82

2485. It is, I think, an indisputable fact that Americans are, as Americans, the most self-conscious people in the world, and the most addicted to the belief that the other nations of the earth are in a conspiracy to under value them.—**Henry James:** *Hawthorne* (1879)

2486. We Americans have no commission from God to police the world.—**President Benjamin Harrison:** address to Congress, 1888

2487. We Americans bear the ark of liberties of the world.—**Mark Twain,** 1835–1910

2488. To me Americanism means an imperative duty to be nobler than the rest of the world.—**Meyer London,** American labor leader: speech to Congress, 18 January 1916

2489. I wish all Americans would realize that American politics is world politics.—**Theodore Roosevelt,** 1858–1919

2490. It isn't the oceans which cut us off from the world—it's the American way of looking at things.—**Henry Miller:** *The Air-Conditioned Nightmare* (1945)

2491. Instead of leading the world, America appears to have resolved to buy it.—**Thomas Mann:** letter, 1947; Joseph R. Conlin *Morrow Book of Quotations in American History* (1984)

2492. America shudders at anything alien, and when it wants to shut its mind against any man's ideas it calls him a foreigner.—**Max Lerner:** *Actions and Passions* (1949)

2493. Some of the more fatuous flag-waving Americans are in danger of forgetting that you can't extract gratitude as you would extract a tooth; that unless friendship is freely given, it means nothing and less than nothing.—**Max Lerner:** *Actions and Passions* (1949)

2494. We cannot reform the world. Uncle Sugar is as dangerous a role for us to play as Uncle Shylock.—**John F. Kennedy:** speech to Boston Chamber of Commerce, 19 November 1951

2495. Whatever America hopes to bring to pass in the world must first come to pass in the heart of America.—**Dwight D. Eisenhower:** address, 20 January 1953

2496. With the supermarket as our temple and the singing commercial as our litany, are we likely to fire the world with an irresistible vision of America's exalted purpose and inspiring way of life?—**Adlai Stevenson:** *Wall Street Journal*, 1 June 1960

2497. The trouble with the Americans is that they hate to lose face.—**Jawarharlal Nehru,** 1889–1964: Colin Bingham (ed.) *Wit and Wisdom* (1982)

2498. The U.S. cannot "lead": for that she is, paradoxically, far too powerful.—**John Mander:** *Encounter*, September 1965

2499. We have earned the slogan, "Yanks, go home!"—**Edmund Wilson:** *Europe Without Baedeker* (1967)

2500. In April 1917 the illusion of isolation was destroyed, America came to the end of innocence, and of the exuberant freedom of bachelor independence. That the responsibilities of world power have not made us happier is no surprise. To help ourselves manage them, we have replaced the illusion of isolation with a new illusion of omnipotence.—**Barbara Tuchman:** *New York Times Magazine*, 5 May 1967

2501. The genius of you Americans is that you never make any clear-cut stupid moves, only complicated stupid moves that leave us scratching our heads wondering if we might possibly have missed something.—**Gamal Abdel Nasser,** 1918–70

2502. Unlike Rome, we have not exploited our empire. On the contrary, our empire has exploited us, making enormous drains on our resources and energies.—**Ronald Steel:** *Imperialists and Other Heroes: A Chronicle of the American Empire* (1971)

2503. The United States is the glory, jest, and terror of mankind.—**James M. Minifie,** 1900–74, Canadian broadcaster: Al Purdy (ed.) *The New Romans* (1988)

2504. The United States has the power to destroy the world, but not the power to save it alone.—**Margaret Mead,** 1901–78: Laurence J. Peter *Peter's Quotations* (1977)

2505. America is the longest argument in the world.—**Bill Moyers**

2506. It bewilders Americans to be hated.—**Lance Morrow:** *Observer*, 13 January 1980

2507. We Americans cannot save the world. Even Christ failed at that. We Americans have our hands full trying to save ourselves.—**Edward Abbey:** *Words From the Land* (1981)

2508. What you have to do is enter the fiction of America, enter America as fiction. It is, indeed, on this fictive basis that it dominates the world.—**Jean Baudrillard:** *America* (1986)

2509. What the United States does best is to understand itself. What it does worst is understand others.—**Carlos Fuentes:** *Time*, 16 June 1986

2510. The problem is that Americans would like to be independent of the rest of the world …. Except the world ain't that way.—**Ben Bova,** 1932–

2511. To the United States the Third World often takes the form of a black woman who has been made pregnant in a moment of passion and who shows up one day in the reception room on the forty-ninth floor threatening to make a scene. The lawyers pay the woman off, sometimes uninformed guards accompany her to the elevators.—**Lewis H. Lapham:** *Money and Class in America* (1988)

2512. So everyone's a fool outside their own country. America, having emerged from World War II as the only country with any money left, got a twenty-year head start on being fools overseas.—**P. J. O'Rourke:** *Observer*, 15 January 1989

2513. America is the world's policeman, all right—a big, dumb, mick flatfoot in the middle of the one thing cops dread most, a "domestic disturbance."—**P. J. O'Rourke:** *Rolling Stone*, August 1990

2514. Americans don't have friends, they have interests.—**Panamanian government official:** "All Things Considered," National Public Radio, 19 December 1990

2515. The world has always felt a long way away to Americans. Its important battles have always been internal, its most feared enemies within.—**Salman Rushdie:** *Independent on Sunday*, 10 February 1991

2516. If America does not wish to end her days in the same nursing home as Britannia she had best end this geobabble about new world orders. Our war, the Cold War, is over. It is time for America to come home.—**Patrick Buchanan:** *Observer*, 15 December 1991

2517. America must be the teacher of democracy, not the advertiser of the consumer society. It is unrealistic for the rest of the world to reach the American living standard.—**Mikhail Gorbachev:** *Parade*, 23 January 1994

2518. America is the number one killer of people; a superpower that the world has never seen before in its history. America made it cool to be violent.—**Ice Cube:** *New Musical Express* (London), 1994

2519. Each American embassy comes with two permanent features—a giant anti–American demonstration and a giant line for American visas. Most demonstrators spend half their time burning Old Glory and the other half waiting for green cards.—**P. J. O'Rourke**, 1947–

POLITICS AND GOVERNMENT

Acheson, Dean (1893–1971), statesman

2520. Washington's number 1 number 2 man. —**Anonymous**

2521. Not only did he not suffer fools gladly; he did not suffer them at all.—**Lester Pearson,** Canadian statesman: *Time*, 25 October 1971

2522. His career was a text book example of the rise of a patrician in the snug embrace of the American establishment.—*Time*: 25 October 1971

2523. Smarter than most of his colleagues in the Truman cabinet, but not smart enough to hide it.—**James B. Reston:** *Deadline* (1991)

Adams, John Quincy (1767–1848), 6th president (1825–29)

2524. A man must be a born fool who voluntarily engages in controversy with Mr. Adams on a question of fact. I doubt whether he was ever mistaken in his life.—**Henry Clay:** 1823

2525. He has peculiar powers as an assailant, and almost always, even when attacked, gets himself into that attitude by making war upon his accuser; and he has, withal, an instinct for the jugular and the carotid artery, as unerring as that of any carnivorous animal.—**Rufus Choate,** 1799–1859: Samuel Gilman Brown *Memoir of Rufus Choate* (1862)

2526. He is no literary old gentleman, but a bruiser, and loves the melee.—**Ralph Waldo Emerson,** 1803–82: *Journal* (1909)

2527. Adams was a short, stout, bald, brilliant and puritanical twig off a short, stout, bald, brilliant and puritanical tree. Little wonder that he took the same view of the office of president as his father.—**Alfred Steinberg:** *The First Ten* (1967)

Bush, George (1924–   ), 41st president (1989–93)

2528. Just a tweedier version of Ronald Reagan.—**John B. Anderson:** *New York Times Magazine*, 17 February 1980

2529. The unpleasant sound emitting from [vice-president] Bush as he traipses from one conservative gathering to another is a thin, tinny "arf"—the sound of a lap-dog.—**George F. Will:** *Washington Post*, 30 January 1986

2530. There are things we can do to give us a little more attention…. I've got to look more frantic.—**George Bush:** speaking to his aides, 1987

2531. What's wrong with being a boring kind of guy?—**George Bush:** *Daily Telegraph*, 28 April 1988

2532. He's the kind of guy you'd like to have around when you want to be alone. With a little effort he could become an anonymity.—**Richard Little:** TV program on night of presidential election, 9 November 1988

2533. Let the others have the charisma. I've got the class.—**George Bush:** comment in California during presidential campaign; *Guardian*, 3 December 1988

2534. We've had triumphs, we've made mistakes, we've had sex.—**George Bush:** of the Reagan–Bush administration; speech at College of Southern Idaho, 6 May 1988; *International Herald Tribune*, 13 May 1988

2535. Poor George, he can't help it—he was born with a silver foot in his mouth.—**Ann Richards:** address to Democratic National Convention; *New York Times*, 19 July 1988

2536. I want a kinder, gentler nation.—**George Bush:** acceptance speech for presidential nomination, New Orleans, 18 August 1988

2537. I'm going to be so much better a president for having been at the CIA that you're not going to believe it.—**George Bush**

2538. A comma in an easy chair.—**Peggy Noonan,** speechwriter: on working with Bush; *Washington Times*, 18 January 1989

2539. All hat and no cattle.—**John B. Connally,** governor of Texas: on president Bush's claim of being a Texan; *New York Times*, 14 February 1989

2540. I will never apologize for the United States of America—I don't care what the facts are.—**George Bush:** said after the *Vincennes* shot down an Iranian airliner; *Newsweek*, 15 August 1989

2541. Gerald Ford without the pizzazz.—**Pat Paulsen:** Robert Byrne *The Fourth 637 Best Things Anybody Ever Said* (1990)

2542. At the moment, he would love to save the planet, though not if it means offending General Motors.—**Simon Hoggart:** *Observer*, 10 December 1989

2543. Bush talked to us like we were a bunch of morons and we ate it up. Can you imagine, the Pledge of Allegiance, read my lips—can you imagine such crap in this day and age? —**John Updike**: *Rabbit at Rest* (1990)

2544. I do not like broccoli, and I haven't liked it since I was a little kid and my mother made me eat it. And I'm president of the United States, and I'm not going to eat any more broccoli! —**George Bush**: *New York Times*, 23 March 1990

2545. He's nice enough not to want to be associated with a nasty remark but not nice enough not to make it. Lacking the courage of one's nastiness does not make one nice. —**Michael Kinsley**: *Time*, 16 July 1990

2546. George Bush has met more foreign heads of state than I have. But a substantial number of them were dead. —**Jesse Jackson**, 1941–

2547. You may think the president is all-powerful, but he is not. He needs a lot of guidance from the Lord. —**Barbara Bush**

2548. I'll be glad to reply to or dodge your questions, depending on what I think will help our election most. —**George Bush**

2549. A toothache of a man. —**Jim Hightower**

2550. I'm conservative, but I'm not a nut about it. —**George Bush**

2551. The only American statesman whose portrait is an authentic classic of Western Art, being of course by Paul Klee and entitled *The Twittering Machine*. —**Murray Kempton** 1917–

2552. You cannot be president of the United States if you don't have faith. Remember Lincoln, going to his knees in times of trial in the Civil War and all that stuff. —**George Bush**

2553. A cross between Rambo and Mary Poppins. —**Peter Fenn**

2554. But let me tell you, this gender thing is history. You're looking at a guy who sat down with Margaret Thatcher across the table and talked about serious issues. —**George Bush**

2555. Every woman's first husband. —**Barbara Ehrenreich** 1941– , and **Jane O'Reilly** 1936–

2556. It's no exaggeration to say that the undecideds could go one way or another. —**George Bush**

2557. The national twit. —**Michael Kinsley**

2558. It's a very good question, very direct, and I'm not going to answer it. —**George Bush**

2559. [Bush] has the look about him of someone who might sit up and yip for a Dog Yummie. —**Mike Royko** 1932–

2560. My theory is that [Bush] has had to tell so many lies—and has such a hard time remembering them—that he sounds dyslexic. —**Gore Vidal**, 1925–

2561. I have opinions of my own—strong opinions—but I don't always agree with them. —**George Bush**

2562. Bush thinks a domestic policy is how much he pays his maid. —**Hank Morris**: *New York Times*, 22 January 1992

2563. Bush's mistake was to run a big-band campaign in a rock'n'roll country. —**Ralph Whitehead**: on losing the presidential election; 1992

2564. A weaseling pragmatist devoid of principle. —**William Safire**: 1992

2565. Patrician, not folksy, and he clanks falsely when he puts on Joe Sixpack nonairs. —**William Safire**: *New York Times*, 18 October 1992

2566. You know, there are a lot of would-be governors of Texas sitting around today who never took the opportunity to get into a race when the time was right. If George is good at anything, it's timing. —**Laura Bush**: 1994

2567. Lincoln is honest, Carter is weak, Reagan is decent but doddering. Bush is a wimp. —**Michael Kelly**: *New York Times*, 31 July 1994

2568. I confess I'm no expert in that [technological know-how]. I just learned how to forward Monica Lewinsky jokes to someone else. —**George Bush**: at a tech convention in Las Vegas; *Newsweek*, 4 June 2001

Bush, George W. (1946–), 43rd president (2001–)

2569. People make suggestions on what to say all the time. I'll give you an example; I don't read what's handed to me. People say, 'Here, here's your speech, or here's an idea for a speech.' They're changed. Trust me.—**George W. Bush:** 2000

2570. This is Preservation Month. I appreciate preservation. It's what you do when you run for president. You gotta preserve.—**George W. Bush:** 2000

2571. I don't make any apologies for what I do on the campaign trail.—**George W. Bush:** 2000

2572. It's exciting; I don't know whether I'm going to win or not. I think I am. I do know I'm ready for the job. And, if not, that's just the way it goes.—**George W. Bush:** asked by a Des Moines, Iowa fifth-grader how it felt to run for president, 2000

2573. I am the right.—**George W. Bush:** campaigning in South Carolina, 2000

2574. He was wearing cowboy boots and dirty jeans and was chewing tobacco that was drooling out of his mouth.—**Andrew Card,** chief of staff-in-waiting to George W. Bush: recalling their first meeting in 1979; *Time*, 11 December 2000

2575. Choosing George W. Bush is like writing a restaurant review after you've ordered your meal but before it has been served.—**Susan J. Berlin:** *Time*, 29 January 2001

2576. And to the C students, I say, you, too, can be president of the United States.—**George W. Bush:** a C student himself, receiving an honorary degree from Yale, his alma mater; *Newsweek*, 4 June 2001

2577. The common European perception of Bush is of a shallow, arrogant, gun-loving, abortion-hating, Christian fundamentalist Texan buffoon.—**A senior administration official:** *Newsweek*, 18 June 2001

2578. I have made this decision with great care, and I pray it is the right one.—**George W. Bush:** announcing that he will allow limited federal funding for stem-cell research; *Newsweek*, 20 August 2001

2579. I have never felt more confident about something. I believe a lot of it has to do with the prayers of the people.—**George W. Bush:** *Newsweek*, 3 December 2001

Carter, Jimmy (1924–), 39th president (1977–81)

2580. Your typical smiling, brilliant, backstabbing, bull-shitting, Southern nut cutter.—**Lane Kirkland:** *New Times*, 3 September 1976

2581. I've looked on a lot of women with lust. I've committed adultery in my heart many times. This is something God recognizes I will do—and I have done it—and God forgives me for it.—**Jimmy Carter:** *Playboy*, November 1976

2582. Jimmy Carter as president is like Truman Capote marrying Dolly Parton. The job is just too big for him.—**Richard Little,** 1932– : attrib.; Fred Metcalf *The Penguin Dictionary of Modern Humorous Quotations* (1986)

2583. Jimmy's basic problem is that he's super cautious. He looks before and after he leaps.—**Joey Adams:** *New York Post*, 1978

2584. I don't know what people have got against Jimmy Carter. He's done nothing.—**Bob Hope:** 2 November 1980

2585. He's a great ex-president. It's a shame he couldn't have gone directly to the ex-presidency.—**Thomas Mann:** *Newsweek*, 27 June 1994

2586. I never really had any affinity for politics. I've always looked on politics as a means to an end. It has never been a natural part of my life.—**Jimmy Carter:** *Guardian*, 7 February 1998

CIA

2587. The CIA claims that secrecy is necessary to hide what it's doing from the enemies of the United States. I claim that the real reason for secrecy is to hide what the CIA is doing from the American people.—**Philip Agee:** *Playboy*, August 1975

2588. No American who works for the CIA is a spy. A spy is a foreign agent who commits treason.—**Jim Keehner,** CIA psychologist: *New Times*, 1976

2589. It had all the earmarks of a CIA operation; the bomb killed everybody in the room except the intended target.—**William F. Buckley,** 1925–

2590. Disinformation is most effective in a very narrow context.—**Frank Snepp,** former CIA agent: *Christian Science Monitor*, 26 February 1985

2591. We have slain a large dragon, but now we must live in a jungle filled with a bewildering variety of poisonous snakes, and in many ways the dragon was easier to keep track of. —**R. James Woolsey,** CIA director: on the CIA after the Cold War; *Forbes*, 25 October 1993

2592. Absolute secrecy corrupts absolutely. —**Fred Hitz,** the Inspector General of the CIA: *New York Times*, 30 July 1995

Clinton, Bill (1946–), 42nd president (1993–2000)

2593. When I was in England I experimented with marijuana a time or two, and I didn't like it. I didn't inhale.—**Bill Clinton:** TV debate with Jerry Brown; *New York Times*, 30 March 1992

2594. The Prince of sleaze.—**Jerry Brown:** 1992

2595. Here sits America, with no appetite and in the wrong restaurant, served up a costly, tasteless, warmed-over dish it didn't order and cannot send back.—**William Safire:** on sexual harassment charges against Clinton; *New York Times*, 5 May 1994

2596. The only focus is the unfocusability. —**Maureen Dowd:** *US News & World Report*, 9 January 1995

2597. The president has kept all the promises he intended to keep.—**George Stephanopolous,** Clinton's aide

2598. I'm not going to have some reporters pawing through our papers. We are the president.—**Hillary Clinton,** 1947–

2599. The sexually charged atmosphere of the White House has lit a thousand points of lust. —**Hugh Hefner,** Playboy founder: on Clinton–Lewinsky sex scandal; *Playboy*, May 1998

2600. Indeed I did have a relationship with Ms Lewinsky that was not appropriate. In fact it was wrong. Even presidents have private lives. —**Bill Clinton:** broadcast to the nation, 17 August 1998

2601. America is a strange country. Most pornographic films are made here, and yet you have the president of the United States on trial for having an affair. Incredible.—**Catherine Deneuve,** French actress: on Clinton–Lewinsky sex scandal; *Time*, 17 August 1998

2602. Clinton smoked marijuana but did not inhale. He had an inappropriate relationship with a woman but did not have sex. He lied but did not commit perjury. So, what else did he not do, this self-defined innocent sinner?—**Lida Bates:** *Newsweek*, 12 October 1998

2603. He is an enormously gifted and richly qualified leader for our nation, but someone who is exasperatingly stupid in his personal life.—**Mike McCurry,** former White House spokesman: *Time*, 2 November 1998

2604. Mr Clinton does not have the strength of character to be a war criminal.—**Henry Kissinger:** *Independent*, 16 January 1999

2605. We elected a president, not a pope. —**Barbra Streisand:** to journalists at the White House, 5 February 1998; BBC Radio 4, 6 February 1998

2606. In his final desperate bid for a place in history, the Commander-in-Chief is in danger of finding he's got all the qualities of leadership except followers.—**Mark Steyn:** on Clinton and Kosovo; *Spectator*, 17 April 1999

2607. A hard dog to keep on the porch.—**Hillary Clinton:** *Guardian*, 2 August 1999

2608. He is a great communicator. The trouble is he has absolutely nothing to communicate.—**Margaret Thatcher:** Iain Dale (ed.) *Memories of Maggie* (2000)

2609. The word "scandal" has been thrown around here like a clanging teapot for seven years.—**Bill Clinton:** *Time*, 10 July 2000

2610. I may not have been the greatest president, but I've had the most fun eight years.—**Bill Clinton:** *Newsweek*, 11 December 2000

Cold War

See also INTERNATIONAL RELATIONS: Cuba; INTERNATIONAL RELATIONS: Russia; INTERNATIONAL RELATIONS: World

2611. Let us not be deceived—we are today in the midst of a cold war.—**Bernard Baruch,** American financier and presidential adviser: speech to South Carolina Legislature, 16 April 1947

2612. We are in the midst of a cold war which is getting warmer.—**Bernard Baruch:** speech before the Senate Committee, 1948

2613. Russia and America may be likened to two scorpions in a bottle, each capable of killing the other, but only at the risk of its own life. —**Julius Robert Oppenheimer,** 1904–67: Colin Bingham (ed.) *Wit and Wisdom* (1982)

2614. We walked to the brink and we looked it in the face.—**John Foster Dulles,** American politician: *Life*, 11 January 1956

2615. Whether you like it or not, history is on our side. We will bury you.—**Nikita Khrushchev,** Soviet premier: to Western diplomats at the Kremlin, 18 November 1956

2616. If we cannot now end our differences, at least we can help make the world safe for diversity.—**John F. Kennedy:** speech, American University, Washington DC, 10 June 1963

2617. The warning message we sent the Russians was a calculated ambiguity that would be clearly understood.—**Alexander Haig,** 1924–

2618. We are now in a war called peace.—**Richard M. Nixon:** *Time*, 10 September 1979

2619. The superpowers often behave like two heavily-armed blind men feeling their way around a room, each believing himself in mortal peril from the other, whom he assumes to have perfect vision. Each tends to ascribe to the other side a consistency, foresight and coherence that its own experience belies. Of course, even two blind men can do enormous damage to each other, not to speak of the room.—**Henry Kissinger:** *Observer*, 30 September 1979

2620. The cold war was not so terrible and détente was not so exalting.—**Henry Kissinger:** *Observer*, 10 February 1980

2621. If the Soviet empire still existed, I'd be terrified. The fact is, we can afford a fairly ignorant presidency now.—**Newt Gingrich,** Republican: 1989

2622. If the Soviet Union can give up the Brezhnev Doctrine for the Sinatra Doctrine, the United States can give up the James Monroe Doctrine for the Marilyn Monroe Doctrine: Let's all go to bed wearing the perfume we like best.—**Carlos Fuentes:** *Times* (London), 23 February 1990

Communism

See also INTERNATIONAL RELATIONS: Cuba; INTERNATIONAL RELATIONS: Russia

2623. If it walks like a duck and it talks like a duck, then it must be a duck.—**Walter Reuther,** 1907–70, American labor leader: suggested method of identifying a communist; William Safire (ed.) *Safire's Political Dictionary* (1978)

2624. McCarthy bought communism in much the same way as other people purchase a new automobile.—**Roy Cohn:** 1950; Jonathon Green (ed.) *The Pan Dictionary of Contemporary Quotations* (1989)

2625. Such pipsqueaks as Nixon and McCarthy are trying to get us so frightened of Communism that we'll be afraid to turn out the lights at night.—**Helen Gahagan Douglas:** speech, 1950; *Ms.*, October 1973

2626. Being America's foremost Socialist is like being the only tall building in Topeka, Kansas.—**William F. Buckley, Jr.,** 1925– : Michael Harrington *The Long-Distance Runner* (1988)

2627. Innate fear and hate of Communism reasserted itself in America. On that dark yeast, grudge, ambition and vindictiveness could feed, and demagogues grow fat.—**Barbara W. Tuchman:** *Stilwell and the American Experience in China* (1970)

2628. [American radicals] must take Communism away from the Communists, and take it without ambiguities, asserting that their ultimate goal is the ownership by the Government of the means of production.—**Edmund Wilson,** 1895–1972: obituary, *New York Times*, 13 June 1972

2629. America's hysterical fear of Communism stems not from any real fear of brutality or oppression—but from the fear of not being able to wear the sloganized T-shirt of your choice, of not being an all-important (literally) individual.—**Julie Burchill:** *Damaged Gods* (1986)

Congress

2630. Oh! The wisdom, the foresight and the hindsight and the rightsight and the leftsight, the northsight and the southsight, and the eastsight and the westsight that appeared in that August assembly.—**John Adams,** 1735–1826

2631. If the present Congress errs in too much talking, how can it be otherwise in a body to which the people send one hundred and fifty lawyers, whose trade it is to question everything, yield nothing, and talk by the hour?—**Thomas Jefferson,** 1743–1826

2632. The American Republic will endure until the day Congress discovers that it can bribe the public with the public's money.—**Alexis de Tocqueville,** 1805–59

2633. I believe if we introduced the Lord's Prayer here, senators would propose a large number of amendments to it.—**Henry Wilson,** 1812–75: Leon A. Harris *The Fine art of Political Wit* (1964)

2634. Though the president is Commander-in-Chief, Congress is his commander; and, God willing, he shall obey. He and his minions shall learn that this is not a Government of kings and satraps, but a Government of the people, and that Congress is the people.—**Thaddeus Stevens:** speech in House of Representatives, 3 January 1867

2635. The weakness of Congress is the strength of the president.—**James Bryce:** *The American Commonwealth* (1888)

2636. They never open their mouths without subtracting from the sum of human knowledge. —**Thomas Brackett Reed,** 1839–1902: Samuel W. McCall *The Life of Thomas Brackett Reed* (1914)

2637. The right of the minority is to draw its salaries, and its function is to make a quorum. —**Thomas Brackett Reed:** Leon A. Harris *The Fine Art of Political Wit* (1964)

2638. I took the Canal Zone and let Congress debate, and while the debate goes on the canal does also.—**Theodore Roosevelt:** speech in Berkeley, California, 23 March 1911

2639. Oh, if I could only be president and Congress, too, for just ten minutes.—**Theodore Roosevelt:** speaking to young Franklin D. Roosevelt, recalled in a letter from FDR to Robert M. Ashburn, 18 August 1928

2640. You can't use tact with a Congressman! A Congressman is a hog! You must take a stick and hit him on the snout!—**Henry Brooks Adams,** 1838–1918

2641. The informing function of Congress should be even preferred to its legislative function.—**Woodrow Wilson,** 1856–1924: Laurence J. Peter (ed.) *Peter's Quotations* (1977)

2642. We have the best Congress money can buy.—**Will Rogers,** 1879–1935

2643. It is the duty of the president to propose and it is the privilege of the Congress to dispose.—**Franklin D. Roosevelt:** press conference, 23 July 1937

2644. We favor putting Congress on a commission basis. Pay them for results. If they do a good job and the country prospers, they get 10% of the extra take.—**Gracie Allen:** *How to Become President* (1940)

2645. Congress is so strange. A man gets up to speak and says nothing. Nobody listens, and then everybody disagrees.—**Boris Marshalov:** *Reader's Digest*, March 1941

2646. These illiterate hacks whose fancy vests are spotted with gravy, and whose speeches, hypocritical, unctuous, and slovenly, are spotted also with the gravy of political patronage. —**Mary McCarthy:** *Commentary*, September 1947

2647. Give us clear vision, that we may know where to stand and what to stand for—because unless we stand for something, we shall fall for anything.—**Peter Marshall,** Senate chaplain: Senate prayer, 1947

2648. Sure the people are stupid: the human race is stupid. Sure Congress is an inefficient instrument of government. But the people are not stupid enough to abandon representative government for any other kind, including government by the guy who knows.—**Bernard De Voto:** *The Easy Chair* (1955)

2649. The Congress is not, was not intended to be, and cannot be an Executive.—**Dean Acheson:** *A Democrat Looks at His Part* (1955)

2650. Don't try to go too fast. Learn your job. Don't ever talk until you know what you're talking about…. If you want to get along, go along.—**Sam Rayburn,** 1882–1961

2651. If you tell Congress everything about the world situation, they get hysterical. If you tell them nothing, they go fishing.—**Harry S Truman,** 1884–1972

2652. The seniority system keeps a handful of old men in control of the Congress. These old men stand implacably across the paths that could lead us toward a better future.—**Shirley Chisholm:** *Unbought and Unbossed* (1970)

2653. In Britain the government has to come down in front of Parliament every day to explain its actions, but here the president never answers directly to Congress.—**Bella Abzug:** 17 June 1971; Mel Ziegler *Bella!* (1972)

2654. Congress is a very *unrepresentative* institution. Not only from an economic class point of view, but from *every* point of view—sex, race, age, vocation.—**Bella Abzug:** Mel Ziegler *Bella!* (1972)

2655. While the Nixon presidency induced a momentary sense of congressional unity, a more skillful president could readily restore the customary situation where members of Congress felt more solidarity with a president of their own party than with colleagues of the opposite party—**Arthur M. Schlesinger, Jr.:** *The Imperial Presidency* (1973)

2656. An institution designed only to react, not to plan or lead.—**Jimmy Breslin:** *How the Good Guys Finally Won* (1975)

2657. Everyone in America seems to be joining an organization of some kind, and in Congress one hears from them all.—**Millicent Fenwick:** newsletter, 1975

2658. It is said that the titles of most bills in Congress are like the titles of Marx Brothers movies ("Duck Soup," "Animal Crackers"): they do not tell much about the contents. —**George F. Will:** *Newsweek*, 3 October 1977

2659. A president and his wise men can only propose; but Congress disposes. It is when president and Congress agree that American history marches forward.—**Theodore H. White:** *In Search of History* (1978)

2660. It is Congress that voters mistrust, not their own congressmen.—**Peter Goldman:** *Newsweek*, 6 November 1978

2661. The bigger the appropriations bill, the shorter the debate.—**James Abourezk:** *Playboy*, March 1979

2662. If you give Congress a chance to vote on both sides of an issue, it will always do it.—**Les Aspin:** *New York Times*, 9 December 1982

2663. Give a member of Congress a junket and a mimeograph machine and he thinks he is Secretary of State.—**Dean Rusk:** *Time*, 6 May 1985

2664. A congressman's first obligation is to get elected; his second is to get reelected.—**Russell Long**

2665. Can any of you seriously say the Bill of Rights could get through Congress today? It wouldn't even get out of committee.—**Francis Lee Bailey,** 1933–

2666. Congress is continually appointing fact-finding committees, when what we really need are some fact-facing committees.—**Roger Allen:** *Grand Rapids Press*

2667. The mistakes made by Congress wouldn't be so bad if the next Congress didn't keep trying to correct them.—**Cullen Hightower**

2668. We may not imagine how our lives could be more frustrating and complex—but Congress can.—**Cullen Hightower**

2669. Talk is cheap—except when Congress does it.—**Cullen Hightower**

2670. I don't think it's the function of Congress to function well. It should drag its heels on the way to decision.—**Barber B. Conable, Jr.,** Congressman

2671. There are so many women on the floor of Congress, it looks like a mall.—**Henry Hyde,** Republican

2672. From early on, everything I did was calculated to being elected to Congress.—**Carl Albert,** Democrat

2673. The idea that a congressman would be tainted by accepting money from private industry or private sources is essentially a socialist argument.—**Newt Gingrich,** 1943– Republican

2674. Privatize Congress!—**Arthur Miller:** *New York Times,* January 1995

2675. Asking an incumbent member of Congress to vote for term limits is a bit like asking a chicken to vote for Colonel Sanders.—**Bob Inglis:** 1995

2676. You need to know that a member of Congress who refuses to allow the minimum wage to come up for a vote made more money during last year's one-month government shutdown than a minimum wage worker makes in an entire year.—**Bill Clinton,** 1946–   , president

2677. The only place on Earth where crocodiles and alligators live side by side.—**President George W. Bush:** *Time,* 18 June 2001

Coolidge, Calvin (1872–1933), 30th president (1923–29)

2678. I think the American people want a solemn ass as a president. And I think I'll go along with them.—**Calvin Coolidge:** to Ethel Barrymore, c. 1924; *Time,* 16 May 1955

2679. Mr. Coolidge's genius for inactivity is developed to a very high point. It is far from being an indolent activity. It is a grim, determined, alert inactivity which keeps Mr. Coolidge occupied constantly. Nobody has ever worked harder at inactivity, with such force of character, with such unremitting attention to detail, with such conscientious devotion to the task.—**Walter Lippmann:** *Men of Destiny* (1927)

2680. Perhaps one of the most important accomplishments of my administration has been minding my own business.—**Calvin Coolidge:** news conference, 1929

2681. He looks as if he had been weaned on a pickle.—**Anonymous:** Alice Roosevelt Longworth *Crowded Hours* (1934)

2682. He slept more than any other president, whether by day or by night. Nero fiddled, but Coolidge only snored.—**H. L. Mencken:** *American Mercury,* April 1933

2683. He's the greatest man who ever came out of Plymouth, Vermont.—**Clarence S. Darrow,** 1857–1938: Jon Winokur (ed.) *The Portable Curmudgeon Redux* (1992)

2684. Calvin Coolidge believed that the least government was the best government; he aspired to become the least president the country had ever had; he attained his desire.—**Irving Stone,** 1903–89: Isabel Leighton (ed.) *The Aspirin Age* (1949)

2685. Coolidge is a faded memory, as unromantic as old commerce statistics, relegated to that remote corner of the national consciousness reserved for quaint and faintly ridiculous characters. This does no credit to the nation which under his stewardship enjoyed a 45 percent increase in the production of ice cream. —**George F. Will:** 2 July 1975; *The Pursuit of Happiness* (1978)

Corruption

2686. When I want to buy up any politician I always find the anti-monopolists the most purchasable—they don't come so high.—**William Vanderbilt,** American industrialist: *Chicago Daily News,* 9 October 1882

2687. I am against government by crony. —**Harold L. Ickes:** speech, February 1946; on resigning as Secretary of the Interior, referring to president Truman's award of government positions to old friends

2688. The press is free to do battle against secrecy and deception in government. But the press cannot expect the Constitution any guarantee it will succeed.—**Potter Stewart,** 1915–85, Associate Justice Supreme Court: Henry O. Dormann *The Speaker's Book of Quotations* (1987)

Cuban Missile Crisis (1962)

2689. They talk about who won and who lost. Human reason won. Mankind won.—**Nikita Khrushchev,** Soviet premier: *Observer,* 11 November 1962

2690. We're eyeball to eyeball, and I think the other fellow just blinked.—**Dean Rusk,** Secretary of State: 24 October 1962; *Saturday Evening Post,* 8 December 1962

2691. In the military operations of Cuba Kennedy did not look for military victory, he sought to change Khrushchev's mind, and he succeeded. —**Peter Gretton:** speech at the Royal United Services Institution, April 1965

2692. There is no evidence to support the belief that Khrushchev ever questioned America's power. He questioned only the president's readiness to use it.—**Elie Abel:** *The Missile Crisis* (1966)

2693. When you solve a problem, you ought to thank God and go on to the next one.—**Dean Rusk:** *Look,* 6 September 1966

Democracy

2694. I know of no country in which there is so little independence of mind and real freedom of discussion as in America.—**Alexis de Tocqueville:** *Democracy in America* (1835–40)

2695. The surface of American society is covered with a layer of democratic paint, but from time to time one can see the old aristocratic colors breaking through.—**Alexis de Tocqueville,** 1805–59

2696. It is by the goodness of God that in our country we have those three unspeakably precious things: freedom of speech, freedom of conscience, and the prudence never to practice either of them.—**Mark Twain:** *Following the Equator* (1897)

2697. The Americans burn incense before it [democracy], but they are themselves ruled by the Boss and the Trust.—**William Ralph Inge:** *Outspoken Essays: First Series* (1919)

2698. All benefits have been poured out upon America and America is using them as a cheerful prodigal; America is conscious of her good fortune and that is why she can afford the manifestation of pride which is called democracy. —**W. L. George:** *Hail Columbia!* (1921)

2699. We have the men, the skill, the wealth, and above all, the will. We must be the great arsenal of democracy.—**Franklin D. Roosevelt:** radio broadcast, 29 December 1940

2700. The typical American of today has lost all the love of liberty, that his forefathers had, and all their disgust of emotion, and pride in self-reliance. He is led no longer by Davy Crocketts; he is led by cheer leaders, press agents, word mongers, uplifters.—**H. L. Mencken,** 1880–1956

2701. It is the American vice, the democratic disease which expresses its tyranny by reducing everything unique to the level of the herd. —**Henry Miller:** *The Wisdom of the Heart* (1947)

2702. We are inclined to confuse freedom and democracy, which we regard as moral principles, with the way in which they are practiced in America—with capitalism, federalism, and the two-party system, which are not moral principles but simply the preferred and accepted practices of the American people. —**J. William Fulbright:** *Old Myths and New Realities* (1964)

2703. In America, through pressure of conformity, there is freedom of choice, but nothing to choose from. —**Peter Ustinov,** 1921–

2704. American democracy is the inalienable right to sit on your own front porch, in your pyjamas, drinking a can of beer and shouting out "Where else is this possible?"—**Peter Ustinov:** *Nova,* 1968

2705. In America you can say anything you want—as long as it doesn't have any effect. —**Paul Goodman,** 1911–72

2706. America did not invent human rights. In a very real sense … human rights invented America. —**Jimmy Carter:** farewell address, 14 January 1981

2707. Americans like to talk about (or be told about) Democracy but, when put to the test, usually find it to be an "inconvenience." We have opted instead for an authoritarian system "disguised" as a Democracy. We pay through the nose for an enormous joke-of-a-government, let it push us around, and then wonder how all those assholes got in there. —**Frank Zappa,** 1940–93

2708. The two greatest obstacles to democracy in the United States are, first, the widespread delusion among the poor that we have a democracy, and second, the chronic terror among the rich, lest we get it. —**Edward Dowling**

2709. Chinks in America's egalitarian armor are not hard to find. Democracy is the fig leaf of elitism. —**Florence King:** *Reflections in a Jaundiced Eye* (1989)

2710. The 1st Amendment has always been dearest to our hearts because it allows us to see

where our hearts are located. —**Roger Rosenblatt:** *Life,* Fall 1991

2711. Leadership has rarely fit comfortably with democracy in America. —**Bruce Miroff:** *Icons of Democracy* (1993)

2712. In the United States the difficulties are not a Minotaur or a dragon—not imprisonment, hard labor, death, government harassment, and censorship—but cupidity, boredom, sloppiness, and indifference. Not the acts of a mighty all-pervading repressive government but the failure of a listless public to make use of the freedom that is its birthright. —**Alexander Solzhenitsyn:** *Policy Review,* Winter 1994

2713. We have an underdeveloped democracy and an overdeveloped plutocracy. —**Ralph Nader:** *Economist,* 30 March 1996

Democrats and Republicans

2714. [The Democrats] see nothing wrong in the rule that to the victors belong the spoils of the enemy. —**William Learned Marcy:** speech to the Senate, 25 January 1832

2715. Republicans are for both the *man* and the *dollar*; but in cases of conflict, the man *before* the dollar. —**Abraham Lincoln:** letter to H. L. Pierce, 6 April 1859

2716. I never said all Democrats were saloonkeepers; what I said was that all saloon-keepers were Democrats. —**Horace Greeley:** c. 1860; Evan Esar (ed.) *The Dictionary of Humorous Quotations* (1949)

2717. The Democratic Party is like a mule. It has neither pride of ancestry nor hope of posterity. —**Ignatius Donnelly:** speech in the Minnesota Legislature, 1860

2718. The Democratic Party is like a man riding backward in a carriage. It never sees a thing until it has gone by. —**Benjamin F. Butler:** c. 1870, attrib.

2719. We are Republicans and don't propose to leave our party and identify ourselves with the party whose antecedents are rum, Romanism, and rebellion.—**Samuel Dickinson Burchard:** speech, 29 October 1884

2720. The Republicans have their splits right after election, and Democrats have theirs just before an election.—**Will Rogers,** 1879–1935: Evan Esar (ed.) *The Dictionary of Humorous Quotations* (1949)

2721. The Democratic Party ain't on speaking terms with itself.—**Finley Peter Dunne,** 1867–1936: Evan Esar (ed.) *The Dictionary of Humorous Quotations* (1949)

2722. There is no Democratic or Republican way of cleaning the streets.—**Fiorella H. La Guardia,** 1882–1947: Charles Garrett *The La Guardia Years* (1961)

2723. Any well-established village in New England or the northern Middle West could afford a town drunkard, a town atheist, and a few Democrats.—**Denis William Brogan:** *The American Character* (1944)

2724. I like a lot of Republicans. Indeed, there are some I would trust with anything—anything, that is, except public office.—**Adlai Stevenson:** *New York Times,* 15 August 1952

2725. If Republicans will stop telling lies about the United States, we will stop telling the truth about them.—**Adlai Stevenson:** speech, Bakersfield, California, 10 September 1952

2726. Every Republican candidate for president since 1936 has been nominated by the Chase National Bank.—**Robert A. Taft:** statement to the press, after defeat in 1952 G.O.P. convention

2727. The Republican Party makes even its young men seem old; the Democratic Party makes even its old men seem young.—**Adlai Stevenson,** 1900–65: Earl Mazo *Richard Nixon* (1959)

2728. The Republicans stroke platitudes until they purr like epigrams.—**Adlai Stevenson**

2729. The Republicans have a "me too" candidate running on a "yes but" platform, advised by a "has been" staff.—**Adlai Stevenson:** Leon Harris *The Fine Art of Political Wit* (1964)

2730. [The Republican Party needs to be] dragged kicking and screaming into the twentieth century.—**Adlai Stevenson:** Kenneth Tynan *Curtains* (1967)

2731. I am invariably and have been since adolescence inimical to the Republican mind which shows at the most inflated size the bad qualities of the bourgeoisie rather than the good qualities of the middle class which the Democrats call forth.—**Janet Flanner,** 1892–1978: Natalia Danesi Murray (ed.) *Darlinghissima: Letters to a Friend* (1960)

2732. The Republican nominee-to-be, of course, is also a young man. But his approach is as old as McKinley. His party is the party of the past. His speeches are generalities from Poor Richard's Almanac. Their platform, made up of left-over Democratic planks, has the courage of our old convictions. Their pledge is a pledge to the status quo—and today there can be no status quo.—**John F. Kennedy:** 1960

2733. Republicans raise dahlias, Dalmatians, and eyebrows. Democrats raise Airedales, kids and taxes.—**Will Stanton:** *Ladies' Home Journal,* November 1962

2734. Republicans sleep in twin beds—some even in separate rooms. That is why there are more Democrats.—**Will Stanton:** *Ladies' Home Journal,* November 1962

2735. I don't belong to any organized party. I'm a Republican.—**E. Roland Harriman:** *New York Times,* 28 June 1964

2736. When a leader is in the Democratic Party he's a boss; when he's in the Republican Party he's a leader.—**Harry S Truman,** 1884–1972: Laurence J. Peter *Peter's Quotations* (1977)

2737. Republican boys date Democratic girls. They plan to marry Republican girls, but feel they're entitled to a little fun first.—**Anonymous**

2738. Republicans employ exterminators. Democrats step on bugs.—**Anonymous**

2739. The Democrats let it all out and love to shout and laugh and have fun. The Republicans have fun but they don't want people to see it. The Democrats, even when they are not having fun, like to appear to be having fun.—**Richard M. Nixon:** *Diary,* 1973

2740. The two real political parties in America are the *Winners* and the *Losers*. The people don't acknowledge this. They claim membership in two imaginary parties, the *Republicans* and the *Democrats*, instead.—**Kurt Vonnegut:** *Wampeters, Foma and Granfalloons* (1974)

2741. I've had much more fun out of life since I became a Democrat.—**W. Averell Harriman:** *Washington Post*, 4 January 1976

2742. Its [the Democratic Party's] leaders are always troubadors of trouble; crooners of catastrophe. A democratic president is doomed to proceed to his goals like a squid, squirting darkness all about him.—**Clare Boothe Luce**, 1903–87: Laurence J. Peter *Peter's Quotations* (1977)

2743. Whenever a Republican leaves one side of the aisle and goes to the other [Democratic], it raises the intelligence quotient of both parties.—**Clare Boothe Luce:** Eileen Mason *Great Book of Funny Quotes* (1993)

2744. We're the party that wants to see an America in which people can still get rich.—**Ronald Reagan:** at a Republican congressional dinner, 4 May 1982

2745. The Republicans believe the wagon train will not make it to the frontier unless some of our old, some of our young, and some of our weak are left behind by the side of the trail. We Democrats believe that we can make it all the way with the whole family intact.—**Mario Cuomo:** speech to the Democrat National Convention, 1984

2746. A conservative Republican is one who doesn't believe anything new should ever be tried for the first time. A liberal Republican is one who *does* believe something should be tried for the first time—but not now.—**Mort Sahl,** 1926–: Fred Metcalf *The Penguin Dictionary of Modern Humorous Quotations* (1986)

2747. Democrats can't get elected unless things get worse, and things won't get worse unless they get elected.—**Jeane Kirkpatrick,** 1926– : Henry O. Dormann *The Speaker's Book of Quotations* (1987)

2748. I'm a Democrat with Republican underpinnings. I'm liberal about a lot of things but I'm bullish about America.—**Steven Spielberg:** *Film Yearbook* (1987)

2749. In every election in American history both parties have their clichés. The party that has the clichés that ring true wins.—**Newt Gingrich:** *International Herald Tribune* (Paris), 1 August 1988

2750. America is a land where citizens vote for Democrats but hope to live like Republicans.—**Anonymous**

2751. A bureaucrat is a Democrat who holds some office that a Republican wants.—**Alben W. Barkley:** Jon Winokur (ed.) *The Portable Curmudgeon Redux* (1992)

2752. God is a Republican and Santa Claus is a Democrat.—**P. J. O'Rourke:** *Parliament of Whores* (1991)

2753. The Democrats are the party that says government will make you smarter, taller, richer, and remove the crabgrass on your lawn. The Republicans are the party that says government doesn't work, and then they get elected and prove it.—**P. J. O'Rourke:** *Parliament of Whores* (1991)

2754. The Republican convention, an event with the intellectual content of a Guns 'n' Roses lyric attended by every ofay insurance broker in America who owns a pair of white shoes.—**P. J. O'Rourke:** *Parliament of Whores* (1991)

2755. The outcome of 25 years of Republican rule (Jimmy Carter was a mere blip in 1976) is that Americans have learnt to hate themselves, like children of repressive, conformist families.—**Cynthia Heimel:** *Independent on Sunday*, 1992

2756. I think one of the great problems we have in the Republican Party is that we don't encourage you to be nasty. We encourage you to be neat, obedient, loyal and faithful and all those Boy Scout words, which would be great around a campfire but are lousy in politics.—**Newt Gingrich,** 1943– , Republican

2757. The greatest leaders in fighting for an integrated America in the twentieth century were in the Democratic Party. The fact is, it was the liberal wing of the Democratic Party that ended segregation. The fact is that it was Franklin Roosevelt who gave hope to a nation that was in despair and could have slid into dictatorship. And the fact is, every Republican has much to learn from studying what the Democrats did right.—**Newt Gingrich**: 1995

2758. God is registered to vote for Hollywood as a Republican. However, Jesus Christ is a Democrat from Santa Monica.—*Wall Street Journal*: 12 July 1995

2759. The thing they struggle with is that their electoral base and their governing base are not the same. The best way to win the Republican Party is to be to the far right in the primary. But it's also the fastest way to lose the general election.—**Thad Mathis**

2760. While Democratic and Republican leaders differ sharply, their voters do not.—**Dick Morris**

2761. Bob Dole revealed he is one of the test subjects for Viagra. He said on *Larry King*, "I wish I had bought stock in it." Only a Republican would think the best part of Viagra is the fact that you could make money off of it.—**Jay Leno, 1950–**

Dissent

See also CULTURE AND MEDIA: Intellectual

2762. America is not a country for a dissenter to live in.—**William A. (Billy) Sunday,** 1862–1935: William G. McLoughlin *Billy Sunday Was His Real Name* (1955)

2763. Discussion in America means dissent.—**James Thurber**: c. 1953; *Lanterns and Lances* (1961)

2764. Here in America we are descended in spirit from revolutionists and rebels—men and women who dare to dissent from accepted doctrine.—**Dwight D. Eisenhower**: address, Columbia University, 31 May 1954

Dulles, John Foster (1888–1959), politician

2765. The wooliest type of useless pontificating American. Heaven help us!—**Alexander Cadogan**: *Diary*, 13 July 1942

2766. The world's longest-range misguided missile.—**Walter Reuther,** 1907–70

2767. Dulles is the only case I know of a bull who carries his china shop with him.—**Winston Churchill,** 1874–1965: *Time*, 27 February 1978

2768. Smooth is an inadequate word for Dulles. His prevarications are so highly polished as to be aesthetically pleasurable.—**Isidor Feinstein Stone:** 1953; Jonathon Green (ed.) *The Pan Dictionary of Contemporary Quotations* (1989)

2769. We hear the Secretary of State [Dulles] boasting of his brinkmanship—the art of bringing us to the edge of the abyss.—**Adlai Stevenson:** speech at Hartford, Connecticut, 25 February 1956; *New York Times*, 26 February 1956

2770. The greatest difficulty with Dulles was his yearning for new and exciting variants in policy.—**John Kenneth Galbraith:** letter to President John F. Kennedy, 9 October 1961

2771. A diplomatic bird of prey smelling out from afar the corpses of dead bodies.—**James Cameron:** 1967

2772. A strong personality with views as narrow as a small-gauge railway.—**Kim Philby:** *Esquire* (New York), 28 March 1978

Eisenhower, Dwight D. (1890–1969), 34th president (1953–61)

2773. Ike is the best damn general the British have got.—**George S. Patton,** 1885–1945, American general: attrib.

2774. He'll make a fine president. He was the best clerk who ever served under me.—**Douglas MacArthur,** American general: *News Summaries*, 31 December 1952

2775. If I talk over people's heads, Ike must talk under their feet.—**Adlai Stevenson:** during the presidential campaign of 1952; Bill Adler *The Stevenson Wit* (1966)

2776. The Tomb of the Well-Known Soldier. —**Emlyn Williams,** 1905–87: the White House in the time of president Eisenhower; James Harding *Emlyn Williams* (1987)

2777. The General has dedicated himself so many times, he must feel like the cornerstone of a public building. —**Adlai Stevenson:** of presidential campaign in 1956; Leon Harris *The Fine Art of Political Wit* (1964)

2778. He'll sit right here and he'll say do this, do that! And nothing will happen. Poor Ike— it won't be a bit like the Army. —**Harry S Truman,** 1884–1972: *Harry S Truman* (1973)

2779. Perhaps [Eisenhower's] particular contribution to the art of politics was to make politics boring at a time when the people wanted any excuse to forget public affairs. —**Arthur M. Schlesinger, Jr.:** *Esquire* (New York), January 1960

2780. I read a very interesting quote by Senator Kerr of Oklahoma. In summing up Ike, he said "Eisenhower is the only living unknown soldier." Even this is giving him all the best of it. —**Groucho Marx:** letter to Goodman Ace, 19 July 1960

2781. As an intellectual [he] bestowed upon the games of golf and bridge all the enthusiasm and perseverance that he withheld from books and ideas. —**Emmet John Hughes:** *The Ordeal of Power* (1963)

2782. The great tortoise upon whose back the world sat for eight years. —**Murray Kempton:** *Esquire*, September 1967

2783. I doubt very much if a man whose main literary interests were in works by Mr. Zane Grey, admirable as they may be, is particularly equipped to be the chief executive of this country, particularly where Indian Affairs are concerned. —**Dean Acheson,** 1893–1971: attrib.; Jon Winokur (ed.) *The Portable Curmudgeon Redux* (1992)

2784. Being criticized ... he never did get it through his head that that's what politics is all about. —**Harry S Truman,** 1884–1972: Merle Miller (ed.) *Plain Speaking* (1974)

2785. Eisenhower was a subtle man, and no fool, though in pursuit of his objectives he did not like to be thought of as brilliant; people of

brilliance, he thought, were distrusted. —**David Halberstam:** *The Best and the Brightest* (1972)

2786. Roosevelt proved a man could be president for life; Truman proved anybody could be president; Eisenhower proved you don't need to have a president. —**Kenneth B. Keating:** Jon Winokur (ed.) *The Portable Curmudgeon Redux* (1992)

2787. Eisenhower [was] reading a speech with his usual sense of discovery. —**Gore Vidal:** *United States Essays: 1952–92* (1994)

Elections

2788. "Vote early and vote often," the advice openly displayed on the election banners in one of our northern cities. —**William Porcher Miles:** in the House of Representatives, 31 March 1858

2789. I don't know much about Americanism, but it's a damn good word with which to carry an election. —**Warren G. Harding,** 1865–1923: Laurence J. Peter *Peter's Quotations* (1977)

2790. The Republicans have their splits right after election and Democrats have theirs just before an election. —**Will Rogers:** newspaper column, 29 December 1930

2791. I never vote for anybody, I always vote against. —**W. C. Fields,** 1879–1946: Robert Lewis Taylor *W. C. Fields, His Follies and Fortunes* (1949)

2792. I am not a politician, I am a citizen. —**Adlai Stevenson:** speech during the 1948 election campaign; Bert Cochran *Adlai Stevenson* (1969)

2793. "Senator, you have the vote of every thinking person!" —Woman.
"That's not enough, madam, we need a majority!"
—**Adlai E. Stevenson:** when running for president, 1956

2794. There is nothing wrong with this country which a good election can't fix. —**Richard M. Nixon:** in Syracuse, New York, 29 October 1968

2795. America is a land where a citizen will cross the ocean to fight for democracy, but won't cross the street to vote in a national election.—**Bill Vaughan,** 1915–77: Laurence J. Peter (ed.) *Peter's Quotations* (1977)

2796. In our system, at about 11:30 on election night, they just push you off the edge of the cliff and that's it. You might scream on the way down, but you're going to hit the bottom, and you're not going to be in elective office.—**Walter F. Mondale:** on loss to Ronald Reagan in 1984 presidential election; *New York Times*, 4 March 1987

2797. It makes no difference who you vote for—the two parties are really one party representing four percent of the people.—**Gore Vidal,** 1925–   : Jon Winokur (ed.) *The Portable Curmudgeon* (1987)

2798. In every election in American history both parties have their clichés. The party that has the clichés that ring true wins.—**Newt Gingrich:** *International Herald Tribune*, 1 August 1988

Fascism

2799. If Fascism came to America it would be on a program of 100 percent Americanism.—**Huey P. Long:** U.S. Army Talk, 24 March 1945

2800. I have often thought that if a rational Fascist dictatorship were to exist, then it would choose the American system.—**Noam Chomsky:** *Language and Responsibility* (1979)

First Lady

2801. I let Ike run the country and I ran the home.—**Mamie Eisenhower,** 1896–1979, First Lady: Carolyn Warner *The Last Word* (1992)

2802. You will feel that you are no longer clothing yourself, you are dressing a public monument.—**Eleanor Roosevelt:** warning to wives of future presidents; *New York Herald Tribune,* 27 October 1960

2803. I do not think it altogether inappropriate to introduce myself. I am the man who accompanied Jacqueline Kennedy to Paris, and I have enjoyed it.—**John F. Kennedy:** speaking to the press during his state visit to France, June 1961; Evelyn Lincoln *My Twelve Years with John F. Kennedy* (1965)

2804. Always be on time. Do as little talking as humanly possible. Remember to lean back in the parade car so everybody can see the president. Be sure not to get too fat because you'll have to sit three in the back seat.—**Eleanor Roosevelt:** on campaign behavior for first ladies; *New York Times*, 11 November 1962

2805. The one thing I do not want to be called is First Lady. It sounds like a saddle horse.—**Jacqueline Kennedy:** advice to her secretary following the inauguration of John F. Kennedy; Peter Collier and David Horowitz *The Kennedys* (1984)

2806. Roughly speaking, the president of the United States knows what his job is. Constitution and custom spell it out, for him as well as for us. His wife has no such luck. The First Lady has no rules; rather each new woman must make her own.—**Shana Alexander:** 1968; *The Feminine Eye* (1970)

2807. The First Lady is, and always has been, an unpaid public servant elected by one person, her husband.—**Lady Bird Johnson:** 14 March 1968; *A White House Diary* (1970)

2808. Being First Lady is the hardest unpaid job in the world.—**Pat Nixon,** First Lady: interview in Monrovia, Liberia, 15 March 1972

2809. I'll have to have a room of my own. Nobody could sleep with Dick. He wakes up during the night, switches on the lights, speaks into his tape recorder.—**Pat Nixon:** Barbara Rowes *The Book of Quotes* (1979)

2810. I have sacrificed everything in my life that I consider precious in order to advance the political career of my husband.—**Pat Nixon:** Betty Medsger *Women at Work* (1975)

2811. The first ladyship is the only federal office in which the holder can neither be fired nor impeached. — **William Safire:** *New York Times*, 2 March 1987

2812. If the president has a bully pulpit, then the First Lady has a white glove pulpit … more refined, restricted, ceremonial, but it's a pulpit all the same. — **Nancy Reagan:** *New York Times*, 10 March 1988

2813. I see the first lady as another means to keep a president from being isolated. — **Nancy Reagan:** *International Herald Tribune*, 26 May 1988

2814. Somewhere out in this audience may even be someone who will one day follow in my footsteps, and preside over the White House as the president's spouse. I wish him well! — **Barbara Bush:** at Wellesley College Commencement, 1 June 1990

2815. It was because I threatened no one. I was old, white-headed and large. — **Barbara Bush:** asked why she thought she was a popular First Lady; *Independent on Sunday*, 4 December 1994

Ford, Gerald R. (1913–   ), 38th president (1974–77)

2816. So dumb that he can't fart and chew gum at the same time. — **Lyndon B. Johnson,** 1908–73: Richard Reeves *A Ford, Not a Lincoln* (1975)

2817. He played football too long without a helmet. — **Jerome Cavanagh:** *Newsweek*, 22 October 1973

2818. I am a Ford, not a Lincoln. — **Gerald R. Ford:** on becoming vice-president, 6 December 1973; *Washington Post*, 7 December 1973

2819. I guess it proves that in America anyone can be president. — **Gerald R. Ford:** referring to his own appointment as president; R. Reeves *A Ford, Not a Lincoln* (1975)

2820. I am the people's man. — **Gerald R. Ford:** speech, Congress, 12 August 1974

2821. A year ago Gerald Ford was unknown throughout America. Now he's unknown throughout the world. — **Anonymous:** *Guardian*, 1974

2822. He looks like the guy in a science fiction movie who is the first to see "The Creature." — **David Frye:** 1975, attrib.; Nigel Rees *A Dictionary of Twentieth Century Quotations* (1987)

2823. Richard Nixon self-impeached himself. He gave us Gerald Ford as his revenge. — **Bella Abzug:** *Rolling Stone*, 2 December 1976

2824. In the Bob Hope Golf Classic, the participation of president Gerald Ford was more than enough to remind you that the nuclear button was at one stage at the disposal of a man who might have either pressed it by mistake or else pressed it deliberately in order to obtain room service. — **Clive James,** 1939–

2825. In our own country, the Republic has been governed by Andrew Johnson, an ineffective drunk; Warren Harding, an ineffective drunk; and Gerald Ford, who didn't even need to be a drunk to be ineffective. — **Joe Queenan:** *Imperial Caddy* (1992)

Foreign Policy

See also WAR AND THE MILITARY; INTERNATIONAL RELATIONS

2826. There is a homely adage which runs, "Speak softly and carry a big stick—and you will go far." If the American nation will speak softly and yet build and keep at a pitch of the highest training a thoroughly efficient navy, the Monroe Doctrine will go far. — **Theodore Roosevelt:** speech as vice-president, Minnesota State Fair, 2 September 1901

2827. The U.S. is having the same trouble as Rome in its search for "defensible frontiers." — **Lord Curzon,** 1859–1925: Laurence J. Peter *Peter's Quotations* (1977)

2828. The United States never lost a war or won a conference. — **Will Rogers,** 1879–1935: following the Versailles Peace Conference, at which president Woodrow Wilson spurned all suggestions that the U.S. should take territory or payment as a result of participating in the

World War I; Jack Lait (ed.) *Wit and Wisdom* (1936)

2829. American diplomacy is easy on the brain but hell on the feet.—**Charles G. Dawes:** speech, Washington, 2 June 1931

2830. Greece is a sort of American vassal; the Netherlands is the country of American bases that grow like tulip bulbs; Cuba is the main sugar plantation of the American monopolies; Turkey is prepared to know-tow before any United States pro-consul and Canada is the boring second fiddle in the American symphony.—**Andrei Gromyko:** *New York Herald Tribune*, 30 June 1953

2831. We cannot be any stronger in our foreign policy—for all the bombs and guns we may heap up in our arsenals—than we are in the spirit which rules inside the country. Foreign policy, like a river, cannot rise above its source.—**Adlai Stevenson:** speech in New Orleans, 4 December 1954; *What I Think* (1956)

2832. Americans think of themselves collectively as a huge rescue squad on twenty-four-hour call to any spot on the globe where dispute and conflict may erupt.—**Eldridge Cleaver:** *Soul On Ice* (1968)

2833. The genius of you Americans is that you never make clear-cut stupid moves, only complicated stupid moves which make us wonder at the possibility that there may be something to them which we are missing.—**Gamal Abdel Nasser,** 1918–70

2834. Next week there can't be any crisis. My schedule is already full.—**Henry Kissinger:** *New York Times*, 28 October 1973

2835. No foreign policy will stick unless the American people are behind it. And unless Congress understands it. And unless Congress understands it, the American people aren't going to understand it.—**W. Averell Harriman,** 1891–1986: Laurence J. Peter (ed.) *Peter's Quotations* (1977)

2836. Every damn president since I can remember has been so in love with foreign policy that they're just like a schoolboy with a new girl.—**Cleveland Amory:** *The Trouble with Nowadays* (1979)

2837. One of the recurrent and dangerous influences on our foreign policy—fear of the political consequences of doing the sensible thing, which in many cases is nothing much at all.—**John Kenneth Galbraith:** *A Life in Our Times* (1981)

2838. We cannot play innocents abroad in a world that is not innocent.—**Ronald Reagan:** speech, 6 February 1985

2839. The American temptation [is] to believe that foreign policy is a subdivision of psychiatry.—**Henry Kissinger:** speech, University of South Carolina; *Time*, 17 June 1985

2840. Whatever it is that the government does, sensible Americans would prefer that the government does it to somebody else. This is the idea behind foreign policy.—**P. J. O'Rourke:** *Parliament of Whores* (1991)

2841. Americans tend to think of foreign affairs in terms of sporting events that allow for unambiguous results. Either the team wins or it loses; the game is over within a reasonable period of time, and everybody can go back to doing something else.—**Lewis H. Lapham:** *Harper's*, March 1991

2842. This is a fact: strength in the pursuit of peace is no vice; isolation in the pursuit of security is no vice.—**George Bush:** 28 January 1992

2843. The American foreign policy trauma of the sixties and seventies was caused by applying valid principles to unsuitable conditions.—**Henry Kissinger:** *Guardian*, 16 December 1992

2844. American *diplomacy*. It's like watching somebody trying to do joinery with a chainsaw.—**James Hamilton-Paterson:** *Griefwork* (1993)

Franklin, Benjamin (1706–90)

2845. He snatched the lightning shaft from heaven, and the sceptre from tyrants.—**A. R. J. Turgot:** inscription for a bust of Franklin, 1778

2846. A philosophical Quaker full of mean and thrift maxims.—**John Keats:** letter, 14 October 1818

2847. Printer, philosopher, scientist, author and patriot, impeccable husband and citizen, why isn't he an archetype? Pioneers, Oh Pioneers! Benjamin was one of the greatest pioneers of the United States. Yet we just can't do with him. What's wrong with him then? Or what's wrong with us?—**D. H. Lawrence:** *Studies in Classic American Literature* (1923)

Government

See also PAST AND FUTURE: Revolution; SOCIAL LIFE: Poverty and Wealth; SOCIAL LIFE: Society; BUSINESS AND ECONOMY: Economy; BUSINESS AND ECONOMY: Taxes

2848. Not wishing to be disturbed over moral issues of the political economy, Americans cling to the notion that the government is a sort of automatic machine, regulated by the balancing of competing interests.—**C. Wright Mills:** *The Power Elite* (1956)

2849. If the Government is big enough to give you everything you want, it is big enough to take away everything you have.—**Gerald R. Ford:** John F. Parker *If Elected* (1960)

2850. In the councils of government, we must guard against the acquisition of unwarranted influence, whether sought or unsought, by the military-industrial complex. The potential for the disastrous rise of misplaced power exists and will persist.—**Dwight D. Eisenhower:** farewell address, 17 January 1961

2851. Government is like a big baby—an alimentary canal with a big appetite at one end and no responsibility at the other.—**Ronald Reagan:** 1965, attrib.

2852. Governments does not solve problems; it subsidizes them.—**Ronald Reagan:** speech, 11 December 1972

2853. It is not that the U.S. government is an entirely comic matter; but to deal in power, ambition, and the people driven by both, a fine madness and sense of humor are handy thing to have.—**Barbara Howar:** *Laughing All the Way* (1973)

2854. A triangle of institutions—parts of Congress, the media, and special interest groups—is transforming and placing out of focus our constitutional balance, particularly in the areas of spending and foreign policy.—**Ronald Reagan:** address, 3 December 1988

2855. There was a time when you could say the least government was the best—but not in the nation's most populous state.—**Dianne Feinstein,** Democrat Mayor of San Francisco: campaign speech, 15 March 1990

2856. Giving money and power to government is like giving whisky and car keys to teenage boys.—**P. J. O'Rourke:** *Parliament of Whores* (1991)

2857. The mystery of government is not how Washington works but how to make it stop. —**P. J. O'Rourke,** 1947–

2858. Thank heavens we do not get all of the government that we are made to pay for.—**Milton Friedman,** 1912– , American economist: attrib.

2859. One of the greatest intellectual failures of the welfare state is the penchant for sacrifice, so long as the only people being asked to sacrificed are working, tax-paying Americans. —**Newton Gingrich:** *USA Today*, 16 January 1995

Harding, Warren G. (1865–1923), 29th president (1921–3)

2860. A tin-horn politician with the manner of a rural corn doctor and the mien of a ham actor.—**H. L. Mencken:** *Lodge* (1920)

2861. I am a man of limited talents from a small town. I don't seem to grasp that I am president.—**Warren G. Harding:** Laurence J. Peter (ed.) *Peter's Quotations* (1977)

2862. Bungalow mind.—**Woodrow Wilson,** 1856–1924: Robert Andrews *The New Penguin Dictionary of Modern Quotations* (2001)

2863. Harding was not a bad man. He was just a slob.—**Alice Roosevelt Longworth:** *Crowded Hours* (1933)

2864. The most bewildered president in our history.—**Samuel Hopkins Adams:** *The Aspirin Age* (1949)

Hoover, Herbert (1874–1964), 31st president (1929–33)

2865. It would be difficult to imagine a less political and popularly ingratiating personality than that of this round, sedentary, factual-minded man who seems incapable of pretending to be anything that he does not know himself to be.—**Herbert Croly:** *New Republic*, 27 June 1928

2866. He wouldn't commit himself to the time of day from a hatful of watches.—**Westbrook Pegler:** c. 1929; Oliver Pilat *Pegler: Angry Man of the Press* (1963)

2867. Hoover, if elected, will do one thing that is almost incomprehensible to the human mind: he will make a great man out of Coolidge. —**Clarence S. Darrow:** remark during the presidential campaign, 1932

2868. Once upon a time my political opponents honored me as possessing the fabulous intellectual and economic power by which I created a worldwide depression all by myself. —**Herbert Hoover:** Laurence J. Peter (ed.) *Peter's Quotations* (1977)

2869. Hoover isn't a stuffed shirt. But at times he can give the most convincing impersonation of a stuffed shirt you ever saw.—**Anonymous:** Eugene Lyons *Herbert Hoover* (1947)

2870. An extremely plain man living in an extremely fancy age.—**James M. Cox:** *Sun*, 10 August 1949

2871. Such a little man could not have made so big a depression.—**Norman Thomas:** letter to Murray B. Seidler, 3 August 1960

House of Representatives

2872. I've said many a time that I think the Un-American Activities Committee in the House of Representatives was the most un-American thing in America!—**Harry S Truman,** 1884–1972

2873. The boiling, churning caldron of America.—**James C. Wright, Jr.:** *Life*, 1987

2874. The House looks like more fun. It's like the *Donahue* show. The Senate is like one of those Sunday morning public service programs. —**Phil Donahue**

2875. The House is a microwave and the Senate a crockpot; they operate differently.—**Jim Trafficant:** CNBC, 15 February 1995

Jackson, Andrew (1767–1845), 7th president (1829–37)

2876. Ignorant, passionate, hypocritical, corrupt, and easily swayed by the basest men who surround him.—**Henry Clay:** letter to Francis T. Brooke, 2 August 1833

2877. Where is there a chief magistrate of whom so much evil has been predicted, and from whom so much good has come?—**Thomas H. Benton:** *Thirty Years' View* vol. 1 (1854)

2878. He was too generous to be frugal, too kind-hearted to be thrifty, too honest to live above his means.—**Vernon Parrington:** *Main Currents in American Thought* vol. 1 (1927)

Jefferson, Thomas (1743–1826), 3rd president (1801–09)

2879. By God, he had rather be on his farm than to be made emperor of the world.—**George Washington,** 1732–99: attrib.

2880. His attachment to those of his friends whom he could make useful to himself was thoroughgoing and exemplary.—**John Quincy Adams,** 6th president: *Diary,* 29 July 1836

2881. A gentleman of thirty-two who could calculate an eclipse, survey an estate, tie an artery, plan an edifice, try a cause, break a horse, dance a minuet, and play the violin.—**James Parton:** *Life of Thomas Jefferson* (1874)

2882. Perhaps the most incapable executive that ever filled the presidential chair.—**Theodore Roosevelt:** *The Naval War of 1812* (1882)

2883. Since the days when Jefferson expounded his code of political philosophy, the whole world has become his pupil.—**Michael Mac-White:** speech at the University of Virginia, April 1931

2884. Jeffersonian Democracy simply meant the possession of the federal government by the agrarian masses led by an aristocracy of slave-owning masses.—**Charles A. Beard,** 1874-1948

2885. I think this is the most extraordinary collection of talent, of human knowledge, that has ever been gathered at the White House—with the possible exception of when Thomas Jefferson dined alone.—**John F. Kennedy:** said at a dinner for Nobel Prizewinners, 29 April 1962; *New York Times,* 30 April 1962

2886. A sterile worshipper of the people.—**John B. McCaster**

2887. The moonshine philosopher of Monticello.—**Timothy Pickering**

2888. The moral character of Jefferson was repulsive. Continually pulling about liberty, equality and the degrading curse of slavery, he brought his own children to the hammer, and made money of their debaucheries.—**Thomas Hamilton**

Johnson, Lyndon B. (1908–73), 36th president (1963–69)

See also WAR AND THE MILITARY: Vietnam War

2889. I am a free man, an American, a United States Senator, and a Democrat, in that order.—**Lyndon B. Johnson:** *Texas Quarterly,* Winter 1958

2890. I don't know anyone who is as vain or more selfish than Johnson.—**Sam Rayburn,** 1882-1961: Robert A. Caro *The Path to Power* (1982)

2891. I know I've got a heart big enough to be president. I know I've got guts enough to be president. But I wonder whether I've got intelligence and ability enough to be president—I wonder if any man does.—**Lyndon B. Johnson:** remark to Hugh Sidey, Spring 1960; Hugh Sidey *A Very Personal Presidency: Lyndon Johnson in the White House* (1968)

2892. Johnson's instinct for power is as primordial as a salmon's going upstream to spawn.—**Theodore H. White:** *The Making of the President* (1964)

2893. Lyndon acts like there was never going to be a tomorrow.—**Claudia "Lady Bird" Johnson,** wife of Lyndon B. Johnson: *New York Times Magazine,* 29 November 1964

2894. I am going to build the kind of nation that president Roosevelt hoped for, president Truman worked for and president Kennedy died for.—**Lyndon B. Johnson:** *Sunday Times,* 27 December 1964

2895. He does not concentrate on thinking programs through but in getting them through.—**James B. Reston:** Michael V. DiSalle *Second Choice* (1966)

2896. I work for him despite his faults and he lets me work for him despite my deficiencies.—**Bill Moyers:** *New York Times,* 3 April 1966

2897. I want *loyalty.* I want him to kiss my ass in Macy's window at high noon and tell me it smells like roses. I want his pecker in my pocket.—**Lyndon B. Johnson:** David Halberstam *The Best and the Brightest* (1972)

2898. To him the shortest distance between two points was a tunnel.—**William Manchester:** *The Death of a President* (1967)

2899. A great raw man of immense girth, wandering as a stranger in the Pepsi generation. Coarse, earthy—a brutal intrusion into the misty

Kennedy renaissance that still clung to the land.—**Hugh Sidey:** *A Very Personal Presidency: Lyndon Johnson in the White House* (1968)

2900. Johnson came into office seeking a Great Society in America and found instead an ugly little war that consumed him.—**Tom Wicker:** *JFK and LBJ* (1968)

2901. An extraordinarily gifted president who was the wrong man from the wrong place at the wrong time under the wrong circumstances. —**Eric F. Goldman:** *The Tragedy of Lyndon Johnson* (1969)

2902. I always felt that every job I had was really too big for me.—**Lyndon B. Johnson:** 1969; Colin Bingham (ed.) *Wit and Wisdom* (1982)

2903. He wanted everyone with him all the time, and when they weren't, it broke his heart. —**Max Frankel:** Richard Harwood and Haynes Johnson *Lyndon* (1973)

2904. Johnson himself turned out to be so many different characters he could have populated all of War and Peace and still had a few people left over.—**Herbert Mitgang:** 15 August 1980

2905. Kennedy promised, Johnson delivered. —**Arthur M. Schlesinger, Jr.:** *Observer*, 20 November 1983

2906. He regarded the press as a conveyor belt that should carry, without question, any baggage he wanted to dump on it.—**James B. Reston:** *Deadline* (1991)

2907. He was our very last frontier president as well as the first we had since Abraham Lincoln and Andrew Johnson.—**Joseph W. Alsop:** *I've Seen the Best of It* (1992)

Kennedy, John F. (1917–63), 35th president (1961–63)

See also WAR AND THE MILITARY: Vietnam War

2908. The enviably attractive nephew who sings an Irish ballad for the company and then winsomely disappears before the table-clearing and dishwashing begin.—**Lyndon B. Johnson,** 1908–73: Harry McPherson *A Political Education* (1972)

2909. Don't buy a single vote more than necessary. I'll be damned if I'm going to pay for a landslide.—**Telegraphed message from his father:** read at a Gridiron dinner in Washington, 15 March 1958, and almost certainly JFK's invention; J. F. Cutler *Honey Fitz* (1962)

2910. It was easy—they sank my boat.—**John F. Kennedy:** to an Ashland, WI, youth who asked in 1958 how he became a war hero; Theodore C. Sorensen *Kennedy* (1965)

2911. Do you realize the responsibilities I carry? I'm the only person between Nixon and the White House.—**John F. Kennedy:** to a liberal supporter in 1960 presidential campaign; Theodore C. Srensen *Kennedy* (1965)

2912. I am not the Catholic candidate for president. I am the Democratic Party's candidate for president, who happens also to be a Catholic.—**John F. Kennedy:** speech to Greater Houston Ministerial Association, 12 September 1960

2913. A new star of tremendous national appeal, the skill of a consummate showman. —**Russell Baker:** on Kennedy's first televised press conference; *New York Times*, 26 January 1961

2914. President Kennedy is a great one for the girls, and during the election his opponents said that if he got to the White House they only hoped he would do for fornication what Eisenhower did for golf.—**Rupert Hart-Davis:** letter, 25 February 1961

2915. I wonder how it is with you, Harold? If I don't have a woman for three days, I get a terrible headache.—**John F. Kennedy:** to Prime Minister Harold Mcmillan who recorded it in his *Diary* 5 March 1961; Alistair Horne *Harold Macmillan* vol. 2 (1989)

2916. I'm an idealist without illusions.—**John F. Kennedy:** Harris Wolford *Of Kennedys and Kings* (1981)

2917. The worse I do, the more popular I get. —**John F. Kennedy:** referring to his popularity following the failure of the US invasion of Cuba; David Wallechinsky *The People's Almanac* (1977)

2918. There is something very eighteenth century about this young man. He is always on his toes during our discussion. But in the evening there will be music and wine and pretty women.—**Harold Macmillan:** *New York Journal—American*, 21 January 1962

2919. Spending half his time thinking about adultery, the other half about second-hand ideas passed on by his advisers.—**Harold Macmillan,** 1894–1986: *Sunday Times*, 4 January 1987

2920. If someone wants to shoot me from a window with a rifle, nobody can stop it.—**John F. Kennedy**

2921. [He] died as a soldier under fire, doing his duty in the service of his country.—**Charles de Gaulle:** 1963; Lois and Alan Gordon *American Chronicle* (1987)

2922. Now, I think that I should have known that he was magic all along. I did know it—but I should have guessed that it would be too much to ask to grow old with and see our children grow up together. So now, he is a legend when he would have preferred to be a man. —**Jacqueline Kennedy:** 1964

2923. [Kennedy] had his ear so close to the ground it was full of grasshoppers.—**Harry S Truman,** 1884–1972: *Time*, 20 March 1978

2924. Jack was out kissing babies while I was out passing bills. Someone had to tend the store. —**Lyndon B. Johnson,** 1908–73: Ralph G. Martin *A Hero for Our Time* (1983)

2925. Both in public and in private, Kennedy had been as direct as his pointed finger at televised press conferences.—**William Manchester:** *The Death of a President* (1967)

2926. He might have envisioned himself being "alone, at the top" but, like [Woodrow] Wilson, be would find out that not even a president moves free of human entanglement, human needs, human illusions; not even a president can be independent of those around him.—**Tom Wicker:** *JFK and LBJ* (1968)

2927. We forgave, followed and accepted because we liked the way he looked. And he had

a pretty wife. Camelot was fun, even for the peasants, as long as it was televised to their huts.—**Joe McGinniss:** *The Selling of the President 1968* (1969)

2928. The secret of the Kennedy successes in politics was not money but meticulous planning and organization, tremendous effort, and the enthusiasm and devotion of family and friends.—**Rose Fitzgerald Kennedy:** *Times to Remember* (1974)

2929. Underneath the beautiful exterior there was an element of ruthlessness and toughness that I had trouble either accepting or forgetting.—**Hubert H. Humphrey:** *The Education of a Public Man* (1976)

2930. Kennedy the politician exuded that musk odor which acts as an aphrodisiac to many women.—**Theodore H. White:** *In Search of History* (1978)

2931. He overwhelmed you with decimal points or disarmed you with a wisecrack.—**James B. Reston,** 1909–95: on Kennedy's news conferences; Ralph G. Martin *A Hero for Our Time* (1983)

2932. Kennedy for a brief time gave their fathers an America where the words of a president were once so grand that they hung in the kitchens of the working class.—**Patrick Fenton:** *New York Times*, 15 March 1988

Kennedy, Robert (1925–68), politician

2933. That was the Kennedy way: you bit off more than you could chew and then you chewed it.—**Gerald C. Gardner:** *Robert Kennedy in New York* (1965)

2934. The highest ranking withdrawn adolescent since Alexander Hamilton in 1794. —**Murray Kempton:** *Newsweek*, 1968

2935. His dealings made Jack Kennedy look like Little Lord Fauntleroy ... a many-faceted man whose relationships were not limited to the domestic front.—**C. David Heymann:** *Publisher's Weekly*, 1 March 1991

Kennedy Family

2936. I don't think they are Christians; they may be Catholics but they are not Christians. —**Mary McCarthy:** *Observer*, 14 October 1979

2937. They were always getting more credit than they deserved, more sorrow than they could bear, climbing into jobs before they were ready and failing just when they were succeeding. —**James B. Reston:** *Deadline* (1991)

2938. We have no one to blame for the Kennedys but ourselves. We took the Kennedys to heart of our own accord. And it is my opinion that we did it not because we respected them or thought what they proposed was good, but because they were pretty. We, the electorate, were smitten by this handsome, vivacious family. We wanted to hug their golden tousled heads to our dumpy breasts. —**P. J. O'Rourke:** *Give War A Chance* (1992)

Kissinger, Henry (1923–   ), politician and diplomat

2939. An eel icier than ice. —**Oriana Fallaci,** 1930–

2940. I've always acted alone. Americans like that enormously. Americans like the cowboy who leads the wagon train by riding ahead alone on his horse, the cowboy who rides all alone into the town, the village, with his horse and nothing else. Maybe even without a pistol, since he doesn't shoot. He acts, that's all, by being in the right place at the right time. —**Henry Kissinger:** interview; Oriana Fallaci *Interview with History* (1970)

2941. I worry about Kissinger. He needed someone like Nixon to keep him on that tough track. He has to have someone around who can keep him from giving away the store. —**Ronald Reagan:** *Time*, 17 November 1975

2942. Kissinger won a Nobel Peace Prize for

watching a war [Vietnam] end that he was for. —**Eugene J. McCarthy:** *New York Times Magazine*, 24 October 1976

2943. Henry likes to say outrageous things. He was fascinated by the celebrity set and he liked being one himself. —**Richard M. Nixon:** *Time*, 23 May 1977

2944. Kissinger has constructed a diplomacy for a Hobbesian world. When he exercised that diplomacy he helped create the kind of world that would justify it. —*New Republic*: 1979

2945. His compulsion to crow is as natural as a rooster's … to preen as normal as a peacock's. —**Robert T. Hartmann:** *Palace Politics* (1980)

2946. He not only knew a lot about foreign affairs, he was a foreign affair. —**James B. Reston:** *Deadline* (1991)

2947. Kissinger became the nation's top foreign-policy strategist despite being born with the handicaps of a laughable accent and no morals or neck. —**Dave Barry,** 1948–

2948. Kissinger may be a great writer, but anyone who finishes his book is definitely a great reader. —**Walter Isaacson:** *The Week*, 20 March 1999

Lincoln, Abraham (1809–65), 16th president (1861–65)

2949. I don't know who my grandfather was; I am much more concerned to know what his grandson will be. —**Abraham Lincoln:** attrib.

2950. Many a time have I stood on one side of the counter and sold whiskey to Mr. Douglas, but the difference between us now is this. I have left my side of the counter, but Mr. Douglas still sticks to his as tenaciously as ever. —**Abraham Lincoln:** during a debate with Stephen A. Douglas in 1858; Leon Harris *The Art of Political Wit* (1965)

2951. A first-rate second-rate man. —**Wendell Phillips:** speech, 2 August 1862; Ralph Korngold *Two Friends of Man* (1950)

2952. Mr. Lincoln's soul seems made of leather, and incapable of any grand or noble emotion. He lowers, he never elevates you.—*New York Post*: 1863

2953. Mr. Lincoln is like a waiter in a large eating house where all the bells are ringing at once; he cannot serve them all at once and so some grumblers are to be expected.—**John Bright,** British radical politician: *Cincinnati Gazette* (1864)

2954. His combination of purest, heartiest tenderness, and native western form of manliness.—**Walt Whitman:** 4 March 1965; *Specimen Days and Collect* (1882)

2955. Now he belongs to the ages.—**Edwin McMasters Stanton:** following his assassination, 15 April 1865; I. M. Tarbell *Life of Abraham Lincoln* (1900)

2956. Lincoln had faith in time, and time has justified his faith.—**Benjamin Harrison:** Lincoln Day Address, Chicago, 1898

2957. Lincoln was a very normal man with very normal gifts, but all upon a great scale, all knit together in loose and natural form, like the great frame in which he moved and dwelt.—**Woodrow Wilson:** address, Chicago, 12 February 1909

2958. Lincoln was not all brooding and melancholy and patient understanding. There was a hard core in him, and plenty of toughness. He could recognize a revolutionary situation when he saw one, and he could act fast and ruthlessly to meet it.—**Bruce Catton:** *This Hallowed Ground* (1956)

2959. Not often in the story of mankind does a man arrive on earth who is both steel and velvet, who is as hard as rock and soft as drifting fog, who holds in his heart and mind the paradox of terrible storm and peace unspeakable and perfect.—**Carl Sandburg:** address to Congress, 12 February 1959

2960. Lincoln was the Christ figure of Democracy's passion play.—**Anonymous:** *McNeil-Lehrer Report*, 17 October 1995

2961. Based on what you know about him in history books, what do you think Abraham Lincoln would be doing if he were alive today? 1) Writing his memoirs of the Civil War.

2) Advising the president.
3) Desperately clawing at the inside of his coffin.
—**David Letterman**

McCarthy, Joseph (1908–57), and McCarthyism

2962. There is a miasma of neurotic fear and internal suspicion.—**Joseph W. Alsop:** on Washington at the beginning of the McCarthyism; *Saturday Evening Post*, 29 July 1950

2963. They'll nail anyone who ever scratched his ass during the National Anthem.—**Humphrey Bogart,** 1899–1957

2964. McCarthyism is Americanism with its sleeves rolled.—**Joseph McCarthy:** speech in Wisconsin, 1952; Richard H. Rovere *Senator Joe McCarthy* (1973)

2965. The only major politician in the country who can be labeled "liar" without fear of libel.—**Joseph W. Alsop** and **Stewart Alsop:** *We Accuse!* (1954)

2966. No one can terrorize a whole nation, unless we are all his accomplices.—**Edward R. Murrow:** "See It Now," CBS-TV, 7 March 1954

2967. He didn't create this situation of fear. He merely exploited it, and rather successfully.—**Edward R. Murrow:** "See It Now," CBS-TV, 7 March 1954

2968. The junior senator from Wisconsin, by his reckless charges, has so preyed upon the fears and hatreds and prejudices of the American people that he has started a prairie fire which neither he nor anyone else may be able to control.—**J. William Fulbright:** speech to the Senate, 30 November 1954

2969. A pathological character assassin.—**Harry S Truman,** 1884–1972: Robert Andrews *The New Penguin Dictionary of Modern Quotations* (2001)

2970. A sadistic bum from Wisconsin.—Hank Greenspun

2971. He was nothing but a damn coward. —Harry S Truman

2972. This Typhoid Mary of conformity. —Richard H. Rovere, 1915– : Jonathon Green (ed.) *The Pan Dictionary of Contemporary Quotations* (1989)

2973. He was a master of the scabrous and the scatological.—Richard H. Rovere: *Esquire* (New York), June 1958

2974. McCarthy invented the Multiple Lie— the lie with so many tiny gears and fragile connecting rods that reason exhausted itself in the effort to combat it.—Richard H. Rovere: *Esquire*, June 1958

2975. The nation that complacently and fearfully allows its artists and writers to become suspected rather than respected is no longer regarded as a nation possessed with humor in depth.—James Thurber: *New York Times Magazine*, 7 December 1958

2976. It will do no good to search for villains or heroes or saints or devils, because there were none; there were only victims.—Dalton Trumbo, 1905– : on the McCarthy witchhunts; Jonathon Green (ed.) *The Pan Dictionary of Contemporary Quotations* (1989)

2977. McCarthyism is the revenge of the noses that for 20 years of fancy parties were pressed against the outside window pane. —Peter Viereck: editorial on charges of Communists in government as an expression of class differences; Time-Life's *This Fabulous Century* (1970)

2978. It was an infringement of liberty but it was only a tiny inconvenience compared with having no job. I weighed it by priority.—Joseph Heller, 1923– : on his signing the "loyalty oath" at Penn State University; Peter Lewis *The Fifties* (1978)

2979. Every age develops its own peculiar forms of pathology, which express in exaggerated form its underlying character structure. —Christopher Lasch: *The Culture of Narcissism* (1979)

McKinley, William (1843–1901), 25th president (1897–1901)

2980. [McKinley has] the backbone of a chocolate éclair.—Thomas Brackett Reed: April 1898

2981. Looking for all the world like a benign undertaker, [McKinley] embalmed himself for posterity. Never permitting himself to be photographed in disarray, he would change his white vests, when wrinkled, several times a day. —Thomas A. Bailey: *Presidential Greatness* (1966)

2982. Why, if a man were to call my dog McKinley, and the brute failed to resent to the death the damning insult, I'd drown it.—William Cowper Brann

NASA

2983. Some agencies have a public affairs office. NASA is a public affairs office that has an agency.—John Pike: Jon Winokur (ed.) *The Portable Curmudgeon Redux* (1992)

Nixon, Richard M. (1913–94), 37th president (1969–74)

See also WAR AND THE MILITARY: Vietnam War

2984. The Republican party did not have to encourage the excesses of its vice-presidential nominee [Richard Nixon]—the young man who asks you to set him one heart-beat from the presidency of the United States.—Adlai Stevenson: speech at Cleveland, Ohio, 23 October 1952; *New York Times*, 24 October 1952

2985. Nixon is the kind of politician who would cut down a redwood tree, then mount the stump for a speech on conservation.—**Adlai Stevenson,** 1900–65: Leon Harris *The Fine Art of Political Wit* (1965)

2986. This is a man of many masks. Who can say they have seen his real face?—**Adlai Stevenson:** 1956

2987. You don't set a fox to watching the chickens just because he has a lot of experience in the hen house.—**Harry S Truman:** on Vice-president Nixon's candidacy for the presidency; speech, 30 October 1960

2988. He was like a kamikaze pilot who keeps apologizing for the attack.—**Mary McGrory:** syndicated newspaper column, 8 November 1962

2989. Nixon is a shifty-eyed goddamn liar. He's one of the few in the history of this country to run for high office talking out of both sides of his mouth at the same time and lying out of both sides.—**Harry S Truman,** 1884–1972: Leo Rosten *Infinite Riches* (1978)

2990. President Nixon's motto was, if two wrongs don't make a right, try three.—**Norman Cousins:** *Daily Telegraph*, 17 July 1969

2991. Avoid all needle drugs. The only dope worth shooting is Richard Nixon.—**Abbie Hoffman:** 1971

2992. Nixon was the artist who had discovered the laws of vibration in all the frozen congelations of the mediocre.—**Normal Mailer:** *St. George and the Godfather* (1972)

2993. [Nixon] has a deeper concern for his place in history than for the people he governs. And history will not fail to note that fact.—**Shirley Chisholm:** *The Good Fight* (1973)

2994. [Nixon] bleeds people. He draws every drop of blood and then drops them from a cliff. He'll blame any person he can put his foot on.—**Martha Mitchell:** *Los Angeles Times*, 28 August 1973

2995. I'm not a crook.—**Richard M. Nixon:** press conference, 17 November 1973

2996. I worship the quicksand he walks in.—**Art Buchwald,** 1925– : Jonathon Green (ed.) *The Book of Political Quotes* (1982)

2997. Certainly he is not of the generation that regards honesty as the best policy. However, he does regard it as a policy.—**Walter Lippmann,** 1899–1974: *Newsweek*, 12 May 1980

2998. Nixon is the kind of guy who, if you were drowning twenty feet from shore, would throw you a fifteen-foot rope.—**Eugene J. McCarthy,** 1916– : Jon Winokur (ed.) *The Portable Curmudgeon Redux* (1992)

2999. Would you buy a second-hand car from this man?—**Mort Sahl,** 1926– : M. J. and J. M. Cohen *Penguin Book of Modern Quotations* (1980)

3000. Nixon's sin, like all sin, was a failure of restraint. It was the immoderate craving for that which, desired moderately, is a noble goal. —**George F. Will:** 8 August 1974; *The Pursuit of Happiness* (1978)

3001. It is quite extraordinary! He will even tell a lie when it is not convenient to. That is the sign of a great artist.—**Gore Vidal,** 1925– : Jon Winokur (ed.) *The Portable Curmudgeon Redux* (1992)

3002. He may be the only genuinely tragic hero in our history, his ruination caused by the flaws in his own character.—**William Safire:** *Before the Fall* (1975)

3003. Our founders did not oust George III in order for us to crown Richard I.—**Ralph Nader:** 1975

3004. The integrity of a hyena and the style of a poison toad.—**Hunter S. Thompson,** 1939– : Jon Winokur (ed.) *The Portable Curmudgeon Redux* (1992)

3005. The trouble with Nixon is that he's a serious *politics junkie*. He's totally hooked and like any other junkie, he's a bummer to have around: especially as president.—**Hunter S. Thompson:** *The Great Shark Hunt* (1979)

3006. For years I've regarded him as a monument to all the rancid genes and broken chromosomes that corrupt the possibility of the American Dream: he was a foul caricature of himself, a man with no soul, no inner convictions, with the integrity of a hyena and the style of a poison toad.—**Hunter S. Thompson:** *The Great Shark Hunt* (1979)

3007. If Richard Nixon was second-rate, what in the world *is* third-rate?—**Joseph Heller:** *Good as Gold* (1979)

3008. A man that had the morals of a private detective.—**William S. Burroughs:** 1980; Jonathon Green (ed.) *The Pan Dictionary of Contemporary Quotations* (1989)

3009. Nixon had three goals: to win by the biggest electoral landslide in history; to be remembered as a peacemaker; and to be accepted by the "Establishment" as an equal. He achieved all these objectives at the end of 1972 and the beginning of 1973. And he lost them all two months later—partly because he turned a dream into an obsession.—**Henry Kissinger:** *Years of Upheaval* (1982)

3010. Richard Nixon means never having to say you're sorry.—**Wilfrid Sheed:** *GQ,* 1984

3011. I think that Nixon will go down in history as a true folk hero, who struck a vital blow to the whole diseased concept of the revered image and gave the American virtue of irreverence and skepticism back to the people.—**William S. Burroughs:** *The Adding Machine* (1985)

3012. He forever perplexes and annoys. Every time you think he is about to show the statesmanship for which his intelligence and experience have equipped him, he throws a spitball.—**Ronald Steel:** *New York Review of Books,* 30 May 1985

3013. I wouldn't trust Nixon from here to that phone.—**Barry Goldwater:** *Newsweek,* 1986

3014. His whole life has been one sustained career of escapology.—**Godfrey Hodgson:** *New York Times,* 10 March 1991

Pierce, Franklin (1804–69), 14th president (1853–57)

3015. A man who cannot be befriended; whose miserable administration admits but of one excuse, imbecility. Pierce was either the worst, or

he was the weakest, of all our presidents.—**Ralph Waldo Emerson,** 1803–82

3016. Many persons have difficulty remembering what president Franklin Pierce is best remembered for, and he is therefore probably best forgotten.—**Richard Armour**

3017. Whoever may be elected, we cannot get a poorer cuss than now disgraces the presidential chair.—**B. B. French**

Politics

See also THE AMERICAN PEOPLE: The Public and Public Opinion; PLACES: Washington; BUSINESS AND ECONOMY: Economy; BUSINESS AND ECONOMY: Money; CULTURE AND MEDIA: Intellectuals; WAR AND THE MILITARY; SOCIAL LIFE: Progress; PAST AND FUTURE: Revolution; INTERNATIONAL RELATIONS: World

3018. The politicians of New York see nothing wrong in the rule, that to the victor belong the spoils of the enemy.—**William Learned Marcy:** speech to the Senate, 25 January 1832; James Parton *Life of Andrew Jackson* vol. 3 (1860)

3019. You can always get the truth from an American statesman after he has turned seventy, or given up all hope of the presidency.—**Wendell Philips:** speech, 7 November 1860

3020. Americans don't think, they calculate; they are amazingly clever, but not very wise; they have no statesman, only politicians.—**Charles Marriott:** *The House on the Sands* (1903)

3021. DELEGATION, n. In American politics, an article of merchandise that comes in sets.—**Ambrose Bierce:** *The Devil's Dictionary* (1911)

3022. The American creed is that most politicians of all parties are bad, the worst ones generally being in the other party, and the good ones all dead or out of office.—**William Allen White:** *Masks in a Pageant* (1928)

3023. Over there [England] politics is an obligation; over here it's a business.—**Will Rogers,** 1879–1935: *Autobiography of Will Rogers* (1949)

3024. America has had gifted conservative statesmen and national leaders. But with few exceptions, only the liberals have gone down in history as national heroes.—**Gunnar Myrdal,** 1898–1987: Laurence J. Peter *Peter's Quotations* (1977)

3025. The American people are quite competent to judge a political party that works both sides of the street.—**Franklin D. Roosevelt:** campaign speech in Boston, 4 November 1944

3026. There are no generalizations in American politics that vested selfishness cannot cut through.—**John Gunther:** *Inside U.S.A.* (1947)

3027. A conservative country without any conservative ideology.—**C. Wright Mills:** *The Power Elite* (1956)

3028. Not everyone is attracted to politics. Scholars found that more than half the adults in Wayne County (Detroit) Michigan thought that politics was dirty and dishonest. Nearly half the political volunteers and political workers in the county thought so, too.—**David Botter:** *Politicians and What They Do* (1960)

3029. Mothers all want their sons to grow up to be president, but they don't want them to become politicians in the process.—**John F. Kennedy,** 1917–63: attrib.; Fred Metcalf *The Penguin Dictionary of Modern Humorous Quotations* (1986)

3030. I probably made a mistake in keeping Allen Dulles on [as CIA Director after the Bay of Pigs in 1961]. It's hard to operate with legendary figures.—**John F. Kennedy:** Peter Grose *Gentleman Spy* (1994)

3031. In America you can go on the air and kid the politicians, and the politicians can go on the air and kid the people. Personal relations are the important thing for ever and ever and not this outer life of telegrams and anger. —**E. M. Forster,** 1879–1970

3032. Controversial proposals, once accepted, soon become hallowed.—**Dean Acheson,** 1893–1971

3033. Scratch any American and underneath you'll find an isolationist.—**Dean Rusk,** 1909–94: Tony Benn *Diary*, 12 January 1968

3034. It is ironic that a nation that has never experienced a coup d'état should be so obsessed with the idea of conspiracy.—**Gore Vidal:** *Reflections Upon a Sinking Ship* (1969)

3035. Everyone else is represented in Washington by a rich and powerful lobby, it seems. But there is no lobby for the people.—**Shirley Chisholm:** *Unbought and Unbossed* (1970)

3036. That's one of my Goddam precious American rights, not to think about politics. —**John Updike:** *Rabbit Redux* (1971)

3037. Politics in the United States consists of the struggle between those whose change has been arrested by success or failure, on one side, and those who are still engaged in changing themselves, on the other.—**Harold Rosenberg:** *Discovering the Present* (1973)

3038. In America, where movements spring up overnight like fastfood outlets, all God's children gotta have ideology.—**Richard Dean Rosen:** *New Times,* 1975

3039. The history of American politics is littered with bodies of people who took so pure a position that they had no clout at all.—**Benjamin C. Bradlee,** 1921– : Studs Terkel *Talking to Myself* (1977)

3040. Ninety percent of the politicians give the other ten percent a bad reputation.—**Henry Kissinger:** 1978, attrib.

3041. The two-party system has given this country the war of Lyndon Johnson, the Watergate of Nixon, and the incompetence of Carter. —**Eugene J. McCarthy:** *Chicago Tribune,* 10 September 1978

3042. What this country needs is more unemployed politicians.—**Edward Langley:** *San Francisco Chronicle,* 24 October 1980

3043. Politics in America is the binding secular religion.—**Theodore H. White,** 1915–86: *Time,* 29 December 1986

3044. It's a country evenly divided between conservatives and reactionaries.—**Gore Vidal:** *Observer,* 16 September 1984

3045. There are two ways to empty a room in Washington. Hold a fund raiser for a defeated candidate, or a debate on federalism.—**Charles S. Robb,** 1939– : Henry O. Dormann *The Speaker's Book of Quotations* (1987)

3046. We should realize that the average family in America spends five minutes a week on politics.—**Celinda Lake:** *Democratic Pollster*

3047. When I have to choose between voting for the people or the special interests, I always stick with the special interests. They remember. The people forget.—**Henry Fountain Ashurst,** American senator

3048. The folks you help won't remember it and the folks you hurt won't ever forget it.—**Bill Clayton,** Texas politician

3049. When buying and selling are controlled by legislation, the first things to be bought and sold are legislators.—**P. J. O'Rourke,** 1947–

3050. The American political system is like a gigantic Mexican Christmas fiesta. Each political party is a huge piñata—a papier-maché donkey, for example. The donkey is filled with full employment, low interest rates, affordable housing, comprehensive medical benefits, a balanced budget and other goodies. The American voter is blindfolded and given a stick. The voter then swings the stick wildly in every direction, trying to hit a political candidate on the head and knock some sense into the silly bastard.—**P. J. O'Rourke**

3051. Our political scene is more volatile and given to sudden switches and memory lapses bordering on soap-opera-type amnesia (epidemic, total and terminal) than any other I know of. We are fickle and we are insatiable in our appetite for new news, new issues, new biases, new clichés. It's not just (as another clichés, lifted from Andy Warhol, has it) that individuals all seem to get their fifteen minutes of celebrity in this country; everything gets only fifteen minutes.—**Meg Greenfield:** *Newsweek,* 1991

3052. We didn't send you to Washington to make intelligent decisions. We sent you to represent us.—**Kent York,** Baptist minister, to U.S. Rep. Bill Sarpalius

3053. I have the most reliable friend you can have in American politics, and that is ready money.—**Phil Gramm,** 1942–   , Republican senator

3054. Although He is regularly asked to do so, God does not take sides in American politics.—**George Mitchell,** Democrat senator

3055. You have to give the press confrontations. When you give them confrontations, you get attention; when you get attention, you can educate.—**Newt Gingrich,** 1943–

3056. What is the primary purpose of a political leader? To build a majority. If [voters] care about parking lots, then talk about parking lots.—**Newt Gingrich**

3057. What is real politics? Who collects what money from whom to spend on whom for what. That's all there is to it, but no politician in the United States dares address that subject for fear we'll discover who bought him and for how much—not to mention how the military got us $5 trillion into debt.—**Gore Vidal:** *Independent,* 19 August 1998

3058. You know what's interesting about Washington? It's the kind of place where second-guessing has become second nature. —**George W. Bush:** speech, 17 May 2002

Power

See also BUSINESS AND ECONOMY: Money

3059. Our country has liberty without license, and authority without despotism.—**James Cardinal Gibbons:** speech in Rome, Italy, 25 March 1887

3060. Power is poison. Its effect on presidents had always been tragic.—**Henry Brooks Adams,** 1838–1918

3061. The United States is like a gigantic boiler. Once the fire is lighted under it, there is no limit to the power it can generate.—**Edward Grey:** 1916; Christopher Hassall *Edward Marsh* (1954)

3062. It is difficult to find a reputable American historian who will acknowledge the crude fact that a Franklin Roosevelt, say, wanted to be president merely to wield power, to be famed and to be feared.—**Gore Vidal:** *Rocking the Boat* (1963)

3063. Can America overcome the fatal arrogance of power?—**J. William Fulbright:** *The Arrogance of Power* (1996)

3064. In the United States, though power corrupts, the expectation of power paralyzes. —**John Kenneth Galbraith:** *New York*, 15 November 1971

3065. Only three men in America understand the use of power. I do. John Connally does. And I guess Nelson [Rockefeller] does. —**Richard M. Nixon:** *American Opinion*, May 1975

3066. What distinguishes America is not its greater or lesser goodness, but simply its unrivalled power to do that which is good or bad. —**Mark Frankland:** *Observer*, 6 November 1977

3067. The trouble in corporate America is that too many people with too much power live in a box (their home), then travel the same road every day to another box (their office). —**Faith Popcorn:** *The Popcorn Report* (1991)

3068. Money is power in American politics. It always has been. —**William Greider:** *Who Will Tell the People* (1992)

Presidency

See also CULTURE AND MEDIA: Television

3069. No man will ever bring out of that office the reputation which carries him into it. —**Thomas Jefferson:** letter, 27 December 1796

3070. The second office of this government is honorable and easy, the first is but a splendid misery. —**Thomas Jefferson:** letter to Elbridge Gerry, 13 May 1797

3071. I have no ambition to govern men; it is a painful and thankless office. —**Thomas Jefferson,** 1743–1826

3072. I had rather be right than be president. —**Henry Clay:** to Senator Preston of South Carolina, 1839; Samuel W. McCall *The Life of Thomas Brackett Reed* (1914)

3073. No president who performs his duties faithfully and conscientiously can have any leisure. —**James K. Polk:** *Diary*, 1 September 1847

3074. As president, I have no eyes but constitutional eyes. —**Abraham Lincoln,** 1809–65: attrib.

3075. All we ask is to be let alone. —**Jefferson Davis:** Inaugural address as president of the Confederate States of America, 18 February 1861, attrib.

3076. There's nothing left ... but to get drunk. —**Franklin Pierce,** 1804–69: when asked what a president should do after leaving office; Harry Barnard *Rutherford B. Hayes and His America* (1954)

3077. [The president is] the last person in the world to know what the people really want and think. —**James A. Garfield,** 1831–81, 20th president

3078. Washington, where an insignificant individual may trespass on a nation's time. —**Ralph Waldo Emerson,** 1803–82

3079. I may be president of the United States, but my private life is nobody's damned business. —**Chester A. Arthur,** 1830–86, 21st president: responding to a visitor asking him about his expensive tastes

3080. Since I came here I have learned that Chester A. Arthur is one man and the president of the United States is another. —**Chester A. Arthur:** James Morgan *Our Presidents* (1958)

3081. The progress of evolution from president Washington to president Grant was alone evidence to upset Darwin. —**Henry Brooks Adams:** *The Education of Henry Adams* (1907)

3082. I want the people to love me, but I suppose they never will. —**Woodrow Wilson,** 1856–1924: Richard Hofstadter *The American Political Tradition* (1948)

3083. My God, this is a hell of a job! I have no trouble with my enemies. 1 can take care of my enemies all right. But my damn friends, my goddamn friends. They're the ones that keep me walking the floor nights! —**Warren G. Harding,** 1865–1923: William Allen White *Autobiography* (1946)

3084. One cannot always be sure of the truth of what one hears if he happens to be president of the United States. —**William Howard Taft,** 1857–1930, 27th president: Archie Butt *Taft and Roosevelt* vol. II (1930)

3085. The presidency does not yield to definition. Like the glory of a morning sunrise, it can be experienced it can not be told.—**Calvin Coolidge,** 1872–1933, 30th president

3086. The presidency is not merely an administrative office. That's the least of it. It is more than an engineering job, efficient or inefficient. It is preeminently a place of moral leadership.—**Franklin D. Roosevelt:** *New York Times,* 11 September 1932

3087. The duty of the president to see that the laws be executed is a duty that does not go beyond the laws or require him to achieve more than Congress sees fit to leave within his power.—**Oliver Wendell Holmes, Jr.,** 1841–1935: Laurence J. Peter (ed.) *Peter's Quotations* (1977)

3088. When I was a boy I was told that anybody could become president; I'm beginning to believe it.—**Clarence S. Darrow,** 1857–1938: Irving Stone *Clarence Darrow for the Defence* (1941)

3089. Brains, integrity, and force may be all very well, but what you need today is Charm.—**Gracie Allen:** *How to Become President* (1940)

3090. The first twelve years are the hardest.—**Franklin D. Roosevelt:** press conference, 19 January 1945

3091. All Coolidge had to do in 1924 was to keep his mean trap shut, to be elected. All Harding had to do in 1920 was repeat "Avoid foreign entanglements." All Hoover had to do in 1928 was to endorse Coolidge. All Roosevelt had to do in 1932 was to point to Hoover.—**Robert E. Sherwood,** 1896–1955: Robert E. Drennan *Wit's End* (1968)

3092. They [the White House staff] should be possessed of high competence, great physical vigour, and a passion for anonymity.—**Thomas Jones,** 1870–1955: Colin Bingham (ed.) *Wit and Wisdom* (1982)

3093. All the president is, is a glorified public relations man who spends his time flattering, kissing and kicking people to get them to do what they are supposed to do anyway.—**Harry S Truman:** letter to his sister, 14 November 1947; *Off the Record* (1980)

3094. A president is best judged by the enemies he makes when he has really hit his stride.—**Max Lerner:** *New York Star,* 9 January 1949

3095. The White House is the finest jail in the world.—**Harry S Truman:** 1949

3096. In my opinion eight years as president is enough and sometimes too much for any man to serve in that capacity. There is a lure in power. It can get into a man's blood just as gambling and lust for money have been known to do.—**Harry S Truman:** 16 April 1950

3097. The best reason I can think of for not running for president of the United States is that you have to shave twice a day.—**Adlai Stevenson,** 1900–65: Fred Metcalf *The Penguin Dictionary of Modern Humorous Quotations* (1986)

3098. They pick a president and then for four years they pick on him.—**Adlai Stevenson:** speech, 28 August 1952

3099. In America any boy may become president, and I suppose it's just one of the risks he takes.—**Adlai Stevenson:** speech in Indianapolis, 26 September 1952; *Major Campaign Speeches of Adlai Stevenson: 1952* (1953)

3100. There is one thing about being president—nobody can tell you when to sit down.—**Dwight D. Eisenhower:** *Observer,* 9 August 1953

3101. Any man who wants to be president is either an egomaniac or crazy.—**Dwight D. Eisenhower,** 1890–1969

3102. Any man who has had the job I've had and didn't have a sense of humor wouldn't still be here.—**Harry S Truman:** 1955, attrib.

3103. Most of the problems a president has to face have their roots in the past.—**Harry S Truman:** *Memoirs* vol. 2 (1955)

3104. A president needs political understanding to *run* the government, but he may be *elected* without it.—**Harry S Truman:** *Memoirs* vol. 2 (1955)

3105. Being president is like riding a tiger … keep on riding or be swallowed.—**Harry S Truman,** 1884–1972: *New York Times,* 28 December 1984

3106. The president is the representative of the whole nation and he's the only lobbyist that all the 160 million people in this country have.—**Harry S Truman:** lecture, Columbia University, 27 April 1959

3107. All presidents grow in office.—**Earl Schenck Miers:** *Saturday Review*, 29 August 1959

3108. Oh, that lovely title, ex-president. —**Dwight D. Eisenhower:** 1959

3109. Roosevelt proved a man could be president for life; Truman proved anybody could be president; and Eisenhower proved we don't need a president.—**Anonymous**

3110. From now on, I think it is safe to predict, neither the Democratic nor the Republican Party will ever nominate for president a candidate without good looks, stage presence, theatrical delivery, and a sense of timing.—**James Thurber:** referring to the Kennedy-Nixon TV debates, 20 March 1961; Michael J. Rosen (ed.) *James Thurber Collecting Himself* (1989)

3111. This is a most presidential country. The tone and example set by the president have a tremendous effect on the quality of life in America.—**Walter Lippmann,** 1899–1974: *Look*, 25 April 1961

3112. When we got into office, the thing that surprised me most was to find that things were just as bad as we'd been saying they were.—**John F. Kennedy:** speech in Washington, 27 May 1961

3113. The American presidency is a formidable, exposed, and somewhat mysterious institution.—**John F. Kennedy,** 1917–63: attrib.

3114. The American presidency will demand more than ringing manifestos issued from the rear of the battle. It will demand that the president place himself in the very thick of the fight; that he care passionately about the fate of the people he leads.—**John F. Kennedy**

3115. Whatever the political affiliation of our next president, whatever his views may be on all the issues and problems that rush in upon us, he must above all be the chief executive in every sense of the word.—**John F. Kennedy:** Tom Wicker *JFK and LBJ* (1968)

3116. When the presidential virus attacks the system there is a tendency for the patient in his fever to move from the Right or the Left to the Center where the curative votes are.—**Gore Vidal:** *Rocking the Boat* (1962)

3117. No *easy* problems ever come to the president. If they are easy to solve, somebody else has solved them.—**Dwight D. Eisenhower:** *Parade Magazine*, 8 April 1962

3118. In the White House, the future rapidly becomes the past; and delay is itself a decision. —**Theodore Sorensen:** *Nation's Business*, June 1963

3119. All presidents start out pretending to run a crusade, but after a couple of years they find they are running something much less heroic, much more intractable: namely, the presidency.—**Alistair Cooke:** *Listener*, 1963

3120. My most fervent prayer is to be a president who can make it possible for every boy in this land to grow to manhood by loving his country—instead of dying for it.—**Lyndon B. Johnson,** 1908–73

3121. One lesson you better learn if you want to be in politics is that you never go out on a golf course and beat the president.—**Lyndon B. Johnson**

3122. Being president is like being a jackass in a hailstorm. There's nothing to do but to stand there and take it.—**Lyndon B. Johnson**

3123. If one morning I walked on top of the water across the Potomac River, the headline that afternoon would read: PRESIDENT CAN'T SWIM.—**Lyndon B. Johnson**

3124. You're asking the leader of the Western world a chickenshit question like that?—**Lyndon B. Johnson:** to reporter, attrib.

3125. A president's hardest task is not *do* what is right, but to *know* what is right.—**Lyndon B. Johnson:** address to Congress, 4 January 1965

3126. The president is the people's lobbyist. —**Hebert H. Humphrey:** address, 8 December 1965

3127. The final greatness of the presidency lies in the truth that it is not just an office of incredible power but a breeding ground of indestructible myth.—**Clinton Rossiter,** 1917–70: Robert I. Fitzhenry *Barnes & Noble Book of Quotations* (1986)

3128. The purpose of presidential Office is not power, or leadership of the Western World, but reminiscence, best-selling reminiscence. —**Roger Jellinek:** *New York Times Book Review*, 1969

3129. Roosevelt, a false witness; Truman, a merchant; Eisenhower, I am told that on the golf links he is better [with a putter] than he is with the long shots and that doesn't surprise me; Kennedy, the style of a hairdresser's assistant—he combed his way through problems; Johnson, a truck driver or a stevedore—or a legionnaire.—**Charles de Gaulle:** *Time*, February 1969

3130. A president moves through his days surrounded by literally hundreds of people whose relationship to him is that of a doting mother to a spoiled child. Whatever he wants is brought to him immediately—food, drink, helicopters, airplanes, people, in fact, everything but relief from his political problems.—**George Reedy:** *The Twilight of the Presidency* (1970)

3131. When you get to be president, there are all those things, the honors, the twenty-one gun salutes, all those things. You have to remember it isn't for you. It's for the presidency.—**Harry S Truman,** 1884–1972: Merle Miller *Plain Speaking: Conversations with Harry S Truman* (1973)

3132. If you wants to get elected president, you've got to think up some memorable homily so's school kids can be pestered into memorizin' it, even if they don't know what it means. —**Walt Kelly,** 1913–73

3133. Every president reconstructs the presidency to meet his own psychological needs. —**Arthur M. Schlesinger, Jr.:** *The Imperial Presidency* (1973)

3134. The answer to the runaway presidency is not the messenger-boy presidency. The American democracy must discover a middle way between making the president a czar and making him a puppet.—**Arthur M. Schlesinger, Jr.:** *The Imperial Presidency* (1973)

3135. Being president is never having to say that you're sorry.—**David Frye:** 1973; Jonathon Green (ed.) *The Pan Dictionary of Contemporary Quotations* (1989)

3136. Anybody who wants the presidency so much that he'll spend two years organizing and campaigning for it is not to be trusted with the office.—**David Broder:** *Washington Post,* 18 July 1973

3137. To be president is to act as advocate for a blind, venomous, and ungrateful client.—**John Updike:** *Buchanan Dying* (1974)

3138. By the time a man gets to be presidential material he's been bought ten times over. —**Gore Vidal:** *Newsweek*, 18 November 1974

3139. I don't want to spend the next two years in Holiday Inns.—**Walter F. Mondale:** on withdrawing from 1976 presidential campaign, 21 November 1974

3140. A president's ability to govern depends partially on his equity in public opinion, partially on his relations with Congress, and largely on his willingness to impose his will on his own Executive Branch.—**William Safire:** *Before the Fall* (1975)

3141. The office of president is such a bastardized thing, half royalty and half democracy, that nobody knows whether to genuflect or spit.—**Jimmy Breslin,** 1929–

3142. It is the president's decision to choose how to impart information to the people.—**John R. Ehrlichman**

3143. The US presidency is a Tudor monarchy plus telephones.—**Anthony Burgess:** George Plimpton (ed.) *Writers at Work* Fourth Series (1977)

3144. The president's decisions make the weather, and if be is great enough, change the climate, too.—**Theodore H. White:** *In Search of History* (1978)

3145. Old men running for the presidency of the United States are like old men who take young brides. It's an exciting idea for a while but it seldom works.—**James B. Reston:** *New York Times*, 26 January 1979

3146. Americans expect their presidents to do what no monarch by Divine Right could ever do—resolve for them all the contradictions and complexities of life. And those who seek the presidency invariably promise—and perhaps really believe—that they can handle our problems for us, at least better than the other guy. —**Robert T. Hartman:** *Palace Politics: An Inside Account of the Ford Years* (1980)

3147. It would be supremely dangerous if a president were to believe in the myth of his own omnipotence. Fortunately, a new president is soon disabused.—**Robert T. Hartman:** *Palace Politics: An Inside Account of the Ford Years* (1980)

3148. Anyone who is capable of getting themselves made president should on no account be allowed to do the job.—**Douglas Adams:** *The Hitchhiker's Guide to the Galaxy* (1980)

3149. One of the little-celebrated powers of presidents (and other high government officials) is to listen to their critics with just enough sympathy to ensure their silence.—**John Kenneth Galbraith:** *A Life in Our Times* (1981)

3150. All a man needs to be elected president is the kind of profile that looks good on a postage stamp.—**Billy Boy Franklin:** Gerald F. Lieberman *3,500 Good Quotes for Speakers* (1983)

3151. You should judge presidents like plumbing fixtures—by whether they flush.—**Joseph W. Alsop:** *W*, 26 February 1982

3152. Carter, Ford, and Nixon—See No Evil, Hear No Evil, and Evil.—**Senator Robert J. Dole:** 1983; William Cole and Louis Phillips (comps.) *Oh, What an Awful Thing to Say!* (1992)

3153. No man could be equipped for the presidency if he has never been tempted by one of the seven cardinal sins.—**Eugene J. McCarthy,** 1916– , Democrat senator

3154. I would rather be a doorkeeper in the house of God than live in that palace at Washington.—**Rachel Donaldson Jackson**

3155. If presidents don't do it to their wives, they do it to the country.—**Mel Brooks:** *2000-Year-Old Man* (1981)

3156. The presidency is a cross between a popularity contest and a high school debate, with an encyclopedia of clichés the first prize.—**Saul Bellow,** 1915– : Jon Winokur (ed.) *The Portable Curmudgeon* (1987)

3157. Any American who is prepared to run for president should automatically, by definition, be disqualified from ever doing so.—**Gore Vidal,** 1925– : attrib.; Fred Metcalf *The Penguin Dictionary of Modern Humorous Quotations* (1986)

3158. I hope we don't lose in America this demand that those of us who want this office … must be prepared not to handle the 10-second gimmick that deals, say, with little things like war and peace.—**Walter F. Mondale:** after losing presidential election, *New York Times*, 8 November 1984

3159. The United States brags about its political system, but the president says one thing during the election, something else when he takes office, something else at midterm, and something else when he leaves.—**Deng Xiaoping,** Chinese Premier: *New York Times*, 2 January 1985

3160. Frankly, I don't mind not being president. I just mind that someone else is.—**Edward M. Kennedy:** Washington Gridiron Club dinner, 22 March 1986

3161. In Washington it is an honor to be disgraced. You have to have *been* somebody to fall.—**Meg Greenfield:** *Newsweek*, 2 June 1986

3162. But there are advantages to being elected president. The day after I was elected, I had my high school grades classified Top Secret.—**Ronald Reagan:** address in New Jersey, 19 June 1986

3163. Being a press secretary [is like] learning to type: You're hunting and pecking for a while and then you find yourself doing the touch system and don't realize it. You're speaking for the president without ever having to go to him.—**Larry Speakes:** *New York Times*, 10 October 1986

3164. Do you want to tear your life apart and get rid of everything you've known as a lifestyle? Like seeing your family? Being with your friends? A fishing trip? A hunting trip? A night's sleep?—**Walter F. Mondale,** politician: comments to prospective presidential candidates; *Newsweek*, 30 March 1987

3165. There's never a dearth of reasons to shoot at the president.—**Don Delillo:** *Libra* (1988)

3166. They are a great tradition … gliding in and out of the corridors of power with the opulent calm of angelfish swimming through an aquarium castle.—**Henry Allen:** on presidential advisers; *Washington Post*, 3 January 1989

3167. The future of America may or may not bring forth a black president, a woman president, a Jewish president, but it most certainly always will have a suburban president. A president whose senses have been defined by the suburbs, where lakes and public baths mutate into back yards and freeways, where walking means driving, where talking means telephoning, where watching means TV, and where living means real, imitation life.—**Arthur Kroker, Marilouise Kroker** and **David Cook:** *Panic Encyclopedia* (1989)

3168. We want a president who is as much like an American tourist as possible. Someone with the same goofy grin, the same innocent intentions, the same naïve trust; a president with no conception of foreign policy and no discernible connection to the U.S. government, whose Nice Guyism will narrow the gap between the U.S. and us until nobody can tell the difference.—**Florence King:** *Reflections in a Jaundiced Eye* (1989)

3169. Speechwriters have a unique distinction in Washington—none of us has ever been indicted.—**Jack Valenti:** Peggy Noon *What I Saw at the Revolution* (1990)

3170. Most presidents come to Washington bright as freshly minted dimes and leave much diminished.—**George F. Will:** *Suddenly: The American Idea Abroad and at Home* (1990)

3171. We need a president who's fluent in at least one language.—**Buck Henry**

3172. When someone becomes president they automatically are funnier because people are readier to laugh.—**Landon Parvin:** *New York Times*, 29 March 1991

3173. The most successful [presidents] were the cheerful optimists, who appointed competent advisers and listened to them: Roosevelt, Truman, and Eisenhower.—**James B. Reston:** *Deadline* (1991)

3174. The least successful presidents were the pessimists who assumed the worst in everybody and didn't listen to anybody: Nixon and Johnson.—**James B. Reston:** *Deadline* (1991)

3175. In our brief national history we have shot four of our presidents, worried five of them to death, impeached one and hounded another out of office. And when all else fails, we hold an election and assassinate their char-

acter.—**P. J. O'Rourke:** *Parliament of Whores* (1991)

3176. The president we get is the country we get. With each new president the nation is conformed spiritually.—**E. L. Doctorow:** *Jack London, Hemingway, and the Constitution* (1993)

3177. When I go into the voting booth, do I vote for the person who is the best president? Or the slime bucket who will make my life as a cartoonist wonderful?—**Mike Peters,** American cartoonist: *Wall Street Journal*, 20 January 1993

3178. What higher obligation does a president have than to explain his intentions to the people and persuade them that the direction he wishes to go is right?—**Arthur M. Schlesinger, Jr.:** *New York Times*, 15 April 1993

3179. What this White House really needs is a chief of staff who can read Machiavelli in the original Italian.—**Mack McLarty:** 1994

3180. Being president is like running a cemetery; you've got a lot of people under you and nobody's listening.—**Bill Clinton:** at Galesburg, Illinois, *US News & World Report*, 23 January 1995

Reagan, Ronald (1911–   ), 40th president (1981–89)

3181. The most ignorant president since Warren Harding.—**Ralph Nader:** *Pacific Sun*, 21 March 1981

3182. Sure, Reagan promised to take senility tests. But what if he forgets?—**Lorna Kerr-Walker:** *Pacific Sun*, 21 March 1981

3183. A triumph of the embalmer's art.—**Gore Vidal:** *Observer*, 26 April 1981

3184. There's a lot to be said for being *nouveau riche*, and the Reagans mean to say it all.—**Gore Vidal:** *Observer*, 1981

3185. He is the first man for twenty years to make the presidency a part-time job, a means of filling up a few of the otherwise blank days of retirement.—**Simon Hoggart**: *Observer*, June 1981

3186. That youthful sparkle in his eyes is caused by his contact lenses, which he keeps highly polished.—**Sheilah Graham**: *Times*, 22 August 1981

3187. I think that Nancy [Reagan] does most of his talking; you'll notice that she never drinks water when Ronnie speaks.—**Robin Williams**: 1982

3188. Reagan won because he ran against Jimmy Carter. Had he run unopposed he would have lost.—**Mort Sahl**, 1926– : Robert Byrne *The Other 637 Best Things Anybody Ever Said* (1984)

3189. Ask him the time, and he'll tell you how the watch was made.—**Jane Wyman**, 1914– , Reagan's first wife: attrib.

3190. I believe that Ronald Reagan will some-day make this country what it once was … an arctic wilderness.—**Steve Martin**, 1945–

3191. What's really worrying about Reagan is that he always seems to be waiting for some-one to say "Cut" and has no idea how they've decided the script should end.—**Katherine Whitehorn**: *Observer*, 1983

3192. Ronald Reagan is attempting a great breakthrough in political technology—he has been perfecting the Teflon-coated presidency. He sees to it that nothing sticks to him.—**Patricia S. Schroeder**: speech in the House of Representatives, 2 August 1983

3193. The presidency is a huge echo chamber magnifying every little thing he does.—**Stephen Hess**: *Time*, 6 February 1984

3194. Are you more likely to tolerate drivel than you were four years ago? I think the an-swer is yes. Four years of Reagan has deadened the senses against a barrage of uninterrupted nonsense.—**Alexander Cockburn**: *Nation* (New York), 27 October 1984

3195. People want to forget. There was Viet-nam, there was Watergate, there was Iran. We were beaten, we were hustled, and then we were humiliated. And I think people got a need to feel good about the country they live in. And you see the Reagan reelection ads on TV.

"It's morning in America." And you say, well, it's not morning in Pittsburgh. It's not morn-ing above 125th Street in New York. It's mid-night, and like, there's a bad moon risin'.—**Bruce Springsteen**: *Rolling Stone*, December 1984

3196. Reagan doesn't dye his hair; he's just prematurely orange.—**Gerald R. Ford**: *Esquire* (New York), January 1985

3197. He has a chance to make somebody move over on Mount Rushmore. He's working for his place on the coins and the postage stamps.—**Henry Graff**: *Newsweek*, 28 January 1985

3198. In the heat of a political lifetime, Rea-gan innocently squirrels away tidbits of misin-formation and then, sometimes years later, casually drops them into his public discourse, like gumballs in a quiche.—**Lucy Howard**: *Newsweek* 1985

3199. When Ronald Reagan's career in show business came to an end, he was hired to im-personate, first a California Governor and then an American president.—**Gore Vidal**: *Arma-geddon? Essays 1983–1987* (1987)

3200. Like much of America [Reagan] con-tained contradictions, but never experienced them.—**Gary Wills**: *Reagan's America: Inno-cents at Home* (1987)

3201. An authentic phony.—**James B. Reston**, 1909–95

3202. He is running not for election but for the history books.—**George J. Church**: *Time*, 29 September 1986

3203. Live by publicity, you'll probably die by publicity.—**Russell Baker**: on president Ronald Reagan's changing image after news of Iranian arms sales; *New York Times*, 3 December 1986

3204. Heads of state are notoriously ill pre-pared for their mature careers; think of Adolf Hitler (landscape painter), Ho Chi Minh (sea-man), and our own Ronald Reagan.—**Barbara Ehrenreich**: *The Worst Years of Our Lives* (1986)

3205. You know, by the time you reach my age, you've made plenty of mistakes if you've lived your life properly.—**Ronald Reagan**: *Ob-server*, 8 March 1987

3206. We've got the kind of president who thinks arms control means some kind of deodorant.—**Patricia S. Schroeder:** *Observer*, 9 August 1987

3207. Washington could not tell a lie, Nixon could not tell the truth; Reagan cannot tell the difference.—**Mort Sahl:** *Observer*, 18 October 1987

3208. To listen even briefly to Ronald Reagan is to realize that he is a man upon whose synapses the termites have dined long and well. —**Christopher Hitchens:** *Prepared for the Worst* (1988)

3209. The president who never told bad news to the American people.—**Garrison Keillor:** *We Are Still Married* (1989)

3210. At his worst, Reagan made the denial of compassion respectable.—**Mario Cuomo:** *Newsweek*, 9 January 1989

3211. All in all, not bad. Not too bad at all. —**Ronald Reagan:** TV speech on his own presidency; *Independent*, 14 January 1989

3212. A rhetorical roundheels, as befits a politician seeking empathy with his audience. —**William Safire:** *Language Maven Strikes Again* (1990)

3213. The battle for the mind of Ronald Reagan was like the trench warfare of World War I: never have so many fought so hard for such barren terrain.—**Peggy Noonan,** Reagan's special assistant and speechwriter: *What I Saw at the Revolution* (1990)

3214. Reagan was a flesh and blood version of any other mute national emblem, say the Statue of Liberty. Everyone knows what she represents, but no one would dream of asking her opinion.—**Simon Hoggart:** *America: A User's Guide* (1990)

3215. He was simply an actor on loan from Hollywood who had entered politics because he wanted to restrain the power of an increasingly intrusive government.—**Lou Cannon:** *President Reagan* (1991)

3216. The American people were like him: cheerful, optimistic, patriotic, inconsistent, and casually inattentive.—**James B. Reston:** *Deadline* (1991)

3217. After four days of speeches a foreign visitor could be forgiven for thinking indoor plumb-ing was a Reagan-era innovation.—**Charles Krauthammer:** *Time*, 10 August 1992

3218. For touching a people who want to forget ugly problems, no politician equals the one who has already forgotten them himself.—**Murray Kempton:** *Rebellions, Perversities, and Main Events* (1994)

Roosevelt, Franklin D. (1882–1945), 32nd president (1933–45)

3219. I pledge to you, I pledge myself, to a new deal for the American people.—**Franklin D. Roosevelt:** acceptance speech, 2 July 1932

3220. A second-class intellect. But a first-class temperament!—**Oliver Wendell Holmes, Jr.:** 8 March 1933

3221. The man who started more creations since Genesis—and finished none.—**Hugh Johnson:** 1937, attrib.

3222. The best newspaperman who has ever been president of the United States.—**Heywood Broun,** 1888–1939: Daniel J. Boorstin *The Image* (1962)

3223. I'd rather be right than Roosevelt.—**Heywood Broun:** Jon Winokur (ed.) *The Portable Curmudgeon Redux* (1992)

3224. Franklin is always interested in any idea that can be written down on one page.—**Eleanor Roosevelt,** 1884–1962: Colin Bingham (ed.) *Wit and Wisdom* (1982)

3225. He would rather follow public opinion than lead it.—**Harry Hopkins,** 1890–1946: attrib.

3226. He was the only person I ever knew, anywhere, who was never afraid.—**Lyndon B. Johnson:** April 1945; *Time*, 13 April 1998

3227. I never think of anyone as the president but Mr. Roosevelt.—**Harry S Truman:** letter to Eleanor Roosevelt nearly six months after Roosevelt's death; Robert H. Ferrell *Off the Record* (1980)

3228. The quality of his being one with the people, of having no artificial or natural barriers between him and them, made it possible for him to be a leader without ever being or thinking of being a dictator.—**Frances Perkins:** *The Roosevelt Knew* (1946)

3229. I used to tell my husband that, if he could make me "understand" something, it would be clear to all the other people in the country. —**Eleanor Roosevelt,** First Lady: newspaper column, "My Day," 12 February 1947

3230. Franklin had a good way of simplifying things. He made people feel that he had a real understanding of things and they felt they had about the same understanding.—**Eleanor Roosevelt:** *PM,* 6 April 1947

3231. In Roosevelt there died the greatest American friend we have ever known and the greatest champion of freedom who has ever brought help and comfort from the New World to the Old.—**Winston Churchill:** *The Second World War* vol. 5 (1953)

3232. A chameleon on plaid.—**Herbert Hoover,** 1874–1964: attrib.; Jon Winokur (ed.) *The Portable Curmudgeon Redux* (1992)

3233. Meeting Roosevelt was like opening your first bottle of champagne: knowing him was like drinking it.—**Winston Churchill:** recalled on his death, 24 January 1965

3234. Two-thirds mush and one-third Eleanor. —**Alice Roosevelt Longworth,** 1884–1980: George Wolfskill and John A. Hudson *All but the People* (1969)

3235. Not since Lincoln had there been such an artful manipulator of the good, the bad, and the bewildered in between. I believe he saved the capitalist system by deliberately forgetting to balance the books, by transferring the gorgeous resources of credit from the bankers to the government.—**Alistair Cooke:** *America* (1973)

3236. A great deal of Roosevelt's almost magical talent for persuading and manipulating the American people lay in his ability to state his thoughts in simple, homely phrases, in the language of the working neighborhood where visitors sat in the kitchen, with puppies frolicking under the stove, husbands wearing working clothes and wives their one-dollar housedresses. —**David Brinkley:** *Washington Goes to War* (1988)

3237. Presidents Harry Truman and Franklin Roosevelt had the strongest cabinets of any other president in this century. Their criterion was, "Never mind personal weaknesses, tell me first what each of them can do."—**Joe L. Griffith**

Roosevelt, Theodore (1858–1919), 26th president (1901–09)

3238. I am as strong as a bull moose.—**Theodore Roosevelt:** letter to Senator Mark Hanna, 27 June 1900

3239. Now look, that damned cowboy is president of the United States.—**Mark Hanna:** on Roosevelt's acceding to the presidency on the assassination of William McKinley, September 1901

3240. A dangerous and ominous jingo.—**Henry James,** 1843–1916

3241. An interesting combination of St. Vitus and St. Paul.—**John Morley,** 1838–1923

3242. The two outstanding natural phenomena of America are Niagara Falls and Theodore Roosevelt.—**John Morley:** Mark Sullivan *Our Times* vol. 2 (1927)

3243. He was pure act.—**Henry Brooks Adams:** *The Education of Henry Adams* (1907)

3244. A charlatan of the very highest skill. —**H. L. Mencken:** *Prejudices* Second Series (1920)

3245. He hated all pretension save his own pretension.—**H. L. Mencken,** 1880–1956: Jon Winokur (ed.) *The Portable Curmudgeon Redux* (1992)

3246. Greatness, generally speaking, is an unusual quantity of a usual quality grafted upon a common man.—**William Allen White:** *Masks in a Pageant* (1928)

3247. If he was a freak, God and the times needed one.—**William Allen White:** *Masks in a Pageant* (1928)

3248. He was a walking day of judgment. —**John Burroughs:** *Forest And Stream*, January 1928

3249. Theodore Roosevelt thought with his hips.—**Lincoln Steffens,** 1866–1936: Jon Winokur (ed.) *The Portable Curmudgeon Redux* (1992)

3250. My father always wanted to be the corpse at every funeral, the bride at every wedding and the baby at every christening.—**Alice Roosevelt Longworth,** 1884–1980: Cleveland Amory and Earl Blackwell (eds.) *Celebrity Register* (1963)

3251. An old maid with testosterone poisoning.—**Patricia O'Toole**

Security

3252. All the security around the American president is just to make sure the man who shoots him gets caught.—**Norman Mailer:** *Sunday Telegraph*, 4 March 1990

3253. The search for perfect security has uglified Washington…. Uniforms everywhere. Ugly concrete excrescences. Barricades, metal detectors, official guns … an air of penitentiary about the place … security so palpable it gave me the fantods, which is what ghostly encounters gave Huckleberry Finn.—**Russell Baker:** *New York Times*, 16 March 1991

3254. We must seek security based on more than the grim premise that we can destroy those who seek to destroy us.—**President George W. Bush:** *Newsweek*, 14 May 2001

The Senate

3255. The survivors of the fittest.—**George Hearst:** 1886; Richard Hofstadter *The American Political Tradition* (1948)

3256. I look at the Senators and pray for the country.—**Edward Everett Hale,** 1822–1909: when asked, "Do you pray for the Senators?"; Van Wyck Brooks *New England: Indian Summer* (1940)

3257. No man, however strong, can serve ten years as schoolmaster, priest, or Senator, and remain fit for anything else.—**Henry Brooks Adams,** 1838–1918

3258. The Senate is the only show in the world where the cash customers have to sit in the balcony.—**Gracie Allen:** *How to Become President* (1940)

3259. The only way to do anything in the American government is to bypass the Senate. —**Franklin D. Roosevelt,** 1882–1945: returning from Yalta; *Chicago Tribune*, 29 May 1977

3260. The U.S. Senate—an old scow which doesn't move very fast, but never sinks.—**Everett Dirksen,** 1896–1969: Robert I. Fitzhenry *Barnes & Noble Book of Quotations* (1986)

3261. The Senate is a place filled with goodwill and good intentions, and if the road to hell is paved with them, then it's a pretty good detour.—**Hubert H. Humphrey,** 1911–78

3262. The Senate is the last primitive society in the world. We still worship the elders of the tribe and honor the territorial imperative. —**Eugene J. McCarthy,** 1916–   : attrib.

3263. If we in the Senate would stop calling each other "distinguished," we might have ten working days a year.—**Senator Edward W. Brooke:** *Reader's Digest*, April 1972

3264. It doesn't require any particular bravery to stand on the floor of the Senate and urge our boys in Vietnam to fight harder, and if this war mushrooms into a major conflict and a hundred thousand young Americans are killed, it won't be U. S. Senators who die. It will be American soldiers who are too young to qualify for the senate.—**George McGovern,** 1922–   , Democrat senator

3265. No man is fit to be a Senator … unless he is willing to surrender his political life for great principle.—**Senator Henry Fountain Ashurst**

3266. Rome had Senators too, that's why it declined.—**Frank Dane**

States

See also HISTORY: Confederacy

3267. Asking one of the states to surrender part of her sovereignty is like asking a lady to surrender part of her chastity.—**John Randolph,** 1773–1833: Russell Kirk *John Randolph of Roanoke* (1951)

3268. I never use the word "Nation" in speaking of the United States; I always use the word "Union" or "Confederacy." We are not a Nation, but a Union, a confederacy of equal and sovereign States.—**John C. Calhoun:** letter to Oliver Dyer, 1 January 1849

3269. The United States themselves are essentially the greatest poem.—**Walt Whitman:** *Leaves of Grass* (1855)

Stevenson, Adlai (1900–1965), politician

3270. The real trouble with Stevenson is that he's no better than a regular sissy.—**Harry S Truman,** 1884–1972

3271. Stevenson himself hasn't even backbone training, for he is a graduate of Dean Acheson's spineless school of diplomacy which cost the free world 600,000,000 former allies in the past seven years of Trumanism.—**Richard M. Nixon:** 1952

3272. Unexceptional as a glass of decent Beaujolais.—*Newsweek*: 26 July 1965

3273. No matter how many holes his shoe soles bore, no matter how steeped he was in the lore of Lincoln, couldn't fool them, he wasn't folks.—*Newsweek*: 26 July 1965

3274. A man who could never make up his mind whether he had to go to the bathroom or not.—**Harry S Truman**

Taft, William H. (1857–1930), 27th president (1909–13)

3275. Taft meant well, but he meant well feebly.—**Theodore Roosevelt,** 1858–1919: Jon Winokur (ed.) *The Portable Curmudgeon Redux* (1992)

3276. The Great Postponer.—**William Jennings Bryan,** 1860–1925

3277. [Taft] can be depended upon to stand for property rights whenever they come into conflict with human rights.—**Anonymous:** *Literary Digest*, 16 July 1921

3278. Figuratively, he used to come out upon the front stoop of the White House and quarrel petulantly with the American people every day.—**William Allen White:** *Masks in a Pageant* (1928)

3279. It's very difficult for me to understand how a man who is so good as Chief Justice could have been so bad as president.—**Louis D. Brandeis,** 1856–1941

3280. With all the confidence of a man dialing his own telephone number.—**John Bell:** on Taft's manner in handling crises; *The Splendid Misery* (1960)

3281. The amiable, good-natured, subthyroid Taft had the misfortune to follow the crusading, club-brandishing, hyperthyroid Roosevelt, much as a dim star follows a blazing comet. The Nation felt let down.—**Thomas A. Bailey:** *Presidential Greatness* (1966)

Terrorist Attack (11 September 2001)

3282. National unity in confronting a crisis is not uniquely American. But it is something we do better than anyone else on earth.—**David L. Denvir:** *Time*, 24 September 2001

3283. What's needed is a unified, unifying, Pearl Harbor sort of purple American fury—a ruthless indignation that doesn't leak away in a week or two.—**Lance Morrow:** *Time*, 24 September 2001

3284. Either you are with us or you are with the terrorists.—**President George W. Bush:** giving all nations of the world a choice; address to Congress; *Newsweek*, 1 October 2001

3285. This nation is peaceful, but fierce when stirred to anger.—**George W. Bush**

3286. What happened on September 11 was horrific, but this patriotic fever can go too far.—**Norman Mailer,** American author: *Newsweek*, 18 February 2002

Truman, Harry S (1884–1972), 33rd president (1945–53)

3287. Truman is short, square, simple, and looks one straight in the face.—**Harold Nicolson:** *Diaries*, 8 August 1945

3288. This country would be all right if Truman were alive.—**Grouch Marx:** 1947, attrib.

3289. If there had been any formidable body of cannibals in the country he would have promised to provide them with free missionaries fattened at the taxpayer's expense.—**H. L. Mencken:** on Truman's success in the 1948 presidential Campaign; *Baltimore Sun*, 7 November 1948

3290. As long as I have been in the White House, I can't help waking at 5 A.M. and hearing the old man at the foot of the stairs calling and telling me to get out and milk the cows.—**Harry S Truman:** to Senator George Aiken; Robert J. Donovan, *Conflict and Crisis* (1977)

3291. I never give them [the public] hell. I just tell the truth, and they think it is hell.—**Harry S Truman:** *Look*, 3 April 1956

3292. The buck stops here.—**Sign on Truman's desk:** Alfred Steinberg *The Man from Missouri* (1962)

3293. The captain with the mighty heart.

—**Dean Acheson:** *Present and the Creation* (1969)

3294. Truman's very ordinariness has today made him something of a folk hero: a plain-speaking, straight-talking, ordinary fellow who did what he saw as his duty without turning his obligation into an opportunity for personal gain.—**Robert H. Ferrell:** *Truman: A Centenary Remembrance* (1984)

Vice-presidency

3295. The most insignificant office.—**John Adams,** first vice-president and second president: letter to Abigail Adams, 19 December 1793

3296. The second office of the government is honorable and easy, the first is but a splendid misery.—**Thomas Jefferson:** letter to Elbridge Gerry, 13 May 1797

3297. His importance consists in the fact that he may cease to be vice-president.—**Woodrow Wilson:** *Congressional Government* (1885)

3298. The vice-president of the United States is like a man in a cataleptic state: he cannot speak; he cannot move; he suffers no pain; and yet he is perfectly conscious of everything that is going on about him.—**Thomas R. Marshall:** c. 1913, attrib.

3299. There were once two brothers. One ran away to sea. The other was elected vice-president and neither was heard of again.—**Thomas R. Marshall,** 1854–1925: Dick Gregory *Dick Gregory's Political Primer* (1972)

3300. The man with the best job in the country is the vice-president. All he has to do is get up every morning and say, "How's the president?"—**Will Rogers,** 1879–1935: Henry O. Dormann *The Speaker's Book of Quotations* (1987)

3301. The vice-presidency isn't worth a pitcher of warm piss.—**John Nance Garner:** c. 1934, attrib.; O. C. Fisher *Cactus Jack* (1978)

3302. A spare tire on the automobile of government.—**John Hance Garner:** to the press, 19 June 1934

3303. He is a man who sits in the outer office of the White House hoping to hear the president sneeze.—**H. L. Mencken,** 1880–1956

3304. Here is one instance in which it is the man who makes the office, not the office the man.—**Harry S Truman:** *Years of Decision* (1955)

3305. The more you stay in this kind of job, the more you realize that a public figure, a major public figure, is a lonely man.—**Richard M. Nixon:** interview when vice-president; Stewart Alsop *Nixon and Rockefeller* (1960)

3306. Anyone who thinks that the vice-president can take a position independent of the president of his administration simply has no knowledge of politics or government. You are his choice in a political marriage, and he expects your absolute loyalty.—**Hubert H. Humphrey,** 1911–78

3307. The president has only 190 million bosses. The vice-president has 190 million and one.—**Hubert H. Humphrey:** *American Salesman Magazine,* 1966

3308. If you are very active as vice-president, everyone in America knows your name. But that is your only property. It is not the same thing as real power—more like being a movie star.—**Norman Mailer:** *Miami and the Siege of Chicago* (1968)

3309. The vice-presidency is sort of like the last cookie on the plate. Everybody insists he won't take it, but somebody always does.—**Bill Vaughan,** 1915–77: Laurence J. Peter (ed.) *Peter's Quotations* (1977)

3310. The vice-presidency is like a Sally Quinn or Oriana Fallaci interview. Each one thinks it's going to be better for him than it was for the others.—**Anonymous:** *New Times,* 10 December 1976

3311. Vice-president—it has such a nice ring to it!—**Geraldine A. Ferraro:** *New York Times,* 13 July 1984

3312. Democracy means that anyone can grow up to be president, and anyone who doesn't grow up can be vice-president.—**Johnny Carson,** 1925–

3313. One word sums up probably the responsibility of any vice-president, and that one word

is "to be prepared."—**J. Danforth Quayle,** 1947–

3314. The sand trap of American politics. —**Howard Fineman:** *Newsweek,* 20 May 1991

3315. You get all the french fries the president can't get to.—**Al Gore,** vice-president: *New York Times,* 8 April 1994

3316. I am Al Gore, and I used to be the next president of the United States of America. —**Al Gore:** address to Bocconi University in Milan; *Newsweek,* 19 March 2001

Washington, George (1732–99), 1st president (1789–97)

3317. I can't tell a lie, Pa; you know I can't tell a lie. I did cut it with my hatchet.—**George Washington:** M. L. Weems *Life of George Washington* 10th ed. (1810)

3318. [Washington] errs as other men do, but errs with integrity.—**Thomas Jefferson:** letter to William B. Giles, 31 December 1795

3319. First in war, first in peace, first in the hearts of his countrymen.—**Henry Lee:** speech, House of Representatives, 26 December 1799

3320. His mind was great and powerful, without being of the very first order; his penetration strong, though not so acute as that of a Newton, Bacon, or Lock; and as far as he saw, no judgment was ever sounder. It was slow in operation, being little aided by invention or imagination, but sure in conclusion.—**Thomas Jefferson:** letter, January 1814

3321. Soldier and statesman, rarest unison. —**James Russell Lowell:** *Under The Old Elm* (1875)

3322. We have exchanged the Washingtonian dignity for the Jeffersonian simplicity, which in due time came to be only another name for the Jacksonian vulgarity.—**Henry Codman Potter:** speech, 30 April 1889

3323. The crude commercialism of America, its materialising spirit are entirely due to that country having adopted for its national hero a man who was incapable of telling a lie.—**Oscar Wilde:** *Intentions* (1891)

3324. Washington, as a boy, was ignorant of the commonest accomplishments of youth. He could not even lie.—**Mark Twain,** 1835–1910: Laurence J. Peter (ed.) *Peter's Quotations* (1977)

3325. One of the few in the whole history of the world who was not carried away by power. —**Robert Frost,** 1874–1963: Laurence J. Peter *Peter's Quotations* (1977)

Watergate (1972–74)

3326. We have a cancer, close to the presidency, that is growing.—**John Dean:** 21 March 1973

3327. I don't give a shit what happens. I want you all to stonewall it, let them plead the Fifth Amendment, cover-up or anything else, if it'll save it, save the plan.—**Richard M. Nixon:** 22 March 1973

3328. Once the toothpaste is out of the tube, it is awfully hard to get it back in.—**H. R. Haldeman,** presidential assistant to Richard Nixon: to John Dean, 8 April 1973; *Hearings Before the Select Committee on Presidential Campaign Activities of US Senate: Watergate and Related Activities* (1973)

3329. There can be no whitewash at the White House.—**Richard M. Nixon:** TV speech, 30 April 1973

3330. Maybe this is like the Old Testament. It was visited upon us and maybe we're going to benefit from it.—**Nelson A. Rockefeller:** speech, New York City, 17 July 1973

3331. The illegal we do immediately. The unconstitutional takes a little longer.—**Henry Kissinger:** *New York Times,* 28 October 1973

3332. When people ask if the United States can afford to place on trial the president, if the system can stand impeachment, my answer is, "Can we stand anything else?"—**George McGovern:** advocating impeachment of Richard M. Nixon; *San Francisco Examiner,* 29 November 1973

3333. The president seems to extend executive privilege way out past the atmosphere. What he says is executive privilege is nothing but executive poppycock.—**Sam Ervin,** 1896–

3334. Watergate is the great liberal illusion that you can have public virtue without private morality.—**Clare Boothe Luce:** *Parade,* 21 April 1974

3335. It was just basic politics.—**G. Gordon Liddy,** American secret service operative: 1974

3336. Our long national nightmare is over. Our Constitution works; our great Republic is a Government of laws and not of men. Here the people rule.—**Gerald R. Ford:** on being sworn in as president in succession to Richard Nixon; speech, 9 August 1974; *Public Papers of the Presidents of the United States* (1974)

3337. An American tragedy in which we all have played a part.—**Gerald R. Ford,** 1913– : announcing pardon of president Richard M. Nixon

3338. The political lesson of Watergate is this: Never again must America allow an arrogant, elite guard of political adolescents to by-pass the regular party organization and dictate the terms of a national election.—**Gerald R. Ford**

3339. I think [Watergate and the McCarthy Era] are deeply connected, with Nixon being the connection, the rope that carries it all through.—**Lillian Hellman:** *New York Times,* 7 November 1975

3340. When you're a lawyer, you expect your client to lie to you, but not when he is the president.—**Dick Houser**

3341. [We want] modified, limited hangout. —**John R. Ehrlichman,** Special Counsel to Nixon White House: *The Company* (1976)

3342. I personally think he did violate the law, that he committed impeachable offenses. But I don't think that he thinks he did.—**Jimmy Carter:** to reporters after press conference, 12 May 1977

3343. When the president does it, that means that it is not illegal.—**Richard M. Nixon:** TV interview with David Frost, 19 May 1977; *Frost's Account of the Nixon Interviews, I Gave Them a Sword* (1978)

3344. I brought myself down. I gave them a sword. And they stuck it in.—**Richard M. Nixon:** TV interview with David Frost, 19 May 1977; *Frost's Account of the Nixon Interviews, I Gave Them a Sword* (1978)

3345. [Watergate] was worse than a crime, it was a blunder.—**Richard M. Nixon:** *Observer,* 3 December 1978

3346. Watergate was an uncanny crisis. There were just too many bodies to be buried too fast, and too many gravediggers digging each other's graves. It was the imperfect crime par excellence. **Milton Mayer:** Colin Bingham (ed.) *Wit and Wisdom* (1982)

3347. It was the daily decay of integrity.—**Seymour Hersch:** *The Price of Power* (1983)

3348. Watergate was one part wrongdoing, one part blundering, and one part political vendetta by my enemies.—**Richard M. Nixon:** *In the Arena* (1990)

3349. In the darkest hour, he gave the press its finest hour.—**Benjamin C. Bradlee:** *A Good Life* (1995)

Webster, Daniel (1782–1852), politician and orator

3350. A terrible, beetle-browed, mastiff-mouthed, yellow-skinned, broad-bottomed, grim-taciturn individual; with a pair of dull-cruel-looking black eyes, and as much Parliamentary intellect and silent-rage in him as I have ever seen in any man.—**Thomas Carlyle:** letter to his brother, 24 June 1824; *New Letters of Thomas Carlyle* (1904)

3351. Daniel Webster struck me much like a steam engine in trousers.—**Sydney Smith,** 1771–1845: Lady Holland *Memoir* vol. 1 (1855)

3352. The gigantic intellect, the envious temper, the ravenous ambition, and the rotten heart of Webster.—**John Quincy Adams,** 1767–1848

3353. God is only the president of the day, and Webster is his orator.—**Henry David Thoreau:** *Walden* (1854)

Wilson, Woodrow (1856–1924), 28th president (1913–21)

3354. The air currents of the world never ventilated his mind.—**Walter Hines Page,** 1855–1918: Patrick Devlin *Too Proud to Fight* (1974)

3355. A Byzantine logothete.—**Theodore Roosevelt,** 1858–1919

3356. Like Odysseus, the president looked wiser when he was seated.—**John Maynard Keynes:** *The Economic Consequences of the Peace* (1919)

3357. Mr. Wilson's name among the Allies is like that of the rich uncle, and they have accepted his manners out of respect for his means. —*London Morning Post:* 1919

3358. God Almighty was satisfied with Ten Commandments. Mr. Wilson requires Fourteen Points.—**Georges Clemenceau,** 1841–1929: during the Peace Conference negotiations in 1919, attrib.; Leon Harris *The Fine Art of Political Wit* (1965)

3359. How can I talk to a fellow who thinks himself the first man in two thousand years to know anything about peace on earth?—**Georges Clemenceau:** Thomas A. Bailly *Woodrow Wilson and the Lost Peace* (1944)

3360. The spacious philanthropy which he exhaled upon Europe stopped quite sharply at the coasts of his own country.—**Winston Churchill:** *The World Crisis* (1923–29)

3361. They say Wilson has blundered. Perhaps he has but I notice he usually blunders forward.—**Thomas Edison,** 1847–1931: John Dos Passos *Mr Wilson's War* (1962)

3362. A sleepy man from a sleepy college [Princeton] in a sleepy little town.—**Nicholas Murray Butler,** 1862–1947

3363. For Wilson, the justification of America's international role was messianic: America had an obligation not to the balance of power, but to spread its principles throughout the world.—**Henry Kissinger:** *Diplomacy* (1994)

LAW AND ORDER

Capone, Al (1899–1947), gangster

3364. This American system of ours, call it Americanism, call it capitalism, call it what you will, gives each and every one of us a great opportunity if we only seize it with both hands and make the most of it.—**Al Capone**

3365. This is virgin territory for whorehouses. —**Al Capone**: about suburban Chicago; Kenneth Allsop *The Bootleggers* (1961)

3366. They can't collect legal taxes from illegal money.—**Al Capone**: objecting to the U.S. Bureau of Internal Revenue claiming large sums in unpaid back tax; John Kobler *Capone* (1971)

3367. I've been accused of every death except the casualty list of the World War.—**Al Capone**: Kenneth Allsop *The Bootleggers* (1961)

3368. Don't you get the idea I'm one of these goddam radicals. Don't get the idea I'm knocking the American system.—**Al Capone**: interview, c. 1929; Claud Cockburn *In Time of Trouble* (1956)

3369. My rackets are run on strictly American lines and they're going to stay that way.—**Al Capone**: interview, c. 1930; Claud Cockburn *Cockburn Sums Up* (1981)

3370. Neapolitan by birth and Neanderthal by instinct.—**Fred D. Pasley:** *Al Capone: The Biography of a Self-Made Man* (1966)

Constitution

See also THE NATION: Founding

3371. Our Constitution was made only for a moral and religious people. It is wholly inadequate to the government of any other.—**John Adams**, 1735–1826

3372. The people made the Constitution, and the people can unmake it. It is the creature of their own will, and lives only by their will. —**John Marshall,** American jurist: *Cohens v. Virginia,* 1821

3373. The Constitution of the United States was made not merely for the generation that then existed, but for posterity—unlimited, undefined, endless, perpetual posterity.—**Henry Clay:** speech in the Senate, 6 February 1850

3374. Your Constitution is all sail and no anchor.—**T. B. Macaulay:** letter to H. S. Randall, 23 May 1857

3375. The American Constitution is the most wonderful work ever struck off at a given time by the brain and purpose of man.—**William E. Gladstone:** *North American Review*, September 1878

3376. The Constitution is what the judges say it is.—**Charles Evans Hughes,** Chief Justice: speech in Elmira, New York, 3 May 1907

3377. The American Constitution, one of the few modern political documents drawn up by men who were forced by the sternest circumstances to think out what they really had to face, instead of chopping logic in a university classroom.—**George Bernard Shaw:** *Getting Married* (1908)

3378. The United States Constitution has proved itself the most marvelously elastic compilation of rules of government ever written. —**Franklin D. Roosevelt:** radio broadcast, 2 March 1930

3379. [The Constitution] was a charter of anarchism. It was not really a Constitution at all.

It was not an instrument of government; it was a guarantee to a whole nation that they never could be governed at all. And that is exactly what they wanted.—**George Bernard Shaw:** speech at Academy of Political Science, New York City, 11 April 1933

3380. The Constitution does not provide for first and second class citizens.—**Wendell Lewis Willkie:** *An American Program* (1944)

3381. The Constitution has never greatly bothered any wartime president.—**Frances Biddle:** *In Brief Authority* (1962)

3382. No patent medicine was ever put to wider and more varied use than the Fourteenth Amendment.—**William O. Douglas,** 1898–1980: Hugo Black, Jr. *My Father: A Remembrance* (1975)

3383. The United States Constitution is law, the Declaration of Independence is not; and it is the Declaration of Independence, not the Constitution, that *legalizes* the overthrow of the government.—**Milton Mayer:** Laurence J. Peter (ed.) *Peter's Quotations* (1977)

3384. For most Americans the Constitution had become a hazy document, cited like the Bible on ceremonial occasions but forgotten in the daily transactions of life.—**Arthur M. Schlesinger, Jr.:** *The Imperial Presidency* (1973)

3385. The Constitution was based on the old English law that a man's home is his castle. It was designed essentially to protect individuals from government intrusion. That is a good deal for men who own castles.—**Abbie Hoffman:** speech, University of South Carolina, 16 September 1987

3386. The Constitution isn't weak because we don't know the answer to a difficult problem. It's strong because we can find that answer. —**Anthony M. Kennedy:** *New York Times*, 15 December 1987

3387. The Constitution is more than literature, but as literature, it is primarily a work of the imagination. It imagined a country: fantastic. More fantastic still, it imagined a country full of people imagining themselves. Within the exacting articles and stipulations there was not only room to fly but also tacit encouragement to fly, even the instructions to fly, traced delicately within the solid triangular concoctions of the framers.—**Roger Rosenblatt:** *The Man in the Water* (1994)

3388. An idea and not quite a reality.—**Nikki Giovanni:** *Racism 101* (1994)

3389. This place specializes in reason.—**Ruth Bader Ginsburg:** "Prime Time," ABC-TV, 30 December 1994

3390. The Constitution does not set up agnosticism as the established non-religion of the United States.—**Daniel P. B. Smith:** 22 February 2000

Crime

3391. The cure for crime is not the electric chair but the high chair.—**J. Edgar Hoover,** 1895–1972, FBI Director: *Chicago Sunday Times* 9 July 1976

3392. The American Dream is, in part, responsible for a great deal of crime and violence because people feel that the country owes them not only a living but a good living.—**David Abrahamsen:** *San Francisco Examiner & Chronicle*, 18 November 1975

3393. Crime is an overhead you have to pay if you want to live in the city.—**George Moscone:** *Newsweek*, 20 December 1976

3394. It is no secret that organized crime in America takes in over forty billion dollars a year. This is quite a profitable sum, especially when one considers that the Mafia spends very little for office supplies.—**Woody Allen,** 1935– : James Charlton *The Executive's Quotation Book* (1983)

3395. Black on black violence now kills more in one year in America than died during all the history of lynching.—**Jesse Jackson:** *Christian Science Monitor*, 3 November 1993

3396. Our crime problem is only our race problem wearing a different face.—**Adam Walinsky:** *New York Times*, 30 October 1994

3397. The job of the police in America, at least for the last 30 years, is to keep "them" away from "us." Nobody wants to know how they do it. They just want it done.—**Adam Walinsky:** *New York Times*, 30 October 1994

3398. The vice industry, since Luciano took over, is highly organized and operates with business-like precision.—**Thomas E. Dewey,** New York City special prosecutor: *Time*, 7 December 1998

Drugs

3399. Alcohol didn't cause the high crime rates of the '20s and '30s, Prohibition did. Drugs don't cause today's alarming crime rates, but drug prohibition does.—**David Boaz:** 27 April 1988

3400. No drugs, not even alcohol, causes the fundamental ills of society. If we're looking for the sources of our troubles, we shouldn't test people for drugs, we should test them for stupidity, ignorance, greed and love of power.—**P. J. O'Rourke:** *Give War a Chance* (1992)

3401. We older citizens regard youth, health and prosperity as ecstasy, while our prosperous, healthy youths resort to a pill to gain it.—**Ed Troster:** *Time*, 14 August 2000

FBI

3402. Truth-telling, I have found, is the key to responsible citizenship. The thousands of criminals I have seen in forty years of law enforcement have had one thing in common: every single one was a liar.—**J. Edgar Hoover:** *Family Weekly*, 14 July 1963

3403. I regret to say that we of the FBI are powerless to act in cases of oral-genital intimacy, unless it has in some way obstructed interstate commerce.—**J. Edgar Hoover,** 1895–1972: *New York*, 6 October 1980

3404. The FBI is filled with Fordham graduates keeping tabs on Harvard men in the State Department.—**Daniel Patrick Moynihan,** 1927– : Jon Winokur (ed.) *The Portable Curmudgeon Redux* (1992)

Hoover, J. Edgar (1895–1972), director of FBI (1924–72)

3405. Whom you wouldn't trust as much as you would a rattlesnake with a silencer in the tail.—**Dean Acheson:** 1960

3406. A pillar of strength in a city of weak men.—**Lyndon B. Johnson,** 1908–73: Fred Emery *Watergate* (1994)

3407. It's probably better to have him inside the tent pissing out, than outside the tent pissing in.—**Lyndon B. Johnson:** on why he kept Hoover at the FBI; *New York Times*, 31 October 1971

3408. A mythical person first thought up by the *Reader's Digest.*—**Art Buchwald,** 1925– : Jonathon Green (ed.) *The Pan Dictionary of Contemporary Quotations* (1989)

3409. That Virgin Mary in pants.—**Mary Bancroft:** Leonard Mosley *Dulles* (1978)

3410. He fashioned his career as an improbable bureaucratic morality play peopled by bad guys and G-men.—*Time*

Law

3411. Every problem in America turns into a legal problem.—**Alexis de Tocqueville,** 1805–59

3412. No people is shrewder than the American in perceiving when a law works ill, nor prompter in repealing it.—**James Bryce:** *The American Commonwealth* (1888)

3413. The government of the United States is and always has been a lawyer's government.—**Chauncey Depew:** speech, 1898

3414. Anglo-Saxon civilization has taught the individual to protect his own rights; American civilization will teach him to respect the rights of others.—**William Jennings Bryan:** speech, 22 February 1899

3415-3434 • Law and Order

3415. [In America] a man is presoomed to be guilty ontil he's proved guilty an' afther that he's presoomed to be innocent.—**Finley Peter Dunne:** "On Criminal Trials," 1901

3416. In America, where law and custom alike are based upon the dreams of spinsters.—**Bertrand Russell:** *Marriage and Morals* (1929)

3417. You simply cannot hang a millionaire in America.—**Bourke Cockran:** Shane Leslie *American Wonderland* (1936)

3418. It has been said that a judge is a member of the Bar who once knew a Governor.—**Curtis Bok,** American federal judge: *The Backbone of the Herring* (1941)

3419. The United States is the greatest law factory the world has ever known.—**Charles Evans Hughes,** 1862–1948: Evan Esar (ed.) *The Dictionary of Humorous Quotations* (1949)

3420. In American justice the suspect is considered guilty until he is proved innocent, but in society the opposite applies.—**Cecil Beaton:** *Portrait of New York* (1948)

3421. Conservative political opinion in America cleaves to the tradition of the judge as passive interpreter, believing that his absolute loyalty to authoritative law is the price of his immunity from political pressure and of the security of his tenure.—**Learned Hand:** *The Spirit of Liberty* (1959)

3422. Our society is a legal state in the sense that almost everything that takes place will sooner or later raise legal questions.—**Felix Frankfurter,** 1882–1965: Martin Mayer *The Lawyers* (1967)

3423. There are not enough jails, not enough policemen, not enough courts to enforce a law not supported by the people.—**Hubert H. Humphrey:** speech at Williamsburg, 1 May 1965; *New York Times,* 2 May 1965

3424. Even an attorney of moderate talent can postpone doomsday year after year, for the system of appeals that pervades American jurisprudence amounts to a legalistic wheel of fortune, a game of chance, somewhat fixed in the favor of the criminal, that the participants play interminably.—**Truman Capote:** *In Cold Blood* (1965)

3425. The contempt for law and the contempt for the human consequences of lawbreaking go from the bottom to the top of American society.—**Margaret Mead:** *Redbook,* April 1974

3426. I don't know if I like the idea of seatbelt laws. Enforcing intelligence seems, somehow, un–American.—**David Pugh**

3427. Confronted with the choice, the American people would choose the policeman's truncheon over the anarchist's bomb.—**Spiro T. Agnew,** 1918–96

3428. In America a court is an assembly of noble and distinguished grafters.—**Gregory Nunn:** Gerald F. Lieberman *3,500 Good Quotes for Speakers* (1983)

3429. Expedience, not justice, is the rule of contemporary American law.—**Abbie Hoffman:** *Square Dancing in the Ice Age* (1981)

3430. As a moth is drawn to the light, so is a litigant drawn to the United States. If he can only get his case into their courts, he stands to win a fortune. At no cost to himself; and at no risk of having to pay anything to the other side. —**Lord Denning:** *Smith Kline and French Laboratories Ltd. v. Bloch,* 1983

3431. If more Americans were aware of how important "due process" is in our system of justice, they wouldn't have allowed it to turn into "overdue process."—**Sydney J. Harris,** 1917– : Lloyd Cory (comp.) *Quotable Quotations* (1985)

3432. Gerry's friends, you see, had no confidence in the United States judicial system. They did not seem comfortable in the courtroom, and this increased their unreliability in the eyes of judge and jury. If you trust the authorities, they trust you better back, it seems. —**Louise Erdrich:** *Love Medicine* (1984)

3433. The name of the game in the United States is to sue. It's a national pastime. We probably sue more than any other country and thank God we do. It's the little guy who brings the little suit that makes life safer for all of us. —**Melvin M. Belli,** 1907– , attorney: Henry O. Dormann *The Speaker's Book of Quotations* (1987)

3434. In America, an acquittal doesn't mean you're innocent, it means you beat the rap. My clients lose even when they win.—**Francis Lee Bailey,** 1933– : Robert I. Fitzhenry *Barnes & Noble Book of Quotations* (1986)

3435. Yale [Law School] is terrific for anything you wanna do, so long as it don't involve people with sneakers, guns, dope, or sloth.—**Tom Wolfe:** *The Bonfire of the Vanities* (1987)

3436. The United States is a nation of laws: badly written and randomly enforced.—**Frank Zappa,** 1940–93

3437. America's favorite indoor sport used to be sex. Now it's litigation.—**Crandall Condra,** 1919– : Eileen Mason *Great Book of Funny Quotes* (1993)

3438. For any twentieth-century American who'd been paying attention at all, the phrase "criminal justice system" should have been warning enough.—**L. Neil Smith:** *Pallas* (film)

3439. I haven't committed a crime. What I did was fail to comply with the law.—**David Dinkins,** New York City mayor

3440. Power over rules is real power. That's why lobbyists congregate when Congress writes laws, and why the Supreme Court, which interprets and delineates the Constitution—the rules for writing the rules—has even more power than Congress.—**Donella H. Meadows:** *Whole Earth Quarterly,* Winter 1997

Prohibition (1920–33)

3441. The South is dry and will vote dry. That is, everybody sober enough to stagger to the polls will.—**Will Rogers:** "Oklahoma City," 1926

3442. Communism is like prohibition, it's a good idea but it won't work.—**Will Rogers,** 1879–1935: November 1927; *The Autobiography of Will Rogers* (1949)

3443. A great social and economic experiment, noble in motive and far-reaching in purpose.—**Herbert Hoover:** letter to Senator W. H. Borah, 23 February 1928; Claudius O. Johnson *Borah of Idaho* (1936)

3444. The prohibition law, written for weaklings and derelicts, has divided the nation, like Gaul, into three parts—wets, drys, and hypocrites.—**Florence Sabin:** speech, 9 February 1931

3445. Once, during Prohibition, I was forced to live for days on nothing but food and water. —**W. C. Fields,** 1879–1946: Fred Metcalf *The Penguin Dictionary of Modern Humorous Quotations* (1986)

3446. I am certain that the good Lord never intended grapes to be made into jelly.—**Fiorello H. La Guardia,** 1882–1947: Fred Metcalf *The Penguin Dictionary of Modern Humorous Quotations* (1986)

3447. Prohibition most dramatically revealed America's ever-restless, tireless experimentation, its inexhaustible will to try something new in the hope of something better.—**Allan Nevins:** Arthur Goodfriend *What Is America?* (1954)

Supreme Court

3448. The people can change Congress but only God can change the Supreme Court. —**George W. Norris,** 1861–1944: Laurence J. Peter *Peter's Quotations* (1977)

3449. Whenever you put a man on the Supreme Court he ceases to be your friend. —**Harry S Truman:** *New York Times,* 1959

3450. The Supreme Court is the oracle which gives an answer requiring several decades of further elucidation.—**Dean Acheson:** *Sketches From Life of Men I Have Known* (1961)

3451. There is about as much danger of the establishment of religion in the USA as there is of the return of sanity to the Supreme Court. —**William F. Buckley, Jr.:** *National Review* 1963

3452. The Court is the creature of the litigation the lawyers bring to it.—**Earl Warren:** *Washington Post,* 15 March 1971

3453. The Court's great power is its ability to educate, to provide moral leadership.—**William O. Douglas:** *Time,* 12 November 1973

3454. The difficulty in modification of the Constitution makes the Supreme Court a very powerful body in shaping the course of our civilization.—**F. D. G. Ribble:** Laurence J. Peter (ed.) *Peter's Quotations* (1977)

3455. The Supreme Court is the greatest single threat to the Constitution.—**Senator James Eastland:** Laurence J. Peter (ed.) *Peter's Quotations* (1977)

3456. The Court is perhaps one of the last citadels of jealously preserved individualism. For the most part, we function as nine, small independent law firms.—**Lewis F. Powell, Jr.:** *Los Angeles Times*, 9 July 1978

3457. The Supreme Court's only cloak of armor is the public trust; its sole ammunition, the collective hopes of our society.—**Irving R. Kaufman** (1910–1992)

3458. One of the best jobs in the world for a pregnant woman would be a position on the Supreme Court. The work is sedentary and the clothing is loose-fitting.—**Patricia Schroeder**

3459. By creating an unjustified principle of immunity through its own overreaching, the court is diminishing the power of the president and Congress.—**Cass Sunstein:** *Svenska Dagbladet* (Stockholm), 8 August 2002

Violence

3460. Violence is as American as cherry pie. —**H. Rap Brown:** *Evening Star*, 27 July 1967

3461. America is still a frontier country of wide open spaces. Our closeness to nature is one reason why our problem is not repression but regression; our notorious violence is the constant eruption of primitiveness, of anarchic individualism.—**Camille Paglia:** *Sex, Art, and American Culture* (1992)

3462. I thank God for all the freedom we have in this country, I cherish it—even the right to burn the flag. But we also have the right to bear arms and if you burn my flag—*I'll shoot you!*—**Johnny Cash:** *Daily Telegraph*, 10 April 1992

BUSINESS AND ECONOMY

Business

3463. The chief business of the American people is business.—**Calvin Coolidge:** speech in Washington D. C., 17 January 1925; commonly misquoted as "The business of America is business"

3464. [Advertising men:] the Robbing Hoods of America.—**Will Rogers,** 1879–1935: Donald Day *Will Rogers: A Biography* (1962)

3465. Advertising is the genie which is transforming America into a place of comfort, luxury and ease for millions.—**William Allen White,** 1868–1944, American journalist and editor

3466. We grew up founding our dreams on the infinite promise of American advertising. —**Zelda Fitzgerald:** *Save Me the Waltz* (1932)

3467. American businessmen strive to make a mass commodity out of almost everything that used to be a class commodity.—**Frederick Martin:** Arthur Goodfriend *What Is America?* (1954)

3468. Perhaps the most revolting character that the United States ever produced was the Christian businessman.—**H. L. Mencken:** *Minority Report* (1956)

3469. America's great achievement has been business.—**Henry R. Luce,** 1898–1967: obituary, *Time,* 1967

3470. Utility is our national shibboleth: the savior of the American businessman is *fact* and his uterine half-brother, *statistics*.—**Edward Dahlberg:** *The Carnal Myth* (1968)

3471. The advertising media in this country continuously informs the American male of his need for indispensable signs of his virility. —**Frances M. Beal:** Robin Morgan *Sisterhood Is Powerful* (1970)

3472. Ours is the country where, in order to sell your product, you don't so much point out its merits as you first work like hell to sell yourself.—**Louis Kronenberger,** 1904–80: Robert I. Fitzhenry (ed.) *The Harper Book of Quotations* (1993)

3473. Big business is basic to the very life of this country; and yet many—perhaps most—Americans have a deep-seated fear and an emotional repugnance to it. Here is monumental contradiction.—**David E. Lilienthal,** 1899–1981: Robert I. Fitzhenry (ed.) *Barnes & Noble Book of Quotations* (1987)

3474. If an American wants an answer he'll pick up the phone. A European will write a memo. The phone call will seem overly aggressive and pushy to the European manager, but the American needs to convey a greater sense of urgency because competition in the United States is so tough.—**Kai Lindholst:** *Time,* 9 October 1989

3475. Operating in America is like swimming in a shark pool.—**Gerald Ronson:** 1992

3476. American businessmen have a love affair with the quick fixes we find in the one-minute manager books.—**Lawrence A. Bossidy:** speech, 14 February 1994

3477. Everything in American advertising is pretty good. It looks the same. It looks American—overfed, oversexed, overpaid.—**Oliviero Toscani:** *New York Time Magazine,* 8 June 1997

Capitalism

3478. American capitalism has been both overpraised and overindicted. It is neither the Plumed Knight nor the monstrous Robber Baron.—**Max Lerner,** 1902–92: Ted Goodman (ed.) *The Forbes Book of Business Quotations* (1997)

3479. And the word is Capitalism. We are too mealy-mouthed. We fear the word Capitalism is unpopular. So we talk about the "free enterprise system" and run to cover in the folds of the flag and talk about the American Way of Life.—**Eric A. Johnston:** Charles Robert Lightfoot (comp.) *Handbook of Business Quotations* (1991)

Disney

3480. Disney World has acquired by now something of the air of a national shrine. American parents who don't take their children there sense obscurely that they have failed in some fundamental way, like Muslims who never made it to Mecca.—**Simon Hoggart,** British journalist: *America: A User's Guide* (1990)

3481. With Epcot Center the Disney corporation has accomplished something I didn't think possible in today's world. They have created a land of make-believe that's worse than regular life.—**P. J. O'Rourke,** 1947– : Jon Winokur (ed.) *The Portable Curmudgeon Redux* (1992)

Dollar

3482. The dollar has become like a hydrant at an international convention of dogs.—**Eliot Janeway:** *Esquire* (New York), 21 November 1978

Economy

See also SOCIAL LIFE: Classes; SOCIAL LIFE: Poverty and Wealth; SOCIAL LIFE: Society; POLITICS AND GOVERNMENT: Government

3483. All the perplexities, confusion and distress in America rise ... from downright ignorance of the nature of coin, credit and circulation.—**John Adams:** letter to Thomas Jefferson, 1787

3484. What this country needs is a really good five-cent cigar.—**Thomas R. Marshall,** vice-president: said to Henry M. Rose; *New York Tribune*, 4 January 1920

3485. Our country has plenty of good five-cent cigars, but the trouble is they charge fifteen cents for them.—**Will Rogers,** 1879–1935: Evan Esar (ed.) *The Dictionary of Humorous Quotations* (1949)

3486. There are plenty of good five-cent cigars in the country. The trouble is they cost a quarter. What this country really needs is a good five-cent nickel.—**Franklin P. Adams,** 1881–1960: Robert E. Drennan *The Algonquin Wits* (1968)

3487. The citizens of the United States must effectively control the mighty commercial forces which they have themselves called into being.—**Franklin D. Roosevelt,** 1882–1945: R. E. Sherwood *Roosevelt and Hopkins* (1950)

3488. America's best buy for a nickel is a telephone call to the right man.—**Ilka Chase,** 1905–78: Evan Esar (ed.) *The Dictionary of Humorous Quotations* (1949)

3489. Give me a one-handed economist! All my economists say, "On the one hand ... on the other."—**Harry S Truman,** 1884–1972: Paul F. Boller *Presidential Anecdotes* (1981)

3490. I stressed to the president the importance of realizing that in economics, the majority is always wrong.—**John Kenneth Galbraith:** c. 1962; *American Heritage*, October 1969

3491. Did y'ever think, Ken, that making a speech on ee-conomics is a lot like pissing down your leg? It seems hot to you, but it never does to anyone else.—**Lyndon B. Johnson,** 1908–73: J. K. Galbraith *A Life in Our Times* (1981)

3492. Every president of the United States since Harry Truman has proclaimed that it is the duty of the citizen to consume.—**Michael Harrington:** *The Accidental Century* (1966)

3493. There's only one place where inflation is made: that's in Washington.—**Milton Friedman:** 1977, attrib.

3494. America ... an economic system prouder of the distribution of its products than of the products themselves.—**Murray Kempton:** *New York Times*, 1977

3495. None of us really understands what's going on with all these numbers.—**David Allen Stockman:** on the U.S. budget; 1981

3496. You ought to shoot all the economists and elect a couple of historians.—**Ernest Hollings:** *New York Times*, 8 June 1983

3497. What is hurting America today is the high cost of low living.—**Brooks Moore:** Lloyd Cory (comp.) *Quotable Quotations* (1985)

3498. The ideology of this America wants to establish reassurance through Imitation. But profit defeats ideology, because the consumers want to be thrilled not only by the guarantee of the Good but also by the shudder of the Bad.—**Umberto Eco:** *Travels in Hyperreality* (1986)

3499. The government's view of the economy could be summed up in few short phrases: If it moves, tax it. If it keeps moving, regulate it. And if it stops moving, subsidize it.—**Ronald Reagan:** address to the White House Conference on Small Business, 15 August 1986

3500. On 16 September 1985, when the Commerce Department announced that the United States had become a debtor nation, the American Empire died.—**Gore Vidal:** *Armageddon? Essays 1983–1987* (1987)

3501. Balancing the budget is like going to heaven. Everybody wants to do it, but nobody wants to do what you have to do to get there. —**Phil Gramm,** Republican politician: TV interview, September 1990

3502. Corporate America has always had a PR problem. We haven't found a way to dress up certain economic realities so we can take them out in public. —**Robert J. Eaton:** speech, 18 March 1996

General Motors

See also SOCIAL LIFE: Cars

3503. For years I thought what was good for our country was good for General Motors and vice versa. The difference did not exist. Our company is too big. It goes with the welfare of the country. —**Charles E. Wilson,** American industrialist: testimony to the Senate Armed Services Committee on his proposed nomination to be Secretary of Defense, 15 January 1953; *New York Times,* 24 February 1953

3504. Gangsters did more advertising of the Cadillac as a fundamental part of the American way of life than General Motors ever did. —**Anonymous:** Kenneth Allsop *The Bootleggers* (1961)

3505. I come from an environment where, if you see a snake, you kill it. At General Motors, if you see a snake, the first thing you do is hire a consultant on snakes. Then, you spend a year talking about snakes. —**H. Ross Perot:** 1988

3506. General Motors is not in the business of making cars. General Motors is in the business of making money. —**Thomas A. Murphy:** Mark Fisher *The Millionaire's Book of Quotations* (1991)

3507. They didn't sell; they took orders. —**Roger B. Smith,** former GM Chairman: on the automative industry in the post–World War II era; Earl Shorris *A Nation of Salesmen* (1994)

McDonald's

3508. The organization cannot trust the individual; the individual must trust the organization [or] he shouldn't go into this kind of business. —**Ray Kroc:** founder and chairman of the McDonald's Corporation, 1958; David Halberstam *The Fifties* (1993)

3509. It [the first McDonald's restaurant] was only the first step in my struggle to build a personal monument to capitalism. —**Ray Kroc,** 1902–84: Mark Fisher *The Millionaire's Book of Quotations* (1991)

3510. McDonald's isn't a job. It's a life. Our employees have ketchup in their veins. —**Paul Preston:** Booz Allen and Hamilton (pub.) *Strategy & Business* (1997)

Microsoft and Bill Gates (1955–)

3511. He follows somebody's taillights for a while, then zooms past. Soon there will be no taillights left. —**Andrew S. Grove:** *Business Week,* 27 June 1994

3512. If they want we will give them a sleeping bag, but there is something romantic about sleeping under the desk. They want to do it. —**Bill Gates:** on his young software programmers; *Independent,* 18 November 1995

3513. Hiroshima '45, Chernobyl '86, Windows '95. —**Anonymous**

3514. America has a hero in Bill Gates. He's everything we all want to be—smart, creative, dedicated, energetic. —**Sharon Mirtaheri:** *Time,* 10 February 1997

3515. Bill Gates wants people to think he's Edison, when he's really Rockefeller. —**Larry Ellison:** *Newsweek,* 4 August 1997

3516. If they embrace Microsoft, they risk getting swallowed. If they fight, they risk getting crushed. —**Julia Pitta:** *Forbes,* 8 September 1997

3517. It's like the British Empire. They felt that if they didn't control the world someone else would.—**Ralph Nader:** *Time*, 1 December 1997

3518. He's relentless, Darwinian. Success is defined as flattening competition, not creating excellence.—**Rob Glaser,** former Microsoft executive: *Time*, 7 December 1998

3519. Microsoft is a corporate culture based on four premises: you work very hard, Bill is always right, it's us versus them, and Bill is always right.—**Michael Gartenberg,** computer industry analyst: *Time*, 17 April 2000

3520. I think he has a Napoleonic concept of himself and his company, an arrogance that derives from power and unalloyed success.—**Thomas Penfield Jackson,** Microsoft trial judge: *Time*, 22 January 2001

3521. In an Internet without doors or walls, who needs Windows or Gates?—**Anonymous**

Money

3522. Hardly anything but money remains to create strongly marked differences between them [Americans] and to raise some of them above the common level.—**Alexis de Tocqueville:** *Democracy in America* (1835)

3523. The almighty dollar is the only object of worship.—**Anonymous:** *Philadelphia Public Ledger*, 2 December 1836

3524. I think that the reason why we Americans seem to be so addicted to trying to get rich suddenly is merely because the *opportunity* to make promising efforts in that direction has offered itself to us with a frequency all out of proportion to the European experience.—**Mark Twain:** *North American Review* (Iowa), January 1895

3525. The American nation in the sixth ward is a fine people; they love the eagle—on the back of a dollar.—**Finley Peter Dunne:** *Mr Dooley in Peace and War* (1898)

3526. The American talks about money because that is the symbol and measure he has at hand for success, intelligence, and power; but, as to money itself, he makes, loses, spends, and gives it away with a very light heart.—**George Santayana:** *Character and Opinion in the United States* (1920)

3527. Too many of us look upon Americans as dollar chasers. This is a cruel libel, even if it is reiterated thoughtlessly by the Americans themselves.—**Albert Einstein:** 1929

3528. In America, money takes the place of God.—**Anzia Yezierska:** *Red Ribbon on a White Horse* (1950)

3529. Rockefeller made his money in oil, which he discovered at the bottom of wells. Oil was considered crude in those days, but so was Rockefeller. Now both are considered quite refined.—**Richard Armour:** *It All Started with Columbus* (1953)

3530. Americans are not materialistic in the money sense: they are too generous and wasteful, too idealistic for that. Yet this idealism is curiously lacking in the spiritual values.—**Cecil Beaton:** *It Gives Me Great Pleasure* (1955)

3531. Americans relate all effort, all work, and all of life itself to the dollar. Their talk is on nothing but dollars.—**Nancy Mitford:** *Noblesse Oblige* (1956)

3532. There is a strange and mighty race of people called the Americans who are rapidly becoming the coldest in the world because of this cruel, maneating idol, lucre.—**Edward Dahlberg:** *Alms for Oblivion* (1964)

3533. The typical American believes that no necessity of the soul is free and that there are precious few, if any, which cannot be bought.—**Joseph Wood Krutch:** *If You Don't Mind My Saying So* (1964)

3534. Every country has peasants—ours have money.—**Gloria Steinem:** *New York Times*, 1964

3535. It's complicated, being an American Having the money and the bad conscience, both at the same time.
—**Louis Simpson:** *Selected Poems* (1965)

3536. The secret point of money and power in America is neither the things that money can buy nor power for power's sake ... but absolute personal freedom, mobility, privacy.— **Joan Didion:** *Slouching Towards Bethlehem* (1967)

3537. It seems to be a law of American life that whatever enriches us anywhere except in the wallet inevitably becomes uneconomic. —**Russell Baker:** *New York Times*, 24 March 1968

3538. Americans want action for their money. They are fascinated by its self-reproducing qualities if it's put to work. Gold-hoarding goes against the American grain; it fits in better with European pessimism than with America's traditional optimism.—**Paula Nelson:** *The Joy of Money* (1975)

3539. I love the United States, but I see here everything is measured by success, by how much money it makes, not the satisfaction to the individual.—**Maria Schell**, 1926– , Austrian actress: Edward F. Murphy (ed.) *2,715 One-Line Quotations for Speakers, Writers & Raconteurs* (1981)

3540. The entire essence of America is the hope to first make money, then make money with money, then make lots of money with lots of money.—**Paul Erdman:** James Charlton *The Executive's Quotation Book* (1983)

3541. The more money an American accumulates, the less interesting he becomes.—**Gore Vidal**, 1925– : James Charlton *The Executive's Quotation Book* (1983)

3542. Americans are optimists. They hope they'll be wealthy someday—and they're positive they can get one more brushful of paint out of an empty can.—**Bern Williams:** *Readers' Digest*

3543. Generations of Americans have proven they'll spare no expense to get more and pay less.—**Kay M. Fishburn**, 1944– : Henry O. Dormann *The Speaker's Book of Quotations* (1987)

3544. Never criticize Americans. They have the best taste that money can buy.—**Miles Kington:** *Welcome to Kington* (1989)

Taxes

3545. The income tax has made more liars out of the American people than golf. Even when you make a tax form out on the level, you don't know when it's through if you are a crook or a martyr.—**Will Rogers:** *The Illiterate Digest* (1924)

3546. I pay my tax bills more readily than any others—for whether the money is well or ill spent I get civilized society for it.—**Oliver Wendell Holmes, Jr.:** letter to Harold Laski, 12 May 1930

3547. Baseball is a skilled game. It's America's game—it, and high taxes.—**Will Rogers,** 1879–1935

3548. Why shouldn't the American people take half my money from me? I took all of it from them.—**Edward A. Filene,** 1860–1937, American businessman: Arthur M. Schlesinger, Jr. *The Coming of the New Deal* (1987)

3549. Whenever Republicans talk of cutting taxes first and discussing national security second, they remind me of the very tired, rich man who said to his chauffeur, "Drive off that cliff, James, I want to commit suicide."—**Adlai Stevenson:** in the presidential campaign of 1952; Bill Adler *The Stevenson Wit* (1966)

3550. We don't pay taxes. Only the little people pay taxes.—**Leona Helmsley,** American hotelier: to her housekeeper, reported at her trial for tax evasion; *New York Times*, 12 July 1983

3551. The United States may become the first great power to falter because it lost its ability to collect taxes.—**American Bar Association:** *Wall Street Journal*, 10 April 1984

3552. The taxpayer—that's someone who works for the federal government but doesn't have to take a Civil Service examination.—**Ronald Reagan:** 1985, attrib.

3553. Compared with other industrialized countries, the United States is undertaxed. —**George F. Will:** "This Week with David Brinkley," ABC-TV, November 1987

Technology

3554. If it weren't for laundromats half the letters in the United States would never get written.—**Louis Phillips**, 1880–1956: William Cole and Louis Phillips (eds.) *Treasury of Humorous Quotations* (1996)

3555. The drive toward complex technical achievement offers a clue to why the U.S. is good at space gadgetry and bad at slum problems.—**John Kenneth Galbraith**, 1908– : Laurence J. Peter (ed.) *Peter's Quotations* (1977)

3556. Silicon Valley is the Florence of the late 20th century.—**Francis Fukuyama:** *Independent*, 19 June 1999

Texas Instruments

3557. The Creation of the Universe was made possible by a grant from Texas Instruments.—**Anonymous**

Wall Street

3558. A thoroughfare that begins in a graveyard and ends in a river.—**Anonymous:** James Charlton *The Executive's Quotation Book* (1983)

3559. There are only two emotions in Wall Street: fear and greed.—**William M. Lefevre:** *Time*, 1 May 1978

3560. On Wall Street he and a few others—how many?—three hundred, four hundred, five hundred?—had become precisely that ... Masters of the Universe.—**Tom Wolfe:** *The Bonfire of the Vanities* (1987)

3561. Wall Street is stress, highly emotional, and loaded with rejection. You have to be able to survive that. That's perhaps why women haven't achieved the record that they have in other areas.—**James E. Cayne:** 1990; David Olive *GenderBabble* (1993)

FOOD

Food and Drink

See also LAW AND ORDER: Prohibition

3562. I found there a country with thirty-two religions and only one sauce.—**Talleyrand**, 1754–1838: Mario C. Pedrazzini *Autant en apportent les mots* (1969)

3563. The average American's simplest and commonest form of breakfast consists of coffee and beefsteak.—**Mark Twain:** *A Tramp Abroad* (1879)

3564. Americans don't dine. They gobble, gulp, and go.—**A 19th century European traveler:** *The Good Old Days—They Were Terrible!*

3565. The American does not drink at meals as a sensible man should. Indeed, he has no meals. He stuffs for ten minutes thrice a day.—**Rudyard Kipling:** *American Notes* (1891)

3566. I judge that the American is more interested in getting drunk than in drinking.—**Giuseppe Giacosa:** *Impressioni d'America* (1908)

3567. [The cocktail is] the greatest of all the contributions of the American way of life to the salvation of humanity.—**H. L. Mencken:** *Americana* (1925)

3568. I might express it somewhat abruptly by saying that most Americans are born drunk, and really require a little wine or beer to sober them. They have a sort of permanent intoxication from within, a sort of invisible champagne … Americans do not need to drink to inspire them to do anything, though they do sometimes, I think, need a little for the deeper and more delicate purpose of teaching them how to do nothing.—**G. K. Chesterton:** *New York Times*, 28 June 1931

3569. I begin to perceive that Americans regard food as something to sober up with. —**James Agate:** *Ego 3*, 5 May 1937

3570. Cannibalism went right out as soon as the American canned food came in.—**Stephen Leacock,** 1869–1944: *The Boy I left Behind Me* (1947)

3571. You can travel fifty thousand miles in America without once tasting a piece of good bread.—**Henry Miller:** *Remember to Remember* (1947)

3572. When you consider how indifferent Americans are to the quality and cooking of the food they put into their insides, it cannot but strike you as peculiar that they should take such pride in the mechanical appliances they use for its excretion.—**W. Somerset Maugham:** *A Writer's Notebook* (1949)

3573. More die in the United States of too much food than of too little.—**John Kenneth Galbraith:** *The Affluent Society* (1958)

3574. An Englishman teaching an American about food is like the blind leading the one-eyed.—**A. J. Liebling,** 1904–63: Michael Cader and Debby Roth *Eat These Words* (1991)

3575. A plentitude of peanut butter and a dearth of hot mustard.—**Patrick Dean,** British ambassador to the US: *Newsweek*, 10 February 1969

3576. Americans can eat garbage, provided you sprinkle it liberally with ketchup, mustard, chili sauce, Tabasco sauce, cayenne pepper, or any other condiment which destroys the original flavor of the dish.—**Henry Miller,** 1891–1980: Michael Cader and Debby Roth *Eat These Words* (1991)

3577. The Americans provide themselves with the best-equipped kitchens in the world, but when the weather permits—or as often as not, when it does not permit—they abandon them, to cook and eat in conditions of unspeakable discomfort, by a method of which the masters could be counted on a single hand.—**Henry Fairlie:** *Manchester Guardian Weekly*, 1 August 1976

3578. The American aversion to meals … is not really an aversion to food. As every statistic shows, Americans consume vast quantities of food. They merely parcel their food into things that can be eaten with the hand.—**Henry Fairlie:** *Manchester Guardian Weekly*, 1 August 1976

3579. Public and private food in America has become eatable, here and there extremely good. Only the fried potatoes go unchanged, as deadly as before.—**Luigi Barzini:** *O America* (1977)

3580. The three-martini lunch is the epitome of American efficiency. Where else can you get an earful, a bellyful and a snootful at the same time?—**Gerald R. Ford:** to National Restaurant Association, Chicago, 28 May 1978

3581. If you're going to America, bring your own food.—**Fran Lebowitz:** *Social Studies* (1981)

3582. At American weddings, the quality of the food is in inverse proportion to the social position of the bride and groom.—**Calvin Trillin:** *Uncivil Liberties* (1982)

3583. Being American is to eat a lot of beef steak, and boy, we've got a lot more beef steak than any other country, and that's why you ought to be glad you're an American. And people have started looking at these big hunks of bloody meat on their plates, you know, and wondering what on earth they think they're doing.—**Kurt Vonnegut:** *City Limits*, 11 March 1983

3584. Popcorn [is] the sentimental good-time Charlie of American foods.—**Patricia Linden:** *Town & Country*, May 1984

3585. You only have food where you have money. And there is no money in France. The money is here in New York. That is why New York is becoming a world center for food. —**Gerard Paugaud,** chef: Henry O. Dormann *The Speaker's Book of Quotations* (1987)

3586. Americans are just beginning to regard food the way the French always have. Dinner is not what you do in the evening before something else. Dinner is the evening.—**Art Buchwald,** 1925– : Michael Cader and Debby Roth *Eat These Words* (1991)

3587. Americans have more food to eat than any other people on earth, and more diets to keep them from eating it.—**Anonymous**

3588. Only in America do people order double cheese burgers, a large fries, and a diet coke. —**Anonymous**

3589. American beer is like sex in a canoe. —**Anonymous**

3590. America is a country where half the money is spent buying food, and the other half is spent trying to lose weight.—**Anonymous**

Restaurants

3591. More and more in American restaurants, advertising has taken over the menu. You are sold on the meal before you have even started. —**Cecil Beaton:** *It Gives Me Great Pleasure* (1955)

3592. In America, even your menus have the gift of language. "The Chef's own Vienna Roast. A hearty, rich meat loaf, gently seasoned to perfection and served in a creamy nest of mashed farm potatoes and strictly fresh garden vegetables." Of course, what you get is cole slaw and a slab of meat, but that doesn't matter because the menu has already started your juices going. Oh, those menus. In America, they are poetry.—**Laurie Lee:** *Newsweek*, 24 October 1960

3593. Not only is New York City the nation's melting pot, it is also the casserole, the chafing dish and the charcoal grill.—**John V. Lindsay:** *New York Times*, 10 November 1966

3594. The national dish of America is menus. —**Robert Robinson:** "Robinson's Travels," BBC-TV program, August 1977

3595. There is nothing as American as a French chef from the Bronx.—**Susan Heller Anderson** and **David W. Dunlap:** *New York Times*, 14 January 1985

AUTHOR AND
SPEAKER INDEX

Abbey, Edward 391, 2507
Abbott, Shirley 951, 952
Abeel, Bill 571
Abel, Elie 2692
Abish, Walter 1078
Abourezk, James 2661
Abrahamsen, David 3392
Aburdene, Patricia 1131
Abzug, Bella 2653, 2654, 2823
Acheson, Dean 127, 135, 254,
    1018, 2240, 2327, 2649, 2783,
    3032, 3293, 3405, 3450
Ackroyd, Peter 1851
Adair, Gilbert 846
Adams, Douglas 866, 3148
Adams, Franklin P. 3486
Adams, Henry Brooks 28, 29,
    198, 1409, 2640, 3060, 3081,
    3243, 3257
Adams, Joey 2583
Adams, John 2087, 2158, 2630,
    3295, 3371, 3483
Adams, John Quincy 7, 2880,
    3352
Adams, Samuel 2150
Adams, Samuel Hopkins 2864
Adler, Leah 1745
Agate, James 1202, 3569
Agee, James 1797
Agee, Philip 2587
Agnew, Spiro T. 537, 1102, 1649,
    2242, 3427
Aiken, George 2225
Albert, Carl 2672
Alda, Alan 462
Aldrich, Thomas Bailey 1921
Alexander, Shana 2806
Algren, Nelson 490, 491, 503,
    1573, 1862
Alinsky, Saul 167
Allen, Fred 410, 423, 494, 768,
    1557, 1558, 2458

Allen, George 1020
Allen, Gracie 2644, 3089, 3258
Allen, Henry 701, 3166
Allen, Henry Southworth 117
Allen, Paula Gunn 363, 364, 365
Allen, Roger 2666
Allen, Woody 624, 869, 1601, 3394
Alsop, Joseph W. 2907, 2962,
    2965, 3151
Alsop, Stewart 2965
Alvarez, A. 451, 1283, 2017
American Bar Association 3551
Ames, Fisher 26
Ames, Russell 1715
Amory, Cleveland 699, 2836
Anderson, Jeremy S. 1372
Anderson, John B. 2528
Anderson, Margaret 1873
Anderson, Rich 633
Anderson, Sherwood 742, 937,
    1943, 1949
Anderson, Susan Heller 3595
Anthony, Evelyn 1031
Antonio, Emile de 1498
Antonioni, Michelangelo 1595
Anzaldúa, Gloria 2472
Apple, R. W., Jr. 376
Appleton, Thomas Gold 397,
    2453
Arden, Harvey 580
Armatrading, Joan 1755
Armour, Richard 3016, 3529
Arnall, Ellis 417
Arnold, Matthew 1344, 2402
Arnold, Oren 2036
Arthur, Chester A. 3079, 3080
Ashurst, Henry Fountain 3047,
    3265
Aspin, Les 2662
Asquith, Margot 2099
Astral, Joanne 452
Atkinson, Alex 989

Atkinson, Brooks 224, 760, 784
Atkinson, Ti-Grace 1222
Atlas, James 1980, 1981
Atwood, Margaret 1268, 1939
Auden, W. H. 57, 62, 247, 661,
    1250, 1270, 1380, 1391, 1470,
    1661, 1861, 1867, 1926, 2164,
    2359, 2360, 2424, 2428
Aykroyd, Dan 386

Bacall, Lauren 1231, 1738
Bach, Richard 1342
Baez, Joan 1530
Bagdikian 1662
Bailey, Francis Lee 2665, 3434
Bailey, Philip James 6
Bailey, Thomas A. 2981, 3281
Baker, Kyle 878
Baker, Russell 825, 826, 1169,
    1434, 1672, 1936, 2070, 2117,
    2913, 3203, 3253, 3537
Baldridge, Letitia 287
Baldwin, James 129, 161, 303,
    304, 328, 346, 1473, 2120,
    2426, 2432
Ballantyne, Sheila 460
Ballard, J. G. 139, 1746
Baltzell, E. Digby 1349
Bancroft, Mary 3409
Bane, Michal 1730
Bangs, Lester 1171
Bankhead, Tallulah 1765
Banks-Smith, Nancy 861
Baraka, Imamu Amiri 1736
Baring, Maurice 1999
Barkley, Alben W. 2751
The Barnard Bulletin 794
Barnes, Djuna 736
Barnet, Correlli 2146
Barr, Alfred H., Jr. 1329
Barr, Ann 1350
Barrett, Rona 639

SUBJECT INDEX